W9-AQX-497

DEC 1974
RECEIVED
OHIO DOMINICAN
COLLEGE LIBRARY
COLUMBUS, OHIO
43219

SHAKESPEARE SURVEY

ADVISORY BOARD

Anne Barton   G. K. Hunter
Nicholas Brooke   J. C. Maxwell
Philip Edwards   T. J. B. Spencer
Bernard Harris   Glynne Wickham

Allardyce Nicoll
Assistant to the Editor: Rhoda Ann Thompson

1. Shakespeare and his Stage
2. Shakespearian Production
3. The Man and the Writer
4. Interpretation
5. Textual Criticism
6. The Histories
7. Style and Language
8. The Comedies
9. Hamlet
10. The Roman Plays
11. The Last Plays (with an index to *Surveys* 1–10)
12. The Elizabethan Theatre
13. King Lear
14. Shakespeare and his Contemporaries
15. The Poems and Music
16. Shakespeare in the Modern World
17. Shakespeare in His Own Age
18. Shakespeare Then Till Now
19. Macbeth
20. Shakespearian and Other Tragedy
21. Othello (with an index to *Surveys* 11–20)
22. Aspects of Shakespearian Comedy
23. Shakespeare's Language
24. Shakespeare: Theatre Poet
25. Shakespeare's Problem Plays
26. Shakespeare's Jacobean Tragedies

SHAKESPEARE SURVEY

AN ANNUAL SURVEY OF
SHAKESPEARIAN STUDY AND PRODUCTION

27

EDITED BY
KENNETH MUIR

CAMBRIDGE UNIVERSITY PRESS

Published by the Syndics of the Cambridge University Press
Bentley House, 200 Euston Road, London NW1 2DB
American Branch: 32 East 57th Street, New York, N.Y.10022

© Cambridge University Press 1974

Library of Congress Catalogue Card Number: 49–1639

ISBN: 0 521 20468 2

First published 1974

Shakespeare Survey was first published in 1948. For the first
eighteen volumes it was edited by Allardyce Nicoll under the
sponsorship of the University of Birmingham, the University
of Manchester, the Royal Shakespeare Theatre and the
Shakespeare Birthplace Trust

Printed in Great Britain
at the University Printing House, Cambridge
(Brooke Crutchley, University Printer)

822.332
N645
v.27

EDITOR'S NOTE

As previously announced, the central theme of *Shakespeare Survey 28* will be 'Shakespeare and the Ideas of his Time'. The theme of Number 29 will be 'Shakespeare's Final Plays'. Contributions on that or on other topics should reach the Editor (University of Liverpool, P.O. Box 147, Liverpool L69 3BX) by 1 September 1975. Contributors are required to provide brief summaries of their articles and they should leave generous margins, use double-spacing, and follow the style and lay-out of articles in the current issue. A style-sheet is available on request. Contributions should not normally exceed 5,000 words. K. M.

92805

CONTRIBUTORS

NIGEL ALEXANDER, *Senior Lecturer in English Literature, University of Nottingham*

ROY BATTENHOUSE, *Professor of English Literature, Indiana University*

JAMES C. BULMAN, Jr, *Yale University*

GARETH LLOYD EVANS, *Senior Lecturer and Staff Tutor in Literature, Extra-Mural Department, University of Birmingham*

HAROLD FISCH, *Professor of English Literature, Bar-Ilan University, Israel*

ROBERT F. FLEISSNER, *Professor of English Literature, Central State University, Wilberforce, Ohio*

G. K. HUNTER, *Professor of English Literature, University of Warwick*

W. NICHOLAS KNIGHT, *Professor of English Literature, Wesleyan University, Connecticut*

FRANK MCCOMBIE, *Senior Lecturer in English, Northumberland College of Education*

JULIET MCLAUCHLAN, *Teacher of English, Aylesbury High School*

D. J. PALMER, *Senior Lecturer in English Literature, University of Hull*

G. M. PINCISS, *Assistant Professor of English, Hunter College, The City University of New York*

LOIS POTTER, *Lecturer in English Literature, University of Leicester*

RICHARD PROUDFOOT, *Lecturer in English Literature, King's College, University of London*

PETER THOMSON, *Lecturer in English Literature, University of Swansea*

WILLIAM B. TOOLE, *Professor of English, North Carolina State University at Raleigh*

ALBERT H. TRICOMI, *Assistant Professor of English, State University of New York at Binghamton*

CONTENTS

List of Plates   *page* viii

Shakespeare's Earliest Tragedies: 'Titus Andronicus' and 'Romeo and Juliet'
    by G. K. HUNTER   1

The Aesthetics of Mutilation in 'Titus Andronicus' *by* ALBERT H. TRICOMI   11

The Motif of Psychic Division in 'Richard III' *by* WILLIAM B. TOOLE   21

The Antic Disposition of Richard II *by* LOIS POTTER   33

The Prince of Denmark and Claudius's Court *by* JULIET MCLAUCHLAN   43

'Hamlet' and the 'Moriae Encomium' *by* FRANK MCCOMBIE   59

The Relation of Henry V to Tamburlaine *by* ROY BATTENHOUSE   71

Shakespeare and the Puritan Dynamic *by* HAROLD FISCH   81

Equity, 'The Merchant of Venice' and William Lambarde *by*
    W. NICHOLAS KNIGHT   93

'Love's Labour's Won' and the Occasion of 'Much Ado' *by*
    ROBERT F. FLEISSNER   105

The Date and Production of 'Timon' Reconsidered *by* JAMES C. BULMAN, Jr   111

Shakespeare, Her Majesty's Players, and Pembroke's Men *by* G. M. PINCISS   129

JUDI DENCH talks to GARETH LLOYD EVANS   137

Shakespeare Straight and Crooked: a Review of the 1973 Season at
    Stratford *by* PETER THOMSON   143

The Year's Contributions to Shakespearian Study:

    1   Critical Studies *reviewed by* D. J. PALMER   155

    2   Shakespeare's Life, Times, and Stage *reviewed by* NIGEL
        ALEXANDER   172

    3   Textual Studies *reviewed by* RICHARD PROUDFOOT   179

Index   193

PLATES

BETWEEN PAGES 128 AND 129

I   *Love's Labour's Lost*, Royal Shakespeare Theatre, 1973. Directed by John Barton, designed by Timothy O'Brien and Tazeena Firth. Catherine Kessler as Maria, Susan Fleetwood as the Princess of France, Janet Chappell as Katherine, Estelle Kohler as Rosaline and Ian Richardson as Berowne
[*Photo: Joe Cocks*]

II   *Love's Labour's Lost*, with Sebastian Shaw as Boyet and Estelle Kohler (Rosaline) in act IV, scene i
[*Photo: Joe Cocks*]

III   *Love's Labour's Lost*, act v, scene ii: the dialogue of the owl and the cuckoo
[*Photo: Joe Cocks*]

IVA   *As You Like It*, Royal Shakespeare Theatre, 1973. Directed by Buzz Goodbody, designed by Christopher Morley. With Maureen Lipman as Celia and Eileen Atkins as Rosalind
[*Photo: Joe Cocks*]

B   *As You Like It*, with Richard Pasco as Jacques
[*Photo: Joe Cocks*]

V   *Romeo and Juliet*, Royal Shakespeare Theatre, 1973. Directed by Terry Hands, designed by Farrah. With Beatrix Lehmann as the nurse and Estelle Kohler as Juliet
[*Photo: Joe Cocks*]

VI   *Richard II*, Royal Shakespeare Theatre, 1973. Directed by John Barton, designed by Timothy O'Brien and Tazeena Firth. With Ian Richardson and Richard Pasco alternating in the roles of Richard and Bolingbroke
[*Photo: Joe Cocks*]

VII   *Richard II*, act I, scene iii
[*Photo: Joe Cocks*]

VIII   *Romeo and Juliet*, Old Vic, 1960. Directed by Franco Zeffirelli. With Judi Dench as Juliet and John Stride as Romeo
[*Photo: Houston Rogers*]

SHAKESPEARE'S EARLIEST TRAGEDIES: 'TITUS ANDRONICUS' AND 'ROMEO AND JULIET'

G. K. HUNTER

It is commonly accepted that Shakespeare's earliest essays in tragic form are *Titus Andronicus* and *Romeo and Juliet*[1] – accepted, that is, among those who allow that Shakespeare was responsible for *Titus Andronicus*. But few critics, even among the accepters, seem willing to go beyond the merely chronological point to take up the critical consequence: that we might expect to be able to analyse here an early but characteristic Shakespearian mode of tragedy.[2] The two plays are so obviously unlike one another that it is hard even to think of adding them together to make up any description of a unified mode. Whatever the reason, it is a clear critical fact that these plays are not normally considered together, or even apart, in a description of Shakespearian Tragedy. Shakespeare, it is implied, had to throw away this dispersed prentice work, set it against experience rather than achievement, when he began to compose the sequence of truly 'Shakespearian' tragedies beginning with *Julius Caesar* and growing out of the political interests of the English history plays.

These pre-judgements bear more heavily against *Titus Andronicus* than *Romeo and Juliet*, for *Romeo* has, whatever its generic implication, the refuge of being a 'well-loved' play, where *Titus* can only be called 'much disliked'. I begin, however, by assuming an equality of interest and importance, taking it that in both plays Shakespeare was writing as well as he knew how. The subsequent reputations of the plays may be thought to tell us

more securely about audience preferences in the period between Shakespeare and the present than about the author's intention. My concern in this paper is not with differences of valuation but with the formal similarities and relationships that can be established between the two tragedies.

In making this point I am not, of course, forgetting that *Titus* is the most horrific of Shakespeare's tragedies. To some minds this

[1] The exact chronology of these early plays is too uncertain to bear any weight of consequential argument. It is worth noticing that modern scholarship (following E. K. Chambers) has tended to keep the two tragedies within two or three years of one another; so there is nothing on this side to impede the idea of a close relationship. I have not included *Richard III* among the 'early tragedies', though it certainly has a tragic dimension. I have excluded it because I see its historical content and its role in completing the stretch of chronicle begun in *I Henry VI* as impediments, which effectively prevent it from being regarded as a straight example of Shakespearian tragic invention. That level of the play which is not dominated by historical sequence is largely concerned with the dominant personality of Richard himself. The creation of dominant personalities is not, of course, to prove uncharacteristic of Shakespeare in his tragic mood; it is, however, an over-tilled field, and in any case is not that with which I am here concerned.

[2] The obvious exception to this blanket statement is Nicholas Brooke (*Shakespeare's Early Tragedies*, London, 1968). Professor Brooke's brief is, however, much larger than mine; he includes *Julius Caesar* and *Hamlet* (also *Richard III* and *Richard II*) within his survey. Brooke's sense of 'the mode of tragedy' is also rather different from that pursued here, so that the question of 'early tragedy' can, I believe, be rehandled without culpable repetition.

implies that it is exceptional and that its evidence about Shakespeare's tragic mode is out of court. The idea that true tragedy is essentially about the mental suffering of noble natures, and therefore unbloody, is, however, probably a delusion, based on the social assumptions of a post-Enlightenment society which has shown itself incapable of writing tragedy. The Victorian sub-genre, 'the tragedy of blood', invented to deal with plays like *Titus Andronicus*, offers us, in fact, only a pointless tautology: the *Oedipus Rex*, *The Bacchae*, *King Lear*, *The Duchess of Malfi*, are all blood-spattered and horrific; but who would be so bold as to confine such plays to a sub-genre?

That Shakespeare when he wrote *Titus* was under the influence of classical exemplars must also be allowed; but this does not mean that his mind can be cleared of responsibility for it. Shakespeare was no doubt like other artists, and achieved his own voice by working through aesthetic enthusiasms and derivative exercises, and in this *Titus* is no different from other early plays. Like *Lucrece* and its comic counterpart, *Venus and Adonis*, *Titus Andronicus* is deeply indebted to Ovid's sense of human mutability, the frailty of man's happiness and of his capacity for reason. In a similar way *The Comedy of Errors* is indebted to Plautus, *The Taming of the Shrew* to Italianate comedy, *Romeo and Juliet* to the atmosphere and conventions of the Italian novella. The real difference between *Titus Andronicus* and *Romeo and Juliet* seems to emerge not from the derivativeness of the one and the originality of the other, but from the different implications of the genres used. If *Titus* is exceptional among Shakespeare's tragedies in its devotion to a hysterically bleak view of human potential, *Romeo* is exceptional also, in its general sunniness, its closeness to comedy. It is, of course, particularly close to the kind of comedy that Shakespeare was

writing in these years, 'Italian', courtly, exploring the romantic sensibilities of well-bred youth. It goes without saying that we are the better able to understand *Romeo and Juliet* because we know these cognate comedies.

The distinction I have so far made between the two plays suggests that Shakespeare's first move in tragedy was to seek to delimit the space within which he could operate, marking out the extreme polarities of his tragic range. He was never again to pursue the image of man's bestiality with the single-mindedness he showed in *Titus*. And likewise he was never, after *Romeo*, to write another tragedy which was so clearly a diversion by malign fate of materials that would normally form the basis of comedy. From time to time hereafter he will, of course, come close to one pole or the other, but always in a manner which invokes the presence of its opposite. *King Lear*, for example, can be regarded as in some ways a reworking of themes from *Titus Andronicus*. We have the same grieved and deprived father, hounded from dignity into madness by a malignant group whose authority comes from his gift, and rescued in the end by a foreign invasion led by his loyal child. We have the same pervading image of man as a beast of prey, the same contrast between extremes of female rapacity and female innocence, the same overlapping of lust and political ambition. But the role of the family in society is very different in the two plays. In both, the good and evil quickly sort themselves out as opposing forces. In *Titus* the social gap between the two groups is what is emphasised: on the one hand we have the barbarian outsiders, on the other the Andronici, the pious Roman family. In *Lear*, however, the opposition of good and bad emerges from the matrix of a single family. Among the sufferings of Titus the fact that Saturninus betrayed the favour he received does not bulk large; but for Lear the ingratitude of the daughters is the central agony.

Thus the social rituals through which the conflict is expressed in *Titus* (feasting, family reading, the birth of a child, etc.) must give way in *Lear* to more unstructured domestic confrontations, and in these the side of Shakespeare's tragic vision represented by *Romeo* re-emerges. Something of Old Capulet's irascible absurdity survives into the very different world of Lear and his daughters.

Not only in *Lear* but throughout Shakespeare's mature tragedies the ritual of *Titus* is complemented by the domesticity of *Romeo*, the hieratic flanked by the familiar. Shakespeare achieves his later tragic centrality not only by diluting the unreality of *Titus* but also by making more remote and overpowering the cosinesses of Verona. Among the later tragedies *Antony and Cleopatra* is probably the one that most closely resembles *Romeo and Juliet*: in both plays the poetic power is centrally involved in projecting the love emotions of a socially significant couple, whose relationship defies the prevailing political and ethical assumptions of their society. Both are plays whose minor characters (Nurse, Mercutio, Enobarbus, Charmian, Alexis) are much given to comic routines. The lovers are finally united by quasi-sacrificial deaths; their deaths open the way to a unification of their society; and they are memorialised by joint tombs of exemplary splendour. But *Antony and Cleopatra*, in spite of its high comedy, does not in any sense give us a comic world wrenched by fate to a tragic conclusion. The characters are not like us; they are colossuses, and their laughter shakes the world. Here there is no private sphere into which lovers can escape from the pressures of other men's expectations. The love gestures of Antony and Cleopatra, all made in the world's eye, have to have the ritual quality of great public occasions. Their quarrels mirror the clash of alternative moral systems, Roman severity and barbarian self-indulgence. And in these respects the play may

be seen to be closer to *Titus Andronicus*, or at least to the pole of tragedy it represents, than to *Romeo and Juliet*.

I have been arguing for a relationship between *Titus Andronicus* and *Romeo and Juliet* and between these two and the rest of Shakespeare's tragedies in terms of the polar characteristics of tragedy they exhibit. But *Titus Andronicus* and *Romeo and Juliet* are not related only as opposites. As one might expect with a playwright finding his way into his craft, similar structural skeletons serve for both plays, though the flesh hung on top of them is very different. We may note how the two plays open:

Flourish. Enter the Tribunes and Senators aloft; and then enter below Saturninus and his followers at one door, and Bassianus and his followers at the other, with drums and trumpets.

The scene that follows fleshes out the diagram thus established: first Saturninus (the elder) speaks, claiming his right to the crown, derived from primogeniture; then Bassianus (the younger) repeats the speech claiming the crown as his right, derived from election. Then

Enter Marcus Andronicus aloft, with the crown.

Marcus tells us that the *populus Romanus* has chosen Titus Andronicus as its representative to take to himself the issue being contested. The contenders then leave the stage to allow Titus to enter in his *triumphus*.

The opening diagram of the forces in *Romeo and Juliet* is extraordinarily similar:

Enter [at one door] Sampson and Gregory, of the house of Capulet . . . Enter [at the other door] two other Servingmen, Abraham and Balthazar [of the house of Montague] . . . Enter [at one door] Benvolio [a nobleman of the house of Capulet] . . . Enter Tybalt [a nobleman of the house of Montague] . . . [they fight] . . . Enter an Officer and three or four citizens . . . Enter [at one door] Old Capulet . . . and his wife . . . Enter [at the other door] Old Montague and his wife . . . Enter [? above] Prince Escalus with his Train.

I-2

In both plays the opening movement establishes discord against rule. The formalised stage-pictures set one competitor for power against another, the greater social range of the representatives of faction in *Romeo and Juliet* measuring the variety of social experience that play will draw on, the more concentrated concern with political power in *Titus Andronicus* marking that play's range of significant action. In both cases power is denied to the competitors. A central justice in the possession of power is demonstrated, and the establishment of this central authority over the brawling factions leads to their departure from the stage at the end of this dramatic phrase or movement.

In both tragedies, however, the remedy for discord which this opening diagram displays is a matter for display rather than acceptance. The failures to accept are, of course, very different. In *Romeo and Juliet* the Prince remains throughout the action an objective and unsubverted guarantor of order. The discord that persists is, in political terms, a hole-and-corner affair, dealt with by easy penalties. In *Titus Andronicus*, however, the supreme authorities of the opening, Marcus and Titus Andronicus, the representatives of the citizens and of the army, quickly lose their central position *aloft*. Titus is soon self-subverted and then hounded into grotesque subservience and madness. Astraea leaves the country; justice and order cease to have a political dimension. The movement by which moral order vanishes from Rome is, of course, without parallel in *Romeo and Juliet*. But the process by which Titus, in his wrong-headed and high-principled choice of Saturninus, his abject surrender of all rights to the new Emperor, falls from arbiter to suppliant does not end by breaking the parallel with *Romeo*. It ends, in fact, by re-forming the opening diagram of strife into a more stable and more exactly parallel shape.

The central conflict of *Titus Andronicus* stabilises itself as the story of two family groupings, whose conflict destroys (or threatens to destroy) the civilisation represented by the city. The opening chorus of *Romeo and Juliet* can easily be adapted to fit the other play:

> Two households, both alike in dignity,
> In Rome's fair city, where we lay our scene,
> From early grudge break to new mutiny,
> Where civil blood makes civil hands unclean.

It must be confessed, of course, that the 'two households' of *Titus* are less obvious than those of *Romeo*. By the middle of act II, however, it is clear that the action is going to hinge on the conflict between the Andronicus family and that alternative 'household' of Saturninus/ Tamora/Aaron with Tamora's assorted children, Chiron and Demetrius (later joined by the black baby). That this latter grouping can only be called a 'family' by a radically deformed definition does not reduce the significance of the parallel; indeed it strengthens it. The family ties of the Andronici suggest the strength of the family unit as the basis of all social order, and particularly that of Rome, demonstrating loyalty, mutual support and above all *pietas*, drawing on the dutifulness of the past to secure the dutifulness of the future. The household of husband, lover and assorted children that clusters round Tamora suggests the opposite: a dreadful burgeoning of uncontrolled nature into a rank and unweeded plot, where parental love cannot compensate for the various disorders and mismatings that result. Within a short time we are shown the wife over-ruling the husband, the mismating of Emperor and enemy, of Empress and slave, of white and black, the mother encouraging the sons to rape and murder, the brothers ready to kill one another until reduced to 'order' by the black lover (acting as surrogate father). Finally we have the black baby itself 'as loathsome as a toad', the complete image of instinctual wickedness.

In the two plays the conflicts of the households are handled, of course, in very different terms. In *Romeo and Juliet* the conflict between Montagues and Capulets has little political reality. It exists to maintain a certain pressure on what the play presents as more real – the personal emotions of the two lovers. In *Romeo and Juliet* evil exists only in so far as the traditional conflict exists. It is not presented as a facet of the normal human will (even in the case of Tybalt); stability and concord are always possible, as a result of spontaneous human action, and we are always aware that peace is only a hand's breadth away. The narrow distance between tragedy and comedy is of course one of the principal effects of the play. But in *Titus* the political conflict remains central and cannot possibly be evaded. It arises from the fact of being human, from the need to resist destruction, the imposition of chaos, the reduction of civilisation to appetite, and man to beast, all of which here grows out of a personal will to evil, deeply implanted in human nature, and requiring for its neutralisation every energy and every resource available in the play. Here no aspect of life can be thought of as merely personal and private, and so exempted from the struggle. The loves of Aaron and Tamora, the rape of Lavinia, are political as well as moral offences. There is no Duke to intervene; the conflict is not simply a relic of past bitternesses, but a monstrous burgeoning of manic energies; death or flight are the only alternatives to absorption into the system.

And in the end, flight is not possible either. The world of the play demands a return to the scene of the struggle. This is equally true of both tragedies: the two plays are (uniquely among Shakespeare's tragedies) tales whose significance is expressed in terms of single cities, though *Rome* has, of course, a very different civic resonance from *Verona*. Verona suggests to us when we hear that it is in 'fair Verona, where we lay our scene' the anticipation of Italian passions, Italian family honour, the hot blood stirring in the sun, balconies, friars, domestic luxury and homely social display, a cosy familiarity of masters and servants, a world poised between the bourgeois and the aristocratic; though we must try to beware of finding in the play an 'Italianism' which entered English literature through *Romeo and Juliet*. Rome on the other hand suggests *ab initio* a military civilisation, severity, self-conscious masculinity, stoical self-denial, the inexorable rule of law – the collection of ethical icons that long dominated the European sense of culture: Horatius defending the bridge, Mutius Scevola burning off his right hand, Regulus returning to Carthage, Lucretia preferring death to dishonour, Manlius Torquatus killing his son for disobedience, etc., etc.

It appears in consequence that the two cities are well chosen by Shakespeare as points of focus, for a love story on the one hand, and on the other hand for a story of civilisation and its enemies, concerned with fortitude and brutality. In both plays the city walls measure the limit of the ordered world.

> There is no world without Verona walls

says Romeo with what might seem merely adolescent exaggeration; but the exaggeration is in fact quite close to truth. Meaning does not exist for the play outside Verona; the only non-Veronese of whom we hear is the Apothecary, who is death's emissary:

> Famine is in thy cheeks,
> Need and oppression starveth in thy eyes,
> Contempt and beggary hangs upon thy back,
> The world is not thy friend, nor the world's law ...
> (v, i, 69–72)

The balance of love and hate, of personal life and public reputation, the context within which meaning exists – this can be found only in Verona.

In *Titus*, very similarly, the play's meaning can only be brought to focus inside the walls of its city. Of course the focus is very different, the city being so different. We are here concerned with self-sacrifice and self-indulgence, rule and disobedience, with suffering and cruelty, with the destructive will to chaos, set against personal commitment to justice as the only meaningful basis for society. Only in Rome, it is implied, can the victory of cosmos or chaos be fully significant; Rome is seen as the hub of things, where final decisions are made and known to be final. This is why at the end of the play:

> As for that ravenous tiger, Tamora,
> No funeral rite, nor man in mourning weed,
> No mournful bell shall ring her burial;
> But throw her forth to beasts and birds to prey.
>
> (v, iii, 195–8)

Rome is here finally returned to the status appropriate to it, a status it has seemed to lose in the course of the action, when the city came to seem no different from the barbarism outside. When, as Titus tells us,

> Rome is but a wilderness of tigers,

when Lucius has to flee to the Goths to raise an army 'to be revenged on Rome and Saturnine', Rome clearly has forgotten how to be Rome. It takes a political convulsion and a blood-bath to re-establish the city as different from the wilderness of tigers. In the meantime Titus is required to carry the role of Rome's speaking conscience, when Rome cannot speak for herself. Where is Astraea gone? Why do the gods not answer, or not listen? Such questions keep continuously before our minds a sense of meaning in the city which is elsewhere out of sight. Meaning cannot be given to the world again, it is implied, till the mind of Rome and the mind of Titus are at one, when Moors and Goths know their place outside the walls and Roman *severitas* rules all within.

The only locale established in *Titus Andronicus* outside the walls of Rome is the forest of act II where the major crimes are committed. It is to be noticed that those who are at home and effective here are Aaron and Tamora, Chiron and Demetrius. For Tamora everything in the forest 'doth make a gleeful boast':

> The snakes lie rolled in the cheerful sun;
> The green leaves quiver with the cooling wind
> And make a chequer'd shadow on the ground;
> Under their sweet shade, Aaron, let us sit . . .
>
> (II, iii, 13–16)

For Lavinia, however, the forest scene is, like Aaron, dark and evil:

> let her joy her raven-coloured love;
> This valley fits the purpose passing well.
>
> (II, iii, 83–4)

Aaron is skilful in the use of forest pits and stratagems; his energy sprouts at the thought of them. The young Andronici, however, grow uncertain and dim of sight:

> *Quintus.*
> My sight is very dull, whate'er it bodes.
> *Martius.*
> And mine, I promise you; were it not for shame,
> Well could I leave our sport to sleep awhile.
> . . . . . .
> *Quintus.*
> I am surprised with an uncouth fear;
> A chilling sweat o'er-runs my trembling joints;
> My heart suspects more than mine eye can see.
>
> (II, iii, 195–7, 211–13)

Within the dim light of the forest meanings change at the whim of the observer; this is no place for the hard clear minds of the Andronici. It is, however, a natural context for Tamora's Gothic deceptions and shifts of role. At one point the forest is for her, as noted above, a place of love and repose. It is also Tamora, however, who expresses most eloquently the idea of the forest as a place of horror – without even the excuse that it is 'another part of the forest':

> A barren detested vale you see it is:
> The trees, though summer, yet forlorn and lean,
> Overcome with moss and baleful mistletoe;
> Here never shines the sun; here nothing breeds,
> Unless the nightly owl or fatal raven.
>
> (II, iii, 93–7)

This description, like the previous one designed to encourage Aaron to acts of love, is, of course, not organised as a scientific account of a place actually there, but presents a rhetorical backdrop, appropriate in this case to murder, rape and mutilation. When Titus asks for 'proof' that his sons performed the murder he brings a Roman attachment to the rules of evidence to a Gothic dream of total personal fulfilment, where the world becomes what the dreamer desires it to be. At the end of act II when the night-world of the forest is giving way again to the daylight clarities of Rome, Marcus Andronicus sees the nightmare figure of his niece; he remarks:

> If I do dream, would all my wealth would wake me!
> If I do wake, some planet strike me down,
> That I may slumber an eternal sleep!
>
> (II, iv, 13–15)

Henceforth in the play, however, such nightmare shadows have to be allowed as part of the daylight population of Rome. The ghosts are only laid, the shadows of the forest dispelled, when nightmare and truth have faced one another in Tamora's last disguise – as Revenge, the mother of Rapine and Murder ('A pair of cursed hell-hounds and their dam' as Titus puts it) – so that mutilators and mutilated can perish together in a shared universe of absurdity and Rome be restored to rule and the daylight processes of justice.[1]

At the centre of the city, as its soul you may say, stands the family of the Andronici, and at the centre of the Andronici's sense of themselves stands one essential object, which the stage-picture should surely highlight – the tomb. The structural use of the family vault or tomb provides another point of correspondence between *Titus* and *Romeo*. We are shown the tomb of the Andronici very early in the play: when Titus first enters in his Roman Triumph, bearing the Gothic family into Rome among his prisoners, the first action he undertakes is the burial of the dead in the family vault:

> Romans, of five and twenty valiant sons . . .
> Behold the poor remains, alive and dead!
> These that survive let Rome reward with love;
> These that I bring unto their latest home,
> With burial amongst their ancestors . . .
> Make way to lay them by their brethren.
> There greet in silence, as the dead are wont,
> And sleep in peace, slain in your country's wars.
> O sacred receptacle of my joys,
> Sweet cell of virtue and nobility,
> How many sons hast thou of mine in store
> That thou wilt never render to me more!
>
> (I, i, 79–95)

And it is the tomb that stimulates the first statement of the conflict that will dominate the play. Lucius demands, in what is clearly part of a controlled ritual:

> Give us the proudest prisoner of the Goths,
> That we may hew his limbs, and on a pile
> Ad manes fratrum sacrifice his flesh
> Before this earthy prison of their bones,
> That so the shadows be not unappeas'd,
> Nor we disturb'd with prodigies on earth.
>
> (I, i, 96–101)

Shakespeare seems here to be dramatising a clear conception of the religious basis of the Roman way of life; there is no suggestion that he is criticising the system. The dead citizen-warriors claim the right to be returned to their family place within the city. There they will rest in peace, provided the appropriate honour is paid to them; and the appropriate honour is

---

[1] In these terms *Titus* looks like a tragic version of the city–forest–city pattern found in *A Midsummer-Night's Dream* – a play which also has close affinities with *Romeo and Juliet*.

that the living should hear their claim for the propitiatory sacrifice of 'the proudest prisoner of the Goths', and be absolutely obliged to fulfil this claim.

Against this Roman ritual Shakespeare sets the personal plea of Tamora:

> Victorious Titus, rue the tears I shed,
> A mother's tears in passion for her son.
>
> (I, i, 105–6)

Modern readers naturally feel more sympathy for the more personal position taken up by Tamora and argued by her with eloquence and passion. But the play hardly supports the view that these Roman rituals are in themselves barbarous, or that Tamora is in some sense 'justified' in taking up revenge against the Andronici. The stern suppression of self in the interest of family, community or state is certainly presented in an extreme form, but it is the extreme form of a value-system consistently preferred in the play before subjective passion or individual emotionalism. The military dead are represented as an essential part of the living family and of the national destiny; they cannot be fobbed off with something less than their right. As in other military civilisations, the valiancy of the living is preserved by the promise that they, too, in their turn will have the right to enter the family tomb, to join the honoured bones of their ancestors and be rewarded with reverence and with sacrificial victims. This is why the tomb becomes the primary focus again at the end of the play. The new conqueror and paterfamilias, Lucius Andronicus, throws out the tiger Tamora for birds to peck at; Aaron is treated very similarly – half buried in the earth and left to the mercies of a Nature that 'swallows her own increase'. Both are replaced in the extra-mural world of unhallowed appetite. But

> My father and Lavinia shall forthwith
> Be closed in our household's monument.
>
> (V, iii, 193–4)

Interment in the tomb validates the efforts of the life preceding, and ensures the continuity of past, present and future under the same standards of civilisation.

The parallel importance of the tomb in *Romeo and Juliet* suggests that the Andronicus 'household's monument' reflects more than Shakespeare's study of Roman antiquities. It implies that Shakespeare found the tomb property a convenient expression of his sense of the tragic importance of family and social continuities. The Capulet family monument is not, of course, a military symbol. But the choice of it as the most appropriate final setting for the tragedy brings out the structure of significances this play shares with *Titus Andronicus*. It is entirely appropriate that the 'public' wedding-bed of Romeo and Juliet (as against their previous private bedding) should be placed in the Capulet tomb, for it is there that Romeo may be most effectively seen to have joined his wife's clan, there where their corporate identity is most unequivocally established:

> Where all the kindred of the Capulets lie,
>
> (IV, i, 112)

> Where for this many hundred years the bones
> Of all my buried ancestors are pack'd.
>
> (IV, iii, 40–1)

The rash and personal passion of Romeo and Juliet can hardly claim a truly tragic significance if it cannot be caught up in the corporate and continuing life of Verona. Here, as in *Titus Andronicus*, the presence of the tomb assures us that the extreme acts of tragic individuals contribute to the past and future as well as to the brilliant present of personal assertion, here where they join the confluence of acts that make up social continuity.

In both plays a woman as well as a man is placed in the tomb at the end of the action. One might have expected the Andronicus tomb to exclude women; but Lavinia is clearly said to be Titus's companion in death. I do not think, however, that this implies any weakening of the military significance of the family monument. Lavinia, too, has like a soldier triumphed over her enemy. The battle has, of course, been a strange and even a grotesque one. The code of military ethics does not provide much guidance for dealing with a wilderness of tigers; and the cunning ploys of the mad Titus are only marginally 'Roman'. But it is worth noticing that the appeal to Roman precedent and tradition returns at the moment of Lavinia's death:

Was it well done of rash Virginius
To slay his daughter with his own right hand,
(v, iii, 36–7)

asks Titus, and, being told by the Emperor, 'It was, Andronicus', he stabs and kills her. This is often seen as yet another senseless butchery; but in the light of the precedent explicitly established one may prefer to see it as the restoration of truly Roman or meaningful death. To have killed Lavinia earlier would have been an act of despair, for the standards by which such an act might be justified seemed to have vanished. To have enclosed her in the tomb then would have devalued the generations of soldiers already inhearsed. Now, with the mutilators mutilated, and with Tamora and Saturninus securely within the grasp of punishment, the practical possibility of justice reappears, the tomb can reopen and receive the honourable dead. Their presence there can now give meaning to the continuing efforts of the living. The persistent *Romanitas* of the family is spelt out in Marcus's submission of the 'poor remainder of Andronici' to the will of the Roman people:

Now have you heard the truth: what say you,
                                        Romans?
Have we done aught amiss, show us wherein,
And, from the place where you behold us pleading,
The poor remainder of Andronici
Will hand in hand all headlong hurl ourselves,
And on the ragged stones beat forth our souls,
And make a mutual closure of our house.
(v, iii, 128–34)

On the contrary, of course, the people exalt the family and the family, in its turn, must exalt the dead. It is in this context that Lavinia, like another Lucrece, comes to represent something like a Roman tutelary deity, raped, mutilated, rendered incapable of crying out against these invasive barbarisms, but, by virtue of family *pietas* and unflinching self-sacrifice, enabled to take up her niche in the household monument and to represent to later ages a mode of tragic experience appropriate to a meaningfully 'Roman' world.

© G. K. HUNTER 1974

THE AESTHETICS OF MUTILATION IN 'TITUS ANDRONICUS'

ALBERT H. TRICOMI

When T. S. Eliot so flamboyantly denounced *Titus Andronicus* as 'one of the stupidest and most uninspired plays ever written', he naturally invited rebuttal.[1] But while an apology for *Titus* can certainly be erected, the fact is that the imputed stupidities of the tragedy attract far more interest than any of its mediocre achievements. Indeed, if we would only persist in the study of those very 'stupidities' that many critics would rather forget, we would discover that the ways in which the figurative language imitates the literal events of plot makes *The Tragedy of Titus Andronicus* a significant dramatic experiment. In the play's spectacularly self-conscious images that keep pointing at the inventive horrors in the plotting, in its wittily-obsessive allusions to dismembered hands and heads, and in the prophetic literalness of its metaphors, *Titus* reveals its peculiar literary importance.

The peculiar language of *Titus Andronicus* is particularly apparent in the literalness of its central metaphors. In a play preeminently concerned with the mutilation of the human body, *Titus* makes nearly sixty references, figurative as well as literal, to the word 'hands' and eighteen more to the word 'head', or to one of its derivative forms.[2] Far from being divorced from the action as many critics claim,[3] the figurative language points continually toward the lurid events that govern the tragedy. The figurative language, in fact, imitates the gruesome circumstances of the plot, thus revealing that Shakespeare sub-ordinates everything in *Titus*, including metaphor, to that single task of conveying forcefully the Senecan and Ovidian horrors that he has committed himself to portraying.

Such a relationship between language and event is really quite strange. Ordinarily meta-

[1] *Selected Essays: 1917–1932* (London, 1932), p. 82. Effective rebuttal has occurred with relative infrequency. See Hereward T. Price, 'The Authorship of *Titus Andronicus*', *The Journal of English and Germanic Philology*, XLII (1943), 55–81; E. M. W. Tillyard, *Shakespeare's History Plays* (New York, 1962), pp. 158–65; Alan Sommers, '"Wilderness of Tigers": Structure and Symbolism in *Titus Andronicus*', *Essays in Criticism*, X (1960), 275–89; and A. C. Hamilton, *The Early Shakespeare* (San Marino, 1967), pp. 63–89. For a superb theory concerning the language of *Titus Andronicus*, see Eugene Waith, 'The Metamorphosis of Violence in *Titus Andronicus*', *Shakespeare Survey 10* (Cambridge, 1957), pp. 39–49.

[2] Laura Jepsen, 'A Footnote on "Hands" in Shakespeare's *Titus Andronicus*', *Florida State Univ. Studies*, XIX (1955), 7–10; *Oxford Shakespeare Concordance: Titus Andronicus* (Oxford, 1972), pp. 95–6, 99.

[3] The works of Muriel Bradbrook, *Themes and Conventions of Elizabethan Tragedy* (Cambridge, Eng., 1935), pp. 98–9, and *Shakespeare and Elizabethan Poetry* (New York, 1952), pp. 104–10; J. Dover Wilson (ed.), *Titus Andronicus* (Cambridge, Eng., 1948), pp. ix–xii; and Wolfgang Clemen, *The Development of Shakespeare's Imagery* (New York, 1951), pp. 22–7, have provided deservedly influential insights into the discontinuity between image and occasion in *Titus Andronicus*, but the sense in which the figurative language embodies the events in *Titus* has never been analyzed. An explanation of the decorous tone of the poetry in *Titus* can, however, be found in Waith's essay, 'Metamorphosis of Violence'.

phor is endowed with the capacity of extending almost infinitely the imaginative compass of a play. Through its embedded metaphors especially, a play usually translates its immediate events in images that reach far beyond the poor limitations of the stage. In *Titus Andronicus*, however, metaphor, for the most part, draws its images directly from the narrower events of plot. It becomes literalized. This is a very daring and even dangerous enterprise to undertake. Deliberately relinquishing its natural prerogatives, metaphor strives instead to unite language and action in an endeavour to render the events of the tragedy more real and painful. When Marcus offers Titus the throne, for example, he employs a peculiar metaphor, saying, 'And help to set a head on headless Rome' (I, i, 186). Since Titus is being offered the throne of Imperial Rome, Marcus's statement seems to be a happy one. As such, the metaphor appears to be just that, an embellished phrase, a polished, if affected, mode of speech. But, as it happens, this mere metaphor, with all its ominous overtones, is later raised to factual reality when Saturninus, ironically made that 'head' of Rome through Titus's support, beheads two of Titus's sons. In a more specific sense as well, the figures employed direct our perceptions toward isolated parts of the human body. When in the first act Lavinia asks her father to bless her, she uses the rather precise phrase, 'with thy victorious hand' (I, i, 163), and Bassianus does likewise when he explains how Titus, 'With his own hand' slew his youngest son (I, i, 418). In both instances the figurative phrasing points ahead to the mutilations of future events, to the shearing off of Lavinia's hands, and then, to Titus's willing sacrifice of his own hand when bargaining for the lives of two of his sons.

But while the keen critic may discover a rather brutal principle of retribution in Titus's loss of a hand for having killed – with his own

hand – one of his sons, I am more concerned here with the oddly alluring relationship between language and event. Constantly pointing toward and underlining the events that we witness upon the stage, metaphor in this tragedy strains to keep the excruciating images of mutilation ever before our imaginations even when the visual spectacle is no longer before us. The words 'hand' and 'head' appear copiously as figures of speech whose effect is to saturate every aspect of the play with remembered or foreshadowed horror. Following the scene of Lavinia's mutilation, Marcus presents his niece to Titus whose first words to her,

> Speak, Lavinia, what accursed hand
> Hath made thee handless in thy father's sight?
> (III, i, 66–7)

recreates the horrible event in the imagination. Of course, the literate response is so artificial as to invite derision, and, no doubt, the whole idea of asking the dumb to speak is a questionable way of inviting pathos. But the pun on hands, which is equally self-conscious and full of artifice, is not without its redeeming features. Titus's paronomasia rests on two notably dissimilar kinds of usage. When he refers to 'the accursed hand', he employs a simple form of synecdoche, but when he speaks of Lavinia's handlessness, he alludes to nothing but the visual reality before him. Furthermore, the paronomasia draws our attention to the image of the rapist using his hand in the act of shearing off Lavinia's own, effectively underlining, Hamlet-like, the 'unkindness' and unnaturalness of the act. So while we may argue that Titus's self-conscious word-play largely replaces genuine personal response, we must acknowledge that the bitter contrast between the mere metaphor and the experienced reality of Lavinia's handlessness is powerfully conceived.

This remark of Titus's illustrates one of the

play's basic concerns – exploring the gulf between metaphoric descriptions of events and the irrefutable realities they purport to communicate. Shakespeare's interest in these matters, so abstract in its way, appears grounded, however, in the dramatist's involvement in the relative merits of words as contrasted with dramatic events. So concerned is the play with the deceptive powers of poetic description that it offers several instructive lessons contrasting the vacuous rhetoric of rape and the palpable reality of Lavinia's ravishment, hands lopped off, mouth bleeding. As the play opens, Saturninus, who has just announced his betrothal to Lavinia, finds that Bassianus has already married her and berates him in an exaggerated rhetorical outburst, saying, 'Thou and thy faction shall regret this rape' (I, i, 404). Bassianus, sensitive to the proper signification of words, rejoins hotly,

> Rape call you it, my lord, to seize my own,
> My true-betrothed love . . . ?   (I, i, 405–6)

In this way the play continually investigates the chasm between the spoken word and the actual fact, an investigation, incidentally, whose meaning is fully experienced only when Lavinia appears before us raped and bleeding in fact. Similarly, this ironic denigration of metaphor occurs again when Lucius, hearing the villainous Aaron explain how,

> They cut thy sister's tongue and ravish'd her,
> And cut her hands and trimm'd her as thou sawest.
>   (v, i, 93)

seizes on the disgustingly prettified figure and retorts, 'O detestable villain! call'st thou that trimming?' (v, i, 93). Far from being used inadvertently then, the language self-consciously focuses upon itself so as to demonstrate the manner in which figurative speech can diminish and even transform the actual horror of events. But since the purpose of the tragedy is not to dilute but to highlight the nightmare that befalls the Andronici, the play deliberately

'exposes' the euphemisms of metaphor by measuring their falseness against the irrefutable realities of dramatized events. On these occasions, the play turns its back on metaphor, rejecting it as a device that tends to dissipate the unremitting terrors of the tragedy. Only in the literalization of its metaphors, it appears, does the tragedy seem to be at ease with itself.

II

Such a self-consciously didactic use of metaphor is really quite distinctive in Elizabethan drama, to say nothing of Elizabethan tragedy, but far more strange is the deliberate constriction of the figurative language as it binds itself to the gory plot. So firmly does the figurative language yoke itself to the action of *Titus* that mere rhetorical flourishes tend, prophetically, to realize themselves in actual events. In the scene where Titus first bears witness to his daughter's mutilation, for example, he expresses his grief, not unexpectedly, in hyperbolic outburst,

> My grief was at the height before thou cam'st,
> . . . .
> Give me a sword, I'll chop off my hands too,
> For they have fought for Rome, and all in vain
>   (III, i, 70–3)

To be sure, the unusual nature of the event goes far to justify the strained pitch of the rhetoric, but the speech fully realizes its tragic possibilities only in subsequent events. For while Titus begins by speaking an exaggerated language of sorrow, Shakespeare forces his hero to live up to the terrible potential of his hyperbolic outburst. Shylock-like, the dramatist takes Titus's speech out of the realm of mere rant and exacts of him the pound of flesh he promises. That is to say, the exaggeration of Titus's rhetorical figure is, through an act of the dramatist's imagination, realized in terms of a hyperbole of plot, which acts as if it were a figure of speech brought to monstrous birth. Thus, in a vain effort to save his two imprisoned sons, Titus renders up his hand to the ravenous Emperor of Rome. The words he speaks at the time explain precisely the bizarre relationship between language and events that typifies the method of the play. 'Come hither, Aaron ...' he says, 'Lend me thy hand, and I will give thee mine' (III, i, 186–7).

Since *The Tragedy of Titus Andronicus* is predicated on the notion that the most excruciating horrors pertain to the experienced reality of events, the metaphoric impact of the tragedy can only be realized by forcing the metaphors to take on dramatic life. Accordingly, hands become powerful dramatic symbols, not simply because they are mentioned sixty times in the text, but because they become *images in action* whose significance we experience visually and not merely verbally, in abstraction. Stated metaphorically, the most profound impulse in *Titus* is to make the word become flesh. That the literary symbolism of hands indeed becomes flesh is obvious, not only in Titus's hand-lopping scene, but also in the scene in which Titus's son Quintus offers to assist his brother Martius after the latter has fallen into a pit that the cunning Aaron has prepared. Trapped inside, Martius implores Quintus's aid, crying, 'O brother, help me with thy fainting hand' (II, iii, 233), and Quintus in turn replies, 'Reach me thy hand, that I may help thee out' (II, iii, 237). After his first effort fails, Quintus again underscores the dramatic significance of hands, saying,

> Thy hand once more; I will not loose again,
> Till thou art here aloft, or I below.
> Thou canst not come to me—I come to thee.
> [*Falls in.*]   (II, iii, 243–5)

Here the hands of Titus's kin, vainly stretched to help one another, epitomize a central tragic movement in the play. Symbols of Rome's defense, civic pride, and filial love, the hands of the Andronici are, in the aftermath of the Gothic war, rendered useless, not metaphorically, but literally.

Moreover, even while Quintus's allusion to hands attunes us to future events, his specific remark about 'loos[ing]' hands becomes, by virtue of the hand mutilations that are to follow, a visual, theatrical device for dramatizing the helplessness of the Andronici. Like Titus's witticism on Aaron's lending him a hand and like his imaginative question to Lavinia, 'What hand hath made thee handless ...,' Quintus's remark reveals again Shakespeare's unstinting exploration of the gap between a metaphoric use of language and a referential use of language anchored in the afflictions of actual events. Indeed, considering the contrast that exists between Quintus's fear of 'losing' his brother's outstretched hand and the actual lopping off of Lavinia's hands, which immediately follows this first event, we must admit that Shakespeare confers upon the ghoulish notion of losing hands, not one, but several literal meanings!

III

This unrelieved and, in truth, witty exploration of the relationship between language and event marks a notably disinterested, even detached, involvement in the values of language with respect to dramatic events. This cool distance between the playwright and his materials helps to explain one of the distinguishing features of *Titus Andronicus* – the odd way that this tragedy leaps with an inextinguishable wittiness toward the multiple perceptions that ordinarily belong to the world of intellectual comedy. From incidents like the one in which Titus asks his mute daughter to speak or like the one in which he wonders whether the Andronici should

> bite our tongues, and in dumb shows
> Pass the remainder of our hateful days
> (III, i, 131–2)

it becomes obvious that these gruesomely ironic perceptions are rooted in an irrepressible wittiness. This witty impulse expresses itself further in a hideously satanic atmosphere that permeates the unbelievable events of the tragedy, and the personification of this atmosphere is Aaron, whose satanic drollery is not unworthy of his spiritual brother, Richard Crookback. When the fiendish blackamoor instructs Tamora's oafish sons to ravish Lavinia in the woods, he employs an evocatively poetic language that lasciviously focuses upon the image of physical violation:

The woods are ruthless, dreadful, deaf, and dull.
There speak, and strike, brave boys, and take
                                        your turns;
There serve your lust, shadowed from heaven's
                                        eye,
And revel in Lavinia's treasury.

(II, i, 128–31)

The source of Aaron's wittiness, we find, emerges from the deliberate exposure of the literal meanings that underlie our figurative use of language. The poetic decorum of the clause, 'And revel in Lavinia's treasury' is savage in that it simultaneously creates, in prurient delight, a literally-imagined picture of Lavinia's ravished chastity at the moment of violation. Enveloped as it is in a dark language of hushed expectancy, the picture creates an ugly beauty. Like Iago and Richard III, Aaron relishes poetic language because he can force it to serve the baser appetites, which is to say that Aaron appropriates the beauties of language for foul purposes, rapes it as it were, so that it may serve the literalness of his own coarse imaginings.

This deliberate transformation of the beauties of lyrical poetry into a house of horrible imaginings is, however, not just Aaron's, but Shakespeare's, for in *Titus Andronicus* brutality, which is always conceived with the utmost literalness of imagination, continually parades in the parodic disguise of metaphoric

loveliness. In the scene where Titus rouses the court and bids them to join him in the sport of hunting a proud panther, Demetrius declines the invitation, saying to his brother,

Chiron, we hunt not, we, with horse nor hound,
But hope to pluck a dainty doe to ground

(II, ii, 25–6)

Expecting to use his time to rape Lavinia in the forest, Demetrius riddles shallowly on the instrument with which he and his brother will 'hunt' Lavinia. But the couplet is more than indecent; it is brutal and obscene. The venereal suggestiveness of the hunt itself, combined with the image of the 'pluck[ed]' doe being brought to the ground, focuses with salacious relish on the anticipated act of violation. Here again, the poetry, which seems at first to offer only a metaphoric suggestion of Lavinia's rape, is in reality shackled – through the salacious wit – to the literal ugliness of the rape itself.

Whatever we may think about the success of this use of figurative language, there is no escaping the fact that *Titus Andronicus* is, in the broadest sense of the term, a very witty play. It is, in fact, as witty in the circumstances of its plotting as it is in its exploitation of metaphor and in its evocation of atmosphere. The two outstanding cases in point occur in the hand-lopping scene in the third act and in the special technique Lavinia uses to reveal her assailants in act IV. The former instance comes about when Aaron convinces Titus to cut off his right hand as ransom for his two sons imprisoned by the Emperor. Throughout the scene Aaron displays an odd kind of detached artistry, a lunatic humor. After Aaron chops off Titus's hand, he commends the old warrior, saying,   for thy hand
Look by and by to have thy sons with thee
[*Aside.*]   Their heads, I mean.   (III, i, 201–3)

A crude joke indeed. In a play filled with the devices of metonymy and synecdoche, especially on the subject of the human body, Aaron employs the same device with respect to the action. Metaphorically speaking, Aaron does engineer the return of Titus's sons in that he returns the part for the whole. Like a literary artist Aaron has created an act of synecdoche. For the two sons he has returned a metaphor!

This irrepressible wit of plotting is, however, only partly explicable as an expression of Aaron's personality, which in some important measure derives from the ingenious vice figures of the medieval moralities. The wit of plot is, finally, much larger than Aaron's; it is Shakespeare's, and it is worth noting that the scene most universally scored for its ludicrous flight of lyric poetry, the one in II, iv, where Marcus first spies the ravished Lavinia wandering in the woods, keeps pointing to its own achievements in rendering Ovid's pathetic tale of Tereus's rape of Philomel even more pathetic:

> Marcus.
> Fair Philomel, why, she but lost her tongue,
> And in a tedious sampler sew'd her mind;
> But, lovely niece, that mean is cut from thee.
> A craftier Tereus, cousin, hast thou met,
> And he hath cut those pretty fingers off
> That could have better sew'd than Philomel.
>
> (II, iv, 38–43)

The explicit allusions to Ovid's tale invite comparison. That 'craftier Tereus' Marcus speaks of is really Will Shakespeare laying claim to having out-witted the Roman poet in the telling of a tale. In Titus the young playwright even invites the audience to ponder how Lavinia, his heroine, unable to 'sew her mind' as Ovid's Philomel did, will be able to reveal her ravisher's identity. Lavinia's rapists, unschooled as they are, make quite a bit of the problem they have raised:

> Chiron. [to Lavinia]
> Write down thy mind, bewray thy meaning so,
> And if thy stumps will let thee play the scribe.
> Demetrius.
> See how with signs and tokens she can scrowl.
>
> (II, iv, 3–5)

But if the shearing off of Lavinia's hands raises a kind of suspense because we are uncertain how she will be able to expose her assailants, the solution to this puzzle is that much more unexpected and original than Ovid's. In having Lavinia scrawl out the names of her ravishers by holding a pole between her stumps and grasping the pole's end inside her mouth, Shakespeare effects a most witty poetic justice. Lavinia's lips do speak; her handless hands, indeed, do write![1]

IV

In this witty competition with Ovid and Seneca, Shakespeare is just what Greene said he was, 'an upstart Crow' striving to overreach his masters in their own vein.[2] In Titus the especial competition with Ovid fully insinuates itself into Shakespeare's poetic statement and is one of the basic reasons why the tragedy sometimes runs aground on the shoals of Ovidian lyricism. As Eugene Waith points out, the play apparently fails to transpose a narrative tale of horror into a convincing

[1] Although Shakespeare courts comparison with Ovid, he makes no effort to disclose his own native sources. The story of Lavinia's scribbling the names of her assailants by the use of her two stumps occurs in a prose narrative, which in all probability Shakespeare knew. The convincing evidence is set forth by Ralph M. Sargent, 'The Source of Titus Andronicus', Studies in Philology, XLVI (1949), 167–84. The prose narrative itself is reprinted by Sylvan Barnet (ed.), The Tragedy of Titus Andronicus (New York, 1963), pp. 135–48. See also, Geoffrey Bullough (ed.), Narrative and Dramatic Sources of Shakespeare (New York, 1966), VI, 7–13. The witty justice that emerges from Lavinia's using her stumps and her mouth to reveal her rapists is, however, Shakespeare's own invention.

[2] G. B. Harrison (ed.), Robert Greene, M.A.: Groats-Worth of Witte (1592; New York, 1966), p. 45. Although the context in which the phrase appears shows that Greene was thinking of Shakespeare as actor as well as playwright, the colorful phrase aptly captures the ambitiousness that is evident in the writing of Titus Andronicus.

dramatic story.[1] The characters, he observes, respond to events with poetic declamations that lack psychological appropriateness or verisimilitude. Yet, the problem is not one of dramatic ineptitude, pure and simple. The scenes derived from Ovid's story are confidently aware of their transposed existence in the added dimension of drama.[2] When Titus first beholds his ravished daughter, he laments,

> Had I but seen thy picture in this plight
> It would have madded me; what shall I do
> Now I behold thy lively body so?
>
> (III, i, 103–5)

So too, when Marcus first spies the mutilated Lavinia wandering in the woods, his monologue effectively underlines the dramatic mode of Shakespeare's story:

> *Marcus.*
> Cousin, a word; . . .
> . . . .
> Speak, gentle niece . . .
> . . . Why dost not speak to me?
> . . . .
> Shall I speak for thee? Shall I say 'tis so?
>
> (II, iv, 12–33)

That the anticipated dialogue is denied Marcus only emphasizes how effectively Shakespeare has exploited the visual resources of drama. Moreover, inasmuch as dialogue is necessarily impossible in this episode, Shakespeare casts the greater focus upon the visual spectacle of the mutilated Lavinia. Through Marcus who acts as commentator on the event, Shakespeare forces us to see, detail by descriptive detail, the spectacle that we are already beholding:

> Speak, gentle niece, what stern ungentle hands
> Hath lopp'd and hew'd and made thy body bare
> Of her two branches . . . ?
> . . . .
> Alas, a crimson river of warm blood,
> Like to a bubbling fountain stirr'd with wind,
> Doth rise and fall between thy rosed lips,
> Coming and going with thy honey breath.

> But, sure, some Tereus hath deflow'red thee,
> And, lest thou should'st detect him, cut thy tongue.
> Ah, now thou turn'st away thy face for shame!
> And, notwithstanding all this loss of blood . . .
>
> (II, iv, 16–29)

Clearly enough, the visual image is intended to be so powerfully immediate that the characters themselves believe the image of Lavinia must be imaginary. Among Marcus's first words in the above speech are, 'If I do dream, would all my wealth would wake me' (II, iv, 13). Later, Titus complains, 'When will this fearful slumber have an end?' (III, i, 252). The fact that the characters often react to the play's events as if they had been transported into another realm altogether demonstrates Shakespeare's endeavor to reach the utmost verge of realizable horror. By utilizing Ovid's already affecting narrative in a theatrical context that exploits Lavinia's presence upon the stage, Shakespeare reaches to outdo the Roman poet for pathos, and Seneca as well for horror.

But despite the resourcefulness of this theater of horrors, there are unavoidable limits in *Titus Andronicus* to dramatic spectacle. For all the severed heads, for all the poignance of Lavinia's mutilated beauty, the one horror the dramatist could not depict upon the stage was the fact of Lavinia's violated chastity, which loss was to Titus the worst violation of all,

> that more dear
> Than hands or tongue, her spotless chastity
>
> (v, ii, 176–7)

In overcoming this necessary limitation, however, Shakespeare chooses to identify Lavinia's violation with the violation of Rome and of all civilized value. It is upon this enlarged conception of violation – Lavinia's and Rome's – that Shakespeare does confer visual life by introducing the enduring and theatrical symbol

---

[1] 'Metamorphosis of Violence', pp. 47–8.
[2] Hamilton, *The Early Shakespeare*, pp. 68–9.

of the middle acts, the pit. As Tamora's premonitory speech indicates –

> And when they show'd me this abhorred pit,
> They told me, here, at dead time of the night,
> A thousand fiends, a thousand hissing snakes,
> Ten thousand swelling toads, as many urchins,
> Would make such fearful and confused cries,
> As any mortal body hearing it
> Should straight fall mad, or else die suddenly
>
> (II, iii, 98–104)

– the pit symbolizes an inferno of evil and is directly associated, as Professor Hamilton has shown, with the classical underworld.[1] The demonic portentousness of the pit is further highlighted by Lavinia's own ironic protestations, made before her captors. Fearing rape, she begs of Tamora,

> one thing more
> That womanhood denies my tongue to tell:
> O, keep me from their worse than killing lust,
> And tumble me into some loathsome pit.
>
> (II, iii, 173–6)

Speaking a language of chaste circumlocution, Lavinia asks to die rather than to be sexually defiled, but her inadvertent pun upon the word 'tumble', meaning, as Eric Partridge records, 'To copulate with (girl or woman), to cause to *fall backward*,'[2] ironically prophesies the circumstances of her later violation. Just ten lines later Lavinia is dragged off the stage to her rape, and the pit, just alluded to, becomes the central image upon the stage.

In the passage immediately following, Bassianus's bloody corpse is heaved into the pit and Lavinia's brothers, Martius and Quintus, deceived by the cunning Aaron, become entrapped within it. Already depicted vividly by Tamora as an abyss in which a world of evil spawns, the pit is now described as a womb, malignant and devouring.[3] Pictured by Quintus and Martius as 'this unhallow'd and blood-stained hole' (II, iii, 210), then as a

fell, devouring receptacle,
As hateful as Cocytus' misty mouth

(II, iii, 235–6)

and, finally, as

> the swallowing womb
> Of this deep pit   (II, iii, 239–40)

the pit reveals the dark recesses of evil and also carries at least a suggestive reminder of the rape of Lavinia that is simultaneously transpiring off-stage. Moreover, with Bassianus's blood upon it, his body within, and the two entrapped Andronici accused of his murder trapped inside, the pit – that is, the trap door at the front of the Elizabethan stage – becomes not only a symbol of the demonic power, but a theatrical embodiment of it. Grotesque then as the image appears, the pit creates, by virtue of its visibility and concreteness as a device of theater, a powerful and synthesizing poetic image of the horrible fecundity of evil.

This éclat in exploiting the resources of the stage is just what we should expect from a wit-enchanted and ambitious poet who has lately discovered the wider world of theater. Just as the young Shakespeare endeavors to out-plot Plautus in *The Comedy of Errors* by doubling the number of identical twins, and just as he tries to out-marvel Marlowe by creating in *Richard III* a villain more joyous in the performance of evil than Barabas, so in *Titus Andronicus* Shakespeare seeks to outdo both

[1] *Ibid.*, pp. 69–72.
[2] *Shakespeare's Bawdy* (1947; rpt., London, 1961), p. 210.
[3] This association is characteristically Shakespearian. Most strikingly, it appears again in *King Lear* (Kenneth Muir (ed.), London, 1959), where Lear imagines the female sexual organs as the pit of hell:

> Down from the waist they are Centaurs,
> Though women all above:
> But to the girdle do the Gods inherit,
> Beneath is all the fiend's: there's hell,
>   there's darkness,
> There is the sulphurous pit – burning, scalding,
> Stench, consumption; fie, fie, fie! pah, pah!
>
> (IV, vi, 123–8)

Seneca and Ovid by utilizing his living stage in the telling of a tale more horrifying and pathetic than that of either of his models.[1] Small wonder that the characters in this earliest of Shakespeare's tragedies appear to participate actively in the dramatist's own ambitious search for ever more fabulous events:

Titus.
> shall we cut away our hands like thine?
> Or shall we bite our tongues, and in dumb shows
> Pass the remainder of our hateful days?
> What shall we do? let us that have our tongues
> Plot some device of further misery,
> To make us wonder'd at in time to come.

(III, i, 130–5)

Whatever our final aesthetic judgment concerning the merits of *Titus Andronicus*, we must understand that we are dealing, not with a paucity of imagination, but with an excess of dramatic witness, with a talent untamed. However flawed the tragedy may be in other respects, we must grant that the playwright has exploited the language of the stage with inventive brilliance and has taxed the resources of drama in making death and mutilation vivid to us.

If we wish, we can, of course, treat this tragedy with orthodox sobriety in order to demonstrate its thematic integrity, but the real vitality and interest of *Titus Andronicus* lies, it seems to me, in just those parts that are in some ways speculative, or even impossible dramatically. By shackling the metaphoric imagination to the literal reality of the play's events, the tragedy strives for an unrelieved concentration of horrific effect. Through its prophetic allusions to physical dismemberment, its incurably literalized figures of speech, and its ambitious use of the stage as a dramatic metaphor, *Titus Andronicus* strives to exhaust the language as well as the events of tragedy. We do not all have to like the tragedy, but we ought to recognize that *Titus* is a uniquely important experiment in drama, for in it Shakespeare is exploring the resources inherent in a referential use of metaphor and is trying to integrate the power of the poetic language with the immeasurable potential of dramatic action itself.

[1] For a close analysis of the influence of these models, see Bullough (ed.), *Narrative and Dramatic Sources*, VI, 23–33.

THE MOTIF OF PSYCHIC DIVISION
IN 'RICHARD III'

WILLIAM B. TOOLE

Generally speaking, *Richard III* carries on the theme of guilt and retribution that in one way or another links eight of Shakespeare's history plays, and concludes the series with the theme of order restored. Motivated by a totally unconscionable ambition for power, the protagonist intensifies the bloody disorder which has plagued England since the deposition of Richard II until he becomes subject to retribution himself at the hands of Richmond, whose success at Bosworth Field is the prelude to peace and unity in England. The deposition of Richard II had led to a division between the houses of York and Lancaster, and this division was responsible for the moral chaos that afflicted England during the Wars of the Roses. When, in *Richard II*, Carlyle protests against the deposition and prophesies its effect—

> Oh, if you raise this house against this house,
> It will the woefullest division prove
> That ever fell upon this cursed earth
>
> (IV, i, 145–7)[1]

– he is, in effect, partially echoing or anticipating[2] Richmond's choric statement at the end of *Richard III* that the marriage of himself and Elizabeth, 'the true succeeders of each royal house', would bring an end to the unnatural division of brother and brother, and father and son. 'The fair conjunction' of 'the white rose and the red' would, he asserted, unify all that 'divided York and Lancaster, / Divided in their dire division' (v, v, 19, 20, 27–8).

The extent to which the motif of division acts as a dramaturgical and thematic principle controlling the framework of *Richard III* has not been fully explained. In this paper I shall be concerned with showing how Shakespeare's treatment of this motif through the delineation of Richard's character is designed to direct his audience to the central ideas of the play and govern its emotional responses to the protagonist.

The general meaning reflected in the motif of division is given direct expression in the despairing reaction of the Duchess of York to the news that the Queen's kindred have been imprisoned by Gloucester and Buckingham. Realizing that this action is the beginning of further bloody division, she at once sums up her experience and anticipates the course of the dynastic feud:

> Accursed and unquiet wrangling days,
> How many of you have mine eyes beheld!
> My husband lost his life to get the crown,
> And often up and down my sons were toss'd,
> For me to joy and weep their gain and loss.
> And being seated, and domestic broils
> Clean over-blown, themselves, the conquerors,
> Make war upon themselves, blood against blood,
> Self against self. O preposterous
> And frantic outrage . . .   (II, iv, 55–64)

The final lines of this passage indicate the concluding stages of the pattern that Shakespeare established through the motif of division in his

---

[1] All Shakespeare quotations are from G. B. Harrison's *Shakespeare: The Complete Works* (New York, 1948).

[2] Depending, of course, upon whether one is speaking of the compositional or historical chronology.

first tetralogy. In the *Henry VI* plays the effects of the division between two houses have been presented. Now through this speech of Richard's mother Shakespeare intensifies our awareness of the unnaturalness of the initial division by showing how it has led inevitably to further unnatural division when the conquerors 'make war upon themselves'; and in the phrase 'self against self' we have an anticipation of the ultimate division, the final logical absurdity, warfare within an individual. The movement in the *Henry VI* plays and *Richard III* then, when seen as a group, is from the division between two branches of a family to division within a family and, finally, to division within an individual.

One of the most striking architectonic features of *Richard III* lies in the relationship between division within an individual and disorder in the state.[1] For the movement from division and disorder in England to unity and peace is inversely paralleled by a movement from what might be called psychological integrity in the character of Richard to a kind of psychic warfare between two parts of his personality, a struggle which is at once the prelude to his destruction and the salvation of England.

Some of the ideas reflected in the final stages of the pattern of absurdity brought about by the movement away from natural order may be illustrated by a well-known passage from a much later play. In *Troilus and Cressida* Ulysses tells Agamemnon that when degree is neglected:

> Then everything includes itself in power,
> Power into will, will into appetite;
> And appetite, a universal wolf,
> So doubly seconded with will and power,
> Must make perforce a universal prey,
> And last eat up himself.
>
> (I, iii, 119–24)

The character of Richard, which is responsible for the division that takes place in the House of York, is delineated in somewhat similar terms in 3 *Henry VI*. There Richard announces that the only pleasure which life can afford him is that of the power which resides in the crown (III, iii, 165–71); there he expresses his ambitious nature in terms of animal appetite (v, vi, 75–7); and there his assertion 'I am myself alone'[2] (v, vi, 83) is presented in a context which makes it clear that respect for order and degree in human relationships will not deter him from the satisfaction of this appetite. The idea of appetite turning finally upon itself provides, in a very interesting way, the basis for the dramatic fulfillment of the concept of self against self; and the effect of this is to show Richard, to his great surprise, that he is not himself alone. Technically speaking, this is accomplished, as we shall see, through the manner in which the play establishes two polarized bases for the metaphor of appetite. Throughout the major part of the drama the imagery of appetite suggests a cruel passion or lust for power; but it is also, though less markedly, associated with the remorse of conscience. The psychological civil war that occurs in the being of Richard, metaphorically speaking, is the result of a conflict between two forms of appetite, one spiritual and the other secular.

The intensity of Richard's passion for power is presented metaphorically in the bestial

[1] The general pattern of the play has been outlined by E. M. W. Tillyard, *Shakespeare's History Plays* (1944; London, 1969), p. 212: 'The emerging of unity from and through discord, the simultaneous change in Richard from accomplished villain to the despairing embodiment of evil.' No one, so far as I am aware, has indicated the careful structural connection which Shakespeare makes between these movements.

[2] For Shakespeare such an assertion reflected the essence of evil, as Donald A. Stauffer observes in *Shakespeare's World of Images: The Development of His Moral Ideas* (Bloomington, 1949), p. 27. And, as John F. Danby points out in *Shakespeare's Doctrine of Nature: A Study of King Lear* (London, 1949), p. 64, it seems to be one of the key sentiments Shakespeare associates with the 'new' or Machiavellian man.

images[1] that are used to describe him throughout the drama and in the manner in which he is associated with a precocious and unconscionable capacity for eating. We hear him called a wolf, a dog, a hellhound, a boar, a hedgehog, and so on. We are reminded that he had his teeth before his eyes and that he could gnaw a crust before he was two hours old. And we find that he takes pleasure in eating just before, or immediately after ordering or planning some cruel action that will further his drive for power. When asked, for example, what he will do with Hastings if he won't go along with the plan for the coup d'état, Richard responds cheerfully, 'Chop off his head' (III, i, 193) and goes on to suggest that he and his confederates 'sup' after which they may 'digest' their 'complots' (III, i, 198, 199). Later he sends out for strawberries just before sentencing Hastings to death on a trumped-up charge and observes that he will not be able to dine until he sees his head. And still later in the play, upon hearing that his order for the murder of the young Princes has been carried out, he orders Tyrell to come to him 'soon at after supper' so that he may tell him 'the process of their death' (IV, iii, 31, 32).

Throughout the first part of the play we find Richard causing unnatural divisions of various kinds. At the outset of the drama he tells us that he has succeeded in separating Clarence from the affections of his brother; then we see him separating Anne from the body of her father-in-law, an action which represents a movement away from natural family loyalty; and later we find that he has successfully separated Hastings's trusted servant Catesby from his master. Such actions, which are moves employed by Richard in his drive to satisfy his appetite for power,[2] call attention to his clever duplicity and ultimately reflect his capacity for surprising his victims as they discover he is not what he pretends to be, a creature of conscience.

Though the Richard we meet at the beginning of the play is, in a very real sense, psychologically whole, we find that he has two personalities. The public Richard alters somewhat the shape of his image from situation to situation, but all of his 'on-stage' shadows have the same moral essence – whether he is presenting himself as a simple artless child who can be led by others, a bluff plain-spoken man who is vulnerable to the slander of subtle time-servers, or an ambitionless saint whose greatest oath is 'by St. Paul'. The private Richard may well be described in his own terms as Iniquity, the personification of selfish demonic energy or appetite. Since Richard uses his public or puppet character as a means of satisfying his desires, we may say that his is a deliberately split personality. And, as everyone would agree, it is largely by means of this divided personality that he presents himself to us as a most engaging fellow.

Indeed if it were not for the zest with which Richard plays the public side of himself and the delight with which he reflects in private over

[1] Since Richard had identified himself as a master Machiavel in *3 Henry VI*, it is interesting to note here the Elizabethan conviction, as disseminated by Gentillet and others, that the Machiavellian prince took beasts as his models because of his preoccupation with satisfying his sensual appetite and sinful passions. See W. A. Armstrong, 'The Influence of Seneca and Machiavelli on the Elizabethan Tyrant', *The Review of English Studies*, 24 (1948), 25–6.

[2] Bernard Spivack, *Shakespeare and the Allegory of Evil* (New York, 1958), p. 397, says that the emphasis in the play is not on Richard's progress toward the crown but on his ability to create dissension in place of unity and love, and to seduce his victims from virtuous allegiances. While I do not disagree with this point, I think it is important to realize that this divisive ability is the factor which allows Richard to progress toward the crown. Similarly, I do not think it is necessary to dissociate Richard's vice-like delight in villainy for its own sake from his 'naturalistic' desire for the crown, as Spivack does (p. 404). Richard takes great pleasure in his clever and cruel actions because of the sense of superiority and power they give him; at the same time these actions are taking him toward the source of ultimate temporal power.

his ability to dupe others, the drama would be almost as dull in its heavy-footed march on the theme of retribution as *Gorboduc*. The tone of Richard's character is responsible for the most remarkable and dramaturgically effective feature of the play.[1] Consider, for example, the dialogue that takes place in the carefully staged scene in which Buckingham, whom Richard has called his 'other self' (II, ii, 151), pleads with him not to allow his 'conscience', his tender-minded concern for the ties of blood and for degree and due process, deter him from the crown. Pretending to be incensed because Richard has refused the offer, Buckingham cries: 'Come, citizens, 'Zounds! I'll entreat no more.' To this Richard responds, 'Oh, do not swear, my Lord of Buckingham' (III, vii, 219–20).

Richard's magnificently mincing distress here is strongly anticipatory of the tone which Falstaff adopts in another kind of play-within-a-play. Everyone will recall how, upon assuming the role of the prince, he defends his loyal and virtuous friend against the ugly charges levelled by the King. Falstaff rises to great heights of eloquence as he defends his own character. With intentional irony he establishes the fact that, in speaking through the character of Hal, he is speaking for himself: 'But to say I know more harm in him than in myself were to say more than I know' (1 *Henry IV*, II, iv, 512–13). He then goes on to observe, 'That he is old, the more the pity, his white hairs do witness it; but that he is, saving your reverence, a whore master, that I utterly deny' (II, iv, 513–16). Since Falstaff has made it clear that he is speaking in his own person – that is to say, in his customary role of defender of the flesh – the inflectional and parenthetical wince in the line just quoted is perhaps the most outrageously amusing rhetorical stroke in the scene.

It is not altogether an exaggeration to say that Richard at times is Falstaff in a sinister key;[2] for, as everyone knows, both characters have their roots in the Vice. At the outset of the play the quality which he has most in common with his comic counterpart is that self-mastery which enables him to captivate the audience and screen it from the moral judgment which the actions that he directs should otherwise compel. Falstaff entertains us and at the same time commands our admiration by the artful and unblushing way in which he extricates himself from the most flagrant exposure of his vices. The mental control which makes this possible is the result of an extraordinary self-containment that makes all values outside those of his worldly or fleshly self meaningless. Because his soul is solid, or not so solid, flesh, he has no conscience and is therefore incapable of the embarrassment or remorse that might interfere with his mental agility. And he delights in inverting conventional morality in order to present himself, for his own amusement as well as that of others, as an admirably virtuous fellow. This quality of self-containment and its concomitant capacity for amusing inversion Richard also possesses; and it is this which draws us to him in the first part of the play in spite of his reptilian ugliness of body and soul.

The kind of control which Richard has over himself is reflected in the opening soliloquy which serves not only to give the audience necessary information about what is to take place but also, by its tone, to establish the character of the protagonist. With cheerful

[1] Richard's wit and demonic gusto, as A. P. Rossiter observes in *Angel with Horns*, ed. Graham Story (New York, 1961), p. 19, win the audience; for, as W. H. Clemen says in *A Commentary on Shakespeare's Richard III*, trans. by Jean Bonheim (1957; London, 1968), p. 6, he is so entertaining we forget how morally reprehensible his actions are.

[2] Cf. Ronald Berman, 'Anarchy and Order in *Richard III* and *King John*', Shakespeare Survey 20, ed. Kenneth Muir (Cambridge, 1967), p. 53, who says that the quality of Richard's sophistry leads to that of Falstaff and Iago.

malevolence Richard explains his intentions. Unsuited because of his ugliness to play the role of lover and 'court an amorous looking glass', the activity most appropriate during a time of peace, he has elected to 'prove a villain' (I, i, 15,30). We should not, of course, seek a modern psychological explanation for Richard's behavior on the basis of this passage.[1] The main purpose of this part of the soliloquy is to indicate that the protagonist has freely chosen to be a villain; and, as we shall see, the delineation of Richard's character is ultimately conditioned more by his structural role in the overall design of the play than by psychological reality.

The success of the scheme which he has under way to separate his brothers is illustrated by the first incident of the play. Richard encounters Clarence, who is being escorted to prison, and condemns the Queen, whom he pretends to believe responsible for his brother's plight. And he goes on to say that

> this deep disgrace in brotherhood
> Touches me deeper than you can imagine.
>
> (I, i, 111–12)

The duality of this statement, of course, reflects the duality of his character as does the explanation which he makes, after Clarence has been led away, of his appearance of love and his promise to deliver his brother:

> Simple, plain Clarence; I do love thee so
> That I will shortly send thy soul to Heaven
>
> (I, i, 118–19)

He next turns his attention to his desire to marry Anne, an event which we are apparently meant to assume will make it easier for him to take the throne when the opportunity arrives.[2] His justification for the marriage is made in a sardonic Falstaffian vein:

> What though I killed her husband and her father?
> The readiest way to make the wench amends
> Is to become her husband and her father.
>
> (I, i, 154–6)

The episode in which he succeeds in winning Anne by convincing her over the body of Henry that his love for her led him to the murders and that he is sincerely penitent is, as has often been observed, one of the most remarkable in the play.[3] Richard's soliloquy at the end of this encounter reflects the delight which he takes in his own personality, the exhilaration which he gets from the contemplation of his misshapen talents:

> Was ever woman in this humour wooed?
> Was ever woman in this humour won?
>
> (I, ii, 228–9)

he cries in mock surprise. As he proceeds to note the details which made what has ensued unbelievable, his tone reinforces the central impression which his character evoked at the outset of the play; this is a man who knows himself. He is not really surprised at what he has accomplished because, as we observed, before undertaking his psychological seduction, he had announced in mock moral terms his intention of marrying Anne. The last lines of the soliloquy are particularly noteworthy because of the way they call attention to Richard's capacity to mock himself. 'I do mistake my person all this while' (I, ii, 253), he says, his body as well as his voice doubtless strutting or striking a pose. He is not, he says sardonically, unfit to be a lover after all. So having changed his opinion of himself, he will adorn himself appropriately for his new role

[1] Clemen, *A Commentary*, p. 6.

[2] The overall design of the play leads me to agree with Clemen's speculation (p. 19) that 'Richard's *secret close intent* may . . . have been left obscure on purpose: it may have been placed there with the sole purpose of suggesting that the wooing-scene which follows is related to Richard's rise to power, although exactly *how* the scene advances Richard's career might be hard to define . . .'

[3] H. B. Charlton, *Shakespearean Tragedy* (Cambridge, 1948), p. 26, calls this action Richard's 'diploma-piece, his warranty that henceforth . . . no limit can be set to the capacity of his genius'.

and, until he can buy a looking glass, will take pleasure in contemplating the sight of his shadow.[1] This elaborate put-on is the ultimate illustration of a mind in absolute control of itself. For though, dramaturgically speaking, Richard here follows the path of the Vice in playing to the audience, it is important to realize that, psychologically speaking, he is playing to himself. And the performance which he puts on for himself ironically parallels the show which he puts on whenever he is with others. His mocking pretension to himself that the shadow of his body is an index of his physical beauty corresponds, in effect, to his mocking pretension to others that his inner being is beautiful.

The kind of control which Richard is able to exercise over others by means of his projection of a beautiful false or shadow personality is more amply illustrated when, in the midst of a quarrel between Richard and Queen Elizabeth's party, Queen Margaret makes her presence known and laments her misfortunes. Richard reminds her of the curse his father had laid upon her when she had given him 'a clout / Steeped in the faultless blood of pretty Rutland' and piously assures her: 'God, not we, hath plagued thy bloody deed' (I, iii, 177–8, 181). His judgment is then echoed, in effect, by Queen Elizabeth and followed by a chorus of sympathy in the remarks of Hastings, Rivers, Dorset, and Buckingham. By evoking the memory of the brutal murder of an innocent child, Richard manages to intensify Margaret's isolation and unify everyone else with him. This leads Margaret to her series of prophetic curses that culminates with the hope that Richard will find himself in time 'beknaw' [ed] by the 'worm of conscience' and bedevilled in his sleep by 'tormenting' dreams (I, iii, 222, 226). As she prepares to conclude her curse by summing up his character – 'Thou rag of honour! Thou detested' (I, iii, 233) – Richard cleverly inserts her name instead of his. Queen

Elizabeth then responds approvingly to Richard's mocking statement that, because of his insertion, Margaret has cursed herself.

In this scene Richard has brought about a divisive unity of hatred. The full extent of his success in duplicity is revealed by Rivers's response to Richard's prayer that God will forgive those responsible for Clarence's plight and his assertion of repentance for any wrong he had done Margaret in the past while attempting to do good for someone else. Impressed by this display of conscience, Rivers finds his attitude most 'virtuous' and 'Christianlike' (I, iv, 316). Richard's triumph here anticipates the virtuoso performance which he puts on when, standing between two priests with a prayerbook in hand, he allows his 'other self' to force him against his conscience to assume the crown for the good of England.

To appreciate more fully the structure of the drama we should observe the way in which the theme of conscience is presented outside the character of Richard and at the same time associated with him. In the scene following Margaret's prophecy that Richard will be gnawed by the worm of conscience, we find Clarence shaken by a dream which reflects the pangs of conscience and which foreshadows his death through the machinations of Richard.[2] Shortly thereafter the two murderers engaged by Richard appear and carry on a highly significant dialogue over the sleeping Clarence: '... shall we stab him as he sleeps?' asks the Second Murderer callously. The tone of the First Murderer's mockingly ironic response reminds us of the voice of Richard, 'No. Then he will say 'twas done cowardly, when he

---

[1] Clemen, *A Commentary* (p. 38), says that this action is symbolic of Richard's 'isolation and self-centredness'.

[2] Aerol Arnold, 'The Recapitulation Dream in *Richard III* and *Macbeth*', *Shakespeare Quarterly*, 6 (1955), 53, notes that the effect of this dream sequence is to provide a contrast between 'repentant Clarence and remorseless Richard'.

wakes' (I, iv, 100, 101). The Second Murderer's rather literal response to this playfulness brings a serious note into the conversation. Clarence would not, after all, awaken until the Judgment Day, he exclaims; but the thought of Judgment Day awakens his sleeping conscience[1] and he momentarily contemplates renouncing his commission. He is teased back into an attitude of unconscionable playfulness, however, when the First Murderer invokes in him, through the name of Richard and the reward he has promised, the mingled feelings of fear and pleasure. Having been converted to his former state of moral callousness, the Second Murderer speaks in a clearly Falstaffian tone;[2] 'conscience', he maintains, is a dangerous thing –

it makes a man a coward. A man cannot steal but it accuseth him; he cannot swear but it checks him; he cannot lie with his neighbour's wife but it detects him. It is a blushing shamefast spirit that mutinies in a man's bosom; it fills one full of obstacles. It made me once restore a purse of gold that I found; it beggars any man that keeps it. It is turned out of all towns and cities for a dangerous thing, and every man that means to live well endeavours to trust to himself and to live without it.

(I, iv, 137–47)

The First Murderer then pretends that his own conscience is now urging him to turn away from the action they have been commissioned to do, and the Second Murderer conducts a mock conversion process that parallels ironically the turnabout that had taken place within him a few minutes earlier. So it is that, as Clarence begins to awaken, the two voices of the murderers are as one in reflecting the exuberant cruelty that we associate with the character of Richard. When the First Murderer suggests that they carry out their mission by drowning Clarence in a barrel of wine, it seems highly significant that the Second Murderer, in gay agreement, should make use of language which describes an act of cruelty in an image of appetite: 'Oh, excellent device! Make a sop of

him' (I, iv, 162). The echo of Richard's thought processes is also heard clearly in the response to 'simple, plain' Clarence's assertion that the Murderers must be mistaken in their conviction that Richard wants him dead since he had promised to 'labour my delivery' (I, iv, 253); 'Why, so he doth,' says the Second Murderer merrily, 'now he delivers thee / From this world's thralldom to the joys of Heaven' (I, iv, 254–5).

A dramatic division in the wills of the two murderers takes place at the end of the scene, one which is justified psychologically by the Second Murderer's initial qualm of conscience. When Clarence, pleading for his life, urges the murderers to relent and save their souls, the First Murderer is not moved: 'Relent! No, 'tis cowardly and womanish' (I, iv, 264). But the conscience of his counterpart 'mutinies'; struck by pity for Clarence, he tries to avert the murder and, having been unsuccessful, repents his part in the deed. The scene ends with the First Murderer calling his comrade a coward and departing to collect his reward. This conscience-created psychological separation of two characters who, throughout the major part of the scene, had spoken in the voice of their master strikingly foreshadows the psychological division that occurs in Richard.

The first suggestion that there is division within the character of Richard is, as has often been observed, presented indirectly when we learn, through Anne, that the masterful control which he displays over himself during his

[1] Robert B. Heilman, 'Satiety and Conscience: Aspects of *Richard III*', in *Essays in Shakespearean Criticism*, ed. James L. Calderwood and Harold E. Toliver (Englewood Cliffs, 1970), pp. 148–9, realizes that the emphasis on conscience in this scene calls attention to the importance which it is to assume but believes that the scene suffers from extensiveness, a result of Shakespeare's interest in a subject outweighing his dramatic judgment. As my discussion indicates, I do not agree with this criticism.

[2] It is interesting to compare this passage with Falstaff's delineation of honor in *1 Henry IV*.

waking hours does not attend his sleep: 'For never yet', she says,

one hour in his bed
Have I enjoyed the golden dew of sleep
But have been waked by his timorous dreams
(IV, i, 84–5)

Since part of Margaret's curse has been fulfilled – Richard is subject to tormenting dreams – the audience is apparently meant to wonder at this point whether the false conscience which the artist of evil has employed so effectively in his rise to power could possibly assume a realistic dimension as an instrument of retribution and thereby surprise the arch-surpriser.

In the scene immediately following Anne's revelation, evidence of psychological attrition in Richard is presented directly and dramatically when a division occurs between himself and Buckingham. Assisted by the hand of the man who had played the orator to gain the crown for Richard as though it were 'for myself' (III, v, 97), Richard ascends the throne and immediately turns his attention to the problem of securing his position. When Buckingham is deterred momentarily by his conscience from responding affirmatively to Richard's suggestion that the Princes must be murdered, Richard overtly displays anger for the first time in the play.[1] Earlier his capacity to mask his true feelings had been presented most effectively and ironically by the remark that the victim of Richard's 'divided councils' (III, i, 179) made just before Richard accused him of witchcraft and sentenced him to death. Secure in his belief that he was loved by Richard, Hastings commented on his cheerful and unruffled appearance:

I think there's never a man in Christendom
That can less hide his love or hate than he,
For by his face straight shall you know his heart.
(III, iv, 53–5)

Now, however, as Richard finds himself out of tune with his other self, his ability to disguise his inner feelings suddenly deserts him. 'The King is angry', says Catesby. 'See, he bites the lip' (IV, ii, 27).[2] Thus we find also for the first time in the drama that Richard's passion, as reflected in this image and action of appetite, has been momentarily turned inward, another instance of dramatic foreshadowing.

Further indication of loss of psychological control is reflected in Richard's disturbed responses to the news that Dorset has fled to Richmond. Contemplating the next step which he must take to strengthen his hold on the crown, he observes:

I must be married to my brother's daughter,
Or else my kingdom stands on brittle glass.
Murder her brothers, and then marry her!

[1] Professor Heilman, 'Satiety and Conscience', pp. 144–5, makes the provocative but I think ultimately uncompelling suggestion that Richard is reflecting a characteristic aversion to someone he has wooed and won. Having served Richard's political lust, Buckingham is now to be discarded like Anne; thus Richard makes his request knowing that Buckingham's response will give him the excuse he wants to dispose of him. It seems to me that the request is sincere and justified psychologically by Richard's desire to make his position secure. But, as my discussion of the 'other self' motif will indicate, this separation probably has more symbolic or structural than psychological significance.

[2] Cf. Polydore Vergil's statement that Richard 'dyd contynually byte his nether lyppe, as thowgh that crewell nature of his did so rage agaynst yt self in that lyttle carkase' [the Furness Variorum edition of *Richard III* (Philadelphia, 1908), p. 291; hereafter referred to as Variorum]. And cf. Hall's specific application of the characteristic in his description of Richmond's move against Hastings: Richard, he says, came into the chamber 'with a sowre angry countenaunce knittyng the browes, frownyng and fretyng and gnawyng on his lips and so set hym doune in his place' (Variorum, p. 473). Though, as Geoffrey Bullough points out in his 'introduction' to *Richard III* in *Narrative and Dramatic Sources of Shakespeare*, III (London, 1960), 225, there is no evidence that Shakespeare knew the *Historia* at first hand, Vergil's phrasing leads me to believe that his passage not only was the source of the line quoted but may also have helped to inspire Shakespeare's development of the 'self against self' theme.

Uncertain way of gain! But I am in
So far in blood that sin will pluck on sin.
Tear-falling pity dwells not in this eye.

(IV, ii, 61–6)

This brooding reflection is a long way from the Falstaffian verve of 'The readiest way to make the wench amends / Is to become her husband and her father.' So too is the anxiety brought about by his memory of the prophecies of Henry VI and an Irish bard concerning Richmond.

Structurally speaking, it is highly significant that the thought of the person who is to bring political integrity to England unsettles the psychological composure of the evil architect of divisiveness. But this loss of emotional control is only momentary. In the next scene we learn through Tyrrel that Dighton and Forrest were so overcome with 'conscience and remorse' (IV, iii, 20) that they could not finish the description of their murders. In marked contrast to their psychological condition is that of Richard. That he is back to his old self is made clear by his cheerful request that Tyrrel come to him after supper to furnish him with the details of the Princes' deaths and by the confident sardonic tone in which he announces his decision to approach Elizabeth as 'a jolly thriving wooer' (IV, iii, 43).

The psychological task of convincing Elizabeth of the advisability of marrying her daughter to him seems as impossible as that which had confronted him when he set about to woo Anne. Earlier Richard had won Elizabeth to his side by piously condemning Margaret's responsibility for the death of young Rutland; now, however, Elizabeth, because of Richard's own slaughter of the innocent, has called upon Margaret to aid her in cursing Richard. The pattern of the debate that takes place is strongly reminiscent, as many commentators have pointed out, of Richard's psychological conquest of Anne. And it appears that he has again been successful when at last the

Queen agrees to win her daughter to his will. But this time it is Richard who becomes the butt of irony when he says contemptuously after Elizabeth's departure, 'Relenting fool, and shallow, changing woman!' (IV, iv, 431). There has been considerable controversy regarding this point,[1] but the design of the play suggests strongly that we are meant to see this action as a reversal for Richard, a prelude to the reversal of the role of conscience that takes place in the soliloquy which follows his dream. It is the arch-deceiver who becomes the dupe of this episode, not the Queen who, we later learn, intends to give her daughter to Richmond.

In the course of his persuasions Richard sounds many of the themes that he had presented in his courtship of Anne. He protests himself repentant for his past misdeeds and swears the purity of his love for the princess. He goes so far as to hope that 'heaven and fortune' (IV, iv, 400) turn against him if his words are false. And, even more dramatically, he prays also that he turn against himself: 'Myself myself confound!' (IV, iv, 399). This statement makes Richard's position analogous to that of his 'other self', who had, earlier in the play, asked that he be 'punished with hate in those where I expect most love' (II, i, 35) should he prove false to his profession of love to the Queen and her family. In the scene immediately following that in which Richard, as a rhetorical tour de force, calls down a curse upon himself if he is not honest, we find Buckingham experiencing the effect of the

[1] See Professor Clemen (*A Commentary*, p. 191) for a list of critics who have debated the interpretation of this point and (p. 192) for his own rather ingenious conclusion that Elizabeth is truly won by Richard but that the irony falls on him since he fails to realize that this changing woman might well turn again. It is only fair to note that Hall's indictment of Elizabeth's 'inconstancie' (Variorum, p. 492) lends support to those critics who believe that we are meant to see this episode as another psychological victory for Richard.

insincere vow which he had made. He has encountered hatred in the person from whom he most expected love, and he acknowledges the justice of what has transpired:

> This, this All Souls' Day, to my fearful soul
> Is the determined respite of my wrongs.
> That high All-seer that I dallied with
> Hath turned my feigned prayer on my head,
> And given in earnest what I begged in jest.
> Thus doth He force the swords of wicked men
> To turn their own points on their masters' bosoms.
>
> (v, i, 18–24)

The fulfillment of the insincere curse which Richard's other self called down upon himself, as we shall see, brilliantly foreshadows and parallels that which Richard hypocritically invoked upon himself.

Richard's psychological attrition appears again in the incident which follows his scornful comment on Elizabeth's apparent acquiescence in his marriage proposal. Upon hearing that Richmond's navy is close at hand, Richard issues instructions to his henchman in a confused manner which indicates the toll his emotions are collecting. Later in the scene his loss of control is again emphasized when he strikes a messenger whom he assumes to be bringing bad news. By the time the scene ends, however, the good news which he has received has given him back his self-mastery. But the audience, no longer spellbound at this point by the cruelly comic wit of Richard, has become increasingly aware of his potentiality for psychological disintegration.

The culmination of this movement occurs in the most dramatic incident of the play, Richard's response to the dream which haunts him on the eve of the battle at Bosworth Field. The change which has gradually taken place in the personality of Richard is, as many have noted, signaled by two highly significant comments that he makes before he retires: 'I will not sup tonight' (v, iii, 48) and 'I have not that alacrity of spirit / Nor cheer of mind,

that I was wont to have' (v, iii, 73–4). His somber mood and his lack of appetite call attention to the loss of those qualities which throughout the major part of the play have reflected the conscienceless control over himself that has enabled him to rise to power. And when Richard awakens from the ghost-shadowed dream he finds himself, as it were, split apart as he carries on a debate with himself that represents the disintegration of his heretofore carefully synchronized private and public personalities.

Appropriately enough, Richard, who had led so many victims to unexpected disaster through the projection of a false conscience that masked a cruel appetite, finds himself surprised by a real conscience that, as Margaret had predicted, gnaws at his inner being. In Richard, to follow other lines in the play, conscience mutinies or, like the swords of wicked men, turns upon the bosom of its master. And, like Buckingham in effect, he discovers that he has been betrayed by the one in whom he most expected love, himself, as he fulfills the curse which he had hypocritically invoked to convince Elizabeth of his sincerity. He does indeed confound himself, if only momentarily, as his conscience becomes a real power in his being.

His reaction to the shadows of the dream that has terrorized his soul provides a profoundly ironic correspondence to his earlier mocking assertion that, having mistaken his potentiality as a lover, he would take pleasure in observing his shadow until he could acquire a looking glass. Then his discovery was a mocking play discovery; and the tone in which he discussed it reflected his psychological integrity, his masterful control of himself and his sureness of self-knowledge. Now he is forced to contemplate a different kind of shadow. The debate which takes place within him reflects a real division of personality that ironically parallels the deliberately split character we met at the outset of the play; and the mocking ironic voice of a man who thought he knew himself perfectly is replaced by the anguished deadly intense tone of a soul at war with itself:

> What do I fear? Myself? There's none else by.
> Richard loves Richard; that is, I am I
> Is there a murderer here? No. Yes, I am.
> Then fly. What, from myself? Great reason why—
> Lest I revenge. What, myself upon myself?
> Alack, I love myself. Wherefore? For any good
> That I myself have done unto myself?
> Oh no! Alas, I rather hate myself
> For hateful deeds committed by myself!
> I am a villain – yet I lie, I am not.
> Fool, of thyself speak well. Fool, do not flatter.
> My conscience hath a thousand several tongues,
> And every tongue brings in a several tale,
> And every tale condemns me for a villain.
>
> (v, iii, 182–95)

In this dialogue-soliloquy of 'self against self', Richard discovers that he is not, as he had once thought, 'himself alone'. By a supreme effort of will, however, he dismisses from his mind the significance of his dream. And we find, too, when he addresses his men just before the battle that he has also dismissed from his mind the implications of the cry which he had uttered just before awakening – 'Have mercy, Jesu!' (v, iii, 178). He urges his followers not to let 'babbling dreams affright our souls' and, following the path of the First Murderer rather than the Second, maintains that 'Conscience is but a word that cowards use' (v, iii, 308, 309). He dies bravely crying out for a horse just as he had in the dream whose significance he had chosen to ignore.

At the outset of *Richard III* we find ourselves forced, in spite of ourselves, to admire the protagonist's energy, wit, and resourcefulness; we find ourselves, that is to say, compelled to admire the power and artistry of conscienceless evil. Since at the end of the play we continue, at least in part, to admire Richard it is obvious that this drama is not medieval in

tone to the same extent that, say, *Dr Faustus* is, even if the rhythm of Richard's soliloquy of anguish suggests the influence of Marlowe.[1] But, by the same token, though the drama strongly reflects the spirit of Renaissance humanism in its projection of Richard's powerful will and courage, we miss a good part of its meaning and intended effect if we dismiss as 'pious twaddle'[2] Richmond's remarks about God and conscience and overlook the implications of Richard's cry for mercy in his misty state of semi-consciousness. Richard's zest and cleverness at first lull the moral judgment that would alienate us from him. But as the play progresses this faculty is reawakened and we find the appropriateness of what happens to Richard appealing to our moral instincts. At the same time, however, when Richard's own

---

[1] Professor Danby (*Shakespeare's Doctrine of Nature*, p. 66) points out that this soliloquy may reflect the influence of Faustus's 'See where Christ's blood streams in the firmament' speech. It is interesting to note in this connection W. A. Armstrong's observation in 'The Elizabethan Conception of the Tyrant', *The Review of English Studies*, 22 (1946), 171, that Richard is presented to us through imagery as a 'soul who has deliberately surrendered himself to the devil'.

[2] John Palmer, *Political Characters of Shakespeare* (London, 1948), p. 116. Several interpreters have adopted similar viewpoints and carried them, sometimes with great force, to conclusions which make the play highly modern in tone or meaning. A. P. Rossiter, *Angel with Horns*, ed. Graham Storey (New York, 1961), pp. 21–2, maintains that the appeal of Richard's volcanic energies undermines the naive Christian principle that informs the action of the play. Nicholas Brooke, 'Reflecting Gems and Dead Bones: Tragedy versus History in *Richard III*', *The Critical Quarterly*, 7 (1965), 134, states that the play is tragic because human will, as represented by Richard, is oppressed by the impersonal force of history. And A. L. French, 'The World of *Richard III*', *Shakespeare Studies*, ed. J. Leeds Barroll, 4 (Dubuque, 1968), 30–1, who speaks of Richmond's 'pious commonplaces' and of a new regime tainted by the time-serving baseness of Stanley, believes that Shakespeare satisfied his artistic conscience under the false face of orthodoxy.

sleeping conscience is awakened and then suppressed, we find outselves experiencing mingled feelings: we are compelled to admire the 'bloody dog' for the strength of his spirit at the same time that we must deplore his perversion of it.[1]

Though carefully foreshadowed in the play, the psychological civil war that takes place in Richard prior to the battle which marks the end of the civil wars that have torn England apart is probably not ultimately convincing enough, when we consider the evolution of his character, to make him a truly tragic figure. This is so primarily because the attack of conscience is anticipated more through external or structural means than through psychological action or internal development. We are, of course, prepared in a general sense for Richard's psychological distintegration because we have seen his lapses into anger and fear dramatized; that is to say, we have come to realize that this is a man who is capable of losing his emotional equilibrium. But we have not been prepared in any real psychological sense for this upheaval to be brought about by a lightning flash of conscience, even one inspired by a Providence-directed dream. The only internal anticipation of this consequence of conscience is to be found in Richard's brief brooding statement about the chain of sin; and this statement, even if we are able to sense a connection between it and his 'timorous dreams', is not enough to carry us to the whole-hearted conviction that the sword of conscience could smite such a man into two disparate selves.[2]

Conceptually, then, the interlude of psychological separation is a masterstroke of theme and structure, but from the standpoint of character development it is not organically sound. The two main external devices used to bridge the gap between the moral ventriloquist we follow throughout the first part of the play and the conscience-divided king who appears briefly near the end are the conscience-created split between Richard and Buckingham, and that between the two murderers who have spoken in the voice of Richard; thus Richard's 'other self' and the Second Murderer dramatically forecast through their experiences the operation of the moral force that brings about the interlude of psychic disintegration in Richard. Yet the subliminal pull of this structural sleight of hand needs the reinforcement of more extensive corresponding psychological dramatization in the protagonist to compel our belief. Such external foreshadowing effects – and we should include in this connection the use to which the imagery of appetite is turned – are not enough to make us feel, in the final analysis, that the mocking Iniquity we first met has the capacity to experience self-rending guilt and remorse. But though Richard's dialogue-soliloquy, from the standpoint of the play as a whole, is more compelling thematically and structurally than psychologically, so powerfully is it presented in itself that the modern reader or viewer may well feel that it succeeds in moving the drama at least a few steps away from fascinating melodrama toward the profundity of tragedy.

[1] John Palmer (*Political Characters*, p. 109) finds Shakespeare anticipating modern psychology in his presentation of conscience welling up in Richard as a subliminal force; but most commentators would agree with Professor Clemen (*A Commentary*, p. 223) that the soliloquy is, psychologically speaking, unprepared for and that, even though it represents a step toward character tragedy, it comes too late to alter the dramatic fabric of the play. M. M. Reese, *The Cease of Majesty: A Study of Shakespeare's History Plays* (New York, 1961), p. 223, sees the passage as a reflection of the morality convention which, he says, is always at odds with psychological realism.

[2] The 'other self' motif, as I have tried to show, is a very significant part of the structure of the play. The inspiration for Shakespeare's development of this point may well have come from Richmond's reference to the Lord of Oxford in *The True Tragedie* as his 'second selfe' (Variorum, p. 540).

THE ANTIC DISPOSITION
OF RICHARD II

LOIS POTTER

Many critical studies of *Richard II*, and a surprising number of productions, start from a curious assumption: that Shakespeare wrote, and asked his leading actor to star in, a long play dominated by a character whose main effect on the audience was to be one of boredom, embarrassment, or at best contemptuous pity. If Richard's part is not a good one, the play is simply not worth seeing; and 'good', in theatrical terms, means not necessarily virtuous but interesting. I want to argue that Richard is in fact rather less virtuous than has often been thought, and, just for that reason, a 'better' dramatic character.

Much of our difficulty with the play is a difficulty of knowing what moral connotations to attach to its highly rhetorical language. It is useful to be reminded by R. F. Hill that 'apparently self-conscious control of language does not, of itself, indicate dispassion and triviality in character', especially since he goes on to show that self-conscious language is by no means confined to Richard.[1] Yet there is no doubt that elaborate language is used as a substitute for action and, to that extent, is a symbol of weakness. 'Give losers leave to talk' is an Elizabethan proverb, and in the first two acts of the play the long speeches do in fact belong to the 'losers' – Mowbray, Gaunt, York, the Duchess of Gloucester, *and* Bolingbroke. They all talk too much, seldom content with one simile where three or four will do (even Bolingbroke's rejection of the consolations of language is itself couched in a series of rhe-

torical repetitions); they all become despondent in adversity, rejecting all attempts to comfort them; and three of them (the Duchess of Gloucester, Mowbray, Gaunt) prophesy, correctly, that they are soon to die. This is the style which, in the second half of the play, is associated with the defeated king and his supporters. It is foreshadowed, even before Richard's return from Ireland, by the fanciful dialogue of the Queen and the favourites as well as by the Welshmen's prophecies of death and disaster.

Yet, though such language may be a sign of weakness in those who speak it, it is itself extremely powerful. This is largely because of its evocation of patriotic and religious sentiments, on which most of the emotional and poetic force of the first two acts depends. It may be disregarded by the other characters but it works on the audience, and the same is true when Richard starts speaking this language halfway through the play.

The other kind of power, later associated with the 'silent king' Bolingbroke, is at first displayed only by Richard. He declares in the opening scene that 'We are not born to sue but to command' (I, i, 196),[2] and his reactions to the eloquence of others are either impatient – 'It boots thee not to be compassionate' (I, iii,

---

[1] 'Dramatic Techniques and Interpretation in *Richard II*', Stratford upon Avon Studies, 3, *Early Shakespeare* (1961), 103.
[2] References are to the Arden edition of the play, ed. Peter Ure (London, 1956).

174); 'Can sick men play so nicely with their names?' (II, i, 84) – or deflationary, as when he asks 'Why, uncle, what's the matter?' after York has spent twenty-two lines trying to tell him (II, i, 186). His few long speeches, such as the description of Bolingbroke's behaviour to the common people and the formal banishment of the two appellants, are almost the only ones in this part of the play that do not make the director reach for his blue pencil. The banishment speech, indeed, may look at first as if it needs shortening, but in performance its rhetoric has an obvious dramatic effect; Richard keeps the two men in suspense during fifteen lines of sonorous clauses – 'For that', 'and for', 'and for' – and then drops his bombshell in the simple phrase 'Therefore we banish you our territories' (I, iii, 139). His shorter utterances, too, are very like the language which, when it appears in connection with Bolingbroke, we associate with confidence, efficiency and power. His reception of Gaunt's death –

> The ripest fruit first falls, and so doth he;
> His time is spent, our pilgrimage must be;
> So much for that   (II, i, 153–5)

– can be compared with Bolingbroke's reaction to Mowbray's, when, as Kenneth Muir has pointed out, he also 'changes the subject in the middle of a line'.[1] Similarly, Richard's flippant-sounding jingle,

> Think what you will, we seize into our hands
> His plate, his goods, his money and his lands,
>   (II, i, 209–10)

falls into the same rhythm as Northumberland's couplet in the final scene:

> The next news is, I have to London sent
> The heads of Salisbury, Spencer, Blunt, and Kent.[2]
>   (V, vi, 7–8)

The change which Richard undergoes in the second half of the play may be explained in terms of language and decorum, but this is not much help to the actor who has somehow to reconcile the two halves. The commonest solution is to play the first two acts in the light of the other three. A foppish or wicked Richard may spend the first scene eating sweetmeats, talking with his favourites, or making clear that he is the real murderer of Gloucester,[3] while a more pathetically conceived Richard may appear in Christ-like make-up, looking frail and helpless among the brawny peers who will obviously be making mincemeat of him within the hour.[4] It has even been argued that such interpretations are necessary: as one reviewer of the 1964 Stratford production put it, in the first part of the play 'Shakespeare only does half the job, and, unless he is helped, we listen amazed at old Gaunt's dying protest about the king's "rash, fierce blaze of riot". What riot?'[5]

Nicholas Brooke has rightly objected to actors trying too hard to establish Richard's personality before Shakespeare lets it emerge in I, iv. His description of this personality – 'a cold politician with atheistic tendencies ... cheap however witty' – [6] seems to me fair enough, except perhaps that it underrates the effectiveness of cheap wit in a formal setting

[1] Note on II, i, 153–5 in Signet edition (New York, 1963).

[2] The first of these couplets apparently derives, rhythm and all, from *The Mirror for Magistrates*; see Peter Ure's note in the Arden edition.

[3] See, e.g., Shaw on Beerbohm Tree, *The Saturday Review*, 11 Feb. 1905, quoted in *Shaw on Shakespeare*, ed. Edwin Wilson (New York, 1961), p. 148; Audrey Williamson on John Neville, *Old Vic Drama*, 2 (London, 1957), 174–5; and A. C. Sprague, *Shakespeare's Histories, Plays for the Stage* (The Society for Theatre Research, London, 1964), pp. 38–9.

[4] E.g., Edwin Booth (Sprague, *Shakespeare's Histories*, pp. 32) and David Warner (Harold Hobson, *Sunday Times*, 19 April 1964).

[5] Felix Barker, *London Evening News*, 16 April 1964.

[6] *Shakespeare's Early Tragedies* (London, 1968), p. 119.

and audience readiness to sympathise with the character who uses it (compare Shakespeare's *other* King Richard). Professor Brooke feels that our awareness of the real Richard confuses our response to the cosmic and political themes which he embodies and expresses;[1] I should prefer to say that the interest of Richard's character lies in his ability to *use*, and not simply to embody, the emotional associations of these themes. This use only gradually becomes conscious and, like Hamlet's antic disposition, co-exists with a capacity for emotional involvement. But irony and a suggestion of duplicity are present in Richard throughout the play.

For the point about Richard's terse style in the opening scenes is that it is also enigmatic; his carefully balanced speeches to Mowbray and Bolingbroke do not, unless slanted by the production, help the audience to decide which of the challengers is right (indeed, we never know). Hence, the difference in their punishments seems not retributive but arbitrary, especially when, simply because Gaunt looks unhappy, four years are casually lopped off Bolingbroke's exile. The latter's response,

> How long a time lies in one little word!
> Four lagging winters and four wanton springs
> End in a word – such is the breath of kings,
>
> (I, iii, 213–15)

introduces the themes, which Gaunt will take up at more length, of time, breath, and the destructive power of kings. But, taken on its own, it suggests rather oddly that Richard has not restored but killed four years of life. A darker purpose is in fact confirmed by the next scene, where the king's first 'private, words express a doubt,

> When time shall call him home from banishment,
> Whether our kinsman come to see his friends.
>
> (I, iv, 21–2)

In other words, he may never repeal Bolingbroke after all. Perhaps the 'hopeless word of

"never to return"', which Richard breathes against Mowbray (I, iii, 152), is likewise *only* a word, another sign that the breath of kings can blow hot and cold.

Evidence of duplicity in Richard's character could have been provided for Shakespeare by Holinshed, who lists among the thirty-three articles alleged against him the charge that his letters were written in a style 'so subtill and darke that none other prince once beléeued him, nor yet his owne subiects'.[2] Equivocation – setting the word against the word – is a common practice of the Machiavellian ruler in drama (compare Mortimer's use of the 'unpointed' message in *Edward II*), and in the later scenes of the play Bolingbroke himself is not free from a suspicion of it. Hence his almost comic difficulty in finding a form of words which will convince the Duchess of York that he really has pardoned Aumerle. Her nervousness is understandable, since her husband has just made the helpful suggestion, 'Speak it in French, king, say "pardonne moy"' (v, iii, 117). But in fact I get the impression throughout the play that Bolingbroke is genuinely trying to say what he means. There is, for instance, a vast difference between his sharp words to his peers,

> Little are we beholding to your love,
> And little look'd for at your helping hands,
>
> (IV, i, 160–1)

and Richard's way of putting the same thing, when York has insisted that both Gaunt and Herford love him well:

> Right, you say true; as Herford's love, so his;
> As theirs, so mine; and all be as it is. (II, i, 145–6)

This kind of irony reveals rather than conceals the speaker's emotions, which is why it is often taken as a sign of weakness. But it also

[1] *Ibid.*, p. 128.
[2] Raphael Holinshed, *Holinshed's Chronicles of England, Scotland and Ireland* (6 vols., London, 1807), III, 860.

enables him to avoid stating his intentions, and thus, as we shall see, to give a great deal of trouble to Bolingbroke.

The transitional scene at Barkloughly Castle is unusual in its lack of this irony. Richard not only takes over the emotionally charged rhetoric which has hitherto been associated chiefly with his opponents, he also takes on their role as spokesman for England and the Church. From the moment when he greets the English earth, it is he alone who embodies the spirit of Mowbray's lament for his native tongue, Bolingbroke's 'English ground, farewell', and Gaunt's famous purple passage. At the same time the presence of Carlisle reminds us that Richard consistently has the support of the Church, something which his successor never gets. This is unhistorical – Holinshed describes the prominent part taken by the Archbishop of Canterbury on Bolingbroke's behalf – and seems to be deliberate. In the early part of the play the values of Church and State are united in frequent evocations of the figure of the Crusader in the Holy Land and the warrior upholding the truth in single combat. Our last vision of this kind of harmony, now already in the past, comes in Carlisle's account of the death of Mowbray who has fought under the colours of 'his captain Christ' (IV, i, 99). Henry IV will never make his intended Crusade, churchmen are frequently involved in rebellions against him, and it is not until the reign of Henry V that Shakespeare again shows Church and State reconciled.

But their values cannot be reconciled in any case. Richard's behaviour at Barkloughly Castle is often taken as an undignified oscillation between two equally reprehensible states of mind, futile rage and morbid despair. It seems to me rather a bringing out into the open of a conflict between the equally valid but contradictory roles of king and Christian. Richard's moods of defeatism, though Carlisle condemns them, can be interpreted as an attempt to achieve that Christian resignation which, in the *Mirror for Magistrates* view, is the only refuge for the victim of Fortune's wheel. Reviewing the 'sad stories of the death of kings', he describes them as 'all murthered' (III, ii, 155–60), because no death can ever be 'natural' for men who have been led to think of themselves as immortal. The failure to bear in mind their own mortality is the chief crime of which the speakers in the *Mirror* accuse themselves; it is also the only sin which Richard lays to his own charge. Hence the special sense given to 'flattery' in the play: Bolingbroke actually receives much grosser adulation than Richard (especially in II, iii), but the latter says that he is being flattered even when the mirror shows him a beauty that is really his, because it fails to show the ultimate truth about the transitoriness of that beauty. Similarly, at the end of the Barkloughly scene, he seems to equate all forms of comfort with flattery. As York said earlier, 'Comfort's in heaven, and we are on the earth' (II, ii, 78), and 'that sweet way I was in to despair' (III, ii, 205) may be sweet because, in one sense, it is the way to salvation.

On the other hand, as the exchanges of defiances, gages, and insults throughout the play remind us, the concepts of nobility and kingliness are not necessarily Christian. Mowbray and Bolingbroke refuse to accept counsels of patience in I, i, while Gaunt, in the scene that follows, opposes Christian patience to his sister-in-law's exhortations to think of family honour and revenge. Her response –

Call it not patience, Gaunt, it is despair . . .
That which in mean men we intitle patience
Is pale cold cowardice in noble breasts.

(I, ii, 29–34)

– is similar to what the Queen says to Richard at their parting:

The lion dying thrusteth forth his paw
And wounds the earth, if nothing else, with rage

To be o'erpow'r'd, and wilt thou, pupil-like,
Take the correction mildly, kiss the rod,
And fawn on rage with base humility,
Which art a lion and the king of beasts?

(v, i, 29–34)

The Barkloughly castle scene is difficult to play because the Lion King and the Christian are juxtaposed too often and too abruptly. But this is not to say that the roles are not sincerely played. They have to be, if the scene is to work at all. The reason why Richard is un-ironic here is that he believes, although we know otherwise, that effective action is still possible; his responses are real responses. To say that Richard is an actor giving a performance is irrelevant: all good dramatic parts allow actors to behave like actors. But to ask an actor to play the part of an actor giving an unconvincing performance is theatrical suicide. No one can possibly take any interest in the future history of a character shown to be as hollow as his crown. Fops are minor figures in drama, and rightly so.

It is when Richard is completely cut off from the possibility of effective action that he begins to make use of the roles of king and Christian for his own purposes; their contradictions no longer matter, because he is concerned only with their effect. The Lion King makes his last gesture when he asks,

Shall we call back Northumberland and send
Defiance to the traitor, and so die?

(III, iii, 129–30)

But he chooses instead to follow the advice of Aumerle:

No, good my lord, let's fight with gentle words,
Till time lend friends, and friends their helpful
swords.

(III, iii, 131–2)

As has been pointed out, this is 'an intention of plain duplicity'.[1] Words are a weapon for Richard, as well as a form of emotional release,

and a closer look at his confrontations with Bolingbroke will show that he does in fact fight very skilfully with them.

In the first of these scenes, III, iii, Richard first makes an impressive speech in the kingly style, then sends a 'fair' (and, as he at once indicates, a lying) message to Bolingbroke, then (possibly for Northumberland's ears as well as Aumerle's) indulges in a fantasy of despair which plays 'idly', as he says, with traditional Christian symbols. To Northumberland, the sarcastic speeches which follow seem the words of 'a frantic man'. Yet when Richard re-enters the 'base court' he does not sound frantic. He picks up his own words, 'Down, down I come' and 'In the base court?' as he addresses Bolingbroke:

Fair cousin, you *debase* your princely knee
To make the *base* earth proud with kissing it ...
Up, cousin, *up* ...

(III, iii, 190–1, 194)

Bolingbroke and the rest treat him gently because he seems so helpless; he is then able to show up their gentleness as hypocrisy by hinting that he knows what they are really after. It is possible to argue that his anticipation of Bolingbroke's intentions makes Richard an accomplice in his own destruction; it is possible similarly, to say that Lear makes his daughters into monsters by treating them as such before they have done anything more unfilial than complaining about his hundred knights. But this seems to me too 'psychological' an approach to the plays. Richard does not, like a predestinating God, make things happen because he foresees them. He foresees them because they are going to happen, and because his awareness of the situation is both a convenient dramatic shorthand (if an event is accepted as inevitable, Shakespeare does not have to explain the precise practical means by

[1] A. R. Humphreys, *Richard II* (Studies in English Literature, London, 1967), p. 49.

which it comes about) and a means by which he can dominate the action.

Typical of the way in which he uses words to transform weakness into strength is his exploitation, at Flint Castle and in Westminster Hall, of conceits on tears. We dislike this sort of language nowadays, so it is tempting to describe as mere self-indulgence Richard's images of making 'foul weather with despised tears' (III, iii, 161), digging a pair of graves with them (III, iii, 165–9), being weighed down with them like a bucket in a well (IV, i, 184–9), and washing away his royal balm in them (IV, i, 207). What all these fantasies emphasise is the power of something which is normally taken to be a symbol of helplessness. The comparison of himself and Bolingbroke to two buckets in a well derives, in its rising-falling pattern, from the idea of Fortune's wheel and the 'Down, down I come' and 'Up, cousin, up' of III, iii.[1] But in his insistence that he outweighs his cousin, who is able to rise so high only because he is essentially hollow, Richard also echoes and reverses the 'balance' image which the Gardener had used to the Queen:

> Their fortunes both are weigh'd;
> In your lord's scale is nothing but himself,
> And some few vanities that make him light.
> But in the balance of great Bolingbroke,
> Besides himself, are all the English peers,
> And with that odds he weighs King Richard down.
> (III, iv, 84–9)

What we see throughout the deposition scene is that Richard alone, in his potently symbolic role as the Man of Sorrows, can in fact outweigh Bolingbroke and the peers.

The chief irony of this scene is one of which Richard himself is quite well aware: only a king can judge a king, and therefore it is he who must depose himself, yet the very fact that he is in this humiliating position is also a proof of his kingship which nothing can eradicate. He makes as much capital as possible

from this two-edged predicament. Bolingbroke, in response apparently to Carlisle's plea, sends for Richard to perform in public what (according to York) he has already agreed to in private. The intention is, first, that the king should be seen to abdicate voluntarily and thus free his successor from the guilt of usurpation, and, second, that he should prove that he is 'worthily deposed' by reading out the articles which contain the charges against him. Richard does neither of these things.

Instead, he continues to employ the technique which we first saw at the end of the Flint Castle scene, that of giving with one hand and taking back with the other:

> Well you deserve. They well deserve to have
> That know the strong'st and surest way to get.
> (III, iii, 200–1)

> What you will have, I'll give, and willing too,
> For do we must what force will have us do.
> (III, iii, 206–7)

His first speech in Westminster Hall shows the same teasing ambiguity:

> God save the king! although I be not he;
> And yet, amen, if heaven do think him me.
> (IV, i, 174–5)

Urged to resign the crown, he invites Bolingbroke to 'seize' it. The series of quibbles which follows has a serious purpose. By claiming, for instance, that he is willing to resign his crown but not the cares that go with it he is transforming a sacramental object into a piece of metal, a 'heavy weight from off my head' (IV, i, 204). He may formally 'undo' himself, in language that seems as thorough as Bolingbroke could wish, but his very exaggeration is suspicious. The renunciation culminates in his insistence that by losing the crown he loses his life since the one is so completely identified with the other. Later he virtually

[1] See Peter Ure's note on IV, i, 184–9 in the Arden edition.

takes everything back when he condemns himself and everyone else as traitors for their part in the ritual undoing. The stress throughout has been on the unalterable fact of his kingliness.

He also, by a well-timed burst of hysteria, avoids having to read the articles. He promises to read his sins, not from the paper Northumberland is brandishing, but from the mirror where he can see them written on his face. But the mirror shows him no sins; it reveals the face of a king. He smashes it because it lies about his situation, the true situation of all men, even kings. Thus, in drawing Bolingbroke's attention to 'the moral of this sport', he may be offering a warning as well as a further statement of the power of sorrow (IV, i, 290–1).

His last gesture is a trick, and apparently a rather pointless one. He will, he says,

> beg one boon,
> And then be gone, and trouble you no more.
>
> (IV, i, 302–3)

But what he begs in fact is permission to be gone. The request is a further move in the power-struggle, both because Richard is able to leave without having read the articles and because he forces Bolingbroke to show his intentions at last by sending him to the Tower.[1] In his parting shot –

> O, good! Convey! Conveyers are you all,
> That rise thus nimbly by a true king's fall.
>
> (IV, i, 317–18)

– he seizes on the unfortunately chosen word 'convey' (which was slang for 'steal') and adds, I think, a characteristic pun on 'true king' (a 'true man' was the opposite of a thief). It is a good exit, but what he wins is not simply a moral victory; by making it clear that he is not willing to resign the crown and still considers himself the rightful king, he has opened the way for just such a conspiracy as we see taking shape at the end of the scene.

Stanley Wells has pointed out the parallel between the ending of the deposition scene and that of II, i.[2] There, too, mere words – those of the dying Gaunt and York – seem to have no effect, yet the scene ends with three onlookers deciding to take action on behalf of an apparently hopeless cause. Richard's pun on 'convey' links the two still further, since it was his own theft of Gaunt's lands which started the rebellion against him. That the rebellion against Bolingbroke is later discovered and crushed does not alter the effect of the rebels' words, coming as they do immediately after the 'woeful pageant'. It is too simple to treat the deposition scene as a triumph of silent, powerful Bolingbroke over verbose, weak Richard. Language *is* a source of power in the play, even though there is also an awareness of its inadequacy. Though Richard's rhetoric successfully appeals to the spectators' reverence for the symbol of England and the Church, the nobles and churchmen who rally to his cause are defeated in a way that is clearly providential: Aumerle has no sooner said that he intends to be in Oxford 'If God prevent it not' (V, ii, 55) than York notices the seal hanging out of his son's doublet. And the less admirable motives which make the old man gallop away to reveal the plot do not detract from his conviction that Bolingbroke's usurpation, however shocking, must somehow be part of a divine plan.

Shakespeare does not attempt to explain this paradox, but he continues to explore it in the last act of the play, largely through the opposing kinds of language he gives to Richard. On the one hand, the deposed king becomes more formal and rhetorical than ever before. After the ceremonial unkinging, which he later

[1] See Brents Stirling, 'Up, Cousin, Up; Your Heart is Up, I Know', from *Unity in Shakespearean Tragedy* (Columbia, 1956), reprinted in P. M. Cubeta (ed.), *Twentieth-Century Interpretations of Richard II* (New Jersey, 1971), p. 95.

[2] See the introduction to his edition of the play (Penguin, 1969), pp. 30–1.

describes as a divorce between him and his crown (v, i, 71–2), comes his equally ritualistic parting with the Queen, when he 'unkisses' his contract with her in an exchange of hearts which is also a marriage with sorrow. Even his dying words are formal, a divorce of soul from body:

> Exton, thy fierce hand
> Hath with the king's blood stain'd the king's
>   own land.
> Mount, mount, my soul! thy seat is up on high,
> Whilst my gross flesh sinks downward, here to die.
>   (v, v, 109–12)

The speech echoes and unites several dominant images of the play: the rising-falling pattern, the sacrificial blood watering the earth, and the stain which cannot be washed away. Richard shows complete certainty both of his kingly status and of his own salvation; Exton, similarly, accepts the view that he himself is damned forever. We have seen the death of a symbol, not a human being.

But alongside this ritualistic King of Sorrows Shakespeare also gives us intriguing glimpses of the other Richard: sharp-tongued, self-mocking and quite unresigned. The pointed realism of his words to Northumberland in v, i, is fully in keeping with his constant anticipation of Bolingbroke's moves, and I am sure the Quartos are right to give him, and not Northumberland, the cynical reply to the Queen's request that the two of them be banished together: 'That were some love, but little policy' (v, i, 84). The symbolic representative of England has little discernible affection for his people ('A king of beasts indeed' [v, i, 35]), and, as the prison soliloquy shows us, God's representative on earth is unsure of his own salvation. Unlike the saintly Henry VI with his crown of content, Richard finds that 'no thought is contented' (v, v, 11) and he now sees death not as the way to 'a new world's crown' (v, i, 24) but as 'being nothing' (v, v, 41). The images in which he personifies

his own thoughts all tend irresistibly toward the grotesque, whether they are quibbling over scriptural contradictions, plotting an impossible escape, or, like beggars in the stocks (not Stoic philosophers, or even the hermit that he once imagined himself), trying to resign themselves to fate.[1] His playing with words, far from providing a consoling substitute for reality, nearly drives him mad. Yet, despite the desire for human love which comes through at the end of the soliloquy, his immediate reaction to the unexpected appearance of the Groom is a stale pun on 'royal' and 'noble'. The familiar tone of this little episode is almost immediately followed by the outbursts against the keeper and the murderers, in which the dominant note seems one of relief that he at last has an object on which to release his pent-up energies. There is relief for the audience as well, not only in the violent action which follows five acts of fighting with words alone, but also in the sheer arrogance of Richard's reaction: 'How now! what means death in this *rude* assault?' (v, v, 105). Nevertheless, one can see why his dying speech had to be modulated into a different tone.

The formality of that speech, and its rhyming couplets, are taken up at once by Exton, establishing the simplified, symbolic view of Richard ('As full of valour as of royal blood' [v, v, 113]) which is to prevail in the final scene. However uninspired poetically, the alternation of speeches reporting the downfall of Henry's enemies with bathetic thank-you couplets from Henry is dramatically effective in that it prepares the entry of Exton, whom the king emphatically does *not* thank. Moreover, Henry's forgiveness of Carlisle, which ought to be the climax of the scene, is immediately and ironically nullified by the appearance of the coffin which, though it contains 'the mightiest of thy greatest enemies' (v, vi, 32), is a source

[1] See Nicholas Brooke's comments on this soliloquy, *Shakespeare's Early Tragedies*, pp. 134–5.

not of triumph but of consternation to him. 'A god on earth thou art', was the Duchess of York's phrase after he pardoned Aumerle (v, iii, 134), but Exton's act has identified him irrevocably with Pilate, wishing in vain both to pardon his victim and to wash the blood off his hands. As Reese has pointed out, 'thy buried fear' (v, vi, 31) has a double meaning, indicating not only an end to fears but a permanent source of them in the coffin of the murdered king.[1] The presence of that coffin lends dignity and resonance even to the stiff couplets of Henry and Exton; in particular, the phrase 'Richard of Burdeaux' has a shock effect which is curiously moving in the theatre. Henry's last speech calls upon the familiar national and religious symbols and attempts to channel potentially dangerous emotions into the ritual of court mourning and the promise of a Crusade. But it is fitting that irony and ambiguity should hang over this solemn ending and that the 'silent king' in the coffin should still present a threat. Richard dominates the scene in his silence as he had dominated it before with words.

[1] *The Cease of Majesty* (London, 1961), p. 255.

© LOIS POTTER 1974

THE PRINCE OF DENMARK
AND CLAUDIUS'S COURT

JULIET McLAUCHLAN

In *King Lear* and *Macbeth*, in different ways, the hero by his own actions sets tragic forces in motion; in *Othello* the hero is gradually 'wrought' to destructive passion; but when *Hamlet* begins, someone other than the hero has already violated the natural order of the kingdom, and the hero, although profoundly disturbed, is only partially aware of the evil which is entrenched. Hamlet's original 'intent' to go back to Wittenberg seems to reflect a feeling of helplessness and a desire simply to escape from Elsinore as it now is. Agreeing to stay, he rightly senses that 'it is not, nor it cannot come to good' (I, 2).[1] Thus, for the hero of *Hamlet*, the situation is from the very start one of tragic disruption: to see the play in terms of a conflict which shatters the prince when he is faced with life in the Denmark of Claudius constitutes a key approach – not a new one, but, as I hope to demonstrate, one which it is illuminating to carry further. In this play Shakespeare creates and intensifies the sense of tragic conflict by particularly subtle and oblique *presentation* of concepts of the universe, the state, and man, which were familiar in his day.[2] As they are also familiar to all students of Shakespeare I wish to draw attention only to points most relevant to subsequent discussion.

The first concept underlying my argument is that of the Great Chain of Being. In this imagined hierarchy of created things, man was thought to enjoy a unique potential: *ni ange ni bête*, he could move upwards, through the exercise and control of reason, towards angelic apprehension and even godlike qualities, or he could move downwards, through the dominance of passion, towards the level of the beast. In *Hamlet*, the inevitable tragic conflict begins with Hamlet's immediate and painful sense of the bestial qualities embodied in Claudius and, what to the prince is worse, his mother's faithlessness to her marriage vows through her hasty union with the 'satyr'. She, too, has been brought down to the brute level – or even lower, for 'a beast, that wants discourse of reason, / Would have mourn'd longer', he cries (I, 2). Hamlet's passionate feeling of revulsion (seemingly an intuitive thing) is further intensified when he is cruelly shocked into awareness of sheer evil, through the revelation that his father has been murdered. My argument will seek to show that Shakespeare presents in *Hamlet* a conflict between the humanistic Wittenberg ideal with its upward aspirations, and the negation of it at Elsinore. He shows this ideal to have been Hamlet's and to have been embodied for him in

[1] All references are to H. H. Furness, New Variorum *Hamlet* (New York, 1963).

[2] I am not maintaining that there was ever any single universally accepted medieval, Renaissance, Elizabethan, or other view of the cosmos and man's place in it; nor am I maintaining that Shakespeare was deliberately presenting in *Hamlet* or any of his plays an 'Elizabethan view' known and accepted by himself and everyone in his audiences. I am suggesting that in *Hamlet* Shakespeare shows certain views (mainly in conflict) which had long been known and discussed, and were therefore familiar to his audiences.

the figure of his father, 'a man, take him for all in all, / I shall not look upon his like again' (I, 2).

Arthur Lovejoy has written of that

> plan and structure of the world which, through the Middle Ages and down to the late Eighteenth Century, many philosophers, most men of science and, indeed, most educated men, were to accept without question – the conception of the universe as a 'Great Chain of Being', composed of an immense, or – by the strict but seldom rigorously applied logic of the principle of continuity – of an infinite number of links ranging in hierarchical order from the meagrest kind of existents, which barely escape non-existence, through 'every possible' grade up to the *ens perfectissimus*.[1]

This unquestioning acceptance did not rule out widely divergent views on cosmography and on man's place in the order of things: sometimes a Ptolemaic universe with the earth at its centre was seen as beautiful and man's position as favoured; sometimes 'the centre of the world was . . . the place farthest removed from the Empyrean, the bottom of the creation, to which the dregs and baser elements sank'.[2] Whether in a Ptolemaic or a Copernican universe, however, man's position remained crucial, for 'this planet alone contained a race of free creatures half material and half spiritual – the middle link in the Chain of Being – for whose allegiances the celestial and the infernal powers compete'.[3] Medieval Christian philosophy, like Neoplatonism before it, was faced with a choice between two concepts of God: one, the goal of the 'way up' for the soul which aspired to regain changeless perfection and rest; the other 'the source of and the informing energy of that descending process by which being flows through all the levels of possibility down to the very lowest'. Choosing the former, it thus

shaped the assumptions concerning man's chief end which dominated European thought down to the Renaissance, and in orthodox theology, Protestant as well as Catholic, beyond it. The 'way up' alone was the direction in which man was to look for the good.[4]

Hamlet has seen life in the idealistic light of this concept of following the 'way up'. To this exalted ideal he suffers a shattering blow, which proves tragic in its effects upon him: we see the disintegration of his own wholeness as a man and, worse, watch his responses to the evil around him, responses which are passionate and ultimately destructive to others and to himself, rather than rational. It is what Hamlet suffers, is, and does in the course of the play, which pre-eminently constitutes the tragedy of *Hamlet*.

The second concept basic to my argument is that the king served (under God) as head of the body politic, and the health of this body depended upon the virtue of the king. This is in line with the medieval and Elizabethan doctrine of the king's two bodies, which Anne Barton (paraphrasing Ernst Kantorowitz in *The King's Two Bodies*) defines as a '*body natural . . . which is mystically united* at the moment of coronation with a *body politic*', this 'dual identity' then belonging to the king for life (italics are mine).[5]

These long-held and much-discussed concepts involved the conviction that a violation of any one part of the natural order of things must bring disruption into the rest. By Shakespeare's day they had been challenged in many ways, but in particular (for the purpose of this discussion): the concept of man's noble potential by Montaigne's deeply cynical writings on the baseness of man's nature and the weakness, even 'imbecillitie of man's

[1] Arthur Lovejoy, *The Great Chain of Being* (Cambridge, Mass. 1936), p. 59.

[2] *Ibid.*, p. 101.

[3] *Ibid.*, p. 103.

[4] *Ibid.*, pp. 83–4.

[5] 'Shakespeare: His Tragedies', Sphere History of Literature in the English Language, vol. 3 (*English Drama to 1710*, ed. Christopher Ricks, London, 1971), p. 219.

reason';[1] the concept of the ideal ruler by Machiavelli's writings on practical and realistic statecraft.

In *Hamlet* we see, mainly through the two protagonists, the shattering of familiar Renaissance (and earlier) ideals through conflict with a Montaigne-Machiavelli world – a world where the weapon of man's reason is not adequately used (by Hamlet) and where, in any case, it seems that reason would be powerless to 'set it right'.

Emphasising the conflict, deep ironies arise from the fact that the traditional positives of kingship and of man's potential are often expressed at Elsinore by those whose behaviour and values are a negation of what is asserted. Furthermore, there is sometimes more than the usual degree of irony when a character speaks more truly than he realises. Claudius, for instance, refers to Fortinbras as:

> Holding a weak supposal of our worth,
> Or thinking by our late dear brother's death
> Our state to be disjoint and out of frame

(I, 2)

His sarcastic words imply his own worth and the health of his state; yet a weak supposal of Claudius would be the right one, and his Denmark *is* 'disjoint' and 'out of frame' precisely by his brother's death – or rather by the manner of it. While the court is completely taken in, Shakespeare would not intend his audience to miss the irony. The appearance of the Ghost in scene I would, for Elizabethans, be enough to make these words suspect; they would thus stand out, and the empty claim would still be resonating as the truth of the situation soon became clear.[2] At the end of the play's first 'movement', Hamlet's words provide a direct echo: 'The time is out of joint' (I, 5), as it now obviously *is*. 'Disjoint' and 'out of frame' are exactly right to suggest painful bodily dislocation which must prevent normal functioning; 'out of frame' brings in

the cosmological order, since such phrases as 'this universal frame',[3] 'this wonderful and incomprehensible huge frame of God's works',[4] 'the universal frame of this world' and 'worldly frame'[5] appeared in many contemporary works.[6]

By Claudius's violation of the natural order,

[1] 'An Apologie of Raymond Sebonde', Ch. XII, Bk Two in Montaigne, *Essays*, as translated by John Florio (London, 1603; Everyman Edition, London, 1935), p. 255. The Nonesuch Edition, ed. J. I. M. Stewart (London, 1936), is the most authoritative, but is not readily obtainable. Frances Yates, in her *John Florio* (Cambridge, 1934), p. 213, points out that Florio's translation was licensed for publication in June 1600, and she mentions written references to it as early as 1600, concluding that it 'must have been circulated in manuscript' around 1598. This means that it could well have been seen by Shakespeare before its publication. Although the whole matter is still the subject of scholarly controversy it is certain that, beginning with the Second Quarto of *Hamlet* (1604), many apparent 'echoes' of the Sebonde essay come into the text; study of these is of the greatest interest.

[2] I do not wish to imply that we should feel here anything like the full extent of Claudius's hypocrisy and villainy. However, the play's first scene (with its unnatural tension, and the foreboding which springs from the intrusion of the supernatural) has suggested strongly the rottenness of Denmark, to which Shakespeare adds important clues – clues which would be less likely to be missed by an Elizabethan audience than a present-day one.

[3] Pierre de la Primaudaye, 'Of Policy and the Good Ordering of Estates', from *The French Academy*, trans. T. Bowes, 1586, reprinted in James Winny (ed.), *The Frame of Order* (London, 1957), p. 113.

[4] Thomas Digges, *A Perfit Description of the Celestiall Orbes*, etc. (London, 1575), reprinted Winny, *ibid.*, p. 152.

[5] Annibale Romei, *The Courtier's Academy*, trans. J. Kepers (London, 1598), Winny, *ibid.*, pp. 200, 207.

[6] Two examples from Florio's translation of the Sebonde essay show (not the generally euphuistic style of his translation but) the general application of these terms. He renders '*toute cette machine*' and '*ce grand bastiment*' (Montaigne, *Essais*, Tome II (Paris (Nelson), 1934, p. 59 and p. 64) by, respectively, 'this vast world's frame' and 'the huge world's frame', Florio (trans.) *Essays*, p. 135 and p. 139.

his state is 'rotten' and evil is established. He has murdered the rightful king, who was also his brother; although his marriage to the dead king's widow has been sanctioned by the court, Elizabethans would see it as incest, and this in itself would cast doubt upon the king's smooth explanations; similarly, although his accession has been formally approved according to Danish custom, the Ghost soon reveals that he is, in the spirit if not the letter, a usurper. The force of the Ghost's words:

> so the whole ear of Denmark
> Is by a forged process of my death
> Rankly abused;   (I, 4)

would be much greater to an Elizabethan audience than to us.[1] The deliberately ambiguous uses of 'Denmark' in *Hamlet* (now referring, as here, to the body politic, now to the murdered king, now to Claudius) work to emphasise the inseparable link between the king and the health, or otherwise, of his state. The most extraordinary thing about Claudius is the blandness with which he assumes that he has become, in the true sense, 'Denmark'. He speaks as if he sees himself firmly within the order which his deeds have grossly violated. Gertrude, too, entirely accepts this; true, she is not aware of his crime, but it is a serious indictment of a weak and obtuse nature that she can beg her grieving son to 'look like a friend on Denmark'. Claudius goes further, even imagining that Hamlet can and will stay on at Elsinore as 'our chiefest courtier, our cousin, and our son'. Publicly making the prince his heir, he appears to see himself as successfully assimilating into his court, and even into the closest family relationship, the devoted son of the king he has murdered. To Hamlet such a relationship can seem only a ghastly parody (and so it should seem to the audience), yet Gertrude again seconds her husband's words with her plea to the prince to stay with 'us'.

To Claudius appearance is the reality of the situation. His murderous plot having gained him the throne, he operates as the epitome of smooth courtly condescension. The court accept the appearance of kingship with no apparent reservations. As 'Denmark' Claudius has a quick success in his diplomatic move *vis à vis* Norway. According to Machiavelli:

fortune, especially when she wants to build up the greatness of a new prince, whose need to acquire standing is more pressing than that of a hereditary ruler, finds enemies for him, so that he may have reason to triumph over them and ascend higher on the ladder his foes have provided.[2]

Fortune provides Claudius with just such an external threat: his triumph comes, characteristically, through a strong diplomatic stand. His manner is such as to reassure the court immediately (long before it is known that his move has succeeded) and this adds much to his appearance of kingship, even to the quite

---

[1] I am grateful to Nigel Alexander for giving me permission to quote a comment in which he develops what he calls the 'enormous dramatic implication' of my 'two bodies' argument: 'Claudius, as usurper (although the legally elected monarch) is trying to take over the body politic of Denmark. The only visible sign that this take-over is unlawful is his clearly unlawful and incestuous taking-over of the body of "the imperial jointress to this state" Queen Gertrude. The rape of the body politic of Denmark is thus truly symbolised by the lustful seduction of the body of Denmark's queen – and Hamlet's deep disgust at that act is partly because he can sense the deep political disorder of which it is so clear a sign.'

[2] Nicolò Machiavelli, *The Prince*, trans. George Bull (London, 1961), Ch. 20. I prefer this translation, but others are readily available, notably the World's Classics, trans. Luigi Ricci (London, 1903), revised E. R. P. Vincent (1935); and the Everyman's, trans. W. K. Marriott (London, 1958). The date of the first known English translation is 1640, so it is impossible to know how Shakespeare became familiar with Machiavelli's ideas. The English notion of Machiavellism was unquestionably 'in the air' in his day and that is enough, although Vincent suggests the existence of manuscript translations, and refers to a known Scots translation between 1580 and 1590.

erroneous belief (accepted by some critics) that he might have made a good ruler if only the Ghost and Hamlet had let well alone. The natural order has been violated in *Hamlet* as surely as in *Macbeth*. If the violation seems less blatant, it is simply because of the 'plastering art' which 'beauties' the 'harlot's cheek' of Claudius and his kingdom. In *Macbeth* the murderous usurper soon turns tyrant and his crimes are so evident that supporters begin to mistrust him, hate him, and desert his service, while Claudius continues to be surrounded by loyal courtiers.

The nature of loyalty at Elsinore is, however, very searchingly investigated. Horatio, alone, is truly loyal (to Hamlet as friend and prince); otherwise loyalty is, unquestioningly, to the *throne*, the worth of its occupant being simply assumed. The suggestive way in which the imagery works in *Hamlet* to show underlying corruption of the accepted ideal is very clear in Claudius's words to Laertes:

The head is not more native to the heart,
The hand more instrumental to the mouth,
Than is the throne of Denmark to thy father.
(I, 2)

The body of Claudius's Denmark functions and is sustained precisely through interdependence of usurper and blind supporters. Significantly, the support which Claudius enjoys is purely *court* support. The people hardly figure at all in the play: that they are not loyal to Claudius is apparent from their readiness to make Laertes king, and the love of the 'general gender' for Hamlet.

Polonius sees and expresses his loyalty in elevated terms:

Assure you my good liege,
I hold my duty as I hold my soul,
Both to my God and to my gracious king
(II, 2)

– unexceptionable words, if addressed to a truly gracious king by a courtier less blind in his loyalty, and less forgetful of past loyalty, for surely he has very recently served another 'Denmark'? Polonius is no Machiavel; he is simply obtuse, and when he maunders on about the folly of expostulating 'what majesty should be, what duty is', he clearly has no conception of either.

When Rosencrantz and Guildenstern arrive they vie with each other in piling phrase upon obsequious phrase. Rosencrantz declares that the 'majesties' of Denmark could by their 'sovereign power' put their 'dread pleasures' into commands instead of simply requesting service. Guildenstern rushes to add: 'But we both obey', finishing off Rosencrantz's line, and the rest of his words follow headlong:

And here give up ourselves, in the full bent,
To lay our service freely at your feet,
To be commanded.
(II, 2)

Embodied in the very movement of this verse is their eagerness to throw themselves, literally if need be, at the feet of the king and queen: the positioning of 'bent' and 'commanded' gives the words weight, and the progressive shortening of the lines, with the breathless repetition of 'To lay ...', 'To be ...' adds to the effect. Blind sycophancy is the more blatant since we learn from Claudius that these young men have been 'of so young days brought up with Hamlet'; the prince first welcomes them warmly as 'My excellent good friends' and 'Good lads', and later appeals to them 'by the consonancy of our youth'; they have long known Hamlet, his parents, and the 'fair state' of the past, yet they know as little as Polonius how to value friendship and love or to assess true worth or majesty. It is part of the subtlety of Shakespeare's presentation of Claudius's court and state that these two consummate toadies should try to express the true positives of kingship, and particularly (again) the mystical unity between king and body politic:

Most *holy and religious* fear it is
To keep those *many many* bodies safe
That *live and feed* upon your majesty.

Rosencrantz immediately takes up this assertion of Guildenstern's and among other fulsome protestations, sees the king as:

That spirit upon whose weal *depends and rests*
The lives of many.

(III, 3; italics are mine)

The most obvious effect of this oblique presentation of the traditional ideal is to force the audience to see the contrast between these declarations and the realities of Elsinore, but the language itself makes this effect more interesting. With one exception, the italicised phrases (and others, 'strength and armour', 'singular and peculiar', even 'mortis'd and adjoin'd') are noticeably less forceful than are many of Shakespeare's complimentary phrases (as Granville Barker has noted).[1] They are intentionally banal, spinning out and weakening the accepted positives, so that in their very words the toadies devalue what they say. The phrase 'live and feed' works differently: it provokes in the audience a response opposite to anything Guildenstern intends. He means the words to describe positive interdependence of people and king;[2] what they actually suggest is the sort of gross parasitism which Rosencrantz and Guildenstern represent. Moreover, what is really living and feeding upon the 'majesty' of Claudius is the 'imposthume' of his crime. Claudius himself (and this is again characteristic of the presentation in *Hamlet*) states the true position, though seeing it in the context of his own need to get rid of Hamlet:

but so much was our love,
We would not understand what was most fit,
But like the owner of a foul disease,
To keep it from divulging, let it *feed*
Even on the pith of *life*. (IV, 1; italics are mine)

Exactly. Claudius, trying to keep secret the foul disease which he owns, has been letting it devour the living substance of his state: 'food' and similar words, recur throughout *Hamlet*, to suggest gross sensual appetite, ugly parasitism, or devouring disease.

If it were not already plain just what sort of courtiers Rosencrantz and Guildenstern are, it would become so when they speak as they do of Claudius, whom they see as a true king in fruitful relationship to the body politic – Claudius, whose guilt has just been confirmed in the play scene, who *is* now to the audience a 'damned smiling villain'. Hamlet's taunting words place the toadies exactly:

Hamlet. Besides, to be demanded of a sponge, what replication should be made by the son of a king?
Rosencrantz. Take you me for a sponge, my lord?
Hamlet. Ay, sir, that soaks up the king's countenance, his rewards, his authorities. (IV, 2)

Claudius's appearance of kingship is shown here in all its worthlessness. Hamlet is, of course, putting into precise perspective the extravagant words of Rosencrantz and Guildenstern, but what is more interesting is that the audience has no need of a nudge from Hamlet in order to judge them. What it does need is to see Hamlet's awareness of the nature of their relationship to the king and to see that this is part of his justified loathing of all that Elsinore has come to stand for since his father's death.

The full title of the play is *The Tragedy of Hamlet, Prince of Denmark*: much of the tragedy lies in the fact that the *prince* has been 'rose' of his father's 'fair state' and its 'expectancy', whereas he is now, against all inclination, crown prince of Claudius's Denmark.

[1] *Prefaces to Shakespeare, Hamlet* (London, 1930 and (Batsford Paperback) 1968), p. 170.
[2] Cf. *Macbeth*, I, 4 for the finest expression of this: the ideal king grateful and bountiful, has 'planted' and will 'labour' to make his loyal subjects 'full of growing'. Malcolm later acknowledges the same ideal, which is also embodied in the saintliness of the English king.

While he cannot and should not acquiesce in such a denial of the natural order as would make him truly heir to a murderous usurping 'uncle-father', he must remain virtually imprisoned in this false court situation so long as he fails to come to terms with the duty laid upon him by his father's spirit. Conflicts within himself delay this so that the state is not finally purged until after Ophelia is dead (largely by Hamlet's fault, although she is not herself blameless) – too late, that is, for any restoration of the 'fair state' with Hamlet at its head, for the link between Ophelia and Hamlet (as the state's 'expectancy') is crucial to the future. Nigel Alexander sees the graveyard scene as one of the play's 'most tragic', precisely 'because the characters are burying the future'.[1]

The court obviously accepts Hamlet as crown prince. Because of Hamlet's position, Laertes warns his sister, and once again the image is of the body politic:

> for on his choice depends
> The safety[2] and health of the whole state.
> And therefore must his choice be circumscribed
> Unto the voice and yielding of that body
> Whereof he is the head. (I, 3)

Polonius's warning has been in similar terms (II, 2).

Hamlet sees the underlying court situation as evil because his ideal of kingship is inseparable from his ideal of 'a man'. The sort of a king a man will make depends upon the sort of man he is. Hamlet mourns his father as 'so excellent a king', with all the force of the word 'excellent', but it is his father as a man and as his mother's husband that he most reveres in memory. Horatio recalls him as 'a goodly king', and 'goodly' goes beyond external appearance to connote the admirable and worthy, but to Hamlet:

> He was a man, take him for all in all,
> I shall not look upon his like again. (I, 2)

Later Hamlet speaks to Gertrude in terms which lift his father's human qualities to the god-like: majesty (Jove, king of gods); valiance (Mars, god of war); old Hamlet's bearing has seemed to his son like that of the gods' messenger at the moment of touching the earth, the earth where it is nearest heaven, the verse suggesting aspiration upwards in 'heaven-kissing hill'. The old king has:

> A combination and a form indeed,
> Where every god did seem to set his seal
> To give the world assurance of a man
>
> (III, 4)

To Hamlet the god-like is a seal set upon the human when man attains his highest potential.

How far is this ideal really established in relation to old Hamlet? How much is it simply the son's idealisation of a beloved father? The words used of the Ghost, 'majestical', 'slow and stately', 'fair and warlike', 'valiant' (while living), 'solemn', 'courteous', 'more in sorrow than in anger', suggest a martial figure of regal dignity. There is little in the text to suggest that his own reference to his 'foul crimes' is more than a formal protestation of general guilt by one who has died without absolution. Some critics hold that the Ghost's demand for vengeance is evil and robs the old king of any nobility. Two points seem relevant: the 'rotten' state must somehow be purged of its evil; the demand of the soldier-king is made in terms of an accepted code, such as is followed without question by Laertes, and which is not questioned even by Hamlet himself. Old Hamlet takes on some of the attributes of the ideal king (and man) simply through deliberate contrasts with Claudius. Claudius's acknowledgement of his crime and his own realisation of its ugliness give weight to the Ghost's assessment of him, and to

---

[1] *Poison, Play and Duel* (London, 1971), p. 151.
[2] First Folio reads 'sanctity'; Theobald, Hanmer, *et al.* 'sanity'.

Hamlet's. It is clear that old Hamlet is *not* invested with the sort of value Shakespeare gives to Duncan; but, perhaps, whether or not he was all that Hamlet believes is less important than the simple existence of Hamlet's ideal, and the ways in which crucial details in the play's imagery link old Hamlet with this ideal.

Most significantly, value is associated with him chiefly through his love for Gertrude, which Hamlet recalls as a sort of gentle and protective devotion:

> so loving to my mother,
> That he might not beteem the winds of heaven
> Visit her face too roughly   (I, 2)

The Ghost's own description (I, 5) is very much in the same key (and see below).

The ideal and the negation of it, which the prince immediately senses at Elsinore, are evoked in his first soliloquy. The 'excellent' king and 'loving' husband was to Claudius 'as Hyperion to a satyr': this lifts the brightness and glory of the rightful king towards the god-like, while the usurper is brought down to the lecherous and beastlike. At the very beginning, therefore, Hamlet links his father with man's upward potential, his uncle with man's potential debasement. By contrast to his father's love, Hamlet recalls his mother's response in grossly sensual terms: 'as if increase of appetite had grown by what it fed on', and then in a key passage links her, too, with man's potentiality for debasement:

> O, God! a beast that wants discourse of reason
> Would have mourn'd *longer* ...
>
>   (I, 2; italics are mine)

Debasement occurs when 'reason panders will', in his later words (III, 4).

This recalls Montaigne's contention that not only was man not superior to beasts, he was indeed inferior to them in some ways, hence my italicised 'longer'. Montaigne wrote:

Brute beasts are much more regular than we, and with more moderation containe themselves within the compasse which nature hath prescribed them ... As some of our nations have wives in common ... so have some beasts; yet some there are that observe their marriage with as great respect as we do ours.[1]

Montaigne tells also of beasts which so mourned the death of masters as to be inconsolable and even to seek their own deaths.[2] We should note that it is for Hamlet, not the audience, that the dichotomy between a bestial Claudius and a godlike father is absolute. Claudius is complex and interesting, precisely because he is not a beast but a man, with considerable human potential, who slips towards the bestial through failure to control passion with reason.

Returning to the Ghost's speech, we can see how Shakespeare contrasts most dramatically, through the pattern of the language, man's upward and downward potential:

> O, Hamlet, what a falling-off was there!
> From me, whose love was of that dignity
> That it went hand in hand even with the vow
> I made to her in marriage: and to decline
> Upon a wretch, whose natural gifts were poor
> To those of mine!
> But virtue, as it never will be moved,
> Though lewdness court it in a shape of heaven,
> So lust, though to a radiant angel link'd,
> Will sate itself in a celestial bed,
> And prey on garbage.
>
>   (I, 5)

The note of pain and grief, coupled with the deliberately shocking contrasts in the imagery, lift this above the vaunting of an unworthy and complacent husband or the whinings of a cuckold. Hamlet's earlier description of his father's love and of his mother's appetite is taken up here in stronger terms. The first line sets the tone, after which the words flow smoothly, complementing one another until,

[1] Florio (trans.), *Essays*, p. 166, p. 174.
[2] *Ibid.*, p. 165.

in the middle of the passage, comes a direct contrast of values, which is intensified and rendered concrete by sharply antithetical words *within the lines* that follow. There is also a movement *from line to line* upwards: 'love', 'dignity', 'hand in hand', 'vow', 'marriage', 'virtue', 'shape of heaven', 'radiant angel', 'celestial'; human values come first and rise to the heavenly. This parallels an ugly movement downwards, which details the 'falling-off': 'decline', 'wretch', 'gifts' . . . 'poor', 'lewdness', 'lust', 'sate', 'prey on garbage'.

The Ghost's mention of the marriage vow is echoed twice by Ophelia (I, 3 and II, I): '. . . almost all the holy vows of heaven' and 'music vows' which Hamlet has made to the 'celestial' Ophelia, his 'soul's idol' suggest that his idealistic sense of love has followed his father's. Hamlet later rebukes Gertrude for her broken vows, which her actions have made 'as false as dicers' oaths'. (Throughout Shakespeare great value is attached to vows and oaths.) The Ghost's last words seem to confirm the value of this husband's love, and the validity of Hamlet's view of it. He forgets his desire to spur his son to revenge and pleads with Hamlet to show compassion to his mother, his last words, 'Speak to her, Hamlet'.

The significance of this is that Hamlet's ideal of his father, and thus of man, seems to have been based upon his ideal view of his parents' marriage; his deep disillusionment with man and with life springs *primarily* from the shock to this ideal. Hamlet rightly sees an ugly degeneration from love to lust in Gertrude's second marriage, and it is certainly this, rather than the political disruption of Denmark, which disturbs Hamlet most and rouses his most passionate outbursts.

Hamlet's magnificent prose speech on the universe and man, in which he evokes a familiar Renaissance ideal in noble terms, is a key passage:

I have of late, – but wherefore I know not, – lost all my mirth, forgone all custom of exercises; and indeed it goes so heavily with my disposition that this goodly frame, the earth, seems to me a sterile promontory; this most excellent canopy, the air, look you, this brave o'erhanging firmament, this majestical roof fretted with golden fire, – why, it appears no other thing to me than a foul and pestilent congregation of vapours. What a piece of work is man! how noble in reason! how infinite in faculty! in form and moving, how express and admirable! in action,[1] how like an angel! in apprehension, how like a god! the beauty of the world! the paragon of animals! And yet, to me, what is this quintessence of dust?

(II, 2)

The words in which Hamlet reveals his own distaste for the beauty and splendour of the universe are meant to shock: the earth now seems not a fruitful and admirable 'frame', framed in turn in an ordered universe, but a 'promontory', exposed and 'sterile'. The air and heaven seem (with the suggestion of a positive stench of corruption) to be 'foul' and plague-ridden 'vapours'. The paradox, 'quintessence of dust' works in a remarkable way. 'Quintessence' first creates the expectation of the distillation of something rare and fine, following on from the high human potential which Hamlet has been outlining. Then comes the terrible deflating effect of the monosyllables, 'of dust' – with all the connotations of mortality, decomposition, and utter worthlessness carried by the word 'dust'.

So, in contact with Elsinore, the Wittenberg student's whole view of the world and of man has degenerated. This accounts for Hamlet's growing obsession with the physical state of death and decomposition, with all that is implied in 'a king may go a progress through the

[1] John Dover Wilson adopts the Q2 punctuation in his *Hamlet* (Cambridge, 1934); in *Shakespeare and the Nature of Man* (Cambridge, 1934), Theodore Spencer calls this the punctuation 'which alone makes sense in terms of Elizabethan psychology'. I prefer it too: '. . . admirable in action; how like an angel in apprehension; how like a god!'

guts of a beggar'. He sees 'your fat king and your lean beggar' as being brought to 'one table', the worm's. 'Degree' has ceased to exist. In the reduction of the noble Alexander to something like 'this' (a stinking skull), and in the phrase 'your worm is your only emperor',[1] not only is there a reversal of man's aspiration (man no longer striving upwards in the chain of being, with the emperor looked upon as highest and most admirable in the human hierarchy) but there is a downward movement, from emperor to base dust. Hamlet has come to see the noble 'piece of work' as fragmented into its component parts or as reduced to its ultimate state of decomposition. He questions the purpose of human birth and life:

and did these bones cost no more the breeding,
but to play at loggats with them?

(v, i)

and his next words, 'Mine ache to think on't', bring his sense of futility and mortality so close that he feels it deep within his own body. Similarly, politician, courtier, lawyer, jester, all are seen as coming to one end, rotting in the earth. By now, Hamlet has made and remade the point, but he goes on musing on a possible ignoble end for the 'noble dust' of Alexander and, against the mild protest of Horatio, stubbornly follows in detail the processes of Alexander's death, burial, return to 'dust', 'earth', his 'loam' finally being used 'to stop a beer-barrel'. And he must still go on to consider in similar fashion the possible fate of 'Imperious Caesar'. This insistence and repetition emphasise his obsession with the negative 'progress' of man. Just then he sees the arrival of the funeral procession, with the king and queen. This rounds off the point ironically: Hamlet had just brought all earthly power and glory down into a precise and infinitely belittling perspective: it is in fact the nature and behaviour of this 'king' ('a thing...

Of nothing') and of his wife, especially the nature of their 'love', which have brought Hamlet's view of kingship and of man so low.

Part of the tragedy of *Hamlet* lies then in our suffering with the prince in his deepening awareness of evil and in his consequent agonising loss of belief in man's potentialities. This is not the whole of it. In Elsinore, Hamlet's own personality, his embodiment of his own ideal, suffers disintegration. Ophelia's words of mournful remembrance are as crucial to the play as is Hamlet's great speech on the Renaissance ideal:

Oh, what a noble mind is here o'erthrown!
The courtier's, scholar's, soldier's, eye, tongue,
          sword,
The expectancy and rose of the fair state,
The glass of fashion, and the mould of form,
The observed of all observers, quite, quite down!
And I, of ladies most deject and wretched,
That suck'd the honey of his music-vows,
Now see that noble and most sovereign reason,
Like sweet bells jangled out of tune, and harsh;
That unmatch'd form and feature of blown youth
Blasted with ecstasy

(III, i)

The more we imagine the whole man, as she recalls him, the more we feel the tragedy. Courtier, soldier, scholar – of this Renaissance prince there are only glimpses.

Soldier – on the battlements Hamlet draws his sword and is ready to use it in order to break free from restraint; he acts quickly in the encounter with the pirates, and fights creditably in the duel. Most significantly, Fortinbras, the soldier-prince who becomes 'Denmark', judges that Hamlet would have 'proved most royally had he been put on', and at the end lays repeated emphasis on the fact that Hamlet is to be accorded the treatment and rites due to a soldier.

[1] Montaigne wrote: 'The heart and life of a mighty and triumphant Emperor, is but the break-fast of a seely little Worme.' Florio (trans.), *Essays*, p. 155.

Scholar – most clearly Hamlet is (or has been) the scholar; above all, the scholar of Wittenberg, that great centre of Renaissance humanistic thought, the first university north of the Alps to go beyond medieval patterns of belief and teaching. We often see the inquiring, active, even playful aspects of Hamlet's mind; much less, as will be seen below, of its reasoning powers.

Courtier – the prince should be Denmark's 'chiefest courtier', not Claudius's, for we cannot imagine Hamlet with the 'candied tongue' capable of 'licking the absurd pomp' of the Danish court. There are flashes of princely behaviour, of a characteristic combination of gracious dignity with frankness and informality, but at Elsinore, where Claudius and his courtiers are parodies of true courtliness, Hamlet's behaviour is deliberately most uncourtly. In keeping with the oblique presentation of positives in this play, we have from Claudius, Elsinore's consummate 'courtier', a view of Hamlet which is revealing:

> he being remiss
> Most generous and free of all contriving,
> Will not peruse the foils.
>
> (IV, 7)

Towards the end of the famous passage in which Machiavelli counsels princes on the necessity of combining the attributes of the lion (strength and courage) and the fox (cunning), he also says that the prince must know how to:

act according to the nature of both man and beast . . . he cannot survive otherwise . . . those princes who have known best how to imitate the fox have come off best. But one must know how to colour one's actions and to be a great liar and deceiver. Men are so simple . . . that the deceiver will always find someone to be deceived.[1]

This is the way Claudius operates; again Shakespeare's presentation is striking. In Claudius's words we recognise at once Hamlet's nature, with an accompanying shock of horror and revulsion, for the 'fox' will triumph through unscrupulous use of knowledge of his victim. There is the usual obvious dramatic irony here, but it is painfully intensified when we see the unsuspecting Hamlet with Laertes a little later, apologising for having hurt his 'brother' and (doubtless offering his hand) agreeing that he 'will this brother's wager play'. Here is a glimpse of Hamlet, courtier of the 'fair state' – generous, frank, trusting.

Shakespeare emphasises the disintegration of the prince by images which show in the world around Hamlet fragmentation of the whole man. Farthest from the prince in every sense, is the soldier; the unreflective, aggressive, forthright man of action, Fortinbras. But old Hamlet, too, is mainly shown as a *soldier*-king, with only minimal suggestions of the courtier, none of the scholar. Perhaps a significant element in the tragedy is that the *whole man* is asked to carry out a command based on the code of the soldier-king. Closest to Hamlet is the scholar: the rational, devoted man of thought, Horatio. All around Hamlet is the courtier: appropriately not compressed into a single figure, but multifaceted, even caricatured, especially in its last incarnation, Osric. Superficial, affected, chameleon-like in his views, a rich land owner, and only one of many on whom the 'drossy' time 'dotes', this 'waterfly' is placed exactly by Hamlet's words; these show the depths to which courtly standards are sinking under Claudius, and the metaphor echoes once again the dominant conflicts of the play:

> let a beast be lord of beasts
> and his crib shall stand in the king's mess
>
> (V, 2)

The tragedy of *Hamlet* goes further than the disintegration of the Renaissance prince. The evil, the 'imposthume' in the Danish royal

[1] *The Prince* (trans. Bull), Ch. 18.

family and state, so horrifies Hamlet that it evokes evil in response. The corruption of personality, family, and state is as ugly as Hamlet thinks it is, but the upsurge of evil within him is ugly too and destructive. Hamlet, whose ideal is 'that man who is not passion's slave', who believes that reason and moderation (like Horatio's) should control passion, becomes almost obsessed by hatred of evil, and is more often swayed by passion than ruled by reason. How can we account for this? Montaigne expressed the desire to make men feel: 'the emptinesse, vacuitie, and no worth of man; and violently to pull out of their hands the silly weapons of their reason'.[1] Is it this 'silly weapon' that fails Hamlet? In his last soliloquy, he passionately and half-despairingly asserts, in very characteristic terms, the value of reason:

> What is a man,
> If the chief good and market of his time
> Be but to sleep and feed? a beast, no more;
> Sure, he that made us with such large discourse,
> Looking before and after, gave us not
> That capability and god-like reason
> To fust in us unus'd. (IV, 4)

Surely, he asks, man should not be just a beast? Surely he must use his reason? And Hamlet has been using his reason. Or has he? Later in this soliloquy he wonders if he may have been thinking 'too precisely upon the event'; if so, there is little evidence of it when we see Hamlet in thought or action, nor have we often seen him reasoning out alternative courses of action. The first soliloquy is no reasoned assessment of the situation but a passionate outpouring of deep grief and bitter disgust, culminating in resigned acceptance of heartbreak and silent inactivity. To the encounter with the Ghost he responds more passionately than rationally. The second soliloquy includes a passionate response to the player's speech, a passionate denunciation of himself, a passionate outburst against Claudius,

then more self-denunciation before he finally does set his brain to work on the idea of the play. 'To be or not to be' leads into a prolonged and complex meditation, rather than to concrete reasoning on specific problems. In the short soliloquy (III, 2) there is little reasoning, for Hamlet characteristically finds here some outlet in words, but is clearly swept by a passionate desire to act violently against his mother. Fear that he may actually do so leads him to resolve to exercise control. What happens as he debates the killing of Claudius, at prayer? Nigel Alexander argues very persuasively that Hamlet has at this stage every intention of acting as Pyrrhus and Lucianus do, and that, ironically, it is only the very blackness of his hatred and of his desire for total revenge which holds him back and saves him from sinking to the level of this type of revenger.[2]

Do we then see in *Hamlet* a twofold failure of reason: (1) to show the prince how to deal with evident external evil and (2) to enable him to control evil within himself? I would argue, rather, that his passionate response to evil is so intense that for the most part reason is simply not invoked at all. Instead of reasoning, Hamlet habitually verbalises the emotions which spring from his deeply-felt failure to come to terms with the problem – *with a problem which in fact reason cannot solve?*[3] Can reason show Hamlet any action which will restore an order which has been brutally and permanently destroyed? Old Hamlet is dead, Gertrude is 'one flesh' with the satyr who murdered him. Can the irreversible be reversed by any rational action? Even if reason should sanction the revenge to which passion prompts Hamlet (and this is never reasoned out) will this put things right?

In this situation Hamlet reacts not with

---

[1] Florio (trans.) *Essays*, p. 137.
[2] Alexander, *Poison, Play and Duel*, pp. 115–18; 196.
[3] David Daiches and L. C. Knights, Sussex Tape on *Hamlet*, discuss this in an illuminating manner.

reason, but swings from passionate outbursts to wry mockery to weary apathy. This last seems to spring from a partial awareness of the hopelessness of any action. His sense of evil and his obsessive hatred of it dominate him and sometimes carry him almost beyond rational control. Gertrude doubtless needs a brutal shock to make her see 'black and grainèd spots' within herself, but Hamlet revels in his rage and disgust, renewing his ugly attack in gross detail even after his mother's conscience has been roused. Much sadder, indeed crucial to the tragedy, is Hamlet's failure to use his reason in the one direction where reason could set something right. Sickened by totally imaginary evil and corruption in Ophelia, Hamlet rails pitilessly at the innocent, infinitely vulnerable girl who loves him. A touch of reason would lead Hamlet to some understanding of her behaviour. His failure to understand her is crucial to the tragedy, because from the moment that he in effect rejects her, there can be no hope of eventual re-establishment of the 'fair state' with Hamlet at its head.

Nigel Alexander, too, sees the Hamlet–Ophelia relationship as crucial and treats it fully and sensitively. Reproducing Titian's painting (Plate 4) *Amor-Pulchritudo-Voluptas*, which he sees as portraying 'an initiation of Beauty into Love',[1] he shows how Hamlet's pervasive sense of evil causes him to take a distorted view of the natural sequence 'from *Pulchritudo* through *Amor* to *Voluptas*'. Similarly, in Raphael's *The Three Graces*, which Alexander also reproduces (Plate 2):

The different qualities of these three female figures together make up the feminine principle ... [and] just as each man must strive, in his choice of life, to be a union of wisdom, power, and pleasure, so every woman must be a combination of chastity, beauty, and passion ... They [the Graces] must all be pursued if the individual is to acquire within his own soul the harmony of the dance which is also in tune with the music of the spheres and the divine order of the world.[2]

Alexander points out that in the nunnery scene the natural progression of Beauty from Chastity to the fullness of sensual pleasure, is perverted to the honesty–beauty–bawd sequence, Hamlet's three terms corresponding to the three Graces (Chastity, Beauty, Pleasure), except that the third becomes lust. Hamlet sees as inevitable 'a progression to lust'.[3]

This provides a splendid and original insight, and once again, from this rather different standpoint, we see the reversal in Hamlet of a familiar Renaissance ideal – another aspect of his obsession with man's *downward progression*. It emphasises, again, the fact that Hamlet's total ideal has been based upon an ideal of love. Once this has been shattered by his mother's 'falling off', he never stops to question his certainty that all women share the same corruption. Significantly, he rails passionately against his mother and the innocent Ophelia. Towards the corrupt court he turns only a mocking wit, never losing control as he does when he thinks of his mother's behaviour.

Hamlet's sense of evil extends, of course, to himself. It is in no sense a pretence (as is Malcolm's in *Macbeth*), but deeply felt, and again he sees it as springing from his mother's corruption. In the nunnery scene, he says he could accuse himself of 'such things', that 'it were better my mother had not borne me', and asks 'what should such fellows as I do crawling between earth and heaven?' Hamlet's disillusionment with man has gone so far that he has come face to face with evil within himself, and by this stage it seems to have paralysed any capacity for love. Real remembrance of his love (involving a kind of realisation of its value) comes only when it is too late: at Ophelia's graveside.

Does *Hamlet*, then, show the failure of

[1] Alexander, *Poison, Play and Duel*, p. 138.
[2] *Ibid.*, p. 139.
[3] *Ibid.*, pp. 140–1.

'Renaissance man' to master through reason the Machiavellian and the beastly in man? Montaigne insists that man's reason alone must fail; he contends (though some doubt his sincerity) that God's grace is essential if 'wretched' man is to raise himself above the brute. The Renaissance ideal did not, as Hamlet seems to do, stop at reason. Reason, working downwards upon sense data, had the task of abstracting from them: 'the immaterial forms which they contain. These forms are then apprehended intuitively, by the *understanding*, or intellect, which is akin to the pure intellect of the angels, and which is therefore a higher power than the "discourse of reason"'. And finally, there is *will*, 'which we use', says Raleigh ('A Treatise of the Soul', in *Works*, ed. Oldys and Birch, (London, 1829), VIII, 586), 'to stir us up to seek God and heavenly things, and are delighted and satisfied in them . . .' (my italics).[1] Hamlet, then, classes reason too high when he calls it 'God-like'. Unnecessary to higher beings, reason was man's distinguishing quality, and was, even so, only a tool to enable him to rise higher. Castiglione puts it like this:

And because in our souls there be three manner waies to know, namely, by sense, reason, and understanding: of sense there arises appetite or longing, which is common to us with brute beastes; of reason ariseth election or choise which is proper to man; of understanding by the which man may be partner with Angels ariseth will.[2]

Hamlet's failure to invoke even reason necessarily prevents his attaining to understanding or to a true sense of will, on which action might properly be based.[3]

There is a curious inversion of the reason–understanding–will sequence in Claudius's long speech to Hamlet (I, 2). Hamlet's grief shows 'a will most incorrect to Heaven', 'an understanding simple and unschooled', and is finally, 'to reason most absurd'. Why does Shakespeare do this? There are obvious ironies in the plain reversal of the traditional upward order by one who personifies man's downward potential. Furthermore, the whole speech constitutes an example of careful but completely specious reasoning, characteristic of Claudius. '[Reason's] cry' cannot be 'This [death of fathers] must be so' when death is murder, disruptive of family and state. Claudius's understanding of himself and of the whole natural order is gravely at fault; his will is 'incorrect to Heaven', incorrigible, indeed, as we see when he fails to pray.

As the truth is presented so obliquely in *Hamlet*, more may be implied even than this. Will Hamlet's will be basically incorrect to Heaven, in that he does not subject it to higher control? Will his understanding remain simple and unschooled, not for the reason that Claudius adduces (his unmanly grief), but because Hamlet simply does not follow the upward course from reason to understanding (a crucial failure in Ophelia's case)? Is Hamlet's grief, with its concomitant bitterness and hatred of evil 'to reason most absurd' (senseless that is) because reason will not be able to control his passion, or to order the situation, or make any sense of it?

Any discussion of *Hamlet* must raise more

---

[1] Spencer, *Shakespeare and the Nature of Man*, pp. 12–13.

[2] Baldesar Castiglione, Book IV of *The Book of the Courtier*, trans. Sir Thomas Hoby (London, 1588); Everyman edition (London, 1928, 1948). A modern translation, Charles S. Singleton (New York, 1959), renders Hoby's 'understanding' (Italian 'intelletto') by 'intellect'. The whole of Book IV is of the greatest interest in the study of *Hamlet*.

[3] As a useful qualification, or corrective, to my whole view here, I quote another comment from Nigel Alexander: 'Hamlet frequently acts on his instincts rather than his reason – but his instincts have led him to the presentation of that union of intellect and emotion, a stage play. It is this act of "conscience" in every sense of that term which I think puts revenge-murder for ever beyond him (despite his instincts) in the prayer scene – it's the catching of the conscience of Claudius, which he had set out to do, which defeats the murderous intentions of Hamlet'.

questions than it answers. One large question will be: how much is put right or changed (in Hamlet) after his return from his voyage? He indulges in no more inconclusive verbalising of his conflicts, no more railing against evil. Although he is still acutely conscious of evil, he now thinks of it in terms of 'perfect conscience' and asks:

> is't not to be damned
> To let this canker of our nature come
> In further evil   (v, 2)

– which is to come much nearer the point, for the state must somehow be purged.

Most significantly, instead of the many references early in the play to Fortune (and indeed Hamlet's tragic situation, so far as he is concerned has been brought about by 'slings and arrows of [a particularly] outrageous fortune'), there are references to Heaven as 'ordinant', to 'divinity', to 'special providence', which seem to show some acceptance of the workings of a higher power. Here is the speech which contains Hamlet's most positive affirmation:

> Rashly,
> And *praised be rashness for it* . . . let us know
> Our indiscretion sometimes serves us well,
> When our deep plots do pall, and *that should teach us*
> There's a divinity that shapes our ends
> Rough-hew them how we will.
> (v, 2; my italics)

To this Horatio gravely replies 'That is most certain'. Curiously Hamlet seems here to link divine guidance with his own rashness and even 'indiscretion' (the very opposite of reasoned action). He also explains that his brain had begun the 'play' 'Ere I could make a prologue' – that is, he acted without planning or reflecting. It is as if, abandoning the rational, he has come to feel the activity of something beyond and above human endeavours; it is after his similarly unreflecting action in killing Polonius that he refers to himself as having been punished by being made 'heaven's scourge and minister'.

There is, however, no such positive sense of heavenly control of affairs in *Hamlet* as we see in, say, *The Winter's Tale*. Despite Hamlet's few positive affirmations, we do not come to the end of the play with any conviction that the prince has attained higher understanding, or even regained wholeness as a human being. In the storm of evil, external and internal, in which he has been caught up, too much has been destroyed. This is not to say that 'the readiness is all' implies merely a fatalistic resignation or exhaustion, but Hamlet does seem in a sense spent. There is simplicity and beauty (but of a very ambiguous kind) in his last words, 'The rest is silence', no real affirmation. It is left to Horatio to confirm our feelings: despite all the degradation, the 'falling off' which we have watched in Hamlet in the course of the play, it is a 'noble heart' which has cracked; a 'sweet prince' has died. These comments do not sentimentalise Hamlet, but like Horatio's last prayer that 'flights of angels sing thee to thy rest', serve directly to link Hamlet once more with the great potential envisaged for Renaissance man. Indeed the whole man is once more evoked as both soldier and scholar praise in their own ways the dead prince. This constitutes a final and infinitely sad irony: in *Hamlet* the waste which is characteristic of tragedy is seen as a failure to fulfil a noble and precisely defined potential.

© JULIET MCLAUCHLAN 1974

'HAMLET' AND THE 'MORIAE ENCOMIUM'

FRANK McCOMBIE

Perhaps the most impressive feature of Shakespeare's *Hamlet* is the way he has managed to transform a crude Norseman of the heroic age into a Renaissance prince of such impressive presence. Speculation about how it was done has led commentators a merry dance through sixteenth-century history and ideas. The place of Erasmus there, which no one familiar with the century would wish to dispute, has not really been taken into sufficient account in such speculation, considering first, how inescapable his influence was in general, and second, how much evidence there is in the plays that Shakespeare was familiar with his work[1] – and especially with the *Moriae Encomium*. Positive proof of first-hand acquaintance has, of course, been lacking; but circumstantial evidence is of sufficient weight to command attention. The *Moriae Encomium* was a grammar-school text in the 1570s and 1580s,[2] and it is perfectly possible that Shakespeare knew it as early as that, having perhaps been set to translate it himself. Schoolboys who were able to get hold of a copy must have been tempted to consult the Chaloner translation as a crib (it was first published in 1549, with subsequent editions in about 1560 and 1577); but there is, of course, no reason to think that Shakespeare did, though in later years he may well have known it. Whatever the truth of that, his acquaintance with the *Moriae Encomium* is supported by a wide range of what seem to be direct echoes of not only its thinking, but also its illustrative material. To mention only a few of the more obvious which have drawn notice. There is a fairly direct relationship between Shakespeare's presentation of wisdom-in-folly in *King Lear* and the particular exposition of that philosophy in the *Moriae Encomium*,[3] both works finding a basis of thought, generally, in paradox, with particularly the animal imagery cast in very similar terms. There are general echoes in the love's-madness theme of *A Midsummer Night's Dream*; in the general conception of the wise fool in *As You Like It*;[4] in the world-as-a-stage motif in *As You Like It* and

[1] On Shakespeare's general acquaintance with the work of Erasmus, see Kenneth Muir, *Notes and Queries* (October 1956), pp. 424–5. John W. Velz, in *Shakespeare and the Classical Tradition* (Minneapolis, 1968), lists many suggestions from critics over the past hundred years, echoes notably being discovered in *As You Like It* and *Troilus and Cressida*, plays roughly contemporaneous with *Hamlet*. A recent instance of such detection – of, apparently, a direct echo of the *Moriae Encomium* – is offered by Jürgen Schäfer in *Notes and Queries* (April 1969), pp. 135–6.

[2] See T. W. Baldwin, *Shakespere's Small Latine* (Urbana, 1944), I, 436. There is further evidence in an unpublished dissertation by William Charles McAvoy on 'Shakespeare's Use of the *Laus* of Aphthonius' (Illinois, 1952). See *Dissertation Extracts*, XIII (1953), 97.

[3] This has been much discussed; the argument is presented at length by Enid Welsford, *The Fool: His Social and Literary History* (London, 1935), pp. 236ff. A more recent discussion appears in Robert H. Goldsmith, *Wise Fools in Shakespeare* (East Lansing, 1955).

[4] See Welsford, *The Fool*, pp. 251–2 *et passim*; also John D. Rea, 'Jaques in Praise of Folly', *Modern Philology*, XVII (1919), 465–9.

The Tempest;[1] and a rather more precise echo in the implications and terminology of Gonzalo's speech on the nature of the island in *The Tempest*, II, i.[2] The general similarity of the turn of thought in the *Moriae Encomium* (probably Lucianic in origin) has always struck readers as being quite startlingly Shakespearian.[3] What I want to suggest, however, is something rather more particular than general similarity.

Although a variety of sources for Shakespeare's humanistic ideas makes better sense than a single source, and though one should not wish to argue for anything so patently absurd, it is nevertheless intriguing that so many of those ideas should echo the *Moriae Encomium* so insistently. It would not, for instance, be absurd to speculate upon how far the *Moriae Encomium* – which was only one example out of a whole field of 'fool' literature – owes its sustained popularity in this country to the fact that Shakespeare has attuned us to its characteristic modes of thought. The relationship is that close.

In proposing Hamlet, then, as a student of Wittenberg, a man in most ways at odds with the atmosphere of his uncle's court, as also – it is at least arguable – he had been with that of his heroic father, Shakespeare required a touchstone. Hamlet had to be given a humanist's turn of mind, even of phrase, to contrast, on the one hand, the world of chivalric heroics voiced by the Ghost and still sustained by Fortinbras, and on the other, that of Machiavellian political chicanery and treachery represented by Claudius and, in the event, by Laertes. What I want to suggest is, quite simply, that Shakespeare knew the *Moriae Encomium*, knew it well, and knew also that it precisely served the need.

The *Moriae Encomium*, written in 1509, first published in 1511, was valued in reformation England for its vigorous attack upon the abuses of the Church of Rome. There was a good deal more to its popularity than that, however. Quite notoriously (as the editing hand of Chaloner found), it was anti-chivalric, anti-heroic, and non-patriotic, in much of its content; and in proposing a specifically Christian view of the roles and duties of the prince, it was anti-Machiavellian. Although Erasmus often regretted the particular fame it brought him (watching propagandists carving it up piece-meal was galling), the *Moriae Encomium* did in fact epitomise the intellectual and moral convictions of the Christian humanists, ranged widely in support of its arguments, and powerfully illustrated a charac-

[1] See, for example, Thomas Woodhouse, 'All the World's a Stage', *Notes and Queries* (October, 1881), p. 311.

[2] Gonzalo plays with the thoughts that led men to name the West Indies 'The Fortunate Isles'. He projects a kind of paradise in impractical terms which could only have a rationale in paradise itself, and is thus an easy target for the wit of worldlings like Antonio and Sebastian. The irony is that the foolish prating old man proves his wisdom, first by showing a holy disposition that may win him salvation, second by recognising that what he is doing is merely (judged in practical terms) a 'merry fooling'. The line of thought followed by Erasmus when he makes the Fortunate Isles the birthplace of Folly (Sir Thomas Chaloner (trans.), *The Praise of Folie*, ed. Clarence H. Miller (EETS, London, 1965), pp. 12–13) is very close to all this, even as to imagery: 'I was brought foorth . . . euen amiddes the Ilandes, whiche of their synguler fertilitee and fruitefulnesse, are called Fortunatae, where as all thynges grow vnsowed and vntilled. In whiche iles neither labour, nor age, nor any maner sickenesse reigneth, nor in the fieldes there dooe either Nettles, Thistles, Mallowes, Brambles, Cockle, or suche lyke bagage grow, but in steede therof Gylofloures, Roses, Lilies, Basile, Violettes, and suche swete smellyng herbes, as whilom grew in Adonis gardeins, dooe on all sides satisfie bothe the sente, and the sight.' We note that of the three plants mentioned in the exchange between Gonzalo and his tormentors (nettles, docks, and mallows), two are in Folly's list; and that mallows are mentioned nowhere else in the plays.

[3] There is an essay on this by Alexander H. Sacton, 'The Paradoxical Encomium in Elizabethan Drama', in *University of Texas Studies in English*, XXVIII (1949), 83–104.

teristically humanist approach to the practical business of day-to-day living. Much of what Erasmus propounded there became, of course, the humanistic small change of the century; but the breadth and complexity of the echoes in *Hamlet* argue a relationship deeper than any mere echoing, and more significant than any echo could be. If, as I shall argue, Shakespeare consciously selected it as a touchstone of humanist thinking for his portrait of a humanist prince, he did particularly well; for the *Moriae Encomium* afforded him not merely a wealth of characterising detail, but a whole ethos of which to make him typical. He derived, in other words, not only a large part of Hamlet's character, but a world out of which he might act: not only a *persona*, but a place for him to stand.

In what follows, I have drawn for quotations particularly upon Kennet's translation (published by Woodward in 1709), as I do not wish to hang any part of the central argument upon Shakespeare's intimate acquaintance with the Chaloner, which at many points is less reliable in any case. Where it seems useful, however, I quote additionally from the Chaloner, in square brackets, sometimes from him instead of from Kennet, where the tone seems to me to have been more nicely caught. I have kept the Wilson translation (published 1668) in mind too, though it is altogether too free (and too politically coloured) to be much use here. The Erasmus text I have occasionally quoted directly, using the Basle edition of 1515.

To start, then, in the most familiar place. The precise quality of Hamlet's mind, it has been commonly felt, is revealed in some of its complexities in the 'To be, or not to be' soliloquy. Here, I hope we can take it, Hamlet is reflecting in a specifically, but also traditionally, humanistic way, less perhaps upon particularities than upon generalities. Quotation of his actual

words is scarcely required to see how the drift and quality of his thinking is broadly similar to that of the following:[1]

And now were any one plac'd on that Tower, from whence *Jove* is fancied by the Poets to Survey the World, he would all around discern how many Grievances and Calamities our whole Life is on every Side encompassed with: How Unclean our Birth, how Troublesome our Tendance in the Cradle, how liable our Childhood is to a Thousand Misfortunes, how Toilsome and full of Drudgery our Riper Years, how Heavy and Uncomfortable our Old Age, and lastly, how Unwelcome the Unavoidableness of Death. Further, in every Course of Life how many Wracks there may be of torturing Diseases, how many unhappy Accidents may casually occurr [sic], how many unexpected Disasters may arise, and what strange Alterations may one Moment produce? Not to mention such Miseries as Men are mutually the Cause of, as Poverty, Imprisonment, Slander, Reproach, Revenge, Treachery, Malice, Cousenage, Deceit, and so many more, as to reckon them all would be as puzz'ling Arithmetick as the numbering of the Sands.
(Kennet, pp. 47–8)

Erasmus goes on to reflect that men can scarcely wonder that the Virgins of Milesia, contemplating such miseries, hanged themselves; and yet men cling to life most foolishly, 'unwilling to die, and mighty hardly brought to take their last Farewel of their Friends'. So far the thought follows that of the soliloquy very closely; but now Hamlet goes on to speculate for himself upon that unwillingness to die (not necessarily by suicide), rightly judging that it is the fear of the unknown that makes us foolish in this regard. What is remarkable here, of course, is not the sharing of the reflection, but the close similarity in the progress of the argument and in the choice of illustrations.

So, too, when Hamlet assures Rosencrantz and Guildenstern that Denmark is no prison for them, 'for there is nothing either good or

[1] See Harry Levin, *The Question of Hamlet* (New York, 1959), p. 72, where he notes this similarity.

bad, but thinking makes it so', he is drawing – as Dover Wilson pointed out[1] – on a humanistic commonplace. But the two points in the *Moriae Encomium* at which this commonplace was given a new currency (Erasmus was paraphrasing Horace, *Satires*, I, i, 66)[2] are relevant in a broader way than the term 'commonplace' would suggest: 'but alas, Slander, Calumny and Disgrace, are no other Way Injurious than as they are Interpreted; nor otherwise Evil, than as they are thought to be so' (Kennet, p. 50). As Chaloner put it: '*For what hurteth thee, the peoples hissing, as longe as thou clappest thy selfe on the backe?* (Chaloner, p. 43). It must, at such a moment of confrontation with fellow-students, have seemed a ludicrously inadequate piece of consolation; and Hamlet's observation, seen as deriving hence, carries a weight of bitterness not immediately perceptible, and perhaps only perceptible when the peculiar appropriateness of the source to his own case is understood. And even more strongly may this be felt to be true when the other reference is recalled:

What Difference is there between them that in the darkest Dungeon can with a *Platonick* Brain Survey the whole World in Idea, and him that stands in the open Air, and takes a less deluding Prospect of the Universe? If the *Beggar* in *Lucian*, that *dreamt* he was a Prince, had never wak'd, his *imaginary* Kingdom had been as great as a *real* one. Between him therefore that *truly* is happy, and him that *thinks* himself so, there is no perceivable Distinction ...

(Kennet, p. 81)

Reading the passage between Hamlet and his friends in the light of this, one might even feel that Rosencrantz had picked up a precise reference, which prompts his jibe about Hamlet's ambition. It is interesting to note how Chaloner renders Erasmus here, '*sittyng in a caue vnder the grounde, to see nothyng but shadowes [uariarum rerum umbras] and representacions of thynges*' (p. 64), for Guildenstern, this time, leads the talk almost at once to the difference between reality and shadow.

Hamlet's surprise at the indifference of the clowns in v, i to the humanistic reflections their occupation might have been expected to evoke – echoing his strange cry at IV, iv, 33ff.[3] – is expressed in a passage which takes its place in a long heritage of similar observations; it is another humanistic commonplace. It is, nevertheless, curiously close to an extended passage in the *Moriae Encomium*, in which Folly sets out to show how fools are not afflicted by the troubles endured by rational men. What is arresting here is the list of illustrations Erasmus gives of experiences which leave the insensitive man untouched:

these Persons in all Circumstances fare best and live most comfortably: As first, they are void of all Fear, which is a very great Priviledge to be exempted from; they are troubled with no Remorse, nor Pricks of Conscience; they are not frighted with any Bugbear Stories of another World; they startle not at the fancied Appearance of Ghosts or Apparitions [old wiues tales of sprites, of diuelles, of hobgoblyne and the fayries];[4] they are not wrack'd with the Dread of impending Mischiefs [neither mournyng to theim selues for feare of euilles and aduersitees impendyng], nor bandied with the Hopes of any expected Enjoyments: In short, they are unassaulted by all those Legions of Cares that War against the Quiet of Rational Souls [thousande thousand cares, wherwith other men are oppressed] they are ashamed of nothing, fear no Man, banish the Uneasiness of Ambition, Envy, and Love ...

(Kennet, p. 57)

Again, one feels that Shakespeare has borrowed not simply a sentiment, but the entire climate in which it blossomed forth.

Immediately following upon this, the Clown turns up the skull of Yorick, and we might wonder by what curious turn of thought

[1] *Hamlet*, the New Cambridge edition (Cambridge, 1934), p. 173.

[2] See Chaloner (trans.), *Praise of Folie*, p. 154.

[3] All references are to the *Complete Works*, edited by Peter Alexander (London and Glasgow, 1951).

[4] Chaloner (trans.), *Praise of Folie*, p. 48.

Shakespeare should have chosen to make the gruesome illustration of humanistic reflection the skull of a court jester: our familiarity with the scene tends to obscure the fact that it was anything but an obvious choice. Whether or not it affords us an explanation, Erasmus, too, proceeds from a discussion of what the insensitive are protected against to a lengthy consideration of the privileges accorded to court fools: 'Yet Fools have so great a Priviledge as to have free leave, not only to speak *bare* Truths, but the most *bitter* ones too [not onely true tales, but euin open rebukes are with pleasure declared]' (Kennet, p. 60).[1] Taken as a whole, the passage presents a remarkably accurate summary of the Fool's role in Shakespearian drama; more immediately, we note how both Hamlet and Erasmus go on to remark how even women will take from a fool what they would not take from others: 'Now get thee to my lady's chamber . . .'

Closely following upon all this in the *Moriae Encomium*, there is Erasmus's famous passage upon the 'two kyndes of madnesse', as Chaloner renders it[2] (*duplex insaniae genus*). 'Shakespearian madness' is here described in some detail, and its relevance is commonly acknowledged. More immediate to our present purpose, however, is the fact that it offers a truly Erasmian gloss upon various kinds of madness in *Hamlet*. These are, first, the true (moral) madness of Old Hamlet and Claudius (*ab inferis*):

the one that which the Furies bring from Hell; those that are herewith possess'd are hurried on to Wars and Contentions, by an inexhaustible Thirst of Power and Riches, inflamed to some infamous and unlawful Lust, inraged to act the Parricide, seduced to become guilty of Incest, Sacrilege, or some other of those Crimson-dy'd Crimes; or, finally, to be so prick'd in Conscience as to be lash'd and stung with the Whips and Snakes of Grief and Remorse [in pectora mortalium inuehunt, siue cum nocentem & conscium animum, furijs ac terriculorum facibus agunt] . . .

(Kennet, p. 62)

second, the assuaging (pathological) madness of Ophelia (*mentis error*): 'the Mind is freed from those Cares which would otherwise gratingly afflict it . . .' (Kennet, p. 63), this being, in the way Erasmus describes it, also the third, Hamlet's semi-feigned (politic) madness.[3] There is a fourth kind of madness proposed by Erasmus in a passage which comes very close to the picture we are given of Polonius, conspicuously in the exchange with Reynaldo in II, i:

There is another very pleasant Sort of Madness, whereby Persons assume to *themselves* whatever of Accomplishment they discern in *others*. Thus the Happy *Rich Churl* in Seneca, who had so short a Memory, as he could not tell the least Story without a Servant's standing by to prompt him . . .

(Kennet, p. 74)

Especially as Hamlet sees him, Polonius is ridiculous in his foolish and inefficient aping of his master, Claudius.

An interesting gloss on Hamlet's eulogy upon Horatio is also provided by the *Moriae Encomium*. Critics over the years have dwelt lovingly upon this passage (much quoted out of context), in which Hamlet expresses his high regard of a man who can take all that comes to him and do nothing about it; yet the same critics have spent considerable effort in accounting for Hamlet as a prince who, under pressure to act, does nothing. The fact is, surely, that it is rather a curious thing that a man like Hamlet should wish to be a man like Horatio. Explanations are not lacking, of course: under the complex of pressures he has to endure, Hamlet might well catch himself envying the sort of man who seems to bear pressures better. That it is no more than such a

[1] *Ibid.*, p. 50.
[2] *Ibid.*, p. 52.
[3] Levin (*The Question of Hamlet*, p. 125) points the conscious adoption by Hamlet of the Erasmian role – 'stooping to folly in the grand Erasmian manner' – in IV, iii, 17 ff.

localised sentiment, however, is suggested by the fact that its expression does not have any verifiable effect upon Hamlet's proceeding. The following expression of a typically humanistic view of stoicism suggests why. Erasmus has spoken of passions as 'diseases of the mynde',[1] but then goes on to say:

This, I suppose, will be stomach'd by the Stoical *Seneca*, who pretends, that the only Emblem of Wisdom is *the Man without Passion*; whereas the supposing any Person to be so, is perfectly to Unman him, or else Transforming him into some fabulous Deity that never was, nor ever will be [*qui nusquam nec extitit unquam, nec extabit*]; nay, to speak more plain, it is but the making him a meer *Statue*, immoveable, sensless, and altogether unactive.

(Kennet, p. 46)

Here is Hamlet's difficulty crystallised: to act in passion is absurd, even diseased, 'like a whore unpack my heart with words'; to be stoical is to be wooden, 'bestial oblivion'. Yet it is not difficult to see how a man with this dilemma, who fears on the one hand to be less than a man, but on the other to become a raving beast in the excess of action, must sometimes envy the stoic, however arid and circumscribed the humanist believes his philosophy to be – 'There are more things in heaven and earth, Horatio . . .'

Hamlet tries to steer a middle course, true humanist that he is, neither denying human feeling nor falling victim to its excessive pressures. It sounds easier in theory, however, than it is in practice: 'In the undertaking any Enterprize the Wise Man shall run to consult with his Books, and doze himself with poring upon musty Authors, while the dispatchful Fool shall rush bluntly on, and have done the Business, while the other is thinking of it' (Kennet, p. 42). To be guilty either way in the pursuit of a crown, even when one has been preparing oneself against the day – the *nouus homo* now to be the *nouus imperator* – must strike the humanist as a particular folly; but

to sin for it, folly in the extreme: 'For certainly none can Esteem Perjury or Parricide a Cheap Purchase for a *Crown*, if he does but seriously reflect on that Weight of Cares a Princely Diadem is *loaded* with' (Kennet, p. 124). Parricide (taken in its broadest sense) is condemned almost as regularly as stoicism throughout the *Moriae Encomium*; but living in a court where none is to be trusted, a wise man, we are told, might well learn to play the dissembling game as others play it, for his own safety: 'First then it is confest almost a Proverb, that the Art of Dissembling is a very necessary Accomplishment . . .' (Kennet, p. 139). And perhaps the safest guise under which to conceal onself is that of a fool: 'Ite alibi, Dulce est desipere in loco . . . delirius, inersque uideri, quam sapere, ringi.' Which is Hamlet's policy, as it had been Hal's in the *Henry IV* plays.

Erasmus goes on to describe the world of the court, in which such policies are called for. It is all familiar to us, of course, but once again the importance of the parallels lies less in the thought than in the mode of expression, and in the choice of illustration. Erasmus pictures the courtier as an ignorant and servile flatterer, skilled in the use of impressive-sounding language, extravagantly dressed, empty-headed, yet with a gift for concealing his true nature, nevertheless: 'If you make a stricter Enquiry after their other Endowments, you shall find them meer Sots and Dolts' (Kennet, p. 127). Kennet's rendering of a passage a few lines later is interesting: 'I have many times took great Satisfaction by standing in the Court, and seeing how the tawdry Butterflies vie upon one another . . .' (Kennet, p. 128). 'Butterflies' doesn't appear in the Chaloner; nor is there any such specific reference in the Erasmus text. What Kennet is taking up, clearly enough, however, is the tone of the whole passage, in which it is the self-display of the courtiers, before each other, but especially before the ladies, that is being

[1] Chaloner (trans.), *Praise of Folie*, p. 39.

satirised: the sense of 'butterfly' is very strong. It is interesting to note, then, Shakespeare's use of the term 'water-fly' to describe Osric, who is the personification of all the contemptible qualities Erasmus lists. Shakespeare never uses 'butterfly' in this sense; and 'water-fly' occurs only three times in the plays: once neutrally (in *Antony and Cleopatra*), and twice in Kennet's way, once by Hamlet of Osric, once by Thersites of Patroclus. Of itself, this coincidence is nothing: in the pattern of echoes in which it occurs, it seems entirely natural.

The prince ought, at any rate, to be sharply aware of how deceptive appearances can be, Erasmus reminds him, going to some lengths to show how a 'profess'd Enemy to Liberty and Truth, careless and unmindful of the common Concerns, taking all the Measures of Justice and Honesty from the false Beam of Self-interest [geuin onely to his peculier profite, addicted all to voluptuousnesse]' (Kennet, p. 126)[1] may dress himself in the regalia and look in no way different from the prince himself, 'whan he hath no maner part of a prince in hym, sauyng onely the clothyng', as Chaloner puts it (p. 94). Erasmus is here returning to an issue which, perhaps above everything else, alarmed him, as it did Shakespeare, that 'all humaine thynges lyke the *Silenes or duble images of Alcibiades*, haue two faces muche vnlyke and dissemblable'. The passage continues (taking here the Chaloner, which is less free than the Kennet):

that what outwardly seemed death, yet lokyng within ye shulde fynde it lyfe: and on the other side what semed life, to be death: what fayre, to be foule: what riche, beggerly: what cunnyng, rude: what stronge, feable: what noble, vile: what gladsome, sadde: what happie, vnlucky: what friendly, vnfriendly: what healthsome, noysome. Briefely the Silene ones beyng vndone and disclosed, ye shall fynde all thynges tourned into a new semblance.

(Chaloner, p. 37)[2]

In order to expound the matter the more plainly, Erasmus goes on to picture court life in terms of a play enacted in a theatre:

If one at a solemne stage plaie, woulde take vpon hym to plucke of the plaiers garmentes, whiles they were saiyng theyr partes, and so disciphre vnto the lokers on, the true and natiue faces of eche of the plaiers, shoulde he not (trow ye) marre all the mattier? and well deserue for a madman to be peltid out of the place with stones?

Here we have, I believe, a significant light upon Hamlet's being 'idle' at the court performance of 'The Mouse-trap', by which he clearly intends 'acting the madman', though we should not in fact think anything he does or says during the performance warrants such a description. The passage continues: 'ye shoulde see yet straightwaies a new transmutacion in thynges: that who before plaied the woman, shoulde than appeare to be a man: who seemed youth, should shew his hore heares: who countrefaited the kynge, shulde tourne to a rascall ... (Chaloner, p. 37). Erasmus, of course, goes on to philosophise upon the world as a stage, in the now familiar manner; but here we have, I believe, the origin of the players in *Hamlet*. 'He that plays the King shall be welcome', Hamlet delightedly cries, though at the time of his making it the remark might well strike us as odd, even inexplicable: it is in the sequel that it becomes clear. Hamlet sets up in play form the drama of Elsinore, and then reduces it, in the manner suggested in the Erasmus passage, even as it is being performed, forecasting the outcome of the living drama, when Claudius, the playerking, 'a king of shreds and patches', will be exposed as the rascal he really is. For, as Erasmus says, quoting the proverb, 'That an Ape will be an Ape, tho' clad in Purple' (Kennet, p. 24); and Claudius, Hamlet would

[1] *Ibid.*, pp. 93–4.
[2] This passage is also cited by Levin (*The Question of Hamlet*, p. 74).

willingly believe, is no more, keeping Rosencrantz and Guildenstern 'like an ape in the corner of his jaw, first mouthed to be last swallowed' (IV, ii).

The world of the court is a debased world, where 'fawning Courtiers' (Kennet, p. 134) will find a way of condoning the murders done by their princes, 'having found out the Way how a Man may draw his Sword, and sheath it in his Brother's Bowels ...' Such men, nevertheless, play with fire, to their own damnation; and here it may be as well to quote Erasmus in the original, since the translations tend to mask his sharpness: 'Etenim siquis beatum existimet principibus placuisse uiris, & inter meos illos, ac gemmeos deos uersari, quid inutilius sapientia, imo quid apud hoc hominum genus damnatius?' The fate of Polonius, Laertes, Rosencrantz, and Guildenstern could scarcely be forecast more plainly than this, nor could the manner of their deaths more graphically illustrate the point Erasmus was making.

This passage follows hard upon Erasmus's discussion of Fortune in the *Moriae Encomium*. We note that there is some slight gesture towards personification of Fortune, and to the extent that there is, it is towards portraying her as an asinine creature, fit companion to Folly, pouring wealth and success into the laps of fools, while wise men go in fear of her. The rash, the foolhardy, the adventurous, these are her favourites, and these she rewards; the wise go (in Erasmus's own words) '*neglectos, inglorios, inuisos*'. Direct references to Fortune in *Hamlet* number eighteen: six of these are by the First Player and need not concern us further here; of the rest, that by the Queen, that by Fortinbras, and four references by Hamlet simply refer to Fortune as luck, the turn of events. Three others of Hamlet's picture Fortune as a meddlesome fool – 'outrageous fortune', 'Fortune's buffets and rewards', 'a pipe for Fortune's finger / To

sound what stop she please'. What we tend to remember, however, is the conversation between Hamlet and his fellow-students, Rosencrantz and Guildenstern, when Fortune is described as a strumpet. It is not characteristic of Hamlet so to picture her, though he is clearly familiar – and bored – with this particular analogy, one propounded, significantly for the sixteenth century, by Machiavelli. For him, Fortune (*fortuna*) was ruthless, daemonic, overwhelming, and characteristically he portrayed her as a whore playing with her wheel. The difference between this pagan view and the Erasmian view typified by Hamlet is caught in the German in the difference between *Rückschlag* and *Glückschlag*. It is significant that the only typically Machiavellian use of the word should occur in Hamlet's brief exchange with two amateur Machiavels. It is a distortion of memory if we recall this use rather than the others, for Hamlet's own view of Fortune is thoroughly Erasmian.

It is not, of course, to luck in any sense that Hamlet resigns himself, but to Providence – 'There is special providence in the fall of a sparrow', says Hamlet, as he goes, sword in hand, to meet his fate, reflecting that, 'If it be not now ... yet it will come.'

It is curiously close to the drift of Erasmus's argument in the *Moriae Encomium*, where he rebukes those who mistake Christ's injunction to the Apostles to buy a sword, on the night of Gethsemane, for a recommendation to arms. Such a person, Erasmus says, speaks: 'As if he had forgot that he encouraged them by the Examples of *Sparrows* and *Lillies* to take [no omitted in error] Thought *for the Morrow* [the small care that thei shuld take for theyr liuyng] (Kennet, p. 150).[1] We might well think that the tragedy of Hamlet lies as much as anywhere in his singular failure to learn how to live till that fateful hour when he learned how to die. Yet he goes to his fate with the

[1] Chaloner (trans.), *Praise of Folie*, p. 113.

whole force of Erasmus's treatise supporting his spirits;[1] as we might see in a remarkable passage in which so much of the situation as well as the thought of this play is set forth. Erasmus (through Folly) pictures a heavenly messenger come to earth to rebuke certain men for foolish *affections*, and asks what sort of reception he would get. I quote here from Chaloner, who has, I feel, captured the mood of the original most aptly:

Here nowe if one of these wisemen, come (I wene) from heauen, did sodeinly appeare, and saie, *howe euin this great prince, whom all men honor as their god and soueraigne, deserueth skarce to be called man, seyng like the brute beastes, he is trained by affections, and is none other than a seruaunt of the basest sort, seyng willyngly he obeith so many, and so vile vices his maisters. Or thanne againe, woulde bidde some other, who mourned for his fathers or friendes decease, rather to laughe, and be merie, because suche diyng to this worlde is the beginnyng of a better life, wheras this here, is but a maner death as it were. Furthermore, wolde call an other gloriyng in his armes and auncestrie, bothe a villaine, and a bastarde, because he is so many discentes disalied from vertue, whiche is the onely roote of true nobilitee.*

(Chaloner, p. 38)

Here, in turn, Claudius, Hamlet, and Old Hamlet are – typically – arraigned: but, as it were, unavailingly. Old Hamlet remains, even beyond the grave, a man 'gloriyng in his armes', crying for the vindication of his 'auncestrie', one for whom the rarer action is in vengeance than in virtue; Claudius dies, we might well think, deserving 'skarce to be called man', obeying to the last those 'vile vices his maisters'; and Hamlet, by a bitter irony, dies a man of chivalry, avenging his too-much-mourned father with poison and the sword. The story of these three Shakespeare has set forth as an investigation into 'the onely roote of true nobilitee'.

Other reflections in *Hamlet* of the *Moriae Encomium* may be no more than reflections, distant and, taken just in themselves, accidental – the inevitably shared data of two works of Christian humanism. But they cannot, I believe, be taken 'just in themselves', and so are worth indicating here for the support they lend to the general contention.

Hamlet's attitude towards the women in his life, for instance, interestingly echoes that expressed in the *Moriae Encomium*, which was not in fact specially typical in this respect of the humanist tradition. Hamlet is not hostile and unaccommodating so much as patronising, once his horror at woman's disloyalty is out of his system. His manner is at all times superior: he is contemptuous of the weaknesses he sees so clearly but cannot find sympathy enough to forgive. Erasmus presents Folly as a woman, and the characteristic note of the work is sounded when he says, 'a Woman will be a Woman *i.e.* a Fool, whatever Disguise she takes up' (Kennet, p. 24). He refers to '*mulierum genus*', speculating upon what likelihood there could be of this species belonging to that of rational man.

A curious reflection of the *Moriae Encomium* may be found in the appearance Hamlet makes at the court gathering (I, ii), and at the play (III, ii). Folly castigates serious, or wise, men for being poor mixers:

For place a formal Wise Man at a *Feast*, and he shall, either by his morose Silence put the whole Table out of Humour, or by his frivolous Questions disoblige and tire out all that sit near him ... Invite him to any Publick Performance, and by his very Looks he shall damp the Mirth of all the Spectators ...

(Kennet, pp. 36–7)

Hamlet, trapped in a court where what is serious can find no obvious place, may well feel that he has been tricked into playing a caricature of the scholar in insisting upon observing proper respect for the recently deceased king

[1] Perhaps even consciously. See Levin (*The Question of Hamlet*, pp. 118–19); he supports the speculation that the book Hamlet is reading in II, ii is the *Moriae Encomium*.

his father. And Claudius, we may well believe, is playing most adroitly on the caricature when, in a long and disreputable speech, he cold-bloodedly debases Erasmus's humanistic argument against undue mourning for the dead and undue elevation of parents ('for what did they more than Generate a Body?' (Kennet, p. 165)).

In his first soliloquy, Hamlet compares his father with Hercules, a suitable analogy for one who seems to have been pre-eminently a man of action. There is no hint of irony: nor is there, curiously enough, in Erasmus's references to Hercules; we might reasonably have expected that there would be: 'Ye shall heare therfore the praise set foorth, not of Hercules, nor yet of Solon, but rather of myne owne selfe, That is to saie of Folie' (Chaloner, p. 8). Hamlet, though he never uses the term 'fool' of himself – reserving it as an expression of contempt for others – nevertheless sees himself most gallingly cast in the role of the fool ('Why, what an ass am I') both in the eyes of the court, and in his own. Hamlet does not himself share Shakespeare's later enthusiasm for the paradox of wisdom-in-folly, though he does begin to approach it, we might think, in v, i. His exaggerated view of his father's merits, however, partake of his general reaction to the picture he entertains of himself:

> Hyperion's curls; the front of Jove himself;
> An eye like Mars, to threaten and command;
> A station like the herald Mercury
> New lighted on a heaven-kissing hill –
> A combination and a form indeed
> Where every god did seem to set his seal,
> To give the world assurance of a man.
>
> (III, iv, 56–62)

No more than Hal could swallow the exaggerated stories about Hotspur can we accept this: no such man ever existed. And almost point by point, the claim is rebuked by Folly:

Few haue the gyfte of beautie through Venus fauour. Fewer haue eloquence at Mercuries handes. Hercules maketh not all men riche. Iupiter graunteth not kyngdomes to euery bodie. Oftentymes Mars fauoureth neither partie. Many retourne discomforted from Apollos oracle. Not seeldome Ioues thunder destroieth men . . . But I Folie am she, that egally dooe comprehende all men vnder the compasse of my so great a good gifte. (Chaloner, pp. 65–6)

Here, too, one can appreciate the gall for Hamlet in being cast – by the need he feels to confirm his faith in his father and to reprove his myopic mother – in a role so remote from the one he would have chosen for himself.

There are, further, several striking verbal echoes of the *Moriae Encomium* in *Hamlet*, striking, more often than not, because the words in question are uncommon in Shakespeare generally, and, where they are not particular to this play, are rarely much removed from it in the time of writing. For example, Shakespeare's choice of a name for Polonius's son may have been dictated by a wish to use Greek names for both son and daughter, and he may have already lighted upon Ophelia. But why Laertes, particularly? The classical Laertes was one of the Argonauts, but Shakespeare may have known him as the father of Odysseus: perhaps the connotations of the name were sufficiently evocative of an adventurous life to seem appropriate. It is interesting, nevertheless, that the name occurs in the *Moriae Encomium*, in a list Erasmus offers of Greek names typical of those appropriated by contemporary authors in a current affectation for things Greek, and perhaps with the hope of sounding more impressive than they would otherwise.

We find Hamlet speaking of some act 'That has no relish of salvation in't' (III, iii). In the *Moriae Encomium*, we find Erasmus using 'gustus' in just this way, rendered by Chaloner as 'taste' sometimes, but more usually as 'smacke'. Both 'smack' and 'relish' are common enough in Shakespeare, but only in *Hamlet* with the sense of 'fore-taste', as in the following, where the context is exactly the same: 'tamen quoniam piorum uita, nihil aliud est, quam illius uitae meditatio, ac uelut umbra quaedam, fit ut praemii quoque illius aliquando gustum aut odorem aliquem sentiant'.[1]

The *Moriae Encomium* may possibly shed some light too upon Shakespeare's sole dramatic use of the term 'quietus', which Steevens (quoted in the Variorum edition) describes as: 'the technical term for the acquittance which every sheriff receives on settling his accounts at the Exchequer' (Variorum, I, 212n). This reading might well sound a little strained to the modern reader, who is so determined to think of death in this soliloquy in terms of a release into peace and quiet; but Steevens, in fact, seems to be much closer than this to the truth. Erasmus (thinking perhaps of Henry VII and his death-bed amnesties) pours scorn on those who think they can wipe out the sinful excesses of a life-time by some slight gesture of reparation, and imagine that all is (as Chaloner put it, p. 57): 'therby as vpon a Quites est redeemed ...' Erasmus has '*uelut ex pacto redimi*', where '*pactum*' clearly calls for some appropriate technical term in the translation; and Chaloner found an obvious one. If Shakespeare knew the Chaloner, his attention would be drawn to the '*Quites est*' on the page, as it was printed in roman. Whatever the truth of that, Shakespeare is clearly using 'quietus' as a version of '*quites est*', and with exactly the same sense of 'contract'.

Other words appearing in Chaloner, and notable in *Hamlet* for their relative rarity are: 'quidditee' – only twice in the plays, once in I *Henry IV* (I, ii), and once in *Hamlet*, in a passage strongly reminiscent of the passage in the *Moriae Encomium* castigating the affecta-

tions of lawyers; 'tropologically' – appearing in *Hamlet* as 'tropically', the only use of this word in the plays: 'Niobe' – only two occurrences in the plays (*Troilus and Cressida* and *Hamlet*); 'camel' – three times in the plays (*Troilus and Cressida*, *Hamlet*, and *Coriolanus*); 'satyr' – occurs only in *Hamlet*; 'quintessence' occurs only twice in the plays (*As You Like It* and *Hamlet*); and Shakespeare's 'the front of Jove' is his only use of Jupiter as a source of description, and is very reminiscent of a similar use by Erasmus: 'Iupiter hym selfe, *with all his depe dissembled chere*, lokyng so sternly, as geueth terrour...' (Chaloner, p. 21).

In conclusion, I can only express my personal conviction that in proposing to himself a Renaissance prince, cast in the humanist mould, confronting the long-familiar but still painful humanist dilemma, Shakespeare turned to an obvious source, and one with which he had probably been long acquainted. The precise nature of the relationship that indubitably exists between these two works suggests to me that the *Moriae Encomium* was drawn upon by one who knew it very intimately, had absorbed a great deal of its feeling into his own outlook and thinking, but who now consulted it again, on the brink, as it were, of his new creation, to see what it might afford him in terms of basic data. The use he made of it was masterly, his absorption of it entire: hence the laborious business of tracing even a little of it out.

[1] The words occur in the Chaloner trans. on pp. 126, 127, and 128.

© FRANK McCOMBIE 1974

THE RELATION OF HENRY V TO TAMBURLAINE

ROY BATTENHOUSE

Echoes of Tamburlaine in Shakespeare's Henry V have frequently been noted by scholars, but without a careful probing of their significance. It has been remarked, for instance, that in Henry's summons to Harfleur 'we seem to hear the voice of Tamburlaine himself', and that the play's opening prologue seems to conjure up a hero sprung from 'the Marlovian sphere'.[1] If so, what was Shakespeare trying to do? Was he merely taking advantage of Elizabethan popular taste for Conqueror plays and borrowing haphazardly from well-known prototypes? Or was he intending, rather, some comparison or contrast? In G. Wilson Knight's view, Shakespeare was here attempting to 'Christianize military conquest' by offering an epic blend of Christian virtue with martial prowess; he was holding up an ideal king 'in opposition to a Tamburlaine or to Hitler's tyranny'.[2] And a similar explanation has been given by Irving Ribner: 'Henry V may well be called Shakespeare's Christian Tamburlaine, noteworthy for his mercy rather than cruelty, and for his submission to the will of God rather than rebellion against it.'[3] Superficially, perhaps so, for on Henry's part there is no overt blasphemy, no threatening to storm heaven such as we see in 2 Tamburlaine. But whether Henry is noteworthy for mercy seems to me questionable, as is likewise the genuineness of his submission to God. Is the ethic we see practiced by Henry really Christian, or is it so only by an invalid claim? After all, Tamburlaine too talked a good deal about obeying God.

Writing more recently, Richard Egan has offered a more complex account than Wilson Knight's or Ribner's. Both Tamburlaine and Henry, in Egan's view, undertake a conqueror's role at the peril of neglecting an inner humanity and responsible love for mankind. Tamburlaine conspicuously denies his humanity when he slaughters the virgins of Damascus, Zenocrate's kinsfolk; and when Zenocrate then withers away, Tamburlaine's 'human part' dies with her, leaving him desperate, mad, and unnatural. Likewise, says Egan, Henry's behavior at Harfleur is antithetical to his humanity as a Christian, providing us in fact an 'ironic commentary on the self-contradictory course he has taken'. But Egan would see a change for the better in Henry after Harfleur. The setback of sickness in Henry's army, he argues, reminds Henry of his mortality, teaches him patience, and is climaxed in a brotherly association and Christian pact with his men. By evincing this 'new awareness of his own humanity', Henry has synthesized 'outward Prince and inward Christian'. He has wrestled 'successfully with the dichotomy that destroyed Tamburlaine, emerging with a newly synthesized identity which is illumined and confirmed in his union with Katherine'.[4]

[1] J. Dover Wilson, New Cambridge edition of Henry V (Cambridge, 1947), p. xxvi.
[2] The Olive and the Sword (Oxford, 1944), pp. 28–30.
[3] The English History Play in the Age of Shakespeare (Princeton, 1957), p. 183.
[4] Richard Egan, 'A Muse of Fire: Henry V in the Light of Tamburlaine', MLQ, XXIX (1968), 15–28.

To this interpretation, however, several objections may be made. For one thing, Henry's most inhumane act, his order to cut the throats of prisoners, comes *after* what Egan has termed Henry's 'Christian pact' of brotherhood. And the pact itself, if we note that it is made on the basis of *coveting* honor (IV, iii, 28), constitutes no brotherhood of a properly Christian kind. Rather, it takes on dramatic irony when Henry dresses it up with references to the Crispin brothers, whose suffering was for a commitment quite different from Henry's. For another thing, Henry's patience, when visiting his soldiers on the night before Agincourt, consists actually of *evading* a prickly question by Williams as to the justice of the war.[1] And a moment afterwards, in soliloquy, Henry's patience takes the form of a self-pitying resignation to a worship of 'idol ceremony' as the grief-giving god to whom Henry's 'proud dream' binds him. It is true that he here accepts the limitations of his own mortality without threatening Heaven as Tamburlaine does. But it must be noted that he is not being faced, as Tamburlaine was, with a wife's death or his immediate own. And more basically, Henry is no superman of Marlovian cast. Whereas Tamburlaine's ambition was to scourge in the name of a God of avenging wrath, Henry's (we may say) is to play a political game for the keeping of his crown and gaining a French one – in the pursuit of which he relies on a 'God of battles' to steel his soldiers' hearts. In the process, as various critics have noted, Henry's own heart becomes somewhat steel-like, by his sacrificing to his chosen role a good deal of the natural humanity evident in his early scenes with Falstaff. And unlike Egan, scholars such as Traversi and Bevington see no reversal of this drift. They see it continuing, rather, as the price Henry's office exacts of him; and Goddard goes further to characterize this office as making Henry, by insensible degrees, 'into something that comes too close for comfort to Machiavelli's ideal prince'.[2]

If seen in the light of these criticisms, is Henry's story much different from Tamburlaine's? The scope of his ambition, although less cosmic than that of Marlowe's hero, is analogous in achieving a triumph that was to prove hollow ultimately. And if we admit A. C. Bradley's view that Henry's too much 'policy' and 'superstition' disqualifies him as Shakespeare's ideal of kingship,[3] we may find in Shakespeare's design more of parallel than of contrast to Tamburlaine. Professor Goddard, I believe, was substantially correct in saying that Henry's Battle of Agincourt is something like a royal equivalent of Gadshill robbery, and that Henry in effect confuses Mars with the Christian God.[4]

Overall similarities in the two heroes are easy to recall. Each during his life-time suffered no military defeat. Tamburlaine, as the chronicler Fortescue said, 'never sawe the backe or frowning face of fortune ... never was vanquished or put to flight by any'. Henry, as Hall's chronicle reports, 'was a captain against whom fortune never frowned nor mischance once spurned'. In this respect both compare with Alexander and (except for a final betrayal) with Julius Caesar, to both of whom both plays make reference. And all four of these conquerors, of course, were crown

---

[1] Various scholars have commented on how Henry's answer to Williams dodges the issue. See, e.g., S. C. Sen Gupta, *Shakespeare's Historical Plays* (Oxford, 1964), p. 148.

[2] Derek Traversi, *Shakespeare from Richard II to Henry V* (London, 1957), pp. 166–98; David Bevington, *Tudor Drama and Politics* (Cambridge, Mass., 1968), pp. 247–8; H. C. Goddard, *The Meaning of Shakespeare* (Chicago, 1951), p. 267.

[3] *Oxford Lectures on Poetry* (London, 1909), pp. 256–8.

[4] *Meaning of Shakespeare*, pp. 255, 260. An even more vigorous critique of Henry can be found in John Bromley's *The Shakespearean Kings* (Boulder, Colorado, 1971), pp. 75–92.

seekers. The Prologue to act II of *Henry V* mentions 'crowns and coronets / Promised to Harry and his followers' as the motive of the French expedition. This motive had been omnipresent in *Tamburlaine*. Audiences would know that eventually each conqueror died prematurely, as did their wives, although by Shakespeare this doubly tragic outcome is not shown. Henry's death in fact was from a fever in the midst of foreign campaigning – thus like Tamburlaine's in part II of Marlowe's play. The Epilogue to *Henry V* mentions simply the loss, under Henry's heir, of the empire the father had gained – the second-generation fate also of Tamburlaine's empire. Is it likely that the irony in these historical situations escaped Shakespeare's notice? England, he lets an Archbishop say early in the play, has made

> her chronicle as rich with praise
> As is the ooze and bottom of the sea
> With sunken wrack . . . (I, ii, 163–5)

Here, as so often in Shakespeare, a decorative trope may be carrying more truth than its immediate speaker intends.

Our sketch so far has been only a bird's-eye view. A closer look into the texts of the two plays reveals further and more tantalizing points of analogy. For convenience, let me organize some of these numerically.

(1) Both heroes aspire to be the wonder of their world by imitating the sun. Tamburlaine's view of himself as 'the chiefest lamp of all the earth' has an echo in Henry's resolve to 'rise . . . with so full a glory / That I will dazzle all the eyes of France'. And Henry's likening of himself to the sun, we recall, is the motif of his very first soliloquy in *1 Henry IV*.

(2) Horseback exploits in place of shepherding roles characterize both heroes. Near the beginning of *Tamburlaine* we have a scene in which the hero disdains his shepherd's weeds, reclothes himself with curtle-axe, and plans to conquer horsemen in order to make himself one

and thus fulfil a dream of conquest. In *Henry V* an opening prologue invites us to see Harry decked out with 'horses . . . Printing their proud hoofs', and we learn in the next prologue that the English youth 'sell the pasture now to buy the horse'. That statement may prompt us to ask incidentally: is this not what Henry himself has done in act I by giving over England to the care of bargaining prelates in return for their approval of his expedition? The drama comes to its end, as does *1 Tamburlaine*, with empire achieved and also a betrothal – in both cases to brides who have been won by combining force and demand with wooing and the lure of a queenship. 'Thou wouldst think', says Henry to Kate (before mentioning 'vaulting into my saddle' as his chief skill), that 'I had sold my farm to buy my crown.' The remark may be truer than Henry knows.

(3) The threatening 'with high astounding terms' which Marlowe dramatizes in Tamburlaine has a parallel in Exeter's telling the French king:

> if you hide the crown
> Even in your hearts, there will he rake for it.
> Therefore in fierce tempest is he coming,
> In thunder and in earthquake, like a Jove,
> That, if requiring fail, he will compel
> (II, iv, 97–101)

Here we may recall Tamburlaine's mocking of the attempt of Mycetes to hide his crown. And more importantly, Tamburlaine's likening himself to Jove (*1 Tamb.*, 1, 2, 98; 1, 7, 17) and to thunder (1, 3, 19; 4, 2, 45) and to earthquake (1, 2, 49) here finds a summary in Henry's stance. Both heroes have peremptory manners.

We later see Henry threatening Harfleur with 'heady murder' and a massacre like that of 'Herod's bloody-hunting slaughtermen' (III, iii). The allusion could have reminded Shakespeare's audience of the Herod of the Coventry mystery-play pageant, who boasted that he resembled Mahomet and was descended from Jupiter. But a Henry who gathers to himself such associations must have given some pause to any auditor who remembered the coronation announcement in *2 Henry IV*:

> This is the English, not the Turkish Court.
> Not Amurath an Amurath succeeds,
> But Harry Harry. (v, ii, 46–8)

Is the difference from the Turk, really, any other than in name only? Henry gives Harfleur a choice between surrender and being buried in ashes. He will allow his 'fleshed' soldiers, he says, a 'conscience wide as Hell'.

(4) Although Henry much more often threatens atrocities than carries them to execution, his ordering every soldier at Agincourt to 'kill his prisoners' is later seconded by his message to the French that he will cut the throat of every man either captured or still to be taken. This threat itself is almost as gruesome as Tamburlaine's procedure at Damascus. And can it be justified – especially when we learn afterwards that the total of English dead from the whole long battle was no more than thirty as compared to ten thousand Frenchmen? The very proportions of this victory sound legendary and Tamburlainean. The only apparent difference from Tamburlaine is Henry's humility afterwards. Piously he attributes everything to God's arm alone, thereby minimizing (and hiding) the hand which he and his soliders had in the business. Yet the English *hand*, as Shakespeare lets us know through Katherine's 'language' lesson, consists of nails, bilbow, nick, and 'de sin'; and in the play's various battle scenes the war is repeatedly presented as a business of throat-cutting, not only by Henry, as we have noted, but also in the talk of officers such as Pistol and Captain MacMorris. To which Captain Jamy adds that, 'By the mess' (i.e., Mass), he'll do good service in such work.

An implication of sacrilege, although not intended by these speakers, is surely Shakespeare's. And is this not the case, equally, in Henry's readiness to proclaim a festival of 'all holy rites' after Agincourt? The situation, if carefully considered, is not unlike Tamburlaine's ordering a ritual banquet after his defeat of Bajazet. Claiming a 'power from the imperial heaven' as his sanction (*1 Tamb.*, 4, 4, 30), Tamburlaine celebrated what a Christian reader can recognize as a travesty of Holy Communion, cates and wine offered to 'the god of war'. By comparison, Henry's mass offered to the God of Battles is overtly Christian, yet under circumstances which tinge it with a Shakespearian irony, more subtle of course than Marlowe's.

Henry before leaving England had mercilessly (although legally) executed three rivals, charging them with 'glistering semblances of piety'. But if we recall John of Lancaster's similar moralizing before and after executing the Gaultree rebels, may we not suspect that Henry's own piety, like his brother's, is as much 'semblance' as that of the opponents? Henry, of course, no more recognizes hypocrisy in any of his actions than does Tamburlaine when invoking a 'Scourge of God' office as sanction for his destroying of enemies. And undoubtedly Henry is the more attractive, since he does not, like the mad Scythian at Babylon, depopulate a whole city and justify the slaughter with crude and overt blasphemy. Yet Henry's motive for a 'courteous' behavior may well derive from the counsel given him by Henry IV, his father, to 'dress' in humility in order to 'pluck allegiance from men's hearts'. A 'robe pontifical' (Henry IV's recipe) serves this purpose best – and indeed is much more effective *politically*, we may say, than Tamburlaine's scandalous impiety. A subtle and hidden kind of blasphemy, however, inheres in the very primacy which the two Henrys, father and son, give to political success as their ultimate motivation. Machiavelli, we may recall, counselled (in *The Prince*, Chs. 17 and 18) that although a prince should pay no attention at all to cruelty when campaigning in wars, he should at all other times never let fall any words not seasoned with the virtues of pity, faith, integrity, humanity and religion. In this respect, Henry is a better Machiavellian than Tamburlaine. Better still, he can arrive at this unawares, by a family aptitude for dodging or repressing self-examination. (And auditors akin to Old Adam will join him in this aptitude.)

(5) One of the exemplary scenes in *Tamburlaine* is that in which the hero instructs his sons that 'Blood is the god of war's rich livery' and ceremonializes this teaching with a covenant-like wounding of his arm. Although there is no scene quite like this in *Henry V*, some degree of analogy to it can be seen in Henry's instructing his followers before the battle at Agincourt. 'He today that sheds his blood with me', says Henry, 'shall be my brother', and he pictures his band as united by the fact that in later years each man will be able to 'strip his sleeve and show his scars' as wounds entitling him to a fame storied 'from this day to the ending of the world'. Henry, of course, dresses up his teaching with a promise of 'flowing cups' at household Crispin feats, rather than the crude reward Tamburlaine holds out of a 'carouse within my tent' afterwards; and also Henry is magnanimously willing to excuse from the enterprise any coward who has no stomach for it. These differences, however, accord either with Henry IV's religious camouflage or with the 'magnanimity' of Alexander, rather than with a specifically Christian ethic.

We remember how, in an earlier scene (III, i), Henry had urged his men to be 'like so many Alexanders' and thus show themselves models 'to men of grosser blood'. The details of his teaching in that scene, nevertheless, echo aspects of Tamburlaine. The men were to 'lend the eye a terrible aspect', put on terrifying

frowns, and imitate the action of the tiger. Furthermore, we may recall Henry's way of proving to his father (in *1 Henry IV*, III, ii) the genuineness of his return to chivalry:

> I will wear a garment all of blood
> And stain my favours in a bloody mask.

Is such a vow unTamburlainean? At least on occasion and for playing the hero, Henry seems willing to both practice and preach a Tamburlainean valor. To 'engross up' Henry's deeds, Hotspur must 'render every glory up . . . Or I will tear the reckoning from his heart'.

(6) A deficient humanity in Henry's sense of brotherhood, many critics have felt, is evident especially in his rejection of Falstaff. In the play itself Mistress Quickly tells us this act killed Falstaff's heart, and Fluellen sees in it a parallel to Alexander's killing of his friend Cleitus. Fluellen does his best to interpret as praiseworthy Henry's turning away of Falstaff, ascribing it to 'good judgement'. Yet is Henry's judgment in this case so very different from the judgment Tamburlaine used in killing his son Calyphas? Calyphas, we may recall, is like Falstaff in several respects: he thinks military honor no cure for a wound, has no 'care for blood when wine will quench my thirst' (*2 Tamb.*, 4, 1, 30), and is therefore considered a coward and a disgrace to the court. In slaying Calyphas, Tamburlaine's motive is to enhance his own self-image by removing this 'scorn of my renown', and at the same time to provide an exemplary punishment of 'folly, sloth, and damned idleness'. Is Henry's motive much different from this?

At least 'figuratively' (to use Fluellen's term), Shakespeare may indeed be rating Henry's motive and behavior as comparable to Tamburlaine's. We cannot but notice, however, a situational difference. Falstaff has been no simple idler like Calyphas; he has been busy all along in concocting humorous and shrewd jests for everyone's entertainment. Hence when

Falstaff dies, his departure is attended by some babblings of an enigmatic kind. Could his 'green fields', for instance, be expressing the Psalmist's hope in God as his shepherd (Psalm 23), whereas on the other hand 'whore of Babylon' (St John's term in Rev. 17) is being mumbled as perhaps a phrase for summing up, figuratively, Falstaff's estimate of Henry's kind of lordship? Whatever answer we may give to this admittedly very speculative question, the 'Babylon' motif in any case is not peculiar to 2 *Tamburlaine* but echoes also as a muted undertone in *Henry V*.

The ramifications of the six points I have listed, if added to the general similarities I mentioned earlier, add up to a rather widespread network of analogy. And besides, any student of Shakespeare's art must consider also the problem of what to make of the Tamburlainean humors so evident in Pistol. Why has this comic Ancient been brought into 2 *Henry IV* to declaim about pack horses,

> And hollow pampered jades of Asia
> Which cannot go but thirty mile a day,

and suggest an equivalence of all this to Caesar and to Cannibals? Pistol's cannabalistic urge, we later note, emerges as his motive for the French expedition in *Henry V*:

> Let us to France, like horseleeches, my boys,
> To suck, to suck, the very blood to suck.

These lines, bombastic but crudely honest, crop up right after Falstaff's death. Their positioning in the play suggests that perhaps Shakespeare has decided to allow Henry chiefly this vile braggart as his interpreter and encomiast, now that he has rejected Falstaff. It is Pistol who later hails Harry as the 'imp of fame' whose dirty shoe he is ready to kiss, so heartily does he love the 'lovely bully'. And Pistol's eagerness to suck blood (i.e., extract loot) is exemplified in the scene in which he plays 'Seigneur Dew' and mercifully allows

Monsieur le Fer to ransom himself with crowns.

Pistol's 'gentlemanly' version of the dew of God's mercy (contrast Portia's 'dropping as the gentle rain' and not strained) strikes us as hugely comic, but also as being very likely Shakespeare's parody of Henry's brand of mercy. It ties in with the 'horseleech' intent confessed earlier by Pistol, and that image itself, the more we think about it, looks like Shakespeare's deliberate counterpointing of the 'beehive' image in the Archbishop's war-apology of act 1. The Archbishop's euphemistic likening of the troops to honeybees who merrily 'Make boot upon the summer's velvet buds' is merely more realistically translated by Pistol. The Archbishop's praise of Henry's 'sweet and honeyed sentences', we know, is covering this prelate's awareness of a gloved threat to the Bishop's own interests, a threat which he has decided to redirect toward France. Toward France, then, let Henry's 'bloody flag' be unfurled! As palatable advice, this accords with the instinct of John of Lancaster who had shrewdly foreseen France as next after Gaultree. Pistol but voices a general English enthusiasm for the project.

Marlowe in *Tamburlaine* had no spokesman for pricking the bubble of the lyricism of Tamburlaine's fellowship with his followers, other than obvious enemies whose testimony could be overlooked. A rapt reader might write off as slander, if he wished, the Soldan of Egypt's reference to Tamburlaine's 'troop of thieves and vagabonds' (*1 Tamb.*, 4, 1, 6), or Meander's earlier comment (2, 2, 22–4):

> This country swarms with vile outrageous men,
> That live by rapine and by lawless spoil,
> Fit soldiers for the wicked Tamburlaine.

But Shakespeare is able to make comically, and hence with a covert effectiveness, much this same point regarding Henry and company, simply by having one of Henry's own idolaters embody the subsurface motives of the campaign of conquest. Pistol, we may say, is one of those 'giddy minds' whom Henry, through a 'discretion' learned from Henry IV, is now busying in foreign wars. But that fact implies a moral giddiness in the discretion of the leader of the band, Henry.

Shakespeare is able to play off against the officialese of English oratory not merely the jibes of French enemies – e.g., that of Orleans, that the English have no 'intellectual armour' but merely a peevish king and fatbrained followers (III, vii, 142–8). More subtly than that, Shakespeare uses the blunt enthusiasms of Henry's lowclass followers as comic counterpoint to the romantic patriotism of the play's official Chorus. The result is a complexity of perspectives, which (if we may borrow the Archbishop's words used in another context) so cohere and harmonize that

> many things, having full reference
> To one consent, may work contrariously

and yet come to one mark, like many lines closing in the dial's center or many actions ending in one purpose. That purpose, if bluntly stated instead of veiled under choral mask, might be said to be the transformation of England, under inspiration from a Marlowe-like Muse of Fire, into a 'playhouse' in which everyone is invited to join 'warlike Henry' on an 'unworthy scaffold', like ciphers added to a 'crooked figure' in imaginary puissance. These prologue phrases are more than decorative trope. They carry an underside of intimation that this warrior may be a crook, his followers moral zeros, and their power largely imaginary, indeed scaffold-bound. Any reader who catches this lurking dramatic irony in the language will find the history's whole action covertly comic[1].

The various comic aspects of Shakespeare's drama give it a spice and variety which Marlowe's drama lacks. They also enable us to take somewhat lightheartedly the vauntings of the opposing sides in the war, as if they were as much charade as epic. Here, after all, is something like a medieval 'field of folk', most of them foolish brothers of fallen 'goodman Adam', and rather laughably pretentious in their hollow grandeur. Early critics of *Henry V* who regarded the play as largely a picturesque spectacle are not entirely wrong. Marlowe's play, too, has perhaps its chief appeal as spectacle, enhanced in Marlowe's case by a heavy use of symbolic scenes after the manner of emblem literature. But in *Tamburlaine* the spectacular too often strikes us as extravagantly barbaric, exotic rather than of homespun credibility. It seems calculated more to warn by shock-horrors (as in the Senecan tradition) than to illumine the complexity of human motivation. A monomaniacal Tamburlaine cannot draw our affection as does a bluff King Henry, with his more flexible role-playing and more down-to-earth adaptation to circumstance. Though Henry may often talk like a Tamburlaine – as for instance, when he declares that by God's help 'we'll bend [France] to our awe / Or break it all in pieces' – he can also be a bit of a clown when wooing Kate, awkwardly mixing Petrarchan flattery with invitations to breeding, scambling, and leapfrog love.

In short, Henry can both puff himself out as a Jove and, at other times, exemplify a jovial good humor. It is for him all pretty much of a game, both the tennis-match war with France and life in general – a matter of playing up to imagined models of heroic nobility, on the one hand, or of a conventional humility as 'king of good fellows' on the other. Exactly because Henry's love of titles and honors is a greed of rather ordinary and common kind, which lacks the metaphysical intensity of Tamburlaine's restless climbing toward the 'sweet felicity

[1] For a fuller study of the play's comic aspects, see my essay on '*Henry V* as Heroic Comedy' in R. Hosley (ed.), *Essays on Shakespeare and Elizabethan Drama* (Columbia, 1962), pp. 163–82.

of an earthly crown', we auditors like Henry better than Tamburlaine as a person. One point of difference is that he is aware of the 'polished perturbation' a crown can bring with it, and in soliloquy laments this burden. Although continuing to link its griefs with duty rather than with his own questionable ambition, Henry comes to feel, somewhat like Macbeth, a loss of happiness plaguing him, but goes on nonetheless to play the man in the only way he knows how. It should be noted that Shakespeare's treatment of ambition's punishment in terms of a gnawing attrition is somewhat different from Marlowe's concept of excessive passions punishing their harborer with a progressive madness and physiological fevers. Shakespeare's hero is less mythologically conceived, less the superman and more credibly human, hence more *like us* in Aristotle's sense of the phrase.

The real point of the Prologue to *Henry V*, I have suggested, is not the inadequacy of the theater (though that is its surface meaning), but rather the likeness of Henry's campaign to a staged play. The whole English community, as Shakespeare sees the situation, is being entranced imaginatively into role-playing, and without regard for the moral meaning of the assumed roles. And Henry, by treating himself as an actor caught up in his own play, is able to blind himself to the moral implications of his action. By concentrating on the skill and satisfaction of playing the role he has assigned himself, he is able to dodge or escape questions as to the rightness of his cause. His final answer to Williams, appropriately, is the lamely conventional one of bestowing on the offended man a monetary gift – which, of course, is all 'glove' as far as moral answer is concerned. It is the only answer a king can give when the basis of his whole government has no higher principle than rule of thumb or *ad hoc* devices.

This interpretation implies also that there is no intentional blasphemy in Henry's use of religion, as compared to the deliberate boasting by Tamburlaine when burning Scriptures. Rather, there is by Henry merely a blindly Pharisaic suppression of self-examination, along with a connivance with the worldly-minded bishops in pursuing a mutual game of self-preservation and *raison d'etat*, at whatever cost, and for the sake of fame as recognized by conventional norms of worthiness, norms as old (and unChristian) as those of Alexander the Great. It is Henry's devotion to a role-playing of these norms which marks him as basically more frivolous than Tamburlaine, more self-defined as 'actor' rather than an agent inspired by goals of missionary dimension. Henry at Harfleur imps Tamburlaine, without committing himself to remaking the map of the world. Yet anyone whose approach to life situations is no more than a diplomatic putting on of acts is of necessity a mask-wearer and in that sense hypocritic.

Scholars who regard the comic scenes of *Henry V* as local color only, or as affording mere comic relief, may query some of the implications I have explored in Shakespeare's text. But in each of his plays, I believe, everything ought to contribute to some total design which overarches wayside entertainment, and our task is therefore to envision if we can how all the parts cohere thematically in a poetic whole. Hence in the present essay my concern has been not merely to assemble the echoes of *Tamburlaine* to be found in *Henry V*, although these constitute a larger catalog than scholars have realized, but also to probe for the comparative dramatic patterning which the echoes subserve. A recent study of the *Henry VI* plays by David Riggs has made evident that Shakespeare had long been interested in analogues to Tamburlaine within England's own history.[1] He was attempting in these earliest of plays, Riggs contends, to evaluate

[1] *Shakespeare's Heroical Histories* (Cambridge, Mass., 1971).

three variant versions of a Tamburlainean aspiration, by bringing the ideal out of its mythical past and discerning analogous formulations of it in a more close-to-home, circumstantially definable span of history. And the result of this poetical testing, Riggs concludes, was a critique of antique dreams of heroism through Shakespeare's showing their inability to resist decline into social chaos.

A continuation of this same insight, I am supposing, underlies Shakespeare's later writing of *Henry V*, the play whose chronological period precedes that of *Henry VI* and foreshadows, historically, the seminal issues and problems of Henry's son. The dramatist is careful not to present this insight bluntly or didactically. Rather, he lets it emerge covertly out of the sub-surface of an overtly epical treatment of the popular Henry. To retain enigma, Shakespeare lets Henry say for instance (at I, ii, 230):

> Either our history shall with full mouth
> Speak freely of our acts, or else our grave,
> Like Turkish mute, shall have a tongueless mouth.

At Agincourt the history speaks with somewhat less than full mouth in Williams, since Henry himself mutes the issue raised. But does not the history speak more freely through inadvertent admissions of his own and of various of his adulators? His acts, although perhaps not as savage as those of Amurath the Turk, are indubitably updated echoes of Alexander and of Tamburlaine.

SHAKESPEARE AND THE
PURITAN DYNAMIC

HAROLD FISCH

Lord Angelo is precise;
Stands at a guard with envy; scarce confesses
That his blood flows; or that his appetite
Is more to bread than stone. Hence shall we see
If power change purpose, what our seemers be.
Measure for Measure, I, iii, 50–4

I

Not to take the term in too narrowly confessional a sense we may identify three Puritans in Shakespeare: they are Shylock, Malvolio, and Angelo. The problem of usury in Shakespeare's time, dramatized in the relation of Shylock to Antonio, is one that had arisen specifically as a result of the new Calvinist social ethics. The capitalist individualism of Shylock and his distance from the aristocratic world of Belmont indicate that he represents to an important degree the new Puritan middle class and their problems.[1] 'Lord Angelo', we are told, is 'precise', i.e., a precisian. As for Malvolio, he is indeed once actually named a Puritan by Maria (though she soon afterwards modifies the charge) but even without this we would have recognized him as a Puritan by his kill-joy attitude to the Twelfth Night celebrations of the merry folk. 'Thinkst thou because thou art virtuous there shall be no more cakes and ale' – could stand as a warning against what Puritanism threatened to do in the seventeenth century to the tradition of Merrie England. As has often been pointed out, Shylock has the same attitude when he warns Jessica against the revelry and masques in the street (*The Merchant of Venice*, II, v, 28) – a

clear reminder of the Puritan dislike of theaters and revels. This aspect of the play has as little real relevance to Jews or Judaism, as Arthur Miller's censure of the McCarthy witch-hunts in *The Crucible* (1953) has to the issues of the Salem trials of 1692.

But these are the more superficial aspects of Puritanism. The first thing I should like to draw attention to in all the three characters mentioned, namely, Angelo, Malvolio, and Shylock, is that they are all three studies in the use or abuse of power. In Angelo Shakespeare studies Puritanism in relation to political power, in Shylock it is studied in relation to economic power, and in Malvolio, in relation to social power. Shakespeare seems to have sensed that here was to be the fundamental issue as well as the fundamental paradox of the Puritan movement as a whole. The Puritan as well as being a saint or a man of God is also paradoxically a power-seeker. And their power-drives are going to be the theme of English history in the years following Shakespeare's death. Shakespeare seems to have had an intuition of this.[2] Thus Malvolio desires to control Olivia's household; he resents the influence of others over his lady. He dreams of marriage with Olivia, not because of an invincible desire for her person, but because he

[1] Cf. Paul N. Siegel, 'Shylock, the Elizabethan Puritan and Our Own World', in *Shakespeare in his Time and Ours* (Notre Dame, Ind., 1968), p. 238f.
[2] Cf. Mary Suddard, 'The Poet and the Puritan', in *The Contemporary Review* (December 1909).

will then be in command. He will 'call my officers about me in my branched velvet gown'. The velvet gown is what he desires instead of the sober black dress of the precisian, because it symbolizes power; and Puritanism is a religion of power. It is hardly necessary to demonstrate in reference to Shylock that his dramatic situation is one that propels him to the height of power, until in acts III and IV his economic advantages give him power of life and death over a citizen of Venice and enable him to dominate the processes of law. Bassanio beseeches Portia to 'curb this cruel devil of his will', and Portia answers by saying that 'there is no power in Venice' that can do so. In this context her earlier speech on the quality of mercy with its reference to the limits of earthly power and the necessity of subjecting it to the power of God becomes especially significant. The irony of the ending both here and in *Twelfth Night* consists in the sudden lapse of the protagonist from power to powerlessness. This is achieved by the witty device of Portia in *The Merchant* and by the mock exorcism of Malvolio by 'Sir Topas' in *Twelfth Night*. We shall return to the mode of exorcism later in reference to *Measure for Measure*. We may note here simply that the plays present in their ending an apparent defusing of the power-keg of Puritanism. But we are too well aware that the problem will not be quite so easily solved in real life. And this accounts for the uneasy feeling that the audience takes away with it. Will Malvolio not perhaps have his revenges on us after all? Will the Rialto and the Exchange not ultimately gain mastery over the moon-lit world of Belmont? In short, can we be sure that the power-drives of Malvolio and Shylock have been permanently curbed and mastered?

In *Measure for Measure* the nature of the test to which Angelo is subjected is clearly announced at the beginning.[1] Angelo is going to be given complete control over Vienna:

> Mortality and mercy in Vienna
> Live in thy tongue and heart.
>
> (I, i, 45–6)

says the Duke in his first speech to Angelo, and later he tells us that he will stand by and 'behold his sway'. The Puritan will achieve the power he seeks, and we shall then see what he does with it.

> Hence shall we see
> If power change purpose, what our seemers be.
>
> (I, iii, 53–4)

Of course Angelo fails, just as Malvolio and Shylock had failed before him. Power changes purpose, until in the end the protagonist is humbled, made to recognize his trespass and failure, and the demon is exorcised. But again it must be insisted that Angelo's trespass is not the sin of concupiscence – or rather that is secondary – it is the abuse of power. His fundamental temptation is not the beauty of Isabel. Had she appeared on the scene before the Duke had placed mortality and mercy in his tongue and heart she would not have led him into sin. It is because she is momentarily within his power that the 'strong and swelling evil of his conception' mounts to overthrow him. Power has betrayed him in an unpredicted, and indeed unpredictable fashion. The demon of power releases the djin of the libido. This is clearly then no simple matter of hypocrisy. A hypocrite is a bad man who pretends to be good. This will not do for Angelo.[2] If Isabel is betrayed, then Angelo is no less betrayed. He is betrayed by something within him, by the contradictions of Puritanism itself. On the one hand it is a religion of power, and on the other

---

[1] On the test or trial as the basis of this and other comedies, see Nevill Coghill, 'Comic Form in *Measure for Measure*', *Shakespeare Survey* I (Cambridge, 1955), p. 19.

[2] F. R. Leavis notes that 'Angelo is not a certified criminal type' (*The Common Pursuit* (London, 1952), pp. 171–2), and G. Wilson Knight asserts that he is no hypocrite (*The Wheel of Fire* (New York, 1957), p. 85).

hand it is a religion which cannot coexist with the exercise of that power in the world. This is the paradox of the Puritan psyche which it will be our task to examine a little more closely, with special reference to *Measure for Measure*.[1]

II

What must be insisted upon is that Shakespeare takes Puritanism very seriously. He is not writing caricature or satire simply, like Ben Jonson in *Bartholomew Fair*. Certainly the men of the theater had reason to dislike the Puritans, but Shakespeare was too deeply aware of the moral and religious issues involved to dismiss the Puritan system lightly. Puritanism was a mighty force and a revolutionary force, and it was also a serious religion raising profound questions about man's nature and his relationship to God. Shakespeare in these plays is imaginatively adopting the Puritan outlook and visualizing the world from within the Puritan sensibility. He is also imaginatively adopting their style. Shakespeare's portrayal of the strenuous inner life of his Puritan characters, of their existential dilemmas, and of their energy of action seeking expression through a direct invasion of the world of material things – all this has a stylistic correlative. The style of Angelo, and to a lesser extent of Shylock consists of balancing antitheses, logical distinctions and a tendency towards plain prose. Brian Vickers speaks of the 'indisputable precision' of Shylock's prose, of its knife-edge quality, and of the 'disjunctive logic' of the play as a whole.[2] Sigurd Burckhardt, drawing attention to the undecorated, blunt quality of Shylock's language, defines it as 'positivism triumphant'. His is the 'language of common use'.[3] Shylock, whose whole personality is shaped by his insistence on the literal meaning of his bond, is given to plainness and literalness. 'Ships are but boards, sailors but men' (I, iii). But neither Vickers nor Burckhardt seems to recognize that these are the aspects of discourse which the

Puritan expositors sought to promote.[4] They did so by adducing with monotonous regularity the text in Paul's first epistle to the Corinthians which says, 'And my speech and my preaching was not with enticing words of man's wisdom, but in demonstration of the spirit and of power' (I Corinthians, 2:4), or that verse in the second epistle which says, 'Seeing then that we have such hope, we use great plainness of speech' (II Corinthians, 3:12). The connection between 'power' (in Paul's special use of this term) and plainness was indeed a Puritan commonplace, as was also the insistence on the literal sense of things. William Perkins in rejecting the traditional four-fold sense of the Scripture declares, 'There is onely one sense, and the same is the literall.'[5] Shylock could have said the same about his bond.

One feature of Puritan discourse which I believe can be demonstrated in these plays is associated with the dialectic of Peter Ramus. There is no need to argue that Ramus appealed in a special degree to the Puritans of Shakespeare's time.[6] All the more intellectually

---

[1] As our guide to Elizabethan Puritanism in this essay we shall take the writings of William Perkins (1558–1602). A leading Puritan intellectual, Perkins was a pupil of Laurence Chaderton and became the most eminent authority on Calvinist method and doctrine in Cambridge during the 1590s. Even if Shakespeare was not actually familiar with his writings he could not have failed to be conscious of the intellectual climate which Perkins and his circle had created. He was something like the Harold Laski of the Puritan movement. On the central position of Perkins at this time, see also F. P. Wilson, *Elizabethan and Jacobean* (Oxford, 1945), p. 49.

[2] *The Artistry of Shakespeare's Prose* (London, 1968), pp. 79, 85.

[3] *Shakespeare's Meanings* (Princeton, New Jersey, 1968), p. 228.

[4] On the plain style of the Puritans, see H. Fisch, *Jerusalem and Albion* (New York, 1964), pp. 30–4.

[5] *The Art of Prophecying* (1592) in *Works* (1612), II, 651.

[6] On Ramus and his influence, especially on the Puritans, there is now, starting with Perry Miller, *The*

sophisticated Puritans were Ramists, and this not only because Ramus provided them with simple logical tools for the interpretation of Scripture, but because he provided them with a specific mode of argument which matched their spiritual outlook and temper. This mode, to which Ramus and his followers gave unusual prominence, was that of the disjunctive syllogism. Dudley Fenner's examples are typical:

Man is iustified by fayth or workes:
But not by workes. Therefore
By fayth.

Or else:

Faythfull men must eyther be saued or condemned.
But they shalbe saued:
Therefore not condemned.[1]

It is not hard to hear the echo of these disjunctions in Shylock's downright and sledge-hammer utterance:

I will buy with you, sell with you, talk with you, walk with you and so following; but I will not eat with you, drink with you, nor pray with you.   (I, iii)

Norman E. Nelson in drawing attention to the dissociative logic of the Ramists and their preference for a dry discourse remarks very aptly that

The disjunctive syllogism as Ramus used it . . . could attain importance only in a system of logic founded on the metaphysical dogma that the universe is divided into pairs of opposites by a symmetrically minded God. Therefore, if it is not day, it must be night. Either God is bad which is absurd, or else he is good, which will be seen at once to be true.[2]

Measure for Measure as a whole is surely poised on the fulcrum of a disjunctive syllogism, one which could be expressed as follows:

Our worldly impulses come from the Devil,
Our otherworldly impulses come from God.
Angelo finds he has worldly impulses,
Therefore he is in the grip of the Devil.

Or else:

If a man succumbs to Nature, he is without Grace.
Angelo succumbs to Nature: therefore he is without
                                         Grace

This is the disjunctive logic of Angelo's thinking and to a lesser extent of Isabella's thinking also. It runs through all the soliloquies and dialogues giving them a sharp antithetical quality which is the hall-mark of the play's style. Thus:

When I would pray and think, I think and pray
To several subjects: Heaven hath my empty words,
Whilst my invention, hearing not my tongue,
Anchors on Isabel.   (II, iv, 1–4)

We may note here also the dichotomizing habit of language so popular among Ramus and the Puritans. Everything is divided into pairs. In the *Works* of Perkins already referred to, the text is interleaved with numerous tables to illustrate points of doctrine. In each of these the argument visibly branches out into balancing pairs. The trick goes back to Ramus himself who had divided Logic into Judgement and Invention and each of these into further doublets. This endless bifurcation of subject matter was a useful method for arranging material, but behind it there was also a metaphysical principle, that of a bisected universe and a bisected psyche. Grace and Nature are divided, the Old Adam and the New Adam. The evangelical principle of rendering to Caesar that which is Caesar's and to God that which is God's dictates a parallelistic view of

New England Mind (Cambridge, Mass., 1954), a considerable literature. As for his impact on Shakespeare, this has been noted by Sister Miriam Joseph (*Shakespeare's Use of the Arts of Language* (New York, 1966), p. 17f.) and others. But no one it seems has studied the Ramist dialectic in specific reference to the plays here discussed.

[1] Dudley Fenner, *The Artes of Logike and Rhetorike* (1584), sig. C3[r–v].

[2] *Peter Ramus and the Confusion of Logic, Rhetoric and Poetry* (Ann Arbor, Mich., 1947), p. 11.

the universe, power often linking itself with evil, and piety with impotence. But both sides of the equation must be taken into account, for ideally the two could be held in a kind of equilibrium. Thus when Angelo makes his infamous proposal to Isabella he tells her that it would be 'equal poise of sin and charity' (II, iv, 69). Her submission to Angelo for the purpose of redeeming her brother from death would represent a kind of fantastic balancing act between the two divided halves of man's nature. There is in this phrase, 'equal poise of sin and charity' an implicit reference to the image of a balancing pair of scales. And the same suppressed image may be detected in Isabella's own disjunctive language earlier on:

There is a vice that most I do abhor,
And most desire should meet the blow of justice;
For which I would not plead, but that I must;
For which I must not plead, but that I am
At war 'twixt will and will not.   (II, ii, 29–33)

To be 'at war 'twixt will and will not' was indeed the Puritan way of life, or rather what the Puritans regarded as the normal condition of humanity. Shakespeare is here echoing and perhaps parodying modes of utterance and habits of thought characteristic of the new ethical culture associated with the Puritans. In her very next speech Isabel suggests that Angelo somehow disjoin Claudio from his fault. Angelo's reaction is to question the validity of this disjunction:

Condemn the fault, and not the actor of it?
(line 37)

The two scenes between Angelo and Isabella are more intensely dialectical than anything Shakespeare has given us apart from some scenes in *Hamlet*. Each character watches for the logical flaws in the arguments of the other whilst seeking to guard himself from falling into logical traps. The result is a combat in which, not points of doctrine, but the very spiritual and moral destiny of each is at stake.

Angelo fares worse than Isabella because he has been more mightily tested. His rope is strung higher up, his exposure to power and its temptations rendering his situation more radical than hers.

It is worth noting that Angelo belongs technically not to the reprobate or carnal class of men but to the *regenerate*. I take this term from Perkins's tract on 'The Combat between Flesh and Spirit'. Perkins, to whom we shall be referring often and with good reason, distinguishes between three classes of men: the Carnall, the Regenerate, and the Glorified. Each class has its own distinct attitude to good and evil. Angelo we shall see clearly belongs to the Regenerate class. (The reader will note the dichotomous structure of the following table and also the underlying disjunctive logic of the whole presentation.)

THE VOICE OF A MAN

1. *Carnall*	Euill. I doe that which is euill. and I will doe it.
	Good. I doe not that which is good and I will not doe it.
2. *Regenerate*	Euill. I doe the euill, which I would not.
	Good. I doe not the good, which I would.
3. *Glorified*	Euill. I doe not that which is euill and I would not doe it.
	Good. I doe that which is good, and I would doe it.[1]

Angelo is without any doubt speaking the language of Perkins's 'regenerate' man when he says,

Alack! when once our grace we have forgot,
Nothing goes right, we would and we would not
(IV, iv, 31–2)

But the fact is that both Perkins and Shakespeare are echoing the same Pauline text which

[1] *Of the Combate of the Flesh and Spirit* (1593), in *Works*, I, 473.

declares of the ordinary man in quest of salvation: 'For the good that I would, I do not: but the evil which I would not, that I do' (Romans, 7:19). The man of whom the apostle speaks is not a man who deliberately chooses the way of evil; on the contrary he is one for whom the inward struggle of Flesh and Spirit is unremitting. For this reason Perkins defines him as 'regenerate'; when he is temporarily vanquished he is vanquished against his will. And given the Puritan metaphysic it is almost inevitable that this will happen to everyone sooner or later. The precarious balancing between Heaven and Hell, God and the Devil, Grace and Nature meant that, if one didn't actually fall like Angelo, one swayed wildly to and fro as one walked the tight-rope.

As a matter of fact Angelo's experience – his defeat in the combat between Flesh and Spirit – is defined by Perkins not as a fall but as a 'foyl' – a term from wrestling signifying a temporary overthrow. Perkins's description of this kind of experience is entirely in conformity with what happens to Angelo in the play:

A foyl is, when the flesh for a time vanquisheth and subdueth the spirit. In this case, the man regenerate is like a souldier that with a blow hath his braine-pan cracked, so as he lies groueling astonished not able to fight: or like him that hath a fit of the falling sickness who for a time lies like a dead man ... so after a grieuous fal the child of God feeles no inward peace and comfort, but is smitten in conscience with the trembling of a spiritual palsie for his offence: and yet indeede still remaines before God a member of Christ in respect of coniunction with him, and shall be restored to his former estate after serious repentance.[1]

This passage not only describes Angelo's trouble, his 'foyl' as Perkins terms it; it also bears significantly on his repentance and restoration in act v.

III

How is Angelo restored, and does the 'serious repentance' of which Perkins speaks have any part in the process? We should first examine a little more closely the nature – in Puritan terms – of Angelo's disease. Since the Puritans based themselves so largely on the apostle Paul that is perhaps where we should start. Now the continuation of the passage from Romans, 7 quoted earlier, in which the apostle described the situation of the man who does the evil which he would not, is as follows: 'Now if I do that I would not, it is no more I that do it, but sin that dwelleth in me' (Romans, 7:20). Angelo's sin surely does operate in this same way. It is not *of* him but *in* him. Like the jealousy of Leontes in *The Winter's Tale* it is felt as an hypostatic entity: it invades his personality unawares and joins itself to him. The suddenness of the invasion and the horror and astonishment which it arouses in the victim are indications that it is 'the cunning enemy' that has him in his power. This helps to explain why Angelo's crisis is a crisis of identity:

What dost thou, or what art thou, Angelo?

Perkins's discussion of what he calls 'satanical molestation' provides an interesting analogue to the psychological state of Angelo:

Those [thoughts] that come from the Deuill, come speedily, as lightning into a house: and they are after a sort, forced into the minde by violence, so as the partie cannot auoid them: and they come into the minde againe and againe, yea a thousand times in a day, as, by their often comming, they weaken the memorie, dull the senses, wearie and confound the braine. These are thoughts that come from the Deuill, and by him are conuaied from without, into the minde of man. And if such cogitations, were from a mans owne selfe, they would not come with so great vehemencie and celeritie, but with leisure; and they would rise with more moderation, and lesse violence: Yea further, the frequent vse of them, would not produce so many, and so fearefull effects as it doth.[2]

[1] *Ibid.*, 472.
[2] *The First Part of the Cases of Conscience* (1604), sigs. K3ᵛ–K4ʳ.

The relevance of this to Angelo's two soliloquies in act II and his subsequent behaviour is evident. Angelo has the clear feeling of being taken by surprise, of being overwhelmed. His invention 'anchors on Isabel' with that obsessive vehemence which Perkins notes as the symptom of 'satanical molestation', the thoughts rising with characteristic violence to overthrow his brain and heart. They then dictate actions for which his previous behavior provides no real clue.

Since therefore we are discussing an evil possession 'conuaied from without' it follows that the method of dealing with it is not moral exhortation or punishment in the normal sense, but very simply – exorcism. The devil has to be driven out, and for this there were well established procedures. The Puritans as it happened, though they believed in the hypostatic nature of evil possession, did not speak much of exorcism or the casting out of devils[1] but rather of the cure of souls, and the methods were accordingly psychological rather than ceremonial. Perkins in a manual published posthumously in 1604, the year of the first performance of *Measure for Measure*, provides a dual formula for the curing of distresses due to sin. The first part of the treatment is to 'make them [the sufferers] grieve for their offences' and he insists that the grief must be for the particular sin of which the party is guilty. And the second part of the cure, no less important, is 'the ministring and conuaying of comfort to the mind of him, that hath confessed his sins, and is truly humbled for them'. And this can be done he explains 'by bringing the partie troubled, within the compasse of the promise of life'.[2] The Duke, it would seem, in his handling of Angelo in act v has followed these instructions to the letter. First Angelo is duly humbled; he lies 'like a dead man' overthrown in the combat with the devil and is made to grieve deeply for his sin:

Immediate sentence, then, and sequent death
Is all the grace I beg.   (v, i, 371–2)

And a little later, to Escalus:

I am sorry that such sorrow I procure,
And so deep sticks it in my penitent heart
That I crave death more willingly than mercy;
'Tis my deserving, and I do entreat it.

(v, i, 472–5)

His sense is of a religious offence, a moral obloquy revealed to him in the about-change of circumstances in act v – and the manifest effect, grief. It is not shame merely that lays him prostrate, but exactly what he says, i.e., the sorrow of a deeply penitent heart repenting of a particular sin. The second part of the cure comes when Claudio is unmuffled on the stage and Angelo realizes that he is now no longer within danger of the death penalty. He has entered into the 'compass of the promise of life'. This is indicated by the phraseology of the Duke's last speech:

By this, Lord Angelo perceives he's safe;
Methinks I see a quickening in his eye.
Well, Angelo, your evil quits you well.
Look that you love your wife: her worth, worth
          yours.
                    (v, i, 492–5)

The 'quickening' corresponds to that coming to life after a 'grieuous fal' of which Perkins had spoken in a passage quoted earlier. 'Your evil quits you well' is usually taken in the sense of 'requites' or 'rewards', good having been repaid him for evil. I am inclined to think, however, that the verb should be taken in the older sense of 'leaves' or 'says farewell'. Angelo has been possessed by evil; that evil has

---

[1] But later on, Richard Baxter, in *The Saints Everlasting Rest*, Part II, Chapter 7 (section 3) speaks of a well-known case of the 'dispossession of the Devil out of many persons together in a room in Lancashire, at the prayer of some godly Ministers' (edition of 1658, p. 265).

[2] *The First Part of the Cases of Conscience*, sigs. E8ᵛ–F1ʳ.

now quitted him, leaving him free. It has been exorcised. The emphasis here on the moral worth of Angelo after all that has occurred and all that he has been guilty of is also a clear sign of how successful the exorcism has been. One can imagine the rest of the cast congratulating him on his cure in the manner of the inhabitants of *Erewhon* when visiting a fellow-citizen who, after due treatment, has recovered from some particularly painful moral infirmity.

IV

Is this, however, quite the whole story? Are we to conclude that the play represents the dramatization of the Puritan formula for trial, sin, and repentance, and that Shakespeare has not only entered into the Puritan psychology and deeply understood it but has also adopted the principles and assumptions on which the system was based? After all the 'cure for distresses of conscience' as described in the Puritan manuals would leave a man still 'regenerate' in the sense understood by Perkins, i.e., caught in the disjunctive logic which would lead him, when a new temptation arose, to do the thing he would not and to not do the thing he would. Is that how Shakespeare views the 'restoration' of Angelo? Is he intended to be the same man at the end that he was at the beginning? Does the play not hint at some profounder process of regeneration not perhaps comprised in the Puritan system?

If we look again at the ritual of exorcism which the Duke practises on Angelo in act v, we shall see that in addition to the features already noted, the action we witness on the stage involves other more characteristically Shakespearian motifs and processes, and that these tend to place the whole scene in a new, and I think non-Puritan perspective. First, we should note the enormous emphasis placed on Isabella's powers of eloquence. Angelo tries to argue that her wits are infirm, but in a storm of forensic eloquence adding up to close on a

hundred lines she 'conjures' her auditors and enchants their minds and hearts. The comments which her discourse arouses are until line 105 *solely* concerned with its formal and stylistic excellence. She seems thus to confront Puritanism at the linguistic level, and her appearance and her speech constitute the first moral shock to which Angelo is subjected. Against her words he has no words. It is the victory of language.

The next serious jolt that Angelo receives is in the sudden appearance of Mariana and the disclosure of a bond contracted five years earlier. This ritual involves the awakening of memory. A similar ritual is practised upon Alonso and his companions (*The Tempest*, III, iii) when through the speech of Ariel, their long-forgotten sin against Prospero is brought to remembrance. This is the beginning of their restoration.[1] The action of time is no mere incidental feature of these plays. The divinity that shapes our ends works through history, punishing us for past crimes but also making those crimes the ground of future blessings and benefits. Here is a dimension transcending the narrow spirituality of the Puritan. The stage is enlarged: the living history of which we are part takes little note of our sensations of Grace or our lack of it, but it does take note of our actions to our fellow-men. For these we continue to bear responsibility before a judge whose dealings with us take place not chiefly in the inner zone of spiritual consciousness to which the manuals of Puritan casuistry had reference but in the outer world of affairs where the business of life is conducted. The sudden remembrance of things past in which he had a part forces Angelo to view himself as a moral agent and not simply as an elected vessel of sainthood or reprobation.

The third feature of the ritual which Shake-

[1] For further comment, see H. Fisch, *Hamlet and the Word: The Covenant Pattern in Shakespeare* (New York, 1971), pp. 219–20.

speare practises on Angelo is closely bound up with the second, and is concerned with the sudden revelation of identities. This has its analogy too in *The Tempest*, in *Pericles* and *The Winter's Tale*. In all these the unveiling of hidden figures, the casting off of disguise and the revealing of true identity have a part to play in the moral action. In *The Tempest*, for instance, the sudden 'discasing' of Prospero and his presenting of himself in his true shape 'as I was sometime Milan' seem to shock his visitors into a new frame of mind and complete the work of moral reform. In *Measure for Measure* we have the successive unconcealing of Mariana and the Duke before the stunned gaze of Angelo. This is more than a convention of the romantic theater. This ritual of visibly casting off a false identity seems to trigger a parallel process in the soul of the observer. Its effect on Angelo is surely to reveal to himself his *own* true identity. He will now be in a better position to answer the question he had asked himself earlier:

What dost thou, or what art thou, Angelo?
(II, ii, 173)

Like Alonso and Leontes he will see himself as he truly is. He is not the saint he thought he was nor are his evil propensities the result of diabolical invasion. His virtues and his weaknesses are alike his own, and, in this moment of truth when all disguises, even those we unconsciously assume, are stripped away, he will have to accept them as part of his native endowment.

But the final feature of the exorcism so typical of this play but also of Shakespeare's art generally, and for which no parallel can be found in the manuals of casuistry is in the extraordinary emphasis on the healing powers of marriage.[1] In the economy of the fifth act of *Measure for Measure* the four marriages have a clear redemptive purpose. They come symbolically to repair the moral chaos of the whole society of Vienna. But Angelo's marriage to Mariana seems to have a more particular curative function than this. At the very instant that Angelo sinks down to the ground in contrition saying

Immediate sentence then, and sequent death
Is all the grace I beg –   (v, i, 371–2)

the Duke asks him,

Say: wast thou e'er contracted to this woman?
(line 373)

On his acknowledgement that this was so, he commands him

Go, take her hence, and marry her instantly.
(line 375)

It is a remarkable juxtaposition. The marriage comes to constitute not a perfunctory mode of tying up the story by pairing off the different couples, but rather the climax of the movement of moral restoration itself. When Angelo returns after the solemnization of his marriage with Mariana it is as though he has now passed the crisis and has become a new man. There is some such suggestion of regeneration in the phrase, 'this new-married man approaching here' (line 398).

The marriages are indeed functional to the play as a whole, representing, if I am not mistaken, a symbolic resolution of the major paradoxes of Puritanism. Grace and Nature, Flesh and Spirit, have come together in an institution which holds within it the possibilities for a social application of those energies and drives which Puritanism had released. It is interesting to note that in offering this symbolic answer Shakespeare uses the terminology of contract. Miss M. C. Bradbrook has remarked with great insight that

The four marriages [at the end of *Measure for Measure*] represent, in descending order of dignity,

1 Cf., *ibid.*, pp. 221–2.

variations upon this basic social contract. In *The Merchant of Venice*, a forerunner of this play in many ways, the marriage contract is symbolized in the story of the rings, and contrasted with Shylock's purely legal bond. Marriage is the highest form of contract, in that it contains subtler possibilities for good and evil, for variety, than other types of contract.[1]

What Miss Bradbrook fails to note is that the use of the language of contract and indeed the whole emphasis in the play on the validity of the pre-contract as the effective element in marriage is a Puritan commonplace. Marriage for the Puritans was less a sacrament than a legal contract. Hence the importance they attached to betrothal. 'The contract', says William Gouge, a Puritan writer of the early seventeenth century, 'is the original agreement . . . marriage is the final agreement to adhere to the contract.'[2] Shakespeare is in fact using the Puritan legal code and the terminology that went with it in order to suggest something better. He is redeeming the terms for his own use, turning a business agreement into a mode of salvation, an entry into the kingdom of heaven. The Duke says to Isabella in his proposal of marriage:

> I have a motion much imports your good,
> Whereto if you'll a willing ear incline,
> What's mine is yours, and what is yours is mine –
> *(ibid., 533–5)*

seemingly offering her a partnership in a business enterprise. But in fact he is offering to wed his power to her piety. His marriage to Isabella is a contract for the redemption of society just as the 'gentle bond' of Portia and Bassanio is the bond which symbolically rejoins the severed links of the social order.

The use of the language of contract, indeed, has extraordinary significance both in this play and in *The Merchant of Venice*. Through it Shakespeare provides his own revaluation of the basic structures of Puritanism, those in which its power-drives were contained and through which they were released. The term 'Covenant' should now be introduced. It is of course a key-term in Puritan theology at the end of the sixteenth century. It is used in connection with marriage, but it is of much wider import than that, embracing as it does the whole life of man in his human and divine relationships. William Perkins whom we have taken as our guide to Elizabethan Puritanism in this paper places it at the center of his theology, and it was to become the dominant feature later on of the writings of his most eminent pupil, William Ames. The idea had quite considerable currency in Puritan circles at the time that Shakespeare was writing his plays: Here then is Perkins:

> Gods couenant is his contract with man, concerning the obtaining of life eternall, vpon certen condition.
> This couenant consists of two parts: Gods promise to man, Mans promise to God.[3]

The Covenant as Perkins says is contractual: there is man's obligation to God, and God's obligation to man. Moreover, it is based on the election of the few (by 'special calling') who were given extraordinary privileges. Entry into it offered salvation and power in return for faith on the part of the human partner. This structure of belief and action, as I have argued elsewhere, has the greatest importance for the study of *Hamlet*.[4] But it is hardly less important for *Measure for Measure*. The covenant form underlies the opening scene of *Measure for Measure* in which Angelo receives a 'commission' from the Duke appointing him as his deputy. The language used is that of the Puritan covenants:

> For you must know, we have with special soul
> Elected him our absence to supply;

[1] M. C. Bradbrook, 'Authority, Truth, and Justice', *Review of English Studies*, XVII (1941), 392.

[2] *Of Domesticall Duties* (1622). Quoted by James T. Johnson in his valuable article, 'The Covenant Idea and the Puritan View of Marriage', *Journal of the History of Ideas*, XXXII (1971), 117.

[3] *A Golden Chaine* (1591), in *Works*, I, 32.

[4] *Hamlet and the Word*, passim.

Lent him our terror, drest him with our love,
And given his deputation all the organs
Of our own power.   (I, i, 18–22)

The overwhelmingly exalted status of the chosen vessel is here emphasized, also the power and opportunity which goes with an *election* by *special* calling. It is a solemn moment, portentous and fraught with destiny as is the covenant moment on Mount Sinai. And that indeed is the kind of analogy the Puritans had in mind. It is significant that in a comic scene later on we hear of a 'sanctimonious pirate, that went to sea with the Ten Commandments but scraped one out of the table' (I, ii, 7–9). This will do as a description of Angelo. Here then is the source of the Puritan's peculiar sense of confidence. He had a written contract containing a divine promise of success. In the biblical sources this carried with it primarily an immense sense of responsibility expressing itself in an active zeal of righteousness. The People of Israel were elected by covenant to be a kingdom of priests and a holy nation (Exodus, 19:5–6). But the Puritans detached the covenant-structure from the doctrine of Works and attached it instead to the evangelical principle of Grace. Over this, Angelo, like so many others stumbled. For in the Covenant of Grace there is an inevitable dissociation – a basic split – between Grace and Nature, so that the power which the covenant yields can easily become unsanctified power. Power changes purpose because power must be wielded in this world which has become the arena of Nature separated from Grace. On this dilemma, as we have seen, Angelo is impaled. But he was not alone. Seventeenth-century Puritanism was to encourage not only the sainthood of Bunyan but also the rapacity of the new *laissez-faire* capitalist. Moreover, the early Puritan expositors were dimly conscious of this danger. Perkins speaks of the possibility of a diabolical covenant, a dark replica of the Covenant with

God,[1] and Shakespeare too in all three plays we are considering seems to interpret the Puritan covenant (either parodically or with more serious emphasis) as a covenant with the Devil. Angelo's career has its darker side as he sees himself in the hands of 'the cunning enemy'. The comic exorcism of Malvolio (*Twelfth Night*, IV, ii) begins with the words, 'Out hyperbolical fiend! how vexest thou this man?'. In *The Merchant of Venice* the covenant-event from which the plot takes its rise is visualized in terms of a bond with Shylock who is eight times identified as 'the devil in person'. The rapacity of the Puritan userers was in Shakespeare's time very often taken as a sign that their powers came from the devil. Indeed, 'the Devil is a Puritan' had become a cant phrase.[2]

Now it was clear to Shakespeare that such immoral use of power as we see demonstrated in Angelo and Shylock, must be curbed. Shakespeare achieves this dramatically by means of symbolism and plot-construction. Thus Shylock's savage bond is annulled, and replaced by a gentler bond, that binding Portia to Bassanio and Gratiano to Nerissa. The parallelism between these two modes of contract has been pointed out by a number of commentators. Mr Burckhardt shows how the language of the bond-story is carried over into the story of the rings which the lovers receive in pledge from their mistresses, and he speaks significantly of 'the covenant of the caskets'.[3] Here then is Shakespeare's poetic answer to the threat posed by the irruption into society of the new economic power of the Puritans. Spirit and Flesh will be united. Without perhaps realizing it Shakespeare has returned to something like the original biblical covenant as visualized in

[1] *Works*, I, 39.
[2] See Siegel, 'Shylock, the Elizabethan Puritan and Our Own World', p. 246.
[3] Burckhardt, *Shakespeare's Meanings*, p. 215. Cf. Bradbrook in the passage quoted above.

the Old Testament prophets. Hosea uses the marriage symbol as the chief, indeed the exclusive symbol for the relations between God and Israel, and marriage itself is raised elsewhere to the level of a spiritual union over which God himself presides. In the second chapter of Malachi God is said to witness 'between thee and the wife of thy youth . . . the wife of thy covenant' (Malachi, 2:14). Marriage is a sacred bond.

Shakespeare's intuition of this relationship is strong throughout the comedies, but never more strong than in *Measure for Measure* where the problem of power and the necessity of sanctifying and curbing it is compounded by the problem of moral anarchy. In Vienna men give their sensual race the rein and corruption overruns the stew. Marriage becomes a remedy for this moral evil as well as a symbolical means of reordering society by setting before men constructive social aims.[1] We may add that here is the dramatist's answer to the Puritan covenant of Grace and one which nevertheless keeps within the categories which the Puritan movement had introduced into men's minds. The ending of the play constitutes a covenant-event as momentous as its beginning. The one cancels the other. And that is why Angelo must enter upon his new role immediately his penance begins. He, along with the rest of the cast, is now directed forward to an active quest, a release of energy, like that of act 1, scene i – but this time a release of energy for high social and religious ends. And this new structure too is founded in contract, in an exchange of vows and obligations that 'imports our good' and the good also of the world we live in.

[1] For some perceptive remarks on the wider significance of the marriages in this play, see J. W. Lever in his valuable introduction to this play, *Measure for Measure* (The Arden Shakespeare, London, 1965), p. xci. And see also, W. L. Godshalk, '*Measure for Measure*: Freedom and Restraint', *Shakespeare Studies*, VI (1970), 148.

EQUITY, 'THE MERCHANT OF VENICE' AND WILLIAM LAMBARDE

W. NICHOLAS KNIGHT

Giles E. Dawson and Joseph Q. Adams, while working on Shakespeare's autograph uncovered in 1938 at the Folger Shakespeare Library in a copy of William Lambarde's *Archaionomia* (1568), expressed their continued puzzlement at why this book was ever in Shakespeare's possession or under what specific circumstances the dramatist would have encountered William Lambarde. Dawson felt the book was a peculiar one for Shakespeare to have: '... the only one [possibility] remaining, is that William Shakespeare wrote his signature on this title page, perhaps because he owned the book – a strange volume indeed for his library'.[1] Adams accounted for the strangeness by indicating the likelihood that some other writing on the page, stating that the book should not be lost, was Lambarde's; thus evidencing that this was a presentation copy from the author to Shakespeare. Adams then opined,

That the two men of letters in the small world of literary London knew each other is hardly to be doubted, and that Shakespeare was interested, as was Ben Jonson, in Anglo-Saxon law seems highly likely. We must be content, however, with the likelihood that here at least we have a volume that was once actually in the possession of the poet.[2]

The following analysis of Shakespeare's relationship to Chancery, equity, mortgages, bonds and forfeitures from 1597 to 1599 provides previously unacknowledged contacts between William Lambarde and Shakespeare; more reasons for why Shakespeare should have Lambarde's law book in his possession;

historical support for the authenticity of the signature; and further evidence of Shakespeare's deep involvement in the legal issues of his day.

Adams, Dawson and others could have been more specific about the chances of the dramatist and jurist meeting at the Inns of Court, when Lambarde, who had selected revels, and Donne were at Lincoln's Inn and Shakespeare was having his *Comedy of Errors* performed at Gray's Inn in the Christmas season of 1594; or at Westminster Hall, while Shakespeare was pursuing a case to obtain his estate of Asbies in the Court of Queen's Bench and Lambarde was head of the Office of Alienations during the period of 1588–91. That a personal connection existed between them is strengthened by Queen Elizabeth's making her only recorded reference to Shakespeare in a private interview with William Lambarde: 'I am Richard II, know ye not that? ... this tragedy was played 4otie times in open streets and houses.'[3] There is now more evidence for a sustained and professional connection between William Lambarde, the leading Master of Chancery, and the dramatist at the time of *The Merchant of Venice* and his being a litigant in Chancery from 1597 to 1599.

[1] Giles E. Dawson, 'Authentication and Attribution of Written Matter', *English Institute Annual* (1942), p. 100.

[2] Joseph Quincy Adams, 'A New Signature of Shakespeare?,' *Bulletin of the John Rylands Library, Manchester,* XXXVII (1943), 259.

[3] As cited in Wilbur Dunkel, *William Lambarde: Elizabethan Jurist 1536–1601* (New Brunswick, 1965), pp. 177–8.

I

Around 1596/7, Shakespeare was anatomizing authority, inheritance, legitimacy and justice in the *Henry IV* plays and doing vignettes of the judicial system from the Monarch to the Lord Chief-Justice of the King's Bench, to the country Justices Shallow and Silence, and even to the Sheriff's Officers, Fang and Snare; all were preserving the Elizabethan order at various levels of the politic's hierarchy. In *The Merchant of Venice* (c. 1596), Shakespeare turned to study the technicalities of legal procedure. When he came to write his most obviously legalistic play, a number of biographical events had taken place touching his legal background and personal matters of inheritance. *The Merchant of Venice* is partly about the game of winning an inheritance by the Christians with someone providing the bankroll; the loss of a daughter and a fortune by Shylock, with a mercantile setting; a court of law attempting to mitigate cut-throat competition; and the aggrandizing spirit. Shakespeare in 1596 and 1597 has personally, at the law, sought to mitigate threats of personal injury in Queen's Bench against Gardner; lost an offspring, his son Hamnet, who would have inherited his estate; and attempted to set up for himself an expanded inheritance through purchases and litigation. A Master of Chancery, William Lambarde, may have been a witness of both the legal actions and the artistic products of this period.

William Lambarde (1536–1601) moves through several offices relating to Shakespeare's litigations up to a moment when it is possible to place him in the audience of *Merchant of Venice*. He had published *Archaionomia* in 1568 and had, since 1590, been working at Lincoln's Inn (where Donne wrote some of his poetry) on a manuscript of the history of the High Court of Chancery to which Shakespeare may have had access. The manuscript was entitled *Archeion* and was published in 1591 with a letter of dedication to Sir Robert Cecil from Lincoln's Inn dated 22 October 1591. He accepted the position of deputy of Lord Burghley (William Cecil) in the Office of Composition for the Alienations of Fines on 4 October 1589 at the time Shakespeare had his case (1588–90) in the Court of Queen's Bench involving the earlier alienation of Asbies estate by his father in 1578. Alienation remained an area of general interest to Lambarde throughout his subsequent appointments. He was made Master Extraordinary of Chancery in June 1592 and was assigned to the Office of Alienations. Four significant cases (in *Acta Cancellaria*) between 4 December 1595 and 15 July 1600 indicate he was consulted for major decisions. The Keeper of the Seal, Egerton, Lord Ellesmere, made Lambarde Keeper of the Records of the Rolls Chapel on 26 May 1597, and Master Ordinary in December 1597; and shortly before his death the Queen appointed him, upon the Lord Keeper's recommendation, Keeper of the Records of the Tower on 21 January 1601. In 1595 Lambarde is the most active Master of Chancery and the Lord Keeper relies upon him heavily.[1]

The information Leslie Hotson has uncovered on an exchange of writs to keep the peace indicates that in 1596 Shakespeare is, as he was from 1588–90, involved with Queen's Bench in Westminster and at this later time is associated with the Swan Theater in Paris Garden, Bankside.[2] In this same year of the applications for the issuances of warrants, William Lambarde publishes his revised edition of *A Perambulation of Kent*, originally

[1] Cf. W. J. Jones, *The Elizabethan Court of Chancery* (Oxford, 1967), pp. 44, 62, 68, 111–13, 116–19, 267, 293, 366, 413, 474, 477, and 489; and Wilbur Dunkel, *William Lambarde, Elizabethan Jurist* (New Brunswick, 1965), pp. 110–80.

[2] Leslie Hotson, *Shakespeare versus Shallow* (Boston, 1931).

printed in 1576. He adds to his 1576 version in his account of the pilgrimages to Boxley, where those who visit the shrine do not get off scot-free, the following passage:

... no more than such as goe to Parisgardein, the Bell Savage, or Theatre, to beholde Beare baiting, Enterludes, or Fence play, can account of any pleasant spectacle, unless they first pay one pennie at the gate, another at the entrie of the Scaffolde, and the thirde for a quiet standing.[1]

This has the sound of a personal complaint. How remarkable to have such direct information that this Master of Chancery attended plays in Surrey Bankside. William Lambarde had seen interludes in Paris Garden, Surrey, by 1596 when Shakespeare was living, writing and performing in the Liberty of the Clink. William Shakespeare was in the Court of Queen's Bench in 1596, and later in Chancery, both located in Westminster Hall where Lambarde held office; and the seventh known Shakespeare signature is in a copy of Lambarde's *Archaionomia*, a translation of Anglo-Saxon law. Therefore, in addition to possibly meeting at the Inns of Court festivities such as the revels of Gray's Inn or in discussions in rooms at Lincoln's Inn, Shakespeare could have encountered Lambarde in Westminster Hall, or Lambarde could have met Shakespeare at the Swan. Shakespeare's company is acting at the newly constructed Swan in Paris Garden, Southwark, in 1596 and it is in this year that the *Merchant of Venice* is thought to have been performed. It is reasonable to assume Lambarde would not pass up seeing *The Merchant of Venice*. Around this time (1596–7) the chances for Shakespeare and Lambarde meeting are very high indeed, as they also are for 1588–91 at Westminster, 1594–5 at the Inns, and 1597–9 in Chancery.

It is at least Mark Edwin Andrew's belief, in his technical study of *The Merchant of Venice*,[2] that the play was not only influenced by Shakespeare's thorough familarity with English jurisprudence, but that the play in turn ultimately affected Egerton as Lord Chancellor, Sir Francis Bacon, and other judicial figures in their thoughts about Chancery and equity. Production of the play clearly affected King James, as in 1604 he had *The Merchant* performed before him twice within three days. To these judicial figures can now be added Egerton's right-hand man, William Lambarde, who was a likely frequenter of the plays at The Swan.

In *The Merchant of Venice*, William Shakespeare is not just dramatizing a generalized court scene and sentimentalizing about mercy; rather he is presenting Chancery procedure and advocating that it be used precisely along its theoretical lines of a superior court with its accompanying appellate function and humane spirit, so as not to abrogate the common law of Queen's Bench and Common Pleas, and thus become merely a rival court. William Lambarde was referring to Chancery in his manuscript of *Archeion* as the 'Gate of Mercie' and he championed reform from within in order to preserve its unique jurisdiction. In *The Merchant*, Shakespeare puts to use readings in William West's *Symboleography* and Christopher St Germain's *Doctor and Student* published at the Inns of Court. The 'mercy' of the High Court of Chancery's equitable decisions by the Lord Chancellor is not to be confused with the simple clemency or empathetic pity of Solinus in *The Comedy of Errors* and Theseus in *A Midsummer Night's Dream*, nor the some-

[1] William Lambarde, *A Perambulation of Kent* (London, 1596), p. 233; cf. E. K. Chambers, *The Elizabethan Stage* (Oxford, 1930), II, 359.

[2] Mark Edwin Andrews, *Law versus Equity in 'The Merchant of Venice'* (Boulder, Colorado, 1965). For one of many points that indicate the precision of Shakespeare's reconstruction of the law of his day, compare *The Merchant of Venice*, III, iii, 26 ff. with the 'Case of Market-Overt' given in Coke's *Reports*, part v, p. 83, and tried in Hilary term 1596 of which Sir Thomas Egerton, Lord Ellesmere, was one of the judges (cf. Andrews, *Law versus Equity*, pp. 28–9).

what easy piety of Germain's *Doctor and Student*, for William West says: 'There is a difference between Equitie and Clemencie: for Equitie is alwaies most firmly knit to the evil of the Law which way soever it bends, whether to clemency, or to severity.'[1]

Seemingly extraneous, biblical directives are most apparent in the Duke of Venice's 'How shalt thou hope for mercy, rendering none?' (IV, i, 88). These, however, are also present in Christopher St Germain's dialogue: 'thou do to another as thou wouldst should be done to thee ... that in every general Rule of the Law thou do observe and keep Equity'.[2] This, in turn, served an institutionalized, judicial function in the procedure of Chancery, which as a Court of Conscience operates *in personam*, upon oath, to insure that the plaintiff has come before the Bench 'with clean hands'. Observe in the familiar passage, operating at the same time, Portia's, and of course Shakespeare's, precise sense of how equity accomplishes justice, how Chancery has a remedial function over the strictures of the common law, how a person within an institution can reflect the hope that the application of its system can transcend the system's own limitations to achieve the idealized purpose for which the institution was constructed:

Portia.
The quality of mercy is not strain'd
It droppeth as the gentle rain from heaven
Upon the place beneath: it is twice blest;
It blesseth him that gives and him that takes:
'Tis mightiest in the mightiest: it becomes
The throned monarch better than his crown;
His sceptre shows the force of temporal power,
The attribute to awe and majesty,
Wherein doth sit the dread and fear of kings;
But mercy is above this sceptred sway;
It is enthroned in the hearts of kings,
It is an attribute to God himself;
And earthly power doth then show likest God's
When mercy seasons justice. Therefore, Jew,
Though justice be thy plea, consider this,

That in the course of justice, none of us
Should see salvation: we do pray for mercy;
And that same prayer doth teach us all to render
The deeds of mercy. I have spoke thus much
To mitigate the justice of thy plea;
Which if thou follow, this strict court of Venice
Must needs give sentence 'gainst the merchant there.

Shylock.
My deeds upon my head: I crave the law,
The penalty and forfeit of my bond.
(IV, i, 185–206).[3]

Portia speaks of the power residing in Chancery. The Lord Chancellor was regarded as the Keeper of the King's Conscience, regulating the monarch's justice with his mercy exercised as equity in Chancery. Equity and mercy as attributes of Chancery are very much in the legal wind of London in 1596 and 1597 with Germain's *Doctor and Student*, West's *Symboleography*, Lambarde's *Archeion*, Spenser's *Faerie Queene*,[4] and Shakespeare's *The Merchant of Venice*.

Portia's famous ' Quality of mercy' speech is not just an idealistic invocation but a reminder that it is a Court of Equity that has been convened where, as she says, 'mercy

---

[1] William West, *Symboleography* (London, 1594), Section 28.
[2] Christopher St Germain, *Doctor and Student* (London, 1715), p. 57. This was a popular treatise from the early sixteenth century and printed at Middle Temple Gate several times during the nineties.
[3] All citations of Shakespeare are from *The Complete Works of Shakespeare*, ed. Hardin Craig (Chicago 1953).
[4] Edmund Spenser, *The Faerie Queene*, eds. J. C. Smith and E. de Selincourt (London, 1970), Book V. Proem, stanza x; Canto X, stanza i; and Book VI, Canto I, stanza xlii. The second instalment of *The Faerie Queene* (Books III–VI) was entered at the Stationers' Hall on 20 January 1596. For an analysis of the Chancery side of the law in the work, see W. Nicholas Knight, 'The Narrative Unity of Book v of *The Faerie Queene*: "That Part of Justice Which Is Equity"', *The Review of English Studies*, New Series, XXI, number 83 (August 1970), 267–94.

seasons justice' and one can come 'to mitigate the justice of [the] plea'. As St Germain recognizes, 'Equity is a right Wiseness that considereth all the particular circumstances of the Deed the which also is tempered with the Sweetness of Mercy.' He continues, 'If thou take all that the words of the Law giveth thee [which is the 'rigorous course' (IV, i, 8) of Shylock's action upon the due and forfeit of his bond (line 35)], thou shalt sometime do against the law' (p. 52). Portia's ruling of a pound of flesh only, and no blood, as the award to be taken from Antonio by Shylock, is a severely precise reading of the letter of the law – the reverse of what is expected when one seeks leniency, a loose interpretation, or a moderated sentence. This is a dramatic and legalistic triumph of Shakespeare's design to illustrate how Chancery should fulfill the instruction that 'Equity followeth the Law in all particular cases where Right and Justice requireth, notwithstanding the general Rule of the Law to be to the contrary.'[1] The very terms of the bond were instructive in the debate between law and justice as Shakespeare would have read in West and was picked up by later writers on equity from Gray's Inn, such as Thomas Ashe: 'For it is to bee understood that the law hath two parts, *Carnem* & *Animam*: the letter resembleth the flesh [and that was Shylock's due], and the intent and reason the soule [Equity is the spirit of the law].'[2] Not only does Portia speak to legal theory but to Shakespeare's biographical past. William's father loses Shakespeare's estate in the Court of Queen's Bench (*Shakespeare* v. *Lambert* 1590), which William was to inherit from his mother; Portia symbolically reverses the condition by functioning as a female mercy-figure employing equity to restore what was, upon a technicality, forfeited by a bond. This loss occurred when John Shakespeare's offer of payment to redeem the estate for £40 on the precise day the debt was due was rejected since

he still owed other debts to his brother-in-law Edmund Lambert of Barton-upon-Heath, the holder of the mortgage at the time in 1580.[3]

Shakespeare, at the end of *The Merchant of Venice*, manages during Shylock's remaining life to provide for both Antonio and Shylock as well as preserve the corpus of the estate for the ultimate use and benefit of Shylock's heirs. *Shakespeare* v. *Lambert* discloses that John Shakespeare had failed to do this for his son, and hence his residual interest was not recognizeable in common law before the Court of Queen's Bench. Only a Court of Equity, such as Chancery might provide, could establish and recognize an instrument for such use.

Nerissa.
  Ay, and I'll give them [comforts] him [Lorenzo]
    without a fee
  There do I give to you and Jessica,
  From the rich Jew, a special deed of gift,
  After his death, of all he dies possess'd of.

  (V, i, 290–3)

This legal construction is precisely what Shakespeare knows to set up in his own will for not only his two daughters, but his grandchild, and in hopes of a grandson or great grandson, yet (but never) to come.

... unto the said Susanna Hall for and during the term of her natural life, and after her decease to the first son of her body lawfully issuing, and for default of such issue to the second son of her body lawfully issuing and to the heirs males of the body of the said second son lawfully issuing; and for default of such heirs to the third son of the body of the said Susanna lawfully issuing and of the heirs males of the body of the said

---

[1] Germain, *Doctor and Student*, p. 52.

[2] Thomas Ashe, *Epeikeia* (Gray's Inn, 1608). Ashe is quoting William West's *Symboleography*.

[3] Documents in the Chancery suit are from the estate records in J. O. Halliwell-Phillipps, *Outlines of the Life of Shakespeare* (London, 1897), II, 14–17, and 204. The Induction of *The Taming of the Shrew* has Christopher Sly from Barton-upon-Heath drinking with the Alewife of Wilmecote (where Asbies was located) and saying he will not budge even if the law is brought against him.

third son lawfully issuing; and for default of such issue the same so to be and remain to the fourth, fifth, sixth and seventh sons of her body lawfully issuing, one after another, and to the heirs males of the bodies of said fourth, fifth, sixth, and seventh sons lawfully issuing in such manner as it is before limited to be and remain to the first, second, and third sons of her body and to their heirs males. And for default of such issue the said premises to be and remain to my said niece [granddaughter] Hall and the heirs males of her body lawfully issuing; and for default of such issue, to my daughter Judith and the heirs males of her body lawfully issuing . . . [1]

Had Shakespeare's son, Hamnet, lived, this verbal search would not have been necessary to establish Shakespeare's line of inheritance. The technicalities Shakespeare had to be aware of in not only his own court case, but also in *The Merchant of Venice*, and in his last will and testament, as the result of the creation of a use after a use, and of the trust, are explicated with details in Mark Edwin Andrews's instructive work.[2]

II

Chancery and equity were mainly concerned with property, conveyance, use, inheritance, and things held in trust. Shakespeare makes a major purchase in 1597, so that finally he possessed a separate residence of his own to replace what he might have had in Asbies. The transaction is in keeping with his acquiring an estate for himself, and replacing his father's losses; looking after the rest of his family, and toward the family's future since no son will. Shakespeare senses the burden from both sides of time ('. . . nothing 'gainst Time's scythe can make defense / Save breed, to brave him when he takes thee hence' – Sonnet XII). He will not inherit, and will have no male inheritor.

Evidenced by his plays' texts, audiences and successes, Shakespeare has at this time the legal knowledge, acquaintances, and financial where-withall to reopen the case over Asbies that has rankled so long. The property was alienated in

1578; the mortgage became due in 1580; the Stratford agreement for compensation for the Shakespeares' residual title was reached in 1587, the breaking of which resulted in the case in the Court of Queen's Bench from 1588 to 1590 at which time the matter was dropped. Now in 1597, Shakespeare's father has his coat of arms pending, and his own house liberated from Will's immediate family. The restoration process is going well and so, as a part of this campaign, the dramatist turns to the reclaiming of Asbies, or to gain at least restitution for the loss.

The Bill of Complaint in the name of John and Mary Shakespeare is filed by J. Stovell on 24 November 1597 in Chancery under the jurisdiction of William Lambarde. It is a plea against John Lambert, who has legitimately inherited Asbies upon his father Edmund's death in 1587, to prevent him from entering upon the property. It says the Shakespeares will '. . . abyde suche order and direction there-in as to your good lordshippe shall seeme best to stande with righte, equytie and good con-scyence . . .' indicating they tendered the £40 in 1580, which they say Edmund refused to accept, and therefore William and his parents feel by subsequent events, like his namesake in *Lear*, Edmund has managed to steal his brother (in-law)'s inheritance, by converting a mortgage agreement on the house and forty odd acres into a sale. Shakespeare, in all likeli-hood the person financing and pursuing the litigation, is pressing Chancery to recognize a verbal agreement arrived at in trust that Asbies would be returned when all the debts were paid as opposed to being forfeited on the day of the bond according to the strictures of the common law as would have been ruled by

[1] Tucker Brooke, *Shakespeare of Stratford* (New Haven, 1926), p. 86 and see E. K. Chambers, *William Shakespeare* (Oxford, 1930), II, 169–80.
[2] Cf. Andrews, *Law versus Equity*, pp. 74–5 for how the creation of a use after a use and a trust work in *The Merchant of Venice*.

Queen's Bench in 1590; 'Have I not seen dwellers on form and favour / Lose all, and more ...' (Sonnet cxxx). John Lambert adamantly resists their attempts at recovery.

This case is pursued with considerable vigor from before 14 November 1597 until after 23 October 1599, during three years in Chancery at the height of William Lambarde's Mastership there from December 1597 to January 1601. During this time Shakespeare may have borrowed, or received, the copy of William Lambarde's *Archaionomia*, which contains the dramatist's signature. Meanwhile the case continues as evidenced by Orders of the Court of Chancery:

Quinto die July [5 July 1598] John Shackspeare and Mary, his wief, plaintiffes, John Lamberte, defendant. A commission [Lear convenes a court of equity with 'Thou robed man of justice, take thy place; / And thou, his yoke-fellow of equity, / Bench by his side: you are o' the commission, / Sit you too. *Edgar.* Let us deal justly' (III, vi, 39–42).] ys awarded to examyne witnesses on bothe partes, directed to Richard Lane ...

Richard Lane of Alveston, esquire and Thomas Green and William Shakespeare joined in 1609 in a plea of equity to the then Lord Chancellor, Egerton, Lord Ellesmere in a Chancery suit to protect the income they received from Stratford tithes. One of the personages they sued was George Lord Carew of Clopton. 'Richard Lane and William Shackspeare, and some fewe others of the said parties, are wholly, and against all equity and good conscience, usually dryven to pay the same.'[1]

and for that it is most agreeable to all reason, equity and good conscience that every person ... should be ratably charged ... and for that your orators have no means, by the order or course of the common laws of this realm, to enforce or compel any of the said parties to yield any certain contribution toward the same, and so are and still shall be remediless therein unless they may be in that behalf relieved by your Lordship's gracious clemency and relief to other in such like cases extended.[2]

Richard Lane on several occasions acted in the capacity of Shakespeare's friend.

In addition to Richard Lane as a witness in Stratford to the commission for the Shakespeares was another of William's friends and business acquaintances, John Combes. John Combes's brother Thomas entered the Middle Temple in 1608. Their family, as had the dramatist John Marston's, attended the Middle Temple for generations, inheriting rooms there. Shakespeare purchased in 1602 and 1610 some 120 acres of land from John and William Combes. John left Shakespeare £5 in his will, and Shakespeare left Thomas his sword. To balance Lane and Combes two other gentlemen – Thomas Underhill and Fraunces Woodward – were selected. Underhill was probably not of the family from whom Shakespeare had just purchased New Place. Underhill and Woodward were selected by John Lambert. Richard Lane and John Combes as William Shakespeare's associates, rather than any of his father's, were selected as witnesses to be examined in Stratford by the commission sent under the Chancery order. This evidences the dramatist's direct involvement in the case, as witnesses contemporary to the transaction of 1580, or familiar with John's business were not selected. Friends and partners of William in legal and financial affairs were chosen. Eccles (p. 29) is incorrect simply to presume the witnesses for the commission were selected by John Shakespeare.

gentlemen, iij or ij. of them, returnable octavis Michaelis, by assente of the attorneyes, Powle and Hubard, and the plaintiefes to give xiij, daies warnings.

These were indeed significant attorneys for this case! Edward Huberd was one of the Six Clerks of Chancery, an office Edmund Spenser, author

[1] Mark Eccles, *Shakespeare in Warwickshire* (Madison, 1963), pp. 105–6.

[2] As quoted in Brooke, *Shakespeare of Stratford*, p. 61.

of *The Fairie Queene*, held for Ireland in the 1580s. One of the chief duties of the Clerks, often neglected but not in this case, was that of acting as attorneys. Stephen Powle, the other attorney in the Chancery order for the Shakespeares, was another of the Clerks. The year before this case was introduced to Chancery, Stephen Powle, as deputy to the Clerk of the Crown, was officially summoned to record the ceremony in which Queen Elizabeth made Egerton Lord Keeper in May 1596. Stephen was the son of Thomas Powle who, along with William Lambarde, was one of the four Masters of Chancery and had been Clerk for examining Letters Patent of Alienation. In his father's later years, from 1596 on, Stephen was also serving as his deputy. Stephen Powle, Thomas Powle and William Lambarde worked together as Clerk and Masters of Chancery involved with Alienations at the time of Shakespeare's case appearing in that department. As his father's deputy, one of William Shakespeare's two London attorneys from 1597 to 1599 would have acted as William Lambarde's Clerk during the same time. This is the major connection between Shakespeare and Lambarde, unknown by any forger, supporting the logicality of Shakespeare's signature appearing in a law book with a Greek title and a Latin and Anglo-Saxon text.

Lambert is not idle, as he continues his defense the next year, 1599, with a lawyer from a famous family. Shakespeare's eagerness to pursue this case has created a complication in so far as two Bills have been filed.

xviij. die Maij. [18 May 1599] John Shakespeare, plaintiff; John Lambard [i.e. Lambert, perhaps Lambarde pricked up his ears at this point], defendant. – Forasmuch as this Court . . .

It would be interesting to know who was presiding.

. . . was this presente day ynformed by Mr. Overbury beinge of the defendantes councell . . .

John Lambert's attorney is none other than Nicholas Overbury. Nicholas was the father of Sir Thomas Overbury, who had just become a member of the Middle Temple in 1597 and wrote in his character of a *Mere Common Lawyer* that 'No way to heaven he thinks so wise as through Westminster-Hall.'[1] Sir Thomas was a courtier, and a series of trials after his death in 1613 disclosed that he had been poisoned in the Tower by the Earl of Somerset.[2] In *The Winter's Tale* (II, iii, 96) Shakespeare cites an old proverb from Sir Thomas Overbury's 'Character of a Sergeant': 'The devil calls him his white son; he's so like him, that he is the worse for it.'[3]

. . . that the plaintiff did fyrst exhibyte a bill unto this Court against the defendant, as well by his owne name as in the name of his wyef . . .

This bill in John's name alone would have presented a legal problem since it was Mary's inheritance which he shared by marriage. It must be technically established as falling to her first before John has any claim, and then he does not have sole interest as he shares it with Mary and his eldest son.

. . . to be relyved towchinge a mortgage of certene landes lyinge in the county of Warr, made to the defendantes father, whose heyre the defendant is, and afterwardes exhibyted a bill in his owne name only concerninge such matter in substaunce as the former bill doth; and althoughe the plaintiff hath taken out severall commisyones upon the later bill [5 July and 10 July 1598], yet he hath not examyned any wytnesses thereupon.

Possibly the year's delay on the Shakespeares' part was the result of knowing that their witnesses had no access to the information they needed corroboration on.

[1] As cited in Catherine Drinker Bowen, *The Lion and the Throne* (Boston, 1956), p. 337.
[2] *Ibid.*, pp. 364–9.
[3] Cf. *The Complete Works of Shakespeare*, p. 1227, l. 96 n.

It is therfore ordered that, yf Mr. D. Hunt, one of the Masters of this Cowrt [i.e. Master Dr John Hunt, Master of Chancery] . . .

John Hunt was one of the four Masters of Chancery, the others being William Lambarde, Sir George Carew (Cary) and Thomas Powle.

A description of the Masters' functions from W. J. Jones (*The Elizabethan Court of Chancery*) illustrated by the names from the case under discussion will be helpful at this point.

Normally, the lawyers chosen were impersonal [Nicholas Overbury for Lambert and J. Stovell for the Shakespeares] and would act in a fairly reserved and formal fashion. Judges, to whom a point of law had been referred [as in the Chancery case in 1599], or to whom the matter in law had been dismissed [as in the case when it was before the Court of Queen's Bench in 1590], might be required to arbitrate and determine the entire matter. The Lord Chancellor [the Lord Keeper, Sir Thomas Egerton, Lord Ellesmere] and the Master of the Rolls [Thomas Heneage and then William Lambarde who was first Keeper of the Records of the Rolls Chapel appointed by Egerton on 26 May 1597 and then Keeper of the Records of the Tower on 21 January 1601 while still retaining his Mastership of Chancery] were ready, if the parties [*Shakespeare* v. *Lambert*] were agreeable, to attempt such an agreement. Sometimes the Master of the Rolls [Lambarde] would co-operate with some of the Masters [Dr John Hunt, Master of Chancery]. At other times, only Masters – perhaps as many as four of them together [William Lambarde, George Carew, John Hunt and Thomas Powle, possibly Stephen Powle as his deputy] – would be appointed to arbitrate [as four did in 1579, 1584, 1593, 1600 and 1602]. It is even possible to find one of the Six Clerks [two of them being at this time Stephen Powle and Edward Huberd] being called upon to play his part in an attempt to determine a case without the necessity of a judicial hearing. If attempts of this nature were unsuccessful, the normal practice of reporting the facts to the court would be employed, and once again the finger of suspicion would point at a litigant who had prevented the achievement of a settlement.

The *Shakespeare* v. *Lambert* suit is settled once again out of court. It appears that Lambert retains the land. Jones continues:

None the less, the Masters [Hunt, who worked with Lambarde on the jurisdiction of St James' Court][1] and often other lawyers [Powle and Huberd, Overbury and Stovell] would try again and again to get the parties to agree, even if they felt that the suit was essentially unfit for the court. An arbitration seemed more effective than a dismission in preventing further litigation in some other place.

When the attempt was being made by judges and other lawyers, or when commissioners were sitting near London . . .

The Shakespeares' three commissions ordered out of Chancery would have sat far from London in Stratford, an expensive operation.

. . . the Lord Chancellor and Master of the Rolls readily offered their services as umpires should the discussions reach a stalemate. The Masters too would act as umpires [Did Hunt and Lambarde meet with Shakespeare and Lambert in 1599, with Powle and Hubard?] and might meet with the arbitrators as often as four times [as they did in 1559, 1562, 1563, 1564, 1575, and 1601]. Many legal conundrums had to be sorted out which in later times might well have been settled out of court from the beginning through consultations of the respective legal advisors. In Tudor times this could rarely happen, and the only sanction of reliability could be found in at least beginning formal proceedings in some court of law.

Only by chance Jones picks up for illustration on a personal level a remark by one of the figures in the *Shakespeare* v. *Lambert* Chancery suit.

We can appreciate the glum comments of Master Hunt [the Master referred to in Shakespeare's Court Order of 18 May 1599] who reported [in *Morgan* v. *ap Williams* (1597)] the successful end of a case with the agreement of the parties, finding them at length weary, one of another, and myself also of them both.

Jones notes that by the 1600s if a case were dismissed to arbitration, any unsatisfactory settlement did not prevent the submission of a new bill on the same matter.

'Mr D. Hunt' turns out, then, to be Master Hunt. Therefore the case has moved, by

[1] Jones, *Elizabethan Court of Chancery*, pp. 365–7.

Huberd's and Powle's consents, from the Clerkship level to that of the Masters for consideration. This investigation into the case resulted from the filing of two Complaints in what was substantially a single action, and the Shakespeares' delaying a year before acting upon the two commissions consequently granted by Chancery.

It is therefore ordered that, yf Mr. D. Hunt, one of the Masters of this Cowrt, shall, upon consideration of the said bills, fynde and report that bothe the said billes doe in substance conteyne one matter, then the defendant [i.e. John Lambert] ys to be dismissed from one of the said billes ...

Hunt probably determined that there was, substantially, 'one matter,' and had one Complaint withdrawn, which would explain why it is no longer extant. So Lambert was correct in his earlier furious claim that

they, the said complainantes, doe now trowble and moleste this defendante by unjuste sutes [note the plural] in lawe, thinkinge therby, as yt shoulde seme, to wringe from him this defendante some further recompence for the said premisses then they have alreddy received ...

This is what John Lambert had charged in his Replication of 24 November 1597, and now on 18 May 1599 Master Hunt was being ordered to look into the matter. John Lambert is to be dismissed from one of the bills

... with such costes as the said Mr. D. Hunt [i.e. Master Hunt, Dr, or Dr John Hunt, Master of Chancery] shall tax and asseasse; and the plaintiff ...

Note the singular; Mary is not mentioned in this court order as she was not in the duplicate bill being dismissed.

... the plaintiff did fyrst exhibyte a bill ... as well by his owne name as in the name of his wyef, [which is in the records] ... and afterwardes exhibited a bill in his owne name only ...

which is not extant. The court continues to speak in very strong language against the delays on the part of the Shakespeares.

... the plaintiff ys to proceede to the hearinge thereof withe effect, and the defendant shal be at lyberty to chaunge his commissyones ...

This is a court favour granted to Lambert, and punitively not to the Shakespeares. The justice Shakespeare expected could have been recognized through the concept, not yet formulated, of 'equity of redemption'. Chancery was not turning a kind ear to their protracted and rather costly suit seeking some action.

The Shakespeares move for a hearing on 23 October 1599, which probably indicates the commission (now lost) had obtained depositions from the witnesses. The matter was probably settled outside court, or by arbitration. However, without a doubt, after having signed Asbies away in 1578 and with litigation at common law from 1588 to 1590 and in Chancery from 1597 to 1599 covering overall a period of some twenty years, what was to be Shakespeare's estate remains with the Lamberts as their possession from Edmund to John. John sold it shortly after the termination of the litigation in 1602 to a Richard Smyth for the familiar sum of £40.[1] Perhaps Chancery had come to the arbitrated settlement that the Shakespeares would not have to pay fines or costs but that Lambert when he sold must sell the land with no unfair advantage, or unreasonable enrichment, that is not to exceed the £40 his father had 'purchased' it at.

Beyond a shadow of a doubt, Shakespeare, demonstrably from the legal actions and in his plays' texts is plagued with a concern for his estate lost, and then his lands and revenue forever lost from the critical adolescent age of fourteen until the height of his career at thirty-five; from the time he had to leave his schooling until just before he lost his father, whose decline had affected Shakespeare's prospects, and whose condition prompted him in his rise to attempt to restore him, as well as himself.

[1] Eccles, *Shakespeare in Warwickshire*, p. 29.

III

As a Master of Chancery, William Lambarde was preparing a manuscript about the court and the actions brought before it. He was pre-occupied by the kind of considerations that Shakespeare's case posed as a problem before the law. After Lambarde died in 1601, one of the other Masters and a close friend, Sir George Carew (Cary), edited the papers and produced Cary's *Reports* out of the labors of Lambarde, as the original title-page indicates. The *Reports* suggest how Chancery might have been lenient toward the Shakespeares had their evidence been sufficient. Jones's discussion of the important passage Carew took from Lambarde indicates the significance this case would have had for the Master of Chancery and, despite the fact that the case was never tried nor won by Shakespeare, the contributing effect of the litigation's content upon legal history. 'The opening words of Cary's *Reports* provide a classic introduction to a jurisdiction which more than any other called for the issue of injunctions for stay of actions or executions in other courts.' Chancery could reverse common law arbitration, or withstand its decisions at the termination of the Court of Queen's Bench case at which time ordering that the land be returned to the Shakespeares upon simple payment of the mortgage according to equity, if undue advantage were being taken, unjust insistence on a technicality were being maintained, or a promise, a matter of oath or conscience, were not being honored. What follows is Lambarde's opinion on the Shakespeare case as he speaks through his editor, Sir George Carew in the opening paragraph of Cary's *Reports*. The passage is embellished with the specifics of the case.

If a man be bound in a penalty [the forfeiture of the Estate of Asbies] to pay money [the £40] at a day [Michaelmas-Day 1580] and place [Edmund Lambert's residence at Barton-on-the-Heath in the Cotswolds]

by obligation [the Fine filed Easter Term, 1579 in Court of Common Pleas], and intending to pay the same [as was John Shakespeare's avowed contention in his Bill of Complaint before Chancery] is robbed by the way; or hath entreated by word some other respite at the hands of the obligee ...

This is almost the Shakespeares' case, but with Edmund Lambert as the accidental cause preventing the tendering of the money becoming a successful payment, through 'entreating by word' that the payment of additional debts on the part of the payee must be made. The requirement was not a part of the original indenture and was initiated by Lambert and John apparently unwittingly accepted. Lambarde continues listing accidents preventing intentions from taking place:

'or cometh short of the place by any misfortune, and so failing of the payment, doth nevertheless provide and tender the money in short time after [which John was willing to pay from the day it was due on, and had offered again in 1587 and for the whole matter in 1597, hence the intent and ability had remained extant from 1580 to 1599], in these and many such like cases the Chancery will compel the obligee [Lambert] to take his principal [the £40] with some reasonable consideration of his damages (*quantum expediat*) [obviously met by the income received from the land from 1580 to 1599] for if this was not, men would do that by covenant which they now do by bond ... The like favour is extendable against them that will take advantage upon strict condition for undoing the estate of another in lands, upon a small or trifling default [which is precisely what John Lambert had succeeded in doing, despite Chancery's claim of equity to John Shakespeare, Mary, his wife, and his son William].'

Relief in respect to penalty and forfeiture, quite apart from the conscience of the defendant who might be deemed to be taking undue advantage, depended on an assessment of the elements of accident, mistake, and ignorance. These were vague concepts, depending on the facts and particulars of each case. In other words, the principles of liability rested upon factors which could not easily be defined in the abstract ...

(Jones, pp. 436–7)

Of the four Masters, Lambarde and Carew (more than Hunt and Powle) were obviously much disturbed by the inequity inherent in Shakespeare's case and those like his. However, at this time in legal history the situation upon which the case rested was particularly difficult to unravel without damaging clear obligations between man and property and faith in the instruments of conveyance. Simply, in the Shakespeares' case they probably could furnish no witnesses to substantiate their claim of Edmund Lambert's promise to return Asbies upon their payment of all the outstanding debts. On the other hand, as Lambarde and Carew recognized, Chancery had not met in any clear way its obligation to the matter in so far as the Shakespeare land remains with Lambert after being settled out of court, or by arbitration, rather than specific remedy (but, possibly contributing ultimately to a change in legal precedent). That it did not change the law at the time is precisely what Lambarde objects to in the forefront of his work. What might have been Edmund Lambert's kind offer, or 'merry bond', as in *The Merchant of Venice*, at John Lambert's hands, allows him to have Shakespeare on his hip. Lambert takes, as Lambarde says, 'advantage upon strict condition for [the purpose of] undoing the estate of another in lands, upon a small or trifling default' (of not meeting the payment on a specific day).

The Shakespeare case, and those like it at this time, rankled not only the dramatist, but William Lambarde and Carew as well. In fact just as Lambarde may have been an influence upon Shakespeare's understanding of the higher courts of law through his treatise, so Shakespeare's case in Chancery may have influenced Lambarde enough to seek equity of redemption principles for Chancery. Lambarde in Cary's *Reports* initiates the move toward that principle; thus, Shakespeare through his *The Merchant of Venice* not only anticipates

the arguments, as Mark Edwin Andrews points out, for the supremacy of equity over the common law, but Shakespeare's case may also have been a factor in bringing the modern legal concept of equity of redemption into existence. Small consolation to Shakespeare, but he may have been out to affect the law at this point. His loss may very well have become the world's gain, in so far as there now exists, to be legally enjoyed, a reasonable grace period pertaining to mortgages; further contributing to the equitable principles of protection against unjust rigorous application of documents in case of hardship, unfair advantage being taken of someone's misfortune, or unjust enrichment upon a technicality. At this time, Shakespeare in his litigations and drama has reached the point where he is doing things not only for personal gain and sustenance, but also to instruct his audience, convert the learned, and have his ideas on law, justice and equity affect his contemporary judicial institutions. These effects, both from his theatre and his law suits, survive his life, his estates, and his theatrical stage, and thus posterity has inherited not only his drama but also his view of justice and equity. The Chief Justice of the United States Supreme Court Harlan F. Stone said, 'Often, in listening to *The Merchant of Venice*, it has occurred to me that Shakespeare knew the essentials of the contemporary conflict between law and equity.'[1] And on a more concrete level, a close analysis of Shakespeare's litigation before the Masters of Chancery reveals, finally, the historical link Adams believed must have been there in order to substantiate externally the already satisfactory internal evidence for the authenticity of the Folger's seventh known Shakespeare signature.

[1] Justice Harlan F. Stone in a letter in 1937 to Mark Edwin Andrews quoted by J. K. Emery, editor, in his preface to Andrews's *Law versus Equity*, p. ix.

'LOVE'S LABOUR'S WON' AND THE OCCASION OF 'MUCH ADO'

ROBERT F. FLEISSNER

That the title *Much Ado About Nothing* has been associated with a pun — so that, in effect, something can come *ex nihilo* – has become a commonplace in Shakespearian scholarship; however, the word-play upon 'noting' and 'nothing' (as in the Don Pedro/Balthasar dialogue in act II)[1] is seemingly too slight for considering that an entire play, or even its title, would have been built upon it. Though this word-play is enhanced through the added meaning of noting – that is, *making* notes in the 'immediate context' of sounding notes in music, but also in the 'larger context' of *taking* notes, or eavesdropping – I submit that the explanation is unsatisfactory for justifying the title, which may unfortunately retain the general impression of flippancy. I propose, however, a more agreeable solution which need not make the audience feel 'taken in' or embarrassed by seeming insincerity or flippancy: it is one that builds upon the inherent insouciance of the title, without having to apologize for it in the least. My view is that the title as we have it was originally the play's sub-title. At some point, then, the main title got lost. If so, the lost title may have been *Love's Labour's Won*, for this is the only title of Shakespeare's which we have without a play to to go with it from this period of his career. Since a number of Shakespeare's other comedies have similarly 'flippant' subtitles, the interpretation here offered would not be setting a new precedent.

Briefly, my proposal is as follows: first, Shakespeare wrote a comedy following *Love's Labour's Lost* entitled *Love's Labour's Won; or, Much Ado About Nothing*. This drama was then referred to by Francis Meres in his *Palladis Tamia* as *Love's Labour's Won* alone, without the subtitle, as was customary; it was likewise referred to without the subtitle in the stationer's stocklist of 1603 published by T. W. Baldwin. But when it was registered, on 4 August 1600, it appeared as 'The Commedie of muche A doo about nothing', and on 23 August 1600 as 'Muche a Doo about nothinge'. But why, it is natural to ask, would the play have been registered according to its subtitle? Why indeed?

I believe that I can provide a completely convincing reason for such an anomalous event, one that has not been suggested before. But first let us consider the various reasons why

1 (*Prince.* Doe it in notes.
Balthasar. Note this before my notes,
Theres not a note of mine that's worth the noting.
Prince.
Why, these are very crotchets that he speaks,
Note notes, forsooth, and nothing.
[Air.]) (II, iii, 56–9)

Line and stage citations are to the Neilson-Hill edition; quotations, from the 1623 Folio.

An alternative explication of the titular pun on *Much Ado About Nothing* is presented in my '"Love" in tennis again', *American Notes and Queries*, 11 (Feb. 1973), 90–1; however, that item was contributed as a query, not a note, and contains editorial emendation; the solution offered is at variance with the present study, but was not intended as definitive. It may be considered complementary.

Much Ado may have been the same drama as *Love's Labour's Won*. For there is ample reason to maintain that *Much Ado* is the best candidate, in spite of recent popular preferences for *All's Well That Ends Well*.

The most comprehensive piece of scholarship on the mystery of *Love's Labour's Won* is that by Albert H. Tolman.[1] After considering every possible relationship he thinks he can find between *Won* and the other comedies, Tolman concludes: 'On the whole, if we are to find [*Won*] among the plays that we now possess, the choice appears to lie between *Much Ado About Nothing* and *The Taming of the Shrew*.'[2] But since Tolman wrote these words the publication of the 1603 stationer's stocklist listing both *Won* and *The Taming of a Shrew* has virtually eliminated Shakespeare's *Shrew* comedy as a candidate,[3] leaving only *Much Ado*. Why, then, has the public failed to press this association, generally opting for *All's Well* instead? Probably because the association with *All's Well* is older, having been made in 1764 by Dr Farmer (though Farmer himself was not so sure of the identification: 'It might have been given very aptly to *All's Well That Ends Well: and indeed to other plays*').[4] It is noteworthy that at least the Variorum Edition of *Much Ado* has given fair coverage to the matter, a point hardly considered by those who would think that *Won* is the same as *All's Well*. But to understand fully the implications of the prime candidacy of *Much Ado*, Tolman's points need to be briefly surveyed.

I

Tolman's arguments relating *Won* to other comedies by Shakespeare are long and complex and need not be fully recounted here. The case for *All's Well* is not very strong, largely on the grounds that the only linkage that seems to make any real sense is that the title, *Love's Labour's Won*, 'fits the theme of *All's Well That Ends Well*'.[5] As Henry David Gray has put it, 'Professor Tolman's objection is that no

[1] *The Views About 'Hamlet' and Other Essays* (New York, 1904) – on microfiche.

[2] *Ibid.*, pp. 312–13.

[3] See T. W. Baldwin, *Shakspere's 'Love's Labor's Won'* (Carbondale, 1957), which provides MS. readings from the day-book of the stationer in which reference is made to *Won*. Baldwin's belief that the play is the same as *All's Well* before it was revised has been questioned in the *TLS* review (21 Feb. 1958, p. 102) on the grounds that *All's Well* would fit better if it 'had been printed in the Folio, as was *King John*, without any entry in the Stationers' Register'. See also F. E. Halliday, *A Shakespeare Companion*, 1564–1964 (Baltimore, 1964): 'But in 1953 a London bookseller discovered a list of the books that the stationer Christopher Hunt had in stock in August 1603, and these include "*marchant of vennis, taming of a shrew, loves labor lost, loves labor won.*" Evidently *Love's Labour's Won* is not another name for *The Taming of the Shrew*' (p. 289) (in spite of the purported differences between *A Shrew* and *The Shrew*) – nor for *Love's Labour's Lost*.

[4] See the New Arden edition of *All's Well*, ed. G. K. Hunter (London, 1959), p. xix (italics mine). The reference to Farmer was originally provided by J. C. Maxwell. Hunter concludes: 'Of late, however, the idea [of identifying *Won* with *All's Well*] has become less compelling. Certainly the whole assumption that incoherencies in the text point necessarily to revision or re-writing is no longer tenable. The other assumption, that variation in stylistic level precludes unified construction, or is best explained as due to different layers of composition, also requires re-examination' (p. xx).

Joseph G. Price, in *The Unfortunate Comedy: A Study of 'All's Well that Ends Well' and its Critics* (Toronto, 1968), cites those who have been involved in the controversy: 'Verplanck, Charles Knight, Halliwell-Phillips, Gervinus, Kenny, Wendell, Brandes, Tolman, Masefield, Herford, Chambers, Lowe, Quiller-Couch, Elton, and Craig' (p. 177). Notable omissions include Fleay and Gray. The standard inference, that Helena's words 'Will you be mine now you are doubly wonne?' (v, iii, 315) reflect the old title ('upon which the curtain might well have closed' according to John Dover Wilson in the New Cambridge edition, p. vii) strikes me as no more convincing than the conceivable echo of *Won* in this line from *Much Ado*: 'heere *Claudio*, I haue wooed in thy name, and faire *Hero* is won' (II, i, 309–10).

[5] Gerald Sanders, *A Shakespeare Primer* (New York, 1950), p. 118. He adds: 'This identification,

preliminary draft of *All's Well That Ends Well* could ever have been a companion piece to *Love's Labour's Lost*. "The central situation of *All's Well*, the desperate venture of the indomitable Helena, would be intolerable if treated in the tone of easy banter that distinguishes *Love's Labour's Lost*."[1] Though Gray tries to answer Tolman's objections, he adds significantly that 'it is certainly demonstrable that a greater difference separates the reputedly early passages in *All's Well* from the undeniably early passages in *Love's Labour's Lost* than can justly be claimed for different passages within the play itself'.[2]

The arguments offered for *A Midsummer Night's Dream*, *The Taming of the Shrew*, and other comedies are even less convincing. And the conjecture that *Won* was simply another name of *Love's Labour's Lost* is simply that – a conjecture without foundation, though it apparently persuaded the German translator, who referred to *Love's Labour's Lost* as *Liebes Leid und Lust*.

Tolman's points regarding the identification of *Won* with *Much Ado* now need to be reconsidered. He shows that the claim was first made in print by A. E. Brae in *Beilage zur Allgemeinen Zeitung* for 14 January 1902.[3] First, he tackles the problem of the dating. How could *Won* have been *Much Ado* if *Won* existed in 1598 and *Much Ado* is first mentioned in 1600? He answers by showing that 'as Furness points out, the two other comedies which were published in 1600, *A Midsummer Night's Dream* and *The Merchant of Venice*, are found in Meres'.[4] Secondly, he indicates that 'Brae would apply the title *Love's Labour's Won* to the story of Benedick and Beatrice. The name *Much Ado About Nothing* plainly applies to the action of Claudio and Hero.'[5] (In this connection, is it possible that a former subtitle of *Much Ado* was *Benedick and Beatrice*? Tolman notes that 'the reference to a play "called Benedicte and Betteris" in an item in the Lord-

Treasurer Stanhope's Accounts for May 20, 1613, suggests "that the present title was not always adhered to"'.[6] I suspect, however, that this was a later subtitle, not the original one.) Tolman concludes: 'The ingenuity and plausibility of Brae's argument caused Fleay to abandon the view of Coleridge . . . In 1877, he declared that Brae had shown that *Much Ado* "is almost certainly the same as *Love's Labour's Won*". In 1866 he was less positive. In 1891 he thought *Much Ado* "probably a rewritten version of *Love's Labour's Won*". The additional arguments by which Fleay attempted in 1886 to strengthen Brae's view are ingenious but not valuable.'[7]

Brae's main arguments are summed up in the Variorum edition. Using Malone's suggestion that *Much Ado* 'formerly passed under the title of "Benedick and Beatrix"', Brae affirmed that *Much Ado* 'is a title that can have reference only to the accusation of Hero, and therefore there is a strong probability – directly confirmed by the above quotation from Malone –

however, is mere conjecture; the title would fit several other comedies as well as this play.'

[1] *The Original Version of 'Love's Labour's Lost' With a Conjecture as to 'Love's Labour's Won'* (Stanford, 1918), p. 44.

[2] *Ibid.*, p. 47. He is acceptably forthright: 'I refuse to believe that any student with an ear for Shakespeare's changing cadence came fresh from the study of *Love's Labour's Lost* and found in *All's Well* a single passage which reminded him of the earlier comedy' (p. 45). His argument favoring the *Won–Twelfth Night* identification (apparently original with him) is based on the separableness of the two plots – a point applying also to *Much Ado*.

[3] Trans. in *Collier, Coleridge, and Shakespeare* (London, 1860), pp. 131 ff. See excerpts in the *New Variorum Edition of Shakespeare Much Ado About Nothing*, ed. Horace Howard Furness (London, 1899), pp. 367–72.

[4] Tolman, *Views about 'Hamlet'*, p. 282.

[5] *Ibid.*

[6] *Ibid.* See Furness (ed.), New Variorum edition, *Much Ado*, pp. xxi, 368.

[7] *Ibid.*, pp. 291–2. I also see no point to be gained by recounting Fleay's additions.

that the present title of the play was not always adhered to'.[1] He added that 'the first and most prominent [of internal connections] is the similarity of the two principal characters in *Much Ado About Nothing*, to Biron and Rosaline in *Love's Labour's Lost*', that 'they have long been spoken of as *first sketch* and *finished portrait*'.[2] Brae himself would prefer the expression 'companion pictures'. Building upon this suggestion, he then provides some verbal echoes, e.g.:

Welcome, pure wit! thou partest a fair fray.
(*Lost*, v, ii, 539)

Welcome, Signior; you are almost come to part almost a fray. (*Much Ado*, v, i, 128)[3]

His main point, one to which Gray apparently is averse, is that the concept of Love in the title of the 'lost' play has to be understood mythologically: '*Love's Labours* in the dramatic writing of that time, would be much more likely to be understood as the gests or exploits of the *deity* Love, in the same sense as the fabled *Labours of Hercules* ... Biron exclaims, when the King enters love-stricken, "Proceed, sweet Cupid ..." In another place, Love is "*a Hercules* ..."' The connection with *Much Ado* is impressive. In that play, Don Pedro exclaims, 'I will undertake one of Hercules' labours, which is to bring Signior Benedick and the Lady Beatrice into a mountain of affection, the one with the other.' And Brae makes the grand finale: 'Here, then, in *Love's Labour's Won* (?), is the same literal reference to the *Labours of Hercules* as that before noted in *Love's Labour's Lost*!'[4]

In support of Brae and Tolman, I would add then to the following interesting remark of Tolman's:

It is a striking fact, which the present writer has not seen noted, that the comedies named by Meres, disregarding the uncertain *Love's Labour's Won*, are printed in the Folio in the order in which he names them, though not consecutively. This is made clear in the following table:

FOLIO ORDER	ORDER IN MERES
The Tempest	
Two Gentlemen of Verona	Two Gentlemen of Verona
The Merry Wives of Windsor	
Measure for Measure	
The Comedy of Errors	The Comedy of Errors
Much Ado About Nothing	
Love's Labour's Lost	Love's Labour's Lost
	Love's Labour's Won
A Midsummer Night's Dream	A Midsummer Night's Dream
The Merchant of Venice	The Merchant of Venice
As You Like It	
The Taming of the Shrew	
All's Well That Ends Well	
Twelfth Night	
The Winter's Tale[5]	

The most interesting feature of this table is that there is a block of five plays in the middle which relates to both the order in the 1623 Folio and the order in Meres. But one play is out of order in this block: *Love's Labour's Won*. To put the play back in order, it is necessary to remove it from its position following *Love's Labour's Lost* and place it in its natural position opposite *Much Ado*. Since the order found in both Meres and the Folio is not one of chronology, placing *Won* before *Lost* would in no wise be causing disarray. What is even more striking than the presentation of these parallel structures by Tolman is that he fails to draw the obvious conclusion from them, namely that which I have just posited. Perhaps Tolman had this in mind in his final conclusion that *Much Ado* remains one of the *two* best candidates for *Won*, but this consideration is doubtful since he then immediately states that

[1] See Furness (ed.), *Much Ado*, p. 368.
[2] *Ibid.*
[3] *Ibid.*, p. 369. Further echoes are cited.
[4] *Ibid.*, p. 370.
[5] Tolman, *Views about 'Hamlet'*, p. 267. (The broken arrow is mine.)

The Taming of the Shrew would seem to have the better claim, a position which he would scarcely take today (because of the finding of the stocklist).

It appears then that the case for *Much Ado* being the same as *Won* is extremely strong, or at least better than that of any other candidate. I now intend to present final confirmatory evidence.

II

Earlier I have stated that there may have been a reason why *Won* would have been registered as *Much Ado*, or by its subtitle, and that that reason could have had something to do with the punning inherent in the latter title. It is, initially, possible that the actors apparently enjoyed the buffoonery in the comedy as associated with the subtitle and may have preferred to have had the play registered in this manner. But what lends particular weight to this point is that the *occasion* of the play's having been registered in the century-year 1600 lent itself easily to another titular pun: 'A doo' and 'a Doo' stand as puns on '1600 *Anno Domini*'.

The problem might now be raised of whether this effect is not too anomalous for Shakespeare. Well it might have been! In spite of the numerous puns on the zero throughout his plays, as in *Two Gentlemen of Verona, King Lear*, and particularly in the Prologue to act 1 of *Henry V*, I am perfectly willing to concede that the occasion for *Won* being registered as *Much Ado* had more to do with the likings of the players than with the dramatist himself. Since he, too, was an actor, he would have understood their predilections for verbal fun. All in all, then, the appeal of the pun was, let us say, to the clientele of the Mermaid.

There is, moreover, another pun inherent in the association of *Won* with *Much Ado*. Is it not noticeable that a play originally called *Love's Labour's Won; or, Much Ado About Nothing* would contain a play upon the words *Won* and *Nothing?* There is the additional alliteration behind the word-play (*Love's Labour's | Ado About*), but the significance of the *Won | Nothing* contrast is not only that it builds upon the time-honored theme of the apparent versus the real (a theme suggested also by the natural contrast of love's labour that is *lost* and *won*), but that it has a foundation in Renaissance numerology. Since the Elizabethans, following the medieval tradition, loved to resort to numerological explanations and devices in their compositions (as evident particularly in Spenser), it is only normal that Shakespeare would have fitted into the same pattern. Numerologically, the contrast between *Won* ('One') and *Nothing* is that between Being and Non-Being, that which is (and by existing is intrinsically unified too) and that which is not, which at best is only potentially existent.[1] Donne punned on something similar when he wrote in his *Nocturnal Upon St Lucy's Day* of the very 'quintessence of nothingness', paradoxically linking up number (*Quinta Essentia*) with nought.

[1] Because of the extraordinary interest in numerology in the Middle Ages and Renaissance, the possibility of deliberate word-play on 1/0 should not be dismissed, though I do not claim to be in an authoritative position to adjudicate upon the extent of recent studies in the numerological arena to determine whether a given author or scholar has provided the more basic input. Alastair Fowler's insistence (in *Triumphal Forms: Structural Patterns in Elizabethan Poetry* [Cambridge, 1970]) on authorial intent appears salutary; however, psychological predilection for certain numbers need not have been conscious. I have had the good fortune to have had another 'numerologist' in this area, A. Kent Hieatt, confirm for me the essential value of the point made in the present study. Cf. Shakespeare's use of word-play on *one* and *none* (as in Sonnet 8 and in *Measure for Measure*, II, iv, 135–6, where the play's title itself lends weight to the counterpoint by suggesting the need for numerical balance and contrast). For further comment, see my article on Chaucer's use of number forthcoming in *The Chaucer Review*, vol. 8, no. 3.

Moreover, if the *Won / Nothing* word-play was intended, as expressive of the Renaissance fondness for paradox as well as numerology, there is a hint that Shakespeare well knew what he was about. For the use of *Nothing* in a subtitle conveys a contrast with the concept of everything (namely, the word *All*) in the 'sub-title' to yet another play of his, *Henry VIII* (*All is True*). Such punning in subtitles is also evident in the subtitle to *Twelfth Night* (*What You Will*). For the suggestion may be not only that the audience may accept what it wants, or that rather the dramatist has discerned in advance what the audience wants, but that what the audience *wills* is precisely what it will have from *Will*.

In designating the occasion of *Much Ado*, then, I refer not to the occasion of Shake-speare's writing of the play, or even to its first performance, but to the occasion of the selection of the subtitle as revealed in the quarto. By the time the Folio was published, the pun on 'a Doo' had either worn thin or been forgotten, and at any rate Shakespeare was no longer at hand to point it out; hence the double 'o' was conservatively changed to 'oe' and the result was *Adoe*. (In the table of contents the earlier spelling is retained.)

My final plea is that since Shakespeare's original or main title made more intrinsic sense than the way the play was registered, the modern producer attempting to remain faithful to the original intent of the dramatist might easily, and validly, switch the title back from the (silly) *Much Ado About Nothing* to *Love's Labour's Won*.

THE DATE AND PRODUCTION OF 'TIMON' RECONSIDERED

JAMES C. BULMAN, JR

I

The comedy known as the 'old *Timon*' is of interest largely because of its possible connection with *Timon of Athens*.[1] Numerous similarities between the two plays have been traced to Lucian's dialogue *Misanthropos*: Timon's extravagant spending; his payment of a friend's debt to release the friend from prison; his loss of wealth and subsequent discovery of gold in the earth; the reappearance of his parasitic friends to feign generosity when he no longer needs it; his driving them away with a spade; and the final implication that his prodigality was unwise and his choice of friends, indiscriminate. All these similarities suggest that both Shakespeare and the anonymous author (or authors; the MS., written in alternating Italian and Secretary hands, indicates that the play may have been a collaboration) had either direct or indirect access to Lucian.[2]

But the two plays have a number of similarities which cannot be accounted for by their sharing of a source – neither Lucian, nor Plutarch, nor any Renaissance treatment of the Timon legend.[3] Among these similarities are a strong emphasis on Timon in prosperity (three acts in each play); scenes in which his parasitic friends refuse to reciprocate his generosity; a mock-banquet at which Timon, destitute, rails at them (he pelts them with stones painted as artichokes in *Timon*; in *Timon of Athens*, stones undisguised); and the pre-

sence of a faithful steward who remonstrates against his extravagance, follows him into exile, and helps him to drive off the parasites.[4] The extent of these similarities, covering as they do structure as well as content, implies a

1 The play survives as MS. 52 of the Dyce Collection at the Victoria and Albert Museum. It was edited by Dyce for publication by The Shakespeare Society (London, 1842) and was reprinted in Hazlitt, *Shakespeare Library* (London, 1875), VI. All page numbers refer to Dyce. The present article is the result of research done at the University College of Wales, where I worked with Mr J. M. Nosworthy on an edition of *Timon* for The Malone Society. I have benefited greatly from Mr Nosworthy's numerous suggestions, the most important of which are recorded in the notes. Professor Eugene M. Waith of Yale University also has given me helpful criticism and guidance.

2 Joseph Quincy Adams, Jr, 'The Timon Plays', *The Journal of English and Germanic Philology*, 9 (1910), 506–24, details the debts of both Shakespeare and 'Anonymous' to Lucian. For brief summaries of Shakespeare's use of all the Timon sources, see the New Cambridge edition of *Timon of Athens*, ed. J. C. Maxwell (Cambridge, 1957), pp. xiv–xxii, and the New Arden edition, ed. H. J. Oliver (London, 1959), pp. xxxii–xl.

3 The legend has been traced from Lucian and Plutarch through the Renaissance by Willard Farnham, *Shakespeare's Tragic Frontier* (Berkeley, 1950), pp. 50–67.

4 George Steevens, *Shakspere* (20 vols., London, 1788), XVII, Annotations pp. 3–4, was the first to remark upon the similarities between the two plays. Malone repeated Steevens's observations some years later; and more recently, R. Warwick Bond, 'Lucian and Boiardo in *Timon of Athens*', *Modern Language Review*, 26 (1931), 65–6, has adequately summarized the major parallels exclusive to *Timon* and *Timon of Athens*.

more than coincidental relationship between the plays.

The question posed by such similarities is, of course, one of influence. Was one Timon play influenced by the other? If so, did Shakespeare borrow from 'Anonymous', or 'Anonymous' from Shakespeare? It is important for anyone trying to answer this question first to establish the date and production of the 'old *Timon*'.

Until recently, scholars have tended to date *Timon* earlier than *Timon of Athens*. Steevens conjectured, without citing evidence, that 'it appears to have been written, or transcribed, about the year 1600' (p. 3). G. C. Moore Smith, who regarded it as a university play influenced by Wingfield's *Pedantius*, dated it accordingly between 1581 and 1590;[1] and Adams, who agreed that it was a school play but thought it closer to *Roister Doister* in style, assigned it a date 'somewhat earlier' than 1600 (p. 511). Most notably, H. C. Hart found enough parallels between *Timon* and Ben Jonson's three 'comicall satyres' to conclude that *Timon* influenced Jonson and must have been written prior to 1599, when *Every Man Out of His Humour* was first performed.[2]

The evidence for dating *Timon* so early has stuck like a thorn in the side of many a Shakespearian who has been unwilling to believe that Shakespeare could have borrowed from so 'wretched' a piece.[3] It is generally agreed that Shakespeare wrote *Timon of Athens* sometime between 1604 and 1609.[4] Those who accept the earlier date of the 'old *Timon*' either have neglected to mention the possibility of Shakespeare's debt to it or have hidden behind the assumption that it was an academic play which Shakespeare never could have seen. Steevens was the first to call it 'the work of an academick' (p. 4); and Dyce soon added that it 'was certainly never performed in the metropolis' (p. vii). Moore Smith thought that *Timon* was acted only at Cambridge (p. 143); and more

recently, Georges A. Bonnard argued that such a play would never have been produced in London.[5] Geoffrey Bullough summarized these opinions in his discussion of Shakespeare's sources: 'It is unlikely that Shakespeare could ever have known the academic *Timon*, since there is no evidence that it was played publicly or at the Inns of Court.'[6]

[1] 'Notes on Some English University Plays', *Modern Language Review*, 3 (1907–8), 143.

[2] *The Works of Ben Jonson*, ed. H. C. Hart (2 vols., London, 1906), I, xliii–xlvi; II, vii–xi. The best study of the Jonsonian parallels since Hart (and this, too, by no means exhaustive) was made by C. H. Herford and Percy and Evelyn Simpson (eds.), *Ben Jonson* (11 vols., Oxford, 1925–52), IX, 482–5, Appendix XX. Hereafter I shall refer to this standard edition of Jonson by the abbreviation H & S.

[3] The epithet is Steevens's. It has stuck to the play, and perhaps unfairly, for there are many scenes of good comedy.

[4] Maxwell follows the lead of Raleigh (1907) in assigning a date to *Timon of Athens* near to that of *King Lear* (1604) and in allowing for the possibility that it may have been written before *Lear*. Oliver argues, on the other hand, that Shakespeare's use of Plutarch as a source for *Timon* indicates a date nearer to that of *Coriolanus* (1608). E. A. J. Honigmann, 'Timon of Athens', *Shakespeare Quarterly*, 12 (1961), 3–20, who bases a large part of his argument on Shakespeare's use of Plutarch's 'Life of Marcus Antonius' in *Timon*, assumes throughout that it was written about the time of the two later Roman plays.

[5] 'Note sur les Sources de *Timon of Athens*', *Études Anglaises*, 7 (1954), 59–69. I ought to note that Adams, on the basis of a few scattered 'city' references, allows that *Timon* may have been suitable for a London audience ('The Timon Plays', pp. 511–12). But this allowance is incidental to his argument that it was primarily a school play.

[6] *Narrative and Dramatic Sources of Shakespeare* (London, 1957–), VI, 235. Maxwell, the one scholar who does confront the issue of Shakespeare's debt head-on, comes unwillingly to this conclusion: 'With some reluctance, I am inclined to suppose, then, that Shakespeare somehow came across the anonymous play. If it was a London school play, as Adams thinks, he could have been dragged to see it by some fond father of his acquaintance' (p. xxi). C. F. Tucker Brooke, *The Tudor Drama* (Boston, 1911), pp. 410–11, acknowledges Shakespeare's probable debt to *Timon* but, like Maxwell, neglects to analyze that debt in detail.

One alternative to which scholars have turned is to date *Timon* later than *Timon of Athens*. This alternative has allowed them to assume that 'Anonymous' borrowed from Shakespeare. Its weakness is that there has been virtually no evidence for them to go on. Bond, who betrayed his attitude towards *Timon* in the remark, 'I felt bound to notice it', openly sought ways to circumvent the issue of Shakespeare's debt: the most convenient way was simply to declare 'Anonymous' the debtor (p. 66). Bonnard seized upon this declaration and bolstered it with further 'proofs' of 'Anonymous's' indebtedness to *King Lear*.[1] Bullough followed suit and dated *Timon* after *Timon of Athens* and the first Quarto of *King Lear* (VI, 235).

Oliver merely repeated the frustration of many scholars when he resorted to speculation about 'a common source', now lost, in order to explain the troublesome similarities between the two plays (p. xxxix). Adams had mentioned this 'common source' as a possibility fraught with difficulties (p. 522). Bond blithely adopted it as his second alternative (p. 66); and Bonnard thought that he had found it in a tale from the *Arabian Nights* (pp. 65ff.). Perhaps Honigmann stated the case of previous scholars most honestly when he admitted, 'since Shakespeare's *Timon* remained apparently unperformed, and unpublished till 1623, since the academic MS. *Timon* would be equally unheard-of, a lost common source might be the easiest explanation of the surprising links between the two plays' (p. 4).

In 1966 M. C. Bradbrook cut through this critical quagmire by arguing persuasively that *Timon* (*pace* Bullough) was a reveling play of the Inner Temple.[2] Citing topical evidence of a 'city' performance, she successfully countered Honigmann's assertion that *Timon* was 'unheard of' and reopened, by implication, the question of Shakespeare's borrowing. Her theory, if true, certainly would make it possible for Shakespeare to have seen *Timon*; but he cannot be said to have used *Timon* as a source for *Timon of Athens* until it is proven that the former predated the latter.

Unfortunately, Bradbrook could not resist speculating that 'Anonymous' was attempting to burlesque Shakespeare's play; and largely owing to this speculation, she dated *Timon c. 1611*. Her argument is based on the flimsy assumption that if two plays of discrepant quality have many points of contact, the worse play must have been written in imitation of the better. Her illogic, which amounts to little more than bardolatry, informs many statements such as this: 'The satiric intentions of the first part of Shakespeare's tragic pageant might have been within this author's grasp, but the lyric ending was quite beyond him . . .' (p. 102). The same attitude prevailed among scholars before her.

I find Bradbrook's article disturbing because it opens and closes the door in one motion. It prepares us to accept Shakespeare's indebtedness to 'Anonymous' only to conclude the opposite. I intend to address myself to two of her conclusions: to substantiate her Inns of Court theory with fresh evidence of my own, and to refute her dating of *Timon* by reassessing the strongest evidence we have to go on, the Jonsonian parallels.

II

Bradbrook found ample evidence within *Timon* itself to support her claim that it was performed during Christmas revels at the Inner Temple. She had no external proof. A

[1] Bonnard, 'Note sur les Sources', p. 65, cites Steevens's discovery of a parallel between Laches and Kent. Recently Robert Hilles Goldsmith, 'Did Shakespeare Use the Old *Timon* Comedy?', *Shakespeare Quarterly*, 9 (1958), 31–8, managed to dredge up a few more parallels between *Timon* and *Lear* but concluded, contrary to Bonnard, that Shakespeare was the borrower.

[2] '*The Comedy of Timon*: A Reveling Play of the Inner Temple', *Renaissance Drama*, 9 (1966), 83–103.

few of the allusions she located seem to me indisputable; others, more tenuous. Taken all together, however, they provide fairly conclusive evidence for her case.

She gleaned her best evidence from one scene which is so crammed full of 'Inn' allusions that it reads like a parody of the traditional mock-court. At Christmastime the barristers of each Inn would appoint their own royalty – often a Prince of Misrule and his attendant courtiers – to hold court until Candelmas. It was the duty of the Prince to issue edicts (parodies of court rhetoric), make state visits to other Inns, host banquets and provide dramatic entertainments.[1] The investiture of Timon with mock-royal prerogative in II, v is, as Bradbrook observes, an unmistakable allusion to the Christmas revels. His parasitic friend Eutrapelus declares,

> Thee, Timon, wee electe as soueraigne,
> Prince and commander of these Bacchanales:
> What lawes dost thou ordaine? (p. 37)

Timon's ordinance that all men 'Drinke much at one draughte, breathe not in their drinke; / That none goe out to pisse, that none doe spew / In any corner' reflects the kind of youthful delight in vulgarity which still characterizes the ordinances of fraternity initiations in America. 'Such laws', comments Bradbrook, 'were commonly enacted at Christmas Revels' (p. 89).

Bradbrook notices legal metaphors in an earlier scene but neglects to connect them with Timon's role as a Christmas prince. It seems to me that these metaphors create a network of satirical commentary on the very nature of the revels. The language at the opening of the play portrays Timon in his princely capacity as assessor of 'benevolences'. It was the duty of a mock-prince and his steward (a prominent character in *Timon* named Laches) to collect enough money from the member barristers to

be able to finance the Christmas entertainments. Laches, having collected the 'rents', warns Timon not to be too prodigal with them:

> *Timon.* Laches, hast thou receau'd my rents?
> *Laches.* Master, I haue,
> And brought in sacks filled with goulden talents:
> Is't your pleasure that I cast them into pryson?
> *Timon.* Into pryson! whye soe?
> *Laches.* Lett your chests be the pryson,
> Your locks the keeper, and your keyes the porter,
> Otherwise they'le fly away, swyfter then birds or
> wyndes.
> (I, i, p. 3)

Timon strengthens the thrust of Laches's metaphor by answering, annoyed, 'I'st euen soe, my learned counsaylor?'; to which Laches, chidden, responds by glancing at legal ethics: 'I'le as silent bee / As any counsaylor without his ffee.' Laches will not be silenced, however, until he once more has admonished Timon in language which strongly suggests Timon's role as a Christmas prince:

> Who beares a princelie mynd needes princelie
> wealth,
> Or ells hee'le wither like a rose in springe,
> Nought wilbe left but thornes of povertie.
> Master, thou art noe kinge, noe prince; doe well
> Vnto thie selfe, and all is well. (pp. 3–4)

[1] Three accounts of the Christmas revels provide virtually all the information extant: *Accedence of Armorie* (London, 1562), a description of the Inner Temple revels of 1561 by member Gerard Legh; the *Gesta Grayorum* (Malone Society Reprints, 1914) which details the activities of Henry Prince of Purpoole in 1594; and *Le Prince d'Amour*, an account of the Middle Temple revels of 1599, published by Sir Benjamin Rudyerd (London, 1660). A. Wigfall Green, *The Inns of Court and Early English Drama* (New Haven, 1931) is a good history of Inns' entertainment; and Philip J. Finkelpearl has written about the revels in his study of *John Marston of the Middle Temple* (Harvard, 1969).

Laches's point is that Timon ought to be aware that he is but playing a part, and that his funds, like his royal prerogative, are limited by his constituents. It is a realistic corrective which he urges upon Timon throughout the play: 'thou art noe kinge, noe prince'.

Charity, according to Green, was of major concern to the Templars (pp. 38–9). Timon himself extols charity frequently: 'Lett poore men somewhat take of my greate plenty . . . I will not see / My pensive freinds to pyne with penurie' (p. 3). We soon discover, however, that the recipients of his charity – these 'pensive freinds' about whom he puns — are not the needy, but reveling parasites who encourage him to spend:

> Why walk'st thou not the streetes?
> Thou scarce art knowne in tenn tavernes yett:
> Subdue the world with gould . . .   (I, ii, p. 5)

The hypocrisy of these 'city' squanderers is essential to the play's satire of legal types.

Lollio, a country clown whom Timon and his companions encounter outside a tavern, is totally ignorant of city affectation. His response to the group of gentlemen before him is humorously naive:

> Joue blesse mee, how many diuells are here!
> Are they philosophers or brabbling lawiers?
> They looke with such soure faces.   (II, v, p. 36)

If the gentlemen in fact were lawyers, the joke would be complete. Timon's answer is, as Bradbrook says, 'a claim which the Templars might feel disposed to put forward' (p. 94): 'Say wee are / The prime men of the cittie.' Lollio persists ignorantly in his legal jest – 'Will they not imprisonne mee?' – and remarks pointedly upon their strange attire – 'What daintie burds doe zitte vppon their hatts!' – a possible allusion to headdress worn during the revels.[1]

Perhaps the most telling clue of all to *Timon*'s being an Inns of Court play is '*The signe of the 7 stars*', which Lollio mistakes for the heavenly Plough: 'Lord, Lord, / How many starres see I! how nere they are!' (p. 36). Pseudocheus's deflating comment, 'Thy hande may touche them with a ladders helpe', assures us that the sign was meant to be the signboard of a tavern; and that the prop itself was fairly prominent in the production is evidenced by the insertion of '7 stars' in Italian hand above the original stage direction (in Secretary) on folio 10 recto, a note probably made during rehearsal.[2] My interest in this allusion to a tavern was spurred when the porter of Lincoln's Inn directed me to a tavern called 'The Seven Stars' on Carey Street, bordering the south wall of Lincoln's Inn. 'Formerly "The Leg (League) and Seven Stars" denoting the United Provinces of the Netherlands', reads a plaque inside, it is said to be the 'Magpie and Stump' of *The Pickwick Papers*. A sign hanging outside the door, showing seven stars on a background of blue, claims that the tavern was opened in 1602. This sign is quite likely a fair copy of all previous signs; there is no reason to doubt the veracity of the date that appears on it. If this is the sign to which Lollio refers – the one beneath which the 'brabbling lawiers' have congregated –

---

[1] Bradbrook, '*The Comedy of Timon*', p. 94, cites a passage from William Dugdale, *Origines Juridiciales* (3rd edn, London, 1680), p. 155, to support her claim that Lollio's remark is a topical allusion: 'In the Grand Christmas of the Inner Temple the Constable-Marshall and the Lieutenant of the Tower are both enjoined to wear "a Nest of feather of all colours upon his Crest or Helm" . . . for the sports of St. Stephen's Day.'

[2] Dyce, p. vi, has found an additional stage direction in v, ii which indicates that the play was actually performed. This direction, which once was '*Enter* TIMON *and* LACHES *with either a spade in their hands*', was changed to '*Enter* TIMON *and* LACHES *with* 3 *spades in their hands*', because a third was needed for Gelasimus when he joined their misanthropic digging later in the scene. This change presumably would only have been made during rehearsal, when the technical problems of production were being worked out.

then the author, as Mr Nosworthy suggested to me, may have been making a topical allusion to a new tavern, and perhaps a tavern popular with the Templars.[1]

It is to Lollio that Timon abdicates his throne and dedicates the ensuing revels:

> Wee longe haue look'd for such a one, whom wee
> Might substitute prince ore the whole country . . .
> This day shall bee a day of sporte and mirthe:
> Bring cuppes of wine; let's welcome our new
> prince.
> (II, v, p. 37)

The mock-heroic revels which Lollio instigates in his turn are similar to those of the more un-ruly Christmas princes. I surmise that young barristers were freer to enjoy this form of revelry within the context of a play such as *Timon* than in the actions of the mock-court itself. Lollio's revelers will devote themselves entirely to drink: 'Weele celebrate the feaste of Bacchus. / To make thee prince, I crowne thee with this bole' (p. 38). Their riot soon runs to bawdy song, a kind of humor indigenous to an exclusively male society:

> Shee alone is amiable,
>   My Sophrony, my Sophrony
> Shee shee alone is tractable
>   ffeele her cony, feele her cony
> Shee is not angry, touche her lippes
> Or els descende betweene her hippes . . .[2]

Adolescent bawdy such as this is present throughout *Timon*. Lollio quickly pushes on to a merrygreek impersonation of Homeric heroes, himself as Achilles and Gelasimus, a city fop, as Hector. This mock-heroism takes on a satirical edge only if it is regarded as the *reductio ad absurdum* of a Christmas court, a burlesque of a burlesque.

The emphasis on food and drink in *Timon* seems more than accidentally akin to Inns' revels.[3] The primary purpose of a Christmas prince was to organize banquets. The menus often were sumptuous; and it is not surprising

that a great percentage of a prince's revenue was spent on food.[4] In *Timon*, the *carpe diem* philosophy behind such banquets is stressed early:

> *Eutrapelus.*
> Wee ffeede on partidge, pheazant, plover, quaile,
> Snipes, woodcocks, larks, ambrosia it selfe.
> *Timon.*
> Is not he madd, that carefullie doth watch
> A thowsand heapes of wheate, and dares not tast
> One graine thereof? or he that drincketh lees,
> Having his cellours fraught with pleasing wynes?
> I'le vse my treasure, and possesse my wealth,
> And spend my dayes in pleasure whilst I lyue . . .
> (I, v, p. 17)

It is logical in context that when Timon plans to avenge himself upon his parasites, he thinks at once of a mock-banquet as a means to insure that they will flock to his house. The way in which they are depicted waiting gluttonously around Timon's table, savoring the thoughts of what foods are to be set before them, may be read as a satire on the Templars' greedy appreciation of their own banquets.[5]

Bradbrook interprets the main plot of *Timon* as follows: 'The story offers a satiric

[1] 'C.T.S.', in a note in *Notes and Queries*, 192 (1947), 236, claims that a list of over twenty-five inns in London with the name 'Seven Stars' can easily be drawn up. Unfortunately, he fails to mention the period to which he is referring.

[2] This verse of the song was discreetly deleted by Dyce, along with several other obscene passages.

[3] Bradbrook, '*The Comedy of Timon*', pp. 95–6, compares the importance of butlers at the revels with the importance of butlers in *Timon*. Lollio, as prince, makes butlers of his whole coterie; and Obba, Timon's butler, plays a sizable part in the banquet scenes.

[4] Green, *The Inns of Court*, pp. 59–60, quotes an extensive food budget from one of these banquets.

[5] See IV, v, p. 72. Honigmann thinks that the banquet scene and the importance of food and drink in *Timon of Athens* were inspired indirectly by Lucian; and he regards them as particularly relevant to his theory that Shakespeare wrote *Timon* as an Inns of Court play (p. 18). But food and drink and the mock-banquet are equally important in the 'old *Timon*' and could easily have served as models for Shakespeare.

reflection of the sports of a Christmas Lord, who often overspent his wealth and at the end of his "reign" became an ordinary student once more' (p. 102). I think her interpretation can be taken further. The plot not only traces the fortune of a Christmas prince from wealth to poverty, but also satirizes rather scathingly the ungenerous nature of many participants in the revels. The 'rents' which Timon collects are ravenously devoured in a feast of parasites. When the 'rents' are used up, the parasites leave their prince, refuse to contribute to his coffers, censure his prodigality, and do not even acknowledge him as an acquaintance (indicative, perhaps, that a prince is no prince if he cannot support his court). Those who enjoy the revels most are those who are least willing to contribute to them: this point is dramatized by Philargurus who, I suggest, is meant to represent a Bencher. He presumes to read Timon a moral lesson on profligacy, as Benchers often did to a Christmas prince –

> Base pouertie doth followe luxury:
> Get home, and liue by mending of olde shoes;
> Spende not whole daies in drunken Bacchus
> cuppes . . .
>
> (III, v, p. 56)

– yet he is the first in line to accept Timon's bounty. If this play was written by a student at the Inns as a topical entertainment, then satire such as this would have been warmly appreciated.

Legal satire does not stop at the main plot, however. *Timon* has a prominent sub-plot involving the gulling of Gelasimus by an opportunist called Pseudocheus in which there are a number of allusions to the Inns. At the outset, Gelasimus voices his vain ambition to be an Areopagite:

> *Gelasimus.* Ha, ha, he! my wytty knaue, dost thinck I shall euer be an Areopagite?
> *Paedio.* But stay awhile till your beard growe bigger; otherwise old men wilbe ashamed to be ouer-

come in counsayle and vnderstanding by one that is barbatulous. (I, iii, p. 9)

The Areopagite here described is probably intended to be a caricature of a Bencher (note that he is involved 'in counsayle'). My interpretation is supported by one further reference to the illustrious body of judges, when the Lucianic orator Demeas, hoping for a reward of gold, vows to speak on Timon's behalf before them: 'Heare, my humane Jupiter, the decree that I haue written concerning thee before the Areopagites' (p. 92). If Timon represents a Christmas prince who has incurred the disfavor of the Benchers by being too extravagant, then Demeas's attempt to intercede for him would be humorously topical.[1]

Pseudocheus has no difficulty in gulling Gelasimus with his tales of adventure and romance.[2] In exchange for a golden ring, he offers Gelasimus a brass one which he claims to have been given by the king of the Antipodes at a banquet:

> *Pseudocheus.* They all amazed were,
> Admire, concurre; they bringe me to theire kinge,
> Where I was feasted, plac'd at his right hand.
> *Gelasimus.* For honours sake.
> *Pseudocheus.* When I departed thence,
> This ring he gaue me.
> *Gelasimus.* Prythee, lett me se it.
> Wilt thou that wee exchainge, my Pylades?
>
> (I, iv, pp. 14–15)

---

[1] A literary club which is now called the 'Areopagus' and which had among its membership men such as Spenser, Harvey, Sidney, Dyer, and Greville, attempted to reform English prosody at the end of the sixteenth century. In a letter to Harvey, Spenser referred to the club in Greek as the 'Areopagus'; but the term may have been merely Spenser's private jest about a 'literary court', and not a name by which the club was known to contemporaries. An allusion to this literary Areopagus would have little point in *Timon*.

[2] Adams demonstrates that many of Pseudocheus's tales were stolen from Lucian's *The True History*, a parody of the old Greek historians.

The gift of rings, I think, was inspired by the Inns' custom that a sergeant at law, when selected, feast his fellow barristers lavishly and bestow rings upon his officers.[1]

Bradbrook ascribes the play to the Inner Temple because Pegasus, of which so much is made in scenes between Gelasimus and Pseudocheus, constitutes the arms of the Inner Temple. I need not repeat her findings here. The various references to the flying horse as a means of transportation to the Antipodes, silly in themselves, come alive with implication when regarded as references to heraldry. As Bradbrook remarks, 'Such a burlesque of the arms of the Inn as Gelasimus shows in his proposed ride on Pegasus would have point and be tolerable only at the Inner Temple' (p. 91).[2]

Numerous other references to law and lawyers are scattered through the play, none of any major importance but all contributing to the satire. Law is associated with usury. Abyssus threatens Eutraprelus, 'Our controuersye law shall soone decide ... I'le make thee looke wormes through the pryson grates, / Vnlesse thou satisfie to me my debt / In good and lawfull mony' (p. 6.) Gelasimus twice invokes the law: once to threaten Timon with a suit for having soiled his new clothes; and once to convey his possessions to Abyssus in a deed which is set out with considerable relish:

... a thousand acres of lande with the appurtenances, all goods and chattells, moueable and immoueable, aliue and deade, of kinde and condicion whatsoeuer, in the possession of any whosoeuer, in any place wheresoeur ...

(IV, ii, p. 61)

Such elaborate mockery of legal rhetoric would have been especially appealing to members of the Inns. In context, the deed makes a satirical barb at law as the protector of vice. Lawyers are interested only in money ('I'le as silent bee / As any counsaylor without his ffee'); and to be in debt is the worst felony of all ('I hate a man that's poore; hees worse than any homicide'). The import of these allusions to law in the sub-plot fits into the pattern of allusion in the main plot and strengthens the contention between money and law in the reign of a Christmas prince.

Having examined the evidence for regarding *Timon* as an Inns of Court play, I now must re-examine the old allegation that it was an academic play. Moore Smith assigned it to the school of *Pedantius* on the basis of a single academic chestnut. Demeas, arguing his way out of arrest, calls himself 'an orator not an arator'; *Pedantius* has the line in Latin, '*Sciebam me Oratorem, non Aratorem ... esse.*'[3] This evidence is too insubstantial by far to classify *Timon* as an academic play; yet Herford and Simpson repeated Moore Smith's conclusion without question.[4] Adams's reason

[1] Green devotes a section of his book (*The Inns of Court*, pp. 48–52) to the Sergeants' Feast. 'The newly elected sergeant was expected to entertain lavishly', says Green. 'Often, apparently following the custom of the Anglo-Saxon host of giving rings to his guests, the sergeants made gifts of valuable rings, instead of money, to the sovereign and to each of his administrative officers' (p. 49).

[2] D. S. Bland, 'Pegasus at the Inner Temple', *Notes and Queries*, 214 (1969), 16–18, argues that the use of Pegasus as a crest for the Inner Temple stems from the revels of 1561 (those recorded by Legh), for which Robert Dudley, having intervened successfully on behalf of the Inner Temple in a property dispute with the Middle Temple, was elected Master of Revels. Conceding that Pegasus was not an especially suitable choice for a legal crest, Bland suggests that the Templars were very casual in 'adopting and formalizing their insignia'. Nosworthy cautions that the manifold references to Pegasus in *Timon* may be the way in which *another* Inn paid a compliment (or worse) to the Inner Temple.

[3] Moore Smith, 'Notes on Some English University Plays', p. 143. The device was a common one in plays of this period: cf. *The Merry Wives of Windsor*, 'proverbes and no-verbes'; or *The Two Angry Women of Abingdon*, 'my death-bed not my breath-bed'.

[4] Briefly listing a few Greek and Latin quotations from *Timon*, H & S judge that 'the style of writing is quite unfitted for the London stage' (IX, 482–3).

for linking *Timon* with *Roister Doister* was similarly weak: certain characters in both plays, he said, are Plautine types (p. 510). Bond considered *Timon* a 'university play' because its author apparently was familiar with Plautus, reproduced parts of Lucian's dialogues, and misquoted an iambic line of Greek preserved by Suetonius (pp. 64–5).

Steevens was right to regard *Timon* as 'academick', for the scholarly allusions and use of classical sources make it so. But subsequent scholars have erred in narrowing the meaning of the word 'academick' to include no more than 'school-plays'. Bonnard's comment is typical of what has happened:

Cette comédie est manifestement l'oeuvre d'un 'pédant' d'un universitaire . . . Il est inconcevable que son auteur ait pu la composer pour le public des théâtres londoniens. Elle n'a pu être jouée, si elle l'a jamais été, que par des étudiants ou des écoliers et pour divertir leurs camarades. Elle appartient au genre des 'school-plays'. (p. 63)

Bradbrook corrects this narrowing of 'academick' by incorporating it into her Inns of Court theory. The Inns were, after all, institutions of higher learning in which the study of literature was second only to the study of law. Finkelpearl shows that nearly half the members of the Inns at this time (1587 to 1603) had attended Oxford or Cambridge (pp. 6–7).

In a society as well-educated as that of the Inns, some mockery of scholarship and university dons was probably expected in the course of the revels. The two philosophers in *Timon* (one of whom is called a 'peripatetick' because he walks) are exuberant lampoons of what then passed for philosophy teachers; and Demeas accurately parodies the Ciceronian rhetoric which was then being taught in school. Even Gelasimus makes a sarcastic reference to the universities: 'I am noe Academian, noe ffoole' (p. 21).

All the references in *Timon* to Lucian, Homer, Horace, Juvenal and Plautus would have been readily recognized at the Inns. The mythological paraphernalia so often incorporated into the revels – Pegasus and the Prince of Palaphilos (Lover of Pallas) at the Inner Temple, for instance – indicates how classically oriented the Inns were. Classical themes, in fact, were regularly used as vehicles for topical satire in Inns of Court plays. The near-certainty that Shakespeare's *Troilus and Cressida* was written for the Inns confirms the appropriateness of classical motifs to an erudite society of lawyers.[1] The legend of Timon, derived from an already satirical dialogue by Lucian, was an ideal vehicle for some young lawyer's wit.

III

Since Hart first recognized a few parallels between *Timon* and Jonson's 'comicall satyres', a minor critical battle has been waged over whether 'Anonymous' borrowed from Jonson, or Jonson from 'Anonymous'. Hart thought that 'the play belongs to the "War of the Theaters" series' as an antecedent to Jonson's plays (*Works of Ben Jonson*, I, xliv). But if Jonson borrowed from *Timon*, the borrowing was spread very thinly over three plays – far more diffusely than if 'Anonymous' echoed Jonson's three in his one. Tucker Brooke decided that the plays must have had a common source (*Tudor Drama*, p. 411, note).[2] But in another camp, Herford and Simpson argued that it was nonsense to think that Jonson

[1] Peter Alexander, 'Troilus and Cressida 1609', *The Library*, 4 (1948), 267, was the first to suggest that *Troilus* was written for performance at the Inns. Leslie Hotson, *Shakespeare's Sonnets Dated* (London, 1949), pp. 37–56, argues a strong case for assigning it to the Middle Temple. He dates *Troilus* c. 1598; the consensus among scholars, however, is 1601–2. Either date allows for the possibility that *Troilus* influenced the merrygreek scenes in *Timon*.

[2] Bradbrook misrepresents Brooke when she says that he posited a common source for *Timon* and *Timon of Athens* ('The Comedy of Timon', p. 83, note).

borrowed from *Timon*: 'The idea of his using it as a dramatic quarry is grotesque – only less grotesque than the suggestion that Shakespeare used it' (H & S, IX, 485).

The verification of *Timon* as an Inns of Court play, I contend, greatly increases the likelihood that 'Anonymous' deliberately echoed Jonson; for, though not a member of an Inn, Jonson was closely associated with the Inns' literary circles. Among his friends at the Inns were, no doubt, John Donne; his 'chamber-fellow' Christopher Brooke; John Hoskyns, his 'intellectual father' according to tradition; and Richard Martin, the distinguished lawyer and wit who saved Jonson from prosecution for *Poetaster* and to whom Jonson dedicated the Folio version of that play.[1]

Jonson may have written his 'comicall satyres' with the young Temple Bar audience in mind. He included a good deal of legal satire in them, especially in the characters of Fungoso, the son of a yeoman farmer in *Every Man Out* who comes to London to study law and instead becomes enamoured of fashion; and young Ovid in *Poetaster*, a student in Rome who is roundly condemned by his father for preferring poetry to lawbooks: 'Ovid, whom I thought to see the pleader, become Ovid the playmaker?' (I, ii, 8–9).[2] Jonson's awareness of the contention between poetry and law as rival vocations at the Inns is nowhere more apparent than in his dedication of the 1616 Folio of *Every Man Out* 'to the noblest nourceries of humanity, and liberty, in the kingdome: The Innes of Court'. He requests that his play not interfere with the 'more noble, and use-full studies' of law, but be enjoyed during revels, 'when the gowne and cap is off, and the Lord of liberty raignes'.

Scholars writing after Hart have tended to play down the parallels between *Timon* and the 'comicall satyres' and thereby avoid the issue of Jonsonian influence. But the number of parallels already discovered is, I think, significant; and furthermore, there are various lesser parallels – not convincing by themselves – which, when added to the others, prove 'Anonymous's' debt to Jonson almost conclusively. Some of the parallels which I shall discuss have been noted by Hart, Herford and Simpson, but without any analysis. These parallels, it seems to me, appear all the more striking when studied in detail.[3]

Jonson's influence on the main plot, though weaker than on the sub-plot, is nevertheless worthy of examination. The word 'macilente' is used in *Timon* as a generic adjective to describe Philargurus's servant, 'Leane, macilente Grunnio' (p. 52). But 'macilente' meant 'lean' and thus was redundant. The author of *Timon* may, however, have used it intentionally to recall the critic named Macilente in *Every Man Out*; for like Macilente, whose humor is envy, Grunnio is a starving wretch who covets the food on Timon's table and envies Obba his position as butler. The word 'macilente' was rarely used. The context of *Timon* suggests that the author was familiar with Jonson's use of it.[4]

[1] See H & S, I, 22–30; and Finkelpearl, *John Marston*, pp. 45–61. Hoskyns and Martin were involved in the famous *Prince d'Amour* revels at the Middle Temple – Martin as the Prince, and Hoskyns as Clerk of Council.

[2] All quotations are from H & S: *Every Man Out of His Humour*, III, 419–604; *Cynthia's Revels*, IV, 27–183; *Poetaster*, IV, 197–324.

[3] Oscar James Campbell, *Comicall Satyre and Shakespeare's 'Troilus and Cressida'* (San Marino, 1938), shows that there is a great deal of overlapping in characters and motifs among Jonson's plays. Such overlapping sometimes makes it difficult to trace an allusion to one particular play. I ascribe each allusion to the play at which the point of contact seems strongest.

[4] The word has been written again in the margin of the MS. by a more recent hand, perhaps that of Hart, who was the first to mention its use in *Timon* (*Works of Ben Jonson*, I, xlv).

There also seems to be a connection between Macilente's shedding of his humor at the conclusion of *Every Man Out* and the singular repetition of this unusual device when 'Timon doffs Timon' in his epilogue (see H & S, IX, 483). Compare the two speeches:

> Why, here's a change! Now is my soule at peace.
> I am as emptie of all enuie now,
> As they of merit to be enuied at . . .
>
> > (*EMO*, v, xi, 54–6)

> I now am left alone; this rascall route
> Hath left my side. What's this? I feele throughout
> A sodeine change; my fury doth abate,
> My hearte growes milde, and laies aside its hate.
>
> > (*Timon*, v, v, p. 95)

The similarity of Macilente and Timon in their misanthropy is underscored by the fact that each of them lies down on-stage to rail satirically at the hypocrisy of his acquaintances (see H & S, IX, 484). Both Jonson and 'Anonymous' parody the older form of tragic rant in the tirades of their misanthropes.

A number of minor parallels indicate a possible link with *Poetaster*. In that play, as in *Timon*, there is a decided emphasis on feasting and role-playing, themes which pervaded the Inns' revels. Woven into the revels of *Poetaster*, Hart found (*Works of Ben Jonson*, I, xliv) a Horatian ode to Bacchus, '*Swell me a bowle with lustie wine*' (III, i, 8–11), which he thought similar to Eutrapelus's song to Bacchus in *Timon*, '*Bring me hither a cupp*' *Of wyne, filld to the bryms*' (I, ii, p. 7). At the banquet in *Poetaster* (IV, iii), where the courtiers and their ladies impersonate gods and goddesses, Jonson inserted a prolonged joke about Venus (aspirant lady Chloe) who wishes to cuckold her husband Vulcan (citizen Albius) by making love to a scoundrel Mars (Captain Tucca). Their banter may have inspired the song sung by Hermogenes in *Timon* which begins,

> *Louelie Venus sported,*
> *And with Mars consorted,*
> *While swarthy Vulcan in his shopp*
> *At his forge did lympe and hopp.*
>
> > (I, v, p. 18)[1]

During that same scene in *Poetaster*, Captain Tucca flatters Albanius by addressing him as various Homeric heroes: 'Give me thy hand, AGAMEMNON; we heare abroad, thou art the HECTOR of citizens' (lines 22–3); and about Chloe, Tucca asks him, 'Which of these is thy wedlocke, MENELAUS? thy HELLEN?' (lines 27–8). This mockery of the *Iliad* may have inspired the merrygreek masquerade in *Timon*, for which Lollio impersonates the protagonist – 'I am Achilles, yee my Myrmidones . . . Hector? art thou Hector?' (II, v, p. 42) – and Callimela and Blatte the nurse are summoned out of the house as Helen and 'olde Hecuba, that bitche'.

Among the parasites who cling to Timon there are many shadows of Jonson's characters. Hart remarked (*Works of Ben Jonson*, I, xlv) that Speusippus and Stilpo, the 'two lying philosophers' in *Timon*, read like parodies of Clove and Orange, the two Paul's men in *Every Man Out*. Aiming to gull would-be gentlemen into employing them, to 'make 'hem beleeue we are great schollers' (III, iv, 8), Clove and Orange invoke non-existent works by Plato and Aristotle in an absurd mishmash of peripatetic twaddle:

ARISTOTLE *in his Daemonologia, approues* SCALIGER *for the best Nauigator in his time: and in his Hypercritiques, he reports him to be Heautontimorumenos: you* vnderstand the *Greeke*, sir?

. . . and whereas our *intellectuall*, or *mincing capreall* (according to the *Metaphisicks*) as you may reade in PLATO'S *Histriomastix* – You conceiue me, sir?

> > (lines 14–17, 27–30)

---

[1] Adams (p. 514) thinks that this song 'is probably a metrical rendering of Lucian's *Dialogues of the Gods*, XVII'.

Speusippus and Stilpo invent and abuse names of philosophical tracts in an almost identical way:[1]

Stilpo. Plato in his Acrostikes saith, it is better to giue than receaue.
Speusippus. Neither doth Aristotle dissent from Plato in his first of the Metaphysicks, the last text saue one.
(v, v, p. 93)

And just as Clove answers astronomical questions in pseudo-peripatetic terms – 'you shall perceiue the *Hypothesis*, or *Galaxia* . . . to be meerely *Pythagoricall*, *Mathematicall*, and *Aristocraticall*' (lines 35–8) – Speusippus and Stilpo argue in 'soloecismes' to try to resolve 'whether there be a man in the moone . . . (as the Greekes will haue it) catapodially, specificatiuely, and quidditatiuely' (IV, iii, p. 66). These similarities are reason enough for us to suspect that 'Anonymous' modelled his 'lying philosophers' on those of Jonson. When we consider in addition that each pair of philosophers uses learning for the sake of material advancement alone, our suspicion grows towards certainty.

Hermogenes, the musician in *Timon*, was probably based on the character of the same name in *Poetaster*, which in turn drew upon Horace's satire I, iii. Scornful of his own 'fiddling' as an art beneath the dignity of Timon's court, however, he aspires to a more courtly refinement; and in a passage which Bradbrook interprets (p. 96) as a further satire on learning, he seeks to buy the vocabulary of the prattling philosophers:

Hermogenes. Stilpo, how wilt thou sell these articles of distinction?
Stilpo. For 20 £.
Hermogenes. For such trifles! how deare are thy wares! wilt take 16?
Stilpo. Dost thinke philosophy is soe litle worth? I cannot.
Hermogenes. Bee it soe; because these phrases please mee, and their terminations ende all alike, thou shalt haue 20 £. Repeate them againe.

Stilpo. A thinge may bee mooued entitatiuely or formally –
(IV, iii, p. 66)

It seems to me that the author echoes here Jonson's theme of 'plagiary' in *Poetaster*. Crispinus (a portrait of Marston), the envious poet who wishes to ape the writings of Horace (Jonson's self-portrait), in the final scene is found guilty of plagiary.[2] Like Speusippus and Stilpo, he is given to speaking 'lewd solecisms'. It will not stretch a point too far, I think, to suggest that the author of *Timon*, in the vocabulary which Hermogenes buys from the philosophers, deliberately parodies the words which Crispinus is forced to spew at his trial.

Another parallel exists between the family grouping of Philargurus, Lollio and Callimela (father, son and daughter) in *Timon*, and that of Sordido, Fungoso and Fallace in *Every Man Out*. Philargurus and Sordido both are Plautine misers – the former a farmer residing in the city; the latter a farmer visiting the city – who humorously dramatize Timon's description of the 'madd' man 'that carefullie doth watch / A thowsand heapes of wheate, and dares not tast / One graine thereof.' Lollio and Fungoso, their impoverished sons, both arrive from the country to spend time at the Inns of Court (Fungoso is a student of law; for Lollio's presence there, see my previous argument). Callimela, Lollio's sister, is in search of a wealthy citizen for a husband whom she can dominate and cuckold. Just such a one Fallace has found in her obsequious Deliro. The Jonsonian resonance in *Timon* swells when we remember, with Hart (*Works of Ben Jonson*, I, xliv), that Philargyrus was the name assigned in *Cynthia's Revels* to Asotus's father who, at death, left his son a citizen's fortune. By borrowing the name for his living miser, the

[1] This point was brought to my attention by Mr Nosworthy.
[2] I adhere to the identifications made by R. A. Small, *The Stage-Quarrel between Ben Jonson and the So-called Poetasters* (Breslau, 1899), pp. 25 ff.

author of *Timon* revitalized Jonson's charactonym, 'love of gold'.

Most of the parallels between the 'comicall satyres' and the main plot of *Timon* appear insubstantial when set beside the parallels which can be drawn with the sub-plot. The characters there involved, Gelasimus and Pseudocheus, are strongly reminiscent of certain characters in *Cynthia's Revels*. Previous scholars have concurred in regarding the sub-plot as the most substantial evidence extant of Jonson's influence on *Timon*.

In the list of 'The Actors Names', Gelasimus is identified as 'a cittie heyre'. He is fond of boasting about the inheritance left him by his father, 'rich Megadorus' (II, i, p. 22).[1] In *Cynthia's Revels*, Asotus is introduced by a boy player in similar words as 'a citizens heire'. He, we soon learn, is 'sonne to the late deceas'd Philargyrus the citizen'. In the same play we find another character, 'the daughter of *folly*', whose name Gelaia means 'laughter'. Thus the name Gelasimus may have a double irony. It not only applies to a supercilious fop who is forever breaking into convulsive 'ha, ha, he''s (an idiosyncrasy which makes the Latin superlative form of his name appropriate), but also identifies him with a humorous character, Gelaia, who is nothing more than 'a wench in boyes attire'. Gelasimus's femininity is underscored by Pseudocheus, who advises him to display his latent talents in courting Callimela: 'What, canst thou daunce and singe? Play thou the girle' (I, v, p. 16).

Himself the 'lying trauailor' in *Timon*, Pseudocheus is patterned directly after Amorphus in *Cynthia's Revels*, 'a trauailer that hath drunke of the fountaine' of self-love (Induction, 62–3). The symbiotic relationship of these travelers with their gulls is the same in the two plays. Asotus '(in imitation of the traueller, who hath the *whetstone* following him) entertaines the *begger*, to be his attendant' (lines 69–71); and likewise Gelasimus, entreating

Pseudocheus to let him embark on a voyage to the Antipodes, employs him as an instructor in the arts of romance.

The nearly identical scenes in which the city heirs make the acquaintance of the travelers are ample testimony in themselves of Jonson's influence on *Timon* (see H & S, IX, 483–4). Aware at once of what a gull he has in Gelasimus, Pseudocheus loudly boasts his travels – 'Pacing the myles of Europe, Asia, / And Affrica, my wearied bones at last / Are here arriued' (I, iv, p. 12) – and concludes with a tactical aside, 'What shall I saye? I saw his face at Thebes / Or Sicilie?' This is precisely the method Amorphus uses to make his approach to Asotus: 'Since I trode on this side the *Alpes*, I was not so frozen in my inuention. Let mee see: to accost him with some choice remnant of *spanish*, or *italian*? ... Faine to haue seene him in *Venice*, or *Padau*?' (I, iv, 79ff.).

One of Amorphus's alternative approaches is to compliment Asotus on his street and house, an approach calculated to appeal to a citizen's vanity. Should he 'praise the cleannesse of the street, wherein hee dwelt? or the prouident painting of his posts against hee should haue been *Praetor*?' (lines 100–2). As if taking this hint from Amorphus, Gelasimus brags of these very things to Pseudocheus in the full bloom of Athenian pride –

You neuer saw my howse in Rhamnuse street?
I spent tenn powndes in paynting of my dores,
To make it knowne whose howse it was.   (p. 13)

– and later, to Callimela: 'Thou shalt my lands and large revenues see ... My parks, and paynted posts before my dores' (II, ii, p. 27).

Of little worldly experience, both city heirs naively attempt to win the respect of the travelers by tempting them with their wealth:

[1] That Gelasimus's father is later called '*Rubicunde of the Ilands*' (IV, ii, p. 61) rather than Megadorus is perhaps yet another clue of dual authorship.

Gelasimus.

> H'st, thou may'st tell him, yf thou wilt, how rich
> My ffather was
>
> (*Timon*, I, iv, p. 12)

Asotus. And withall, you may tell him what my father was, and how well he left me, and that I am his heire.

(*CR*, I, iv, 69–70)

The person addressed in each case is a 'critic' figure whom the heir uses as an intercessor to arrange the introduction. Crites, begrudgingly performing this service for Asotus, takes the opportunity to comment on the hypocrisy of such absurd fashions. Paedio, employed by Gelasimus in a like service, takes the opportunity to expose the imposture of Pseudocheus, and thus shows himself to be just as devastating a critic as Crites.

The heirs finally become acquainted with the travelers through the medium of clothing, central to the 'fashion' metaphor in both plays. Amorphus hits upon the idea first: 'I haue it: Thanks, gracious MINERVA ... 'Tis a most curious, and neatly-wrought band, this same, as I haue seene, sir', he flatters Asotus (lines 104 ff.). Gelasimus likewise tenders his cloak to Pseudocheus as a gesture of friendship: 'What yf I send and gyue to him my cloake? ... Ile send it' (p. 12).

The ensuing protestations of affection ultimately lead to an exchange of gifts. Asotus presents Amorphus with the prized beaver which the latter has so admired; but in return, Amorphus gives only a cheap hat to Asotus, who remarks with dismay upon the disparity, 'Slid, this is not worth a crowne, and mine cost mee eight but this morning' (lines 178–9). Amorphus, however, assures him that the hat has magical powers, and moreover that it 'was giuen mee by a great man (in *Russia*) as a especiall-priz'd present' (lines 193–4). This motif is picked up in *Timon* when Gelasimus and Pseudocheus exchange rings of disparate value. Though Pseudocheus admits in an aside, 'By Joue, my ringe is made of brasse,

not gould', Gelasimus is satisfied with the exchange; for Pseudocheus has assured him that the ring once belonged to foreign royalty: 'O happie me, that weares the kings owne ringe / Of th'Antipodes!' (p. 15).

The influence of *Cynthia's Revels* on this one scene is, I think, incontestable. There are further parallels to be drawn with succeeding scenes. Amorphus volunteers to instruct Asotus in the art of courtship (III, v) and insists that Asotus repeat the oaths of love as they are recited to him. Pseudocheus instructs Gelasimus to woo by using the same technique (I, v). Herford and Simpson noticed that Gelasimus and Amorphus, spurned by their ladies, respond in a similar way to failure in love (H & S, IX, 484). Forsaken by Echo, Amorphus cannot believe that his person is to blame:

What should I inferre? If my behauiours had beene of a cheape or customarie garbe; my accent, or phrase vulgar; my garments trite; my countenance illiterate ... then I might (with some change of colour) haue suspected my faculties ...

(I, iii, 24 ff.)

Gelasimus likewise cannot conceive that Callimela's rejection is in any way a reflection on himself:

> Soe the gods loue mee, I doe nothing see
> That this fonde foolishe girle can blame in mee:
> I am not redde hair'd, and I am noe dwarfe;
> What, then, can shee dislike? (III, iii, p. 49)

These complaints are remarkably alike in their emphasis on vain self-justification rather than remorse over the loss of the lady.

The sub-plot in *Timon* bears sufficient resemblance to certain situations in *Every Man Out* to warrant our attention. Like Gelasimus, Puntarvolo fancies himself as something of a traveler; and just as the former plans a fantastic voyage to the Antipodes, the latter decides to embark on a journey to Constantinople, the success of which he wagers with

Fastidious Briske. Puntarvolo's journey and the terms of indenture which his notary draws up (IV, iii) are parodied in the scene of Gelasimus's departure, which contains the deed wherein he signs over all his property to Abyssus (IV, ii).

This pairing of Gelasimus with Puntarvolo is markedly strengthened by the fact that Puntarvolo, like Gelasimus, woos his lady with laughter:

Sogliardo. O, yes sir: first, the gentlewoman, shee lookes out at the window.
Carlo Buffone. After the trumpet has summon'd a parle? not before?
Sogliardo. No, sir, not before: and then saies he – ha, ha, ha, ha, &c.
Carlo Buffone. What saies he? be not rapt so.
Sogliardo. Saies he – ha, ha, ha, ha, &c.
Fastidious Briske. Nay, speake, speake.
Sogliardo. Ha, ha, ha, saies he: God saue you, saies he: ha, ha, &c.
Carlo Buffone. Was this the ridiculous motiue to all this passion?
Sogliardo. Nay, that, that comes after, is – ha, ha, ha, ha, &c.   (II, i, 157 ff.)

This scene, I suggest, directly inspired Pseudocheus's sage advice to Gelasimus: 'After this manner, then, woe thou the maid: / When first thou dost behould her, laugh aloud' (p. 16). Gelasimus takes the advice to heart:

Gelasimus. What is't? I remember, I remember. – Ha, ha, he!
Philargurus. Why laugh'st thou soe?
Gelasimus. Ha, ha, he!
Philargurus. Do'st mock my daughter?
Gelasimus. Ha, ha, he! – he knowes not the manner of the Antipodes, – ha, ha, he!   (II, i, p. 23)

This unusual reference to laughter as a mode of courtship, described in *Every Man Out* and actually executed in *Timon*, surely indicates more than a coincidental connection between the two plays.

The less fantastical elements in Gelasimus's character are partially indebted to a more sober

prototype, Sogliardo. A rich citizen who manifests all that is crass about the English middle class, Sogliardo wishes to acquire 'a most prodigious coat' of arms in order to pass for an aristocrat. Coats of arms had become so easy to buy that they were ceasing to have any real significance. Jonson satirized such middle-class pretension through the mouth of Carlo Buffone:

Sogliardo. Nay, my humour is not for boyes, Ile keepe men, and I keepe any; and Ile giue coats, that's my humour: but I lacke a cullisen.
Carlo Buffone. Why, now you ride to the citie, you may buy one, Ile bring you where you shall ha' your choise for money.
Sogliardo. Can you sir?
Carlo Buffone. O, I: you shall haue one take measure of you, and make you a *Coat of armes*, to fit you of what fashion you will.   (I, ii, 143–51)

Later on Sogliardo, still suffering under the delusion of the clothing metaphor, describes his new coat in all its vulgarity. It has a 'varietie of colours in it', and as for the crest, 'it is your Bore without a head *Rampant*' (III, iv, 57–61). Like Sogliardo, Gelasimus is a citizen enamoured of his heraldic claim to aristocracy. He delights in having Paedio recite the motif of his arms: 'Three guilded thistles ... Three fatt asses, / Drawn out the desarts of Arabia ... Two boares with gilded stones in a feild. / Bloudy' (I, iii, pp. 10–11). Herford and Simpson argue that the vulgarity of Gelasimus's arms rivals that of Sogliardo's (IX, 484: actually they mistakenly ascribe the grotesque coat of arms to Sordido); but it seems to me that Gelasimus's arms bear a stronger resemblance to those of another aspirant courtier, Crispinus:

Yet, I pray you, vouchsafe the sight of my armes, Mistresse; for I beare them about me, to haue 'hem seene: my name is CRISPINVS, or CRI-SPINAS indeed; which is well exprest in my armes (a Face crying *in chiefe*; and beneath it a blouddie Toe, betweene three Thornes *pungent.*)   (*Poetaster*, II, i, 94–9)

Gelasimus's 'three guilded thistles' are quite like the 'three Thornes', or *spinas*, of Crispinus; and the presence of the word 'bloudy'in both descriptions (it functions in *Timon* as *pungent* does in *Poetaster*, as a single adjective placed after the noun for special emphasis) supports my argument that the author of *Timon* was spoofing Jonson's satire of middle-class heraldry.

The last parallel to be considered here is the cap made of ass's ears, which Pseudocheus awards to the gulled Gelasimus. When he learns that Pseudocheus has shipped out to sea with all his gold, Gelasimus in resignation dons the ears and admits, 'Theis were the true armes of my graundfather' (p. 83), an amusing recollection of the 'Three fatt asses' in his own heraldry. The cap also recalls the threat in Timon's revelling ordinance that anyone who failed to drink would 'weare infixt / Vppon his hatte an asses eares' (p. 38). The final de-humoring of the 'two lying philosophers' also is caused by a 'metamorphosis' when Gelasimus transfers the cap from his own head to Stilpo's:

Hermogenes. This philosopher is chainged into an asse.
Stilpo. A chainge is made either essentially or accidentallie; I am made an asse accidentallie.

(v, v, p. 88)

Although Herford and Simpson claim that no parallel can be validly made here with Jonson (IX, 484: they err once again in thinking that the cap has been sent to Timon), I contend that the cap of ass's ears was a device borrowed directly from *Poetaster*. In that play, Asinius Lupus identifies himself with the ass of Horace's emblem: 'An Asse? Good still: That's I, too. I am the asse. I mean me by the asse –' (v, iii, 96–7); and he is finally punished by Caesar with a pair of ass's ears for his 'fierce credulitie' – the very reason Gelasimus is awarded his. The same punishment is dealt to Demetrius by Virgil:

DEMETRIVS FANNIVS, thou shalt here put on
That coate, and cap; and henceforth, thinke thy selfe
No other, then they make thee ...   (lines 576–8)

But the device is not put aside until the play's closing song, '*Blush*, folly, *blush*: here's none that feares / The wagging of an asses eares' (lines 626–7). As a comic device, the cap of ass's ears is too prominent in *Poetaster* for the author of *Timon* to have arrived at it independently. He makes just enough of it to recall its importance in *Poetaster* and thereby enriches its use in his own play with Jonsonian reverberation.

IV

The plots in *Timon*, therefore, have close affinities with characters and situations in Jonson's 'comicall satires'. These affinities, I believe, are the best evidence we now have for dating *Timon*. They point to a date shortly after the production of the last of the satires, *Poetaster*, in 1601, at which time the more striking parallels would have been topical.

It would be convenient, of course, if we could prove that Jonson's three plays lost popularity quickly and were not performed any later than 1601: we could then be assured that *Timon* was written not long thereafter. Unfortunately, no such evidence exists. All we can do is apply logic to the evidence we do have: that *Every Man Out*, first produced in the autumn of 1599, took direct aim at *Histriomastix*, which was produced that same autumn; and that *Poetaster*, acted 'sundry times' in 1601, was promptly answered that year by *Satiromastix*. For plays such as these, in which humor depended in large measure upon timely barbs, speed was essential. What Herford and Simpson say of *Poetaster* may logically be said of the other 'comicall satyres' as well: 'The ephemeral character of the satire ... made later performances impossible.'[1] Thus it may be

[1] Herford and Simpson (IX, 185–9) essentially repeat the stage history of the three plays detailed by

assumed that *Timon*, riddled as it is with Jonsonian allusion, was performed at the Inns of Court no later than 1602.

It is regrettable that Bradbrook, who argues her Inns of Court theory so convincingly, is bent upon interpreting *Timon* as a burlesque of *Timon of Athens*; for by proposing 1611 as a date to suit her interpretation, she all but disregards the parallels which prove that the author of *Timon* was inspired, at least in part, by Jonson's 'comicall satyres' of 1599 to 1601 – parallels which by 1611 would have been stale indeed. Even the parallel she finds between *Timon* and *Twelfth Night*, acted at the Middle Temple on Candlemas 1602, tends to verify the earlier rather than the later date (p. 96).[1]

Scholars for years have been inclined, like Bradbrook, to believe that Shakespeare never could have seen *Timon*. But if *Timon* was performed at the Inns of Court *c.* 1601–2, it is likely that Shakespeare did see it; for he had close associations with the Inns, and especially with the Middle Temple, where his own *Twelfth Night*, and perhaps *Troilus and Cressida* and *Timon of Athens*, were performed. This likelihood leaves incredulous scholars naked of their alibi. Shakespeare could have seen *Timon*; thus he could have borrowed from it.

These conclusions, I think, should reopen the question of influence. They suggest at least three possibilities which hitherto have not been explored seriously enough: that the troublesome similarities between *Timon* and *Timon of Athens* which have caused scholars to conjecture a lost common source may in fact indicate Shakespeare's indebtedness to *Timon*; that Shakespeare may have derived most, if not all, of his Lucian source material through *Timon*;[2] and that he may have written *Timon of Athens* quite a bit earlier than the Roman plays, perhaps even earlier than *King Lear*.

E. K. Chambers, *The Elizabethan Stage* (Oxford, 1923), III, 360–6. There is no record that *Every Man Out* was performed at the Globe after Twelfth Night, 1600. It was revived at court on 8 January 1605. *Cynthia's Revels* was acted at court, apparently without success, on 6 January 1601. *Poetaster* followed *Cynthia's Revels* by only a few months.

[1] Bradbrook's observation that Gelasimus behaves much like Sir Andrew Aguecheek is too tenuous to support her implication that the two plays are somehow connected.

[2] This idea was suggested to me by Mr Nosworthy. The anonymous author of *Timon* borrowed from Lucian far more frequently and literally than Shakespeare did; and the fact that he did not use Plutarch's account of Timon makes it all the more unlikely that he was imitating Shakespeare. T. W. Baldwin, *William Shakespere's Small Latin & Lesse Greeke* (Urbana, 1944) I, 732–5, imagines that Shakespeare may have read Lucian's dialogues in grammar school, in either Latin translation or the original Greek. The 'old *Timon*', then, may have reminded Shakespeare of a text he had studied some twenty-five years before.

1 *Love's Labour's Lost*, Royal Shakespeare Theatre, 1973. Directed by John Barton, designed by Timothy O'Brien and Tazeena Firth. With (left to right) Catherine Kessler as Maria, Susan Fleetwood as the Princess of France, Janet Chappell as Katherine, Estelle Kohler as Rosaline and Ian Richardson as Berowne

II *Love's Labour's Lost*, with Sebastian Shaw as Boyet and Estelle Kohler (Rosaline) in act iv, scene i:
Boyet. And who is your deer?
Rosaline. If we choose by the horns, yourself.

III *Love's Labour's Lost*, act v, scene ii: the dialogue of the owl and the cuckoo

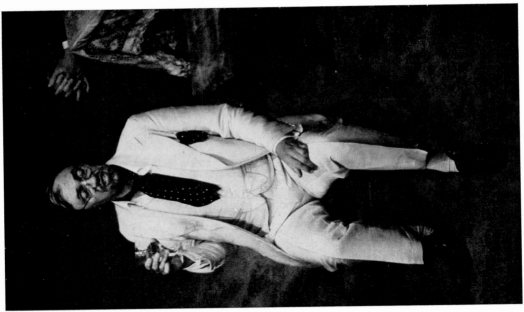

IVв *As You Like It*, with Richard Pasco as Jacques

IVA *As You Like It*, Royal Shakespeare Theatre, 1973. Directed by
Buzz Goodbody, designed by Christopher Morley. With Maureen
Lipman as Celia and Eileen Atkins as Rosalind

V *Romeo and Juliet*, Royal Shakespeare Theatre, 1973. Directed by Terry Hands,
designed by Farrah. With Beatrix Lehmann as the Nurse and Estelle Kohler as Juliet

VI *Richard II*, Royal Shakespeare Theatre, 1973. Directed by John Barton, designed by Timothy O'Brien and Tazeena Firth. With Ian Richardson (left) and Richard Pasco alternating in the roles of Richard and Bolingbroke

VII *Richard II*, act I, scene iii

VIII   *Romeo and Juliet*, Old Vic, 1960. Directed by Franco Zeffirelli. With Judi Dench as Juliet and John Stride as Romeo

SHAKESPEARE, HER MAJESTY'S PLAYERS AND PEMBROKE'S MEN

G. M. PINCISS

I

The history of the Queen's Men spans the years 1583–92. After that date the remnants of what was for a time the first acting company in the land are like the down-at-heels players in *Histrio-mastix* 'that travel with pumps full of gravell' carrying their few props and costumes, and performing 'base-brown-paper-stuffe'. The decade in which the Queen's Men were most influential coincides so exactly with the most obscure period of William Shakespeare's life that the possibility of Shakespeare's having received his introduction to the theater as a trainee with them is worthy of close scrutiny.

Shakespeare probably joined a troupe of actors sometime shortly after leaving Stratford about the mid 1580s; in any case, his talent and success were sufficiently recognized by 1592 for him to be attacked in print as an upstart, 'the onely Shakescene in a country'.[1] But what company did he join and in what capacity? J. Q. Adams suggests that Shakespeare received his training with Pembroke's Men as a hireling, first cast in minor roles – this, at least, would parallel the careers of such actor–playwrights as Thomas Heywood and Samuel Rowley.[2] A. F. Pollard claimed Shakespeare was a member of Leicester's company about 1587;[3] T. W. Baldwin, interpreting the 'Shakescene' passage, finds it an attack on Shakespeare and his company, Strange's Men.[4] Edmund Malone thought Shakespeare may have joined the Queen's Men as early as 1586 when they appeared in Stratford,[5] and

some contemporary scholars argue for a more varied apprenticeship involving a combination of acting troupes: the Queen's Men, Pembroke's and Strange's.[6]

II

There is some rather strong evidence of Shakespeare's association with the Queen's Men.[7] The advice in the *Groatsworth of Wit*,

[1] E. K. Chambers, *William Shakespeare* (2 vols., Oxford, 1930). The biographical details are also laid out in Peter Alexander's *Shakespeare* (London, 1964).
[2] *A Life of William Shakespeare* (London, 1923), pp. 129 ff.
[3] 'The History of England from the accession of Edward VI to the death of Elizabeth', *The Political History of England*, ed. W. Hunt and R. Poole, VI (London, 1929), 451.
[4] *On the Literary Genetics of Shakspeare's Plays, 1592–1594* (Urbana, 1959), p. 47.
[5] *Plays and Poems of William Shakespeare*, II (London, 1821), p. 166.
[6] Alexander, *Shakespeare*, p. 78; E. B. Everitt, *The Young Shakespeare* (Copenhagen, 1954), p. 186. Dover Wilson speculates that by 1592 Shakespeare was working for Strange's Men, that through the Strange–Essex friendship he met Southampton, and that during most of 1593 and part of 1594 he was a member of Southampton's household – *The Essential Shakespeare* (Cambridge, 1932), pp. 64 ff. See also Mark Eccles, *Shakespeare in Warwickshire* (Madison, 1961). Eccles notes (p. 82) that the Queen's were probably seeking to replace an actor in the summer of 1587.
[7] For a summary of the arguments that Shakespeare worked with the Queen's Men, see A. W. Pollard's introduction to Peter Alexander's edition of *Shakespeare's Henry VI and Richard III* (Cambridge, 1929), and Karl Wentersdorf's 'Shakespeare's Erste Truppe', *Shakespeare-Jahrbuch* (1950), pp. 114–30.

warning Marlowe, Nashe, and Peele against writing for the stage, does not imply that these three men all wrote for the same acting company. Greene – if he is, in fact, the real author – is citing his own case as an example to other university-trained playwrights, counseling them to seek 'better Maisters'.[1] His anger is justified he feels because the actors who receive more profit from a playbook than the author were now presuming to pen their own texts. And obviously, one of these upstarts was achieving some success at moving out of his class, for Greene finds that 'I, to whom they all have been beholding . . . have beene at once of them forsaken.' Greene's dealings with the Queen's Men are questionable at least on one occasion. Cuthbert Cony-catcher accuses the playwright of selling *Orlando Furioso* both to Her Majesty's Players and the Lord Admiral's Men. Greene would no doubt excuse these sharp practices by pointing out that there is no honesty even among thieves, and it is in this profession that he would place actors, a thankless tribe. His specific comments, 'were yee in that case as I am now', must apply to some more particular situation regarding the company with which he had the closest connections, but since most if not all his work was performed by the Queen's Men, his remarks may be directed at them in part, for his fortunes were linked to a falling star. Refused in his need by men he thought ill-educated vagabonds, puppets, and apes, by men for whom he had prostituted his talents, Greene is indignant that a 'Crow, beautified with our feathers' could compete in song. Shakespeare was to write, perhaps not very long after and possibly as a gloss on Greene's words, that '"beautified" is a vile phrase'; but even had Greene lived, the Stratford upstart was too busy writing successful plays to indulge in the sports of a Thomas Nashe or a Gabriel Harvey.[2]

With Greene's plays for the Queen's Men Shakespeare shows some general familiarity. Orlando in *As You Like It* hangs verses from the trees; his mad namesake in *Orlando Furioso* finds them in the forest. And from *James IV* Shakespeare may have learned that Oberon is king of the fairies. *Alphonsus, King of Aragon* is perhaps the original source dimly remembered of the Player King's opening lines in *Hamlet*. Greene wrote,

> Thrise ten times Phoebus with his golden beames,
> Hath compassed the circle of the skie,
> Thrise ten times Ceres, hath her workmen hir'd,
> And fild the barnes with frutefull crops of corne,
> Since first in Priesthood I did lead my life.
>
> (1,259–63)

Shakespeare may have recalled these words when he intended to write in a style distinct from the ordinary dialogue of his play.[3]

> Full thirty times hath Phoebus cart gone round
> Neptune's salt wash and Tellus' orbed ground,
> And thirty dozen moons with borrowed sheen
> About the world have times twelve thirties been,
> Since Iove our hearts and Hymen did our hands
> Unite commutual in most sacred bands.
>
> (III, ii, 150–5)

Hamlet also seems to bear some traces of the Greene and Lodge morality, *A Looking-Glass*

[1] Warren B. Austin, *A Computer-Aided Technique for Stylistic Discrimination: The Authorship of Greene's Groatsworth of Wit* (U.S. Department of Health, Education, and Welfare, Washington, 1969) argues that Henry Chettle actually forged this work.

[2] Muriel Bradbrook speculates that *Venus and Adonis* may have been Shakespeare's response to the attack in *Groatsworth of Wit*; she also suggests that this poem reflects Shakespeare's familiarity with the writing of Robert Wilson, an actor–playwright with the Queen's Men. See 'Beasts and Gods: *Groatsworth of Witte* and the Social Purposes of *Venus and Adonis*', *Shakespeare Survey 15* (Cambridge, 1962), pp. 62–72.

[3] G. L. Kittredge in his edition of *Hamlet* (Boston, 1939), p. 224, noted this similarity as well as that appearing later in *Alphonsus*, lines 1,394–400, and a brief passage in *Selimus* that is vaguely reminiscent. The text cited here is the Malone Society edition (1926).

for London and England, in which the Smith tells the Clown, 'Alas, sir, your father, why sir mee-thinks I see the Gentleman stil, a proper youth he was faith, aged some foure & ten, his beard ...' (lines 211–13).

Other plays in the repertory of the Queen's Men may have influenced Shakespeare even more strongly.[1] Elizabeth's company had acted a romance, *The History of Felix and Philomena*, before the sovereign in the 1584–5 season. Shakespeare would have found in this play, probably based on a French translation of Montemayor's *Diana*, the techniques of a whole genre dramatized, techniques he was to employ in *The Merchant of Venice, Romeo and Juliet, Twelfth Night*, and *As You Like It*. Not only does *Two Gentlemen of Verona* share the same source as *Felix and Philomena*, but the devices of Montemayor's tale reappear in Shakespeare's plays: the girl disguised as a boy and employed as her lover's ambassador to a rival; banishment; rope ladders; forests; outlaws; witty maids and friars. Without an extant text of the Queen's Men's play we must consider these elements simply standard romance fare. Launce's rebuking of his dog, Crab, in *Two Gentlemen*, however, finds a precedent in a popular Queen's work, *Sir Clyomon and Sir Clamydes*, and this play like *2 Henry IV* uses a choral figure called Rumour. The bombast of Alexander the Great in *Sir Clyomon*, who is to enter on-stage 'as valiantly set forth as may be' and who is anything but a man of God's making, may be the original of Sir Nathaniel's 'Alisander' in the pageant of *Love's Labour's Lost*, an Alexander that is so easily o'er-parted.

Detailed comparison of Shakespeare's history plays and those in the repertory of the Queen's have been attempted many times. The success of such ventures is limited. The common ground of sources, of proverbs, and of theatrical techniques would naturally result in similarities, and the complex textual prob-lems surrounding the early histories do not permit a definite solution to the question of indebtedness.

Shakespeare's three plays on the reigns of Henry IV and V draw on *The Famous Victories* as one of their sources. The extent to which Shakespeare's work relies on the earlier chronicle play has been variously interpreted. Although one critic has argued for Shakespearian authorship of *The Famous Victories*, the accumulated evidence is not convincing.[2] On the contrary, occurrences in the Shakespeare canon and in this play of commonly paired words, particular turns of phrase, and figures of speech could reflect constant exposure to the earlier work had Shakespeare been an actor in the Queen's Company. Further, the text of *The Famous Victories* seems to be a shortened, memorially-reconstructed version prepared in the early 1590s when plague closed the theaters. That the play was entered on the Stationers' Register in 1594 and that the edition of 1598 is the first known, suggests a 1594 printing may be lost; 'that it was not the existing patchwork is suggested by, first, *The Famous Victories*' almost imbecile nature ... and, second, the fact that Oldcastle must have been more familiar to Elizabethan audiences when Shakespeare took him up than he could possibly be from *The Famous Victories*'.[3] But Shakespeare was evidently acquainted with some form of this play as the many parallels show, incidents and incidental information he could not have acquired from reading Stow, Holinshed, or Daniel.

The relationship between the two King John plays is complicated by the problem of

[1] For a discussion of the repertory of the Queen's Men, see my article 'Thomas Creede and the Repertory of the Queen's Men 1583–1592', *Modern Philology*, LXVII (May 1970), 321–30.

[2] Seymour Pitcher, *The Case for Shakespeare's Authorship of The Famous Victories* (New York, 1961).

[3] *The First Part of King Henry IV*, ed. A. R. Humphreys (Cambridge, Mass., 1960), p. xxxiv.

dating. The Queen's version, *The Troublesome Raigne*, was first published in two parts in 1591; it was reprinted in 1611 and 1622, when the title-pages claimed Shakespeare's authorship. Shakespeare's *King John* appeared first in the 1623 Folio. 'The absence of *King John* from the S.R. entry for F1 suggests that, like *Taming of the Shrew*, it was regarded as commercially identical with its predecessors.'[1] This play has been traditionally regarded as based upon *The Troublesome Raigne* and written sometime between 1589 and 1597. It is one of the twelve plays mentioned by Meres in *Palladis Tamia* in 1598. Chambers suggests that 'the winter of 1596–7 is not an unlikely date'.[2] More recently, it has been argued that *John* was composed earlier, earlier, in fact, than *Troublesome Raigne*.[3] To accommodate this theory, Shakespeare's work is placed about 1590, and the text of *Troublesome Raigne* is labeled 'debased'. Yet there is nothing unplayable about it; indeed, F. J. Furnivall declared it superior to Shakespeare's version.[4] A number of alleged parallel passages place the author of *Troublesome Raigne* in debt to Marlowe (*Edward II*, *Massacre at Paris*, *Jew of Malta*, *Dido*); Peele (*Edward I*); Greene (*Friar Bacon*, *James IV*) and the writer of *Arden of Feversham*.[5] But so large a number of plays weakens the charge of indebtedness and, in fact, expressions like 'loath to leave' or 'dazzle my eyes' are the wide world's commonplaces. Although it would be exceptional for Shakespeare to have used 'no other source whatsoever'[6] in redrafting *The Troublesome Raigne*, he completely changed the dialogue except for one line:

> For that my grandsire was an Englishman.

The difference of tone between the two plays is striking, but the organization of the material is similar, the same episodes being repeated in the same order with little exception.

The argument for Shakespeare's association with the Queen's Men is hardly weakened if the text for *Troublesome Raigne* is derivative and dependent on *King John*; an intimate knowledge of Shakespeare's play, were that the earlier version, could be acquired most easily by actors in the company which had performed it, and *Troublesome Raigne* was acted by Her Majesty's Servants. The same reasoning applies to the relationship of *The True Tragedy of Richard III* and the Shakespearian *Richard III*. The text of the former is chaotic and evidently involved an oral stage in its transmission. In its original form the play may have preceded Shakespeare's treatment; in preparing the version printed in 1594, however, the reporter absorbed reminiscences of Shakespearian lines. One line in *True Tragedy* appears in *Hamlet*:

> The screeking Raven sits croking for revenge

and similar incidents and phrasing not found in the chronicle history are shared by the two Richard plays. A convincing answer to the question of who is the borrower and who the lender has yet to be given, but these similarities can hardly be called 'coincidence' or explained by some shared 'shaping ideas behind the two plays'.[7]

[1] E. K. Chambers, *William Shakespeare* (2 vols., Oxford, 1930), I, 365.

[2] *Ibid.*, p. 366.

[3] Peter Alexander, *Shakespeare's Life and Art* (London, 1939), p. 85. *King John*, ed. E. A. J. Honigmann (Cambridge, Mass., 1965), pp. xliv ff.

[4] *The Troublesome Raigne of King John*, ed. C. Praetorius with a foreword by F. J. Furnivall (London, 1888), p. iv.

[5] Rupert Taylor, 'A Tentative Chronology of Marlowe's and Some Other Elizabethan Plays', *Publications of the Modern Language Association of America*, LI (1936), 643 ff. See also Shakespeare's *3 Henry VI*, ed. Andrew S. Cairncross (Cambridge, Mass., 1964), pp. xliv ff. Cairncross finds *Troublesome Raigne* derives phrases from *Arraignment of Paris*, *Battle of Alcazar*, *2* and *3 Henry VI* and *Richard III*.

[6] *King John*, ed. John Dover Wilson (Cambridge, 1936), p. xxiv.

[7] Baldwin, *Literary Genetics*, p. 393. John Dover Wilson in his edition of *Richard III* (Cambridge,

Whatever Shakespeare's debt to the *True Tragedy of Richard III* or vice versa, *King Leir* is another Queen's play that became transformed by Shakespeare's art. Not only was the older version remolded, but the scene of the attempted murder of Leir and Perillus (xix) closely resembles *Richard III* (I, iv), Clarence's dream and death. The account of the dream, the stage business, the situations, and even occasionally the language are so alike that one could not have been written without the other.[1] Since Leir was not a new play when performed by the joint Queen's-Sussex's combination for Henslowe in April 1594, it may be either older or younger than *Richard III*. Two passages in *Leir* (1,476ff.; 2,453–62) are also found in *Hamlet* (III, iii; v, i), though these like the 'screeching Raven' line in *True Tragedy* may have the *Ur-Hamlet* behind them.

The writing of *King Lear* is usually assigned to 1604–5, and the printing of *Leir* in 1604 is considered an attempt to sell the older play as Shakespeare's work. The influence of the older play is so strong that some scholars prefer to date Shakespeare's version after a copy of the printed *Leir* was available, or assume that he acquired a manuscript of that play. If Shakespeare acted in *King Leir* the numerous verbal parallels are readily understandable, and as Sir Walter Greg has reasoned from his examination: 'Ideas, phrases, cadences from the old play still floated in his memory below the level of conscious thought, and ... now and again one or another helped to fashion the words that flowed from his pen'.[2] This unconscious memory was stirred perhaps not by a careful reading of *King Leir*, as Sir Walter thinks, but rather by the many hearings of the play some ten or fifteen years before. Kenneth Muir in the Arden edition of *Lear* even suggests that 'as Perillus is on stage when all save one of the ... parallel passages are spoken, that may have been Shakespeare's role' in the Queen's production of *Leir*.[3]

To recapitulate, the hypothesis that Shakespeare's initial training in the theater was acquired with the Queen's Men rests on the attack in the *Groatsworth of Wit*, and the close interconnection and cross-absorption of at least four plays in the Queen's repertory with works that are unquestionable Shakespearian.[4]

III

If Shakespeare had, in fact, been a member of Her Majesty's Players, how long might he have remained with this company and what were his associations during the early 1590s when the Queen's were rapidly losing ground to rival troupes?[5] The organization and status of the royal company began to deteriorate in the late 1580s. Weakened by the death of Tarlton and possibly in difficulty over their involvement in the Marprelate controversy, the Queen's made an extended trip to the North, for they reached Carlisle by September 1589 and pushed on to Scotland, perhaps at the invitation of James. On their return to London the players again only managed to match the Admiral's Men for command performances.

1954), p. xxxi agrees with R. A. Law that Shakespeare is indebted to *True Tragedy*. See Law's article, '*Richard III*: A Study in Shakespeare's Composition', *Publications of the Modern Language Association of America*, LX (1954), 689–96.

[1] R. A. Law, '*Richard III*, Act I, Scene 4', *PMLA* XXVII (1912), 117–41.

[2] *King Lear*, ed. Kenneth Muir (Cambridge, Mass., 1959), p. xxxii.

[3] *Ibid.*

[4] It should be pointed out that Shakespeare was influenced by plays other than those in the Queen's Men's repertory. For example, J. M. Nosworthy in his edition of *Cymbeline* (Cambridge, Mass., 1960), which he dates about 1608–9, thinks 'Shakespeare had read or seen or acted' in *The Rare Triumphs of Love and Fortune* and in *Cymbeline* 'he fashioned past experience to present needs' (p. xxviiff). *Love and Fortune* was presented at Court by Derby's Men in December 1582.

[5] The history of the company is examined in greater detail in my article, 'The Queen's Men, 1583–1592', *Theatre Survey*, XI (May 1970), 50–65.

Though John Lanham and John Dutton are named as the company payees for the two court appearances of 1589–90, in the following year the Dutton brothers, John and Lawrence, were given 40 pounds for four performances by 'her mates players & their companye', and John Lanham was paid by separate warrant 10 pounds for a New Year's Day appearance of 'his companye her mates players'. The separate listings, payees, and pay warrants to what is in name the same company are difficult to explain though town records in Southampton, Coventry, and Gloucester for 1590–1 provide some assistance in reconstructing the history of this period.[1]

The joint Dutton–Lanham directorship of 1589–90 was evidently split between the Dutton brothers and Lanham, and according to provincial notices Lanham and his followers joined forces with Sussex's Men. The company as a whole was clearly in difficulty. Alleyn with Strange's Men gave six performances in the court season of 1591–2 while the Queen's and an unnamed payee were rewarded for only one play. And in the abbreviated court season of 1592–3 the Queen's Men for the first time since their founding ten years earlier were not invited to appear.

It was during these plague-troubled days that a new acting company, the Servants of the Earl of Pembroke, was first mentioned in the provinces. Though they twice entertained Elizabeth when her own players were absent, the troupe vanished within a year, Henslowe remarking that by early fall, 1593, they were near bankruptcy.[2] With the theaters closed by the plague, Pembroke's was probably an offspring of a large company formed for touring.[3] Since the whereabouts of the major troupes can be accounted for during this period, it is only the disappearance of the Lanham-directed branch of the Queen's that synchronizes perfectly with the short life of Pembroke's Men.[4] Two traveling companies both called

the Queen's Men were no doubt in direct competition, and the patronage of the Earl of Pembroke who had been made the Lord President of Wales meant the possibility of richer rewards in the towns of the Welsh Marches. The rewards clearly were not so lavish as the players had hoped, for their royal name was resumed not later than the spring of 1594 when Lanham's branch of the Queen's again acted with their former associates, Sussex's Men.

IV

If Pembroke's Company is to be explained as a division of the Queen's Men, Greene's attack on Shakespeare may carry additional weight. Had Shakespeare followed that section of the Queen's that worked under Pembroke's patronage, Greene's advice to three of his fellow playwrights is more intelligible – and Greene, it must be remembered, had sold most if not all of his writing to the Queen's. Although Greene does not clearly state that

[1] See 'Records of Plays and Players in Kent 1450–1642', ed. Giles Dawson, *Malone Society Collections*, VII (1965).

[2] *Henslowe's Diary*, ed. R. A. Foakes and R. T. Rickert (Cambridge, 1961), p. 280.

[3] The Pembroke's Company which agreed to an engagement at the Swan in 1597 had in all likelihood no connection with the troupe which had blossomed so briefly three years earlier. Chambers suggests this later Pembroke's may have been derived from the Chamberlain's Men (*Elizabethan Stage*, II, 131).

[4] The suggestion of Chambers (*ibid.*, p. 129) or Baldwin (*Literary Genetics*, p. 330) that Pembroke's Men consisted of actors from Strange's and the Admiral's does not account for the appearance in provincial records of both these troupes after 1591. If the men in Pembroke's Company had been a part of the Strange's–Admiral's combination, would enough actors remain to cast works in Strange's and the Admiral's repertory when they went on tour? In effect, the dubious claim is made that the combined company had membership large enough to divide into three independent troupes, for the Admiral's and Strange's and Pembroke's played separately during the plague years.

Marlowe, Nashe, and Peele wrote for the company to which Shakespeare was attached, Marlowe's *Edward II* was performed by Pembroke's Men, and Nashe may well have penned a satiric comedy for the Queen's players during the Marprelate controversy. Certainly Nashe is well informed of anti-Martin burlesques, and his *Summer's Last Will and Testament* was performed before Archbishop Whitgift in the early 1590s. The title-page attribution of Peele's *Old Wives' Tale* is questionable, but *Edward I* is generally assigned either to the Queen's or Pembroke's, and a passage in this play provides ground for further speculation:

Now brave John Balioll Lord of Gallaway,
And king of Scots shine with thy goulden head,
Shake thy speres in honour of his name
Under whose roialtie thou wearst the same.

(lines 759–62)

especially about the player who is said to have had a preference for royal parts.[1]

Shakespeare's association with Pembroke's Men can be argued from the plays in their repertory. According to their title-pages *The True Tragedy of Richard Duke of York*, and Marlowe's *Edward II* were acted by this company. Since Professor Alexander has shown that *The True Tragedy* and the *First Part of the Contention betwixt the two famous Houses of York and Lancaster* are not original works but memorially reconstructed versions of *2* and *3 Henry VI*, it is evident that both of Shakespeare's plays were acted by Pembroke's or originally performed by men who joined this company.[2] This is confirmed by the lines and passages of Marlowe's history that a confused memory has inserted into the debased texts of the *Henry* play.

Two other works bear title-page ascription to Pembroke's company: *The Taming of A Shrew*, and *Titus Andronicus*. The relationship of *A Shrew* to the First Folio's *Taming of the Shrew* is in dispute. Critical opinion divides mainly into two schools: the Alexander–Wilson–Hosley position that *A Shrew* is a 'bad quarto' of *The Shrew*; the older view supported by Chambers that *A Shrew* was a source of Shakespeare's version.[3] The conclusive evidence that Alexander revealed in his comparison of *2* and *3 Henry VI* with *True Tragedy* and the *Contention* is conspicuously absent in the case of the *Shrew* plays. 'The nomenclature, which at least a memorizer can recall, is entirely different. The verbal parallels are limited to stray phrases.'[4] Whatever the verdict, a close connection between these plays cannot be doubted, and this is sufficient to strengthen the argument for Shakespeare's association with Pembroke's Men.

The 1594 Quarto of Shakespeare's *Titus Andronicus* states that it was 'Plaide by the Right Honourable the Earle of Darbie, Earle of Pembrooke, and Earle of Sussex their Servants'. Henslowe's *Diary* records a production of 'Titus & ondronicus' by Sussex's Men on 24 January 1594, and John Danter the printer entered the book in the Stationers' Register on 6 February 1594.[5] Since Pembroke's company flourished only during 1593, Danter may

---

[1] Ben Jonson makes the same pun in his dedicatory poem in the First Folio: 'In each of which, he seems to shake a Lance.'

[2] *Shakespeare's Henry VI and Richard III*. A. S. Cairncross in 'Pembroke's Men and Some Shakespearian Piracies', traces the source of the corrupt Quartos of *Richard III* and *Romeo and Juliet* to Pembroke's Men as well – *Shakespeare Quarterly* (Summer 1960), pp. 335–49.

[3] Peter Alexander, *Times Literary Supplement*, 16 September 1926; Richard Hosley, 'Sources and Analogues of *The Taming of the Shrew*', *Huntington Library Quarterly* (1963–4, pp. 289–308; Chambers, *William Shakespeare*, I, 327.

[4] *Ibid.*

[5] Henslowe's mysterious notation 'ne' which marks this performance may signify only that the play was receiving its first presentation by this company. Jonson's vague dating of the work in the

have listed the companies who had performed the play in chronological order.[1] Too, Danter was trying to sell his publication by pointing out its popularity; for this reason his words, like his editions, are never very reliable. The connection between Pembroke's and Sussex's is hardly surprising if the assumption that Pembroke's and members of the Queen's Company are identical. The Queen's, or at least one section of it, could have played this work in the provinces with Sussex's as early as 1590–1, and the two companies were to resume their association under Henslowe in April 1594. A play that had been in the Queen's/Pembroke's repertory could easily have found its way into Sussex's hands. Strange's men – who became the Earl of Derby's when their patron succeeded to the title in September 1593 – also performed this play according to Danter, though where and when are more difficult questions to answer.[2]

Many of the plays in the Queen's/Pembroke's repertory are later found in the possession of Henslowe or Strange's Men. Henslowe records performances by this company in 1592 of *Friar Bacon*, *Orlando*, and *Looking-Glass*, along with a 'iiij plays in one' which may be part of Tarlton's *Seven Deadly Sins*. In addition, if the *Henry VI* recorded as acted by Strange's at the Rose in 1592 is Shakespeare's, it would have passed to Strange's 'from a company to which Shakespeare belonged before he joined Pembroke's.

Just as *Titus Andronicus* after the failure of Pembroke's Men is found at the Rose, so the first part of *Henry VI* may have been written at an earlier period of Shakespeare's career for a company that he had acted with before joining Pembroke's'.[3] This company appears to have been the Queen's Men.

The bridge connecting Shakespeare, the Chamberlain's and Henslowe is found in the *Diary* for the short season at Newington Butts where the Admiral's and Chamberlain's played in June 1594. Henslowe notes performances of three works by the Chamberlain's Men in which Shakespeare may have had a hand: *Titus Andronicus*, a *Hamlet*, and *The Taming of the Shrew*. It was probably on a substantial body of past successes some of which were very likely with the Queen's Men that Shakespeare was named a payee of the Chamberlain's in the court season of 1594. His reputation and his name were secure.

---

induction to *Bartholomew Fair* would also place it earlier than this. *Titus* was acted as well in Rutland at Burley-on-the-Hill as part of the New Year's festivities in 1595/6 for Sir John Harington by a professional London company, but which one is unknown. See Gustav Ungerer's 'An Unrecorded Elizabethan Performance of *Titus Andronicus*', *Shakespeare Survey 14* (Cambridge, 1961), pp. 102–9.

[1] Q2 printed in 1600 by James Roberts names the companies in a different order: Pembroke's, Derby's, Sussex's, and the Lord Chamberlain's.

[2] *Titus Andronicus*, ed. J. C. Maxwell (Cambridge, Mass., 1963), p. xxiv f.

[3] Alexander, *Shakespeare*, p. 80.

JUDI DENCH TALKS TO
GARETH LLOYD EVANS

GLE: I've got an image of you – as an actress, that is – as a sort of loner. Although at the time of talking you are associated with the Royal Shakespeare Company, when I look back on your career I get the impression that you like to cut loose from time to time. I mean that you don't seem to like to be closely tied to any company style or ensemble for too long. Is this impression correct?

JD: Yes, it is correct. I think it doesn't evolve out of wanting specifically to be on my own – to be not connected with something. It doesn't really involve that. Very early on someone once said to my agent, 'Well we can't cast Judi in that, because that's a part for a leading lady and she's a soubrette.' I'm not going to be that. I've never wanted to be cast as one type of person. For instance I've lately read it twice that people have a rather serious image of me. They didn't use the word 'chilling' but they meant a rather serious, rather tragedienne person. Well that is so unlike me. I think things most probably happen most successfully in comedy, funnily enough. So, Gareth, it's not so much not wanting to be tied down to a company, it's rather not wanting to be tied down to an image. And so if anything like *Cabaret* and playing Sally Bowles came up, that was just like getting the most wonderful present, and everything else beside it appeared dross. Each time some kind of challenge like that comes up and somebody takes a gamble on me, then I want to do it.

GLE: I think most people would agree that, certainly so far as Shakespeare is concerned, we are living in a director's theatre, with all the pros and cons that are implied by that. I don't know whether you'd agree, but one tends nowadays to remember the name of the director of a particular production and sometimes struggle to recall who was in it.

JD: Absolutely. That is very true.

GLE: As very much an individualist, how do you get along with director's theatre?

JD: I don't think I've necessarily worked with people, with directors, who want very much to put their stamp on the play, to the exclusion of the author, but I think there are directors who want to do that. Zeffirelli is a director . . . well, they call it Zeffirelli's *Romeo and Juliet* – which isn't quite right. Working with him was the most amazing and extraordinary experience. I learned a great deal from him doing that play for a year. I do think that at Stratford in the recent years I've been there, although they say it's a director's theatre, I don't feel, for instance that when Trevor Nunn did *The Winter's Tale*, despite what many people said, that he was trying to put a stamp on it. I don't believe it in any way. I do believe that Trevor, faced with a very difficult play indeed, was trying to find some kind of solution which I felt very much part of. All in the production felt very much part of it, regardless of the fact that they remember it as Trevor's production. I thought it was an extraordinary kind of insight into that play, and it made the play very much clearer. I haven't honestly felt that any play I was in was being stamped to the exclusion of what the author was trying to say.

GLE: I'd like to take up the two parts that

you've just mentioned. Juliet first. I think this was the first production I ever saw you in, when John Stride played Romeo and Zeffirelli directed. It seems to me that this production captured all the passion, the tremendous heat of the play – both geographical and psychological, so to speak. It captured the young poignancy of the play, too . . .

JD: . . . But forgot the poetry, you're going to say!

GLE: That is exactly what I was going to ask you. How is it that Zeffirelli got away with it, as it were, by so much cutting of the poetry – especially since you, yourself, and others acting with you are so sensitive to it?

JD: No, he didn't get away with it as far as I was concerned, because I got really panned in the part. What he did get away with was this – for a long time people had got used to the poetry being 'used'. In actual fact Zeffirelli used us (John Stride and I) because we were very very young – and we didn't know. I'd been at the Vic since 1957 and that was 1960, and although I was learning about the poetry I didn't understand about it as I understand now, after so many years. Therefore, it took up all our energies, in this production, in order to play the passion and the emotions. In fact, after a year, I was so exhausted I couldn't go to America with it. In the place of the poetry he did offer something that nobody had seen for probably a long time, or perhaps it was a unique thing that he did to offer two extremely young people playing Romeo and Juliet – it has been done many times since, but it hadn't been done till then.

GLE: You mean that until then it had been done by the Leslie Howard age group?

JD: Absolutely – rather static, extremely beautiful, very romantic, very classical. Now, suddenly, with us, you had, I suppose you could say, a hippie pair. It wasn't so all the time, but it was two very young people, and I suppose the passion carried it through. Of course there were many many people who simply couldn't take that – because there was no poetry. I would love to play it again, but I'm too old now, alas. I would love to play it again now because I do know about the poetry, and I think I could still retain the passion.

GLE: You said you learned from Zeffirelli. What did you learn?

JD: I learned something about updating and emotion. He used to say, for example, 'Don't cry like that, cry like a child.' And a child uses its hands in its eyes, and it doesn't stand up to cry, it crouches down to cry; Juliet's is the crying of a young girl who might cry even when she's happy. He really did enlighten me tremendously about non-classical passion, about real hot-blooded passion – perhaps it's because he's a Mediterranean. Also, the amazing thing is that you'll be rehearsing, and suddenly out of the corner of your eye you'll see him standing beside you doing it much better than you, actually. But he made you *feel* something with an intense, incredible passion. Now, of course, somebody else can do that, and I long for somebody else to come along and say that – but to have the classical and poetic approach to it as well.

GLE: I'd like, now, to ask you about the second role – or, rather the double-role. I mean Hermione and Perdita, which you performed in Trevor Nunn's production. The process of doubling is not often found in twentieth-century theatre, but the evidence suggests that it was far from uncommon in the Elizabethan theatre. From the sixteenth-century point of view it would seem natural to double these two parts. I saw this production and it was a most notable piece of acting. What problems did you encounter in the doubling – quite apart I mean from the obvious one about being on stage at the same time?

JD: When Trevor Nunn asked me to do it he asked me to play Hermione, and I made a joke and said, 'Good gracious, is it Mother parts already?' And he said 'Yes it is!' So I thought 'If I'm going in *The Winter's Tale* that is about the only part I can play because I'm much too old to play Perdita now.' So then he came back a few weeks later and said, 'I've had an extraordinary thought'. He said 'I think you should double it and play Perdita as well.' Then he said 'Just leave it to me, but either say yes or no.' So I said 'Yes, I'll do it, I'll do it!' We had quite a long time to rehearse – six or eight weeks – and what Trevor did was to make it quite clear compartments in my mind. We rehearsed Hermione totally and solely for the first fortnight or three weeks; we didn't even set Perdita. So, by the time I came to setting Perdita it was as if I were doing another play, almost. And then we solely rehearsed Perdita. So then I had two total compartments. Then the last week or ten days or two weeks doing the two together was simply very straightforward. What did happen to me was that I used to get ready for Hermione, and people would come into my room and talk to me, and I would walk about and stay quiet in the wings. In the interval I got ready to play Perdita and I used to go and visit everybody, and I used to go in the wings and dance, and I felt a totally different person – just totally different. I'm sure it was because we divided it into the two compartments. Had he set the whole thing I'm sure I'd be still trying to puzzle it out.

GLE: I'd like to go back to your use of a word when you were talking about Zeffirelli – you said 'updating'. I assume you mean 'bringing up to date' or 'immediate response'. Thinking of this in terms of Hermione/Perdita, I've always felt that you excelled in these later heroines. I recall with great pleasure the marvellous vitality (the 'up-datedness'?) and yet, at the same time, the serene innocence of Perdita. In the production there seemed to me to be a Botticelli *Primavera* quality

(visually that is) about the way you looked. My question is this (keeping the word 'updating' in mind). Accepting, as I do, that the production was one of the most successful interpretations, using certain twentieth-century idioms, that I have ever seen, what did you find in Perdita which enabled you simultaneously to encompass this wonderful Renaissance Botticelli quality, and an essentially modern spirit? Was it something you took from the director, or something in the part itself?

JD: Do you think it was because Trevor Nunn set it in the way he did?

GLE: I think it was partly that, but I do not think it accounts for everything.

JD: It was the juxtaposition between Bohemia and Sicily. The latter was very cool, very sophisticated, quiet, pale. There were the white suits, and the pale grey and the pale green and the silk dresses – and everything about those rather cultured people. Then he did suddenly give you a terrible shock with Bohemia, in that it was all orange and yellow, and beads and long hair and tremendous vitality and the way they all practically smelt of sheep-shearing, and things like that. In itself the production had this material difference. I think I was slightly Yorkshire, too, as Perdita, and Trevor and I both thought we should bring this slightly earthy quality into her. Yet the very things she says, in fact, make her more of a Renaissance character than, for instance, Dorcas and Mopsa.

GLE: When you are preparing a role is there any sort of general policy that you follow?

JD: I do a lot of homework that you don't see, and now, living with Michael [Williams, her husband] who sits down when he comes in and works on the part. He often says to me 'when do you do it?', and I know from the moment I say I'm going to do a part there's something inside me that starts working then. Then, from the moment I actually start rehearsing, there is something that is totally pre-occupied with the part, and although I come back and might do the cottage or look after the baby or be in the garden, by the morning, if there's a problem, usually it's resolved itself in some way. By then, you know, it's very much an internal kind of working, a machine.

GLE: This process involves thinking?

JD: Yes, but not necessarily reading or studying at all. I'll have done that beforehand.

GLE: But it's something deep inside and does not communicate?

JD: No it doesn't. And I might be a bit pre-occupied and not quite listen to somebody who's talking to me. But I doubt if anyone would see it. *I* recognise that the process is going on because many many things have really adjusted themselves and answered themselves.

GLE: What if the answers don't come?

JD: They don't always come, and sometimes they come only after a long, long time. You mustn't think that they're always going to come on the first night. I've got over that now, I think. The nicest thing is perhaps when it's recognised that nothing has jelled, and that a critic can say that it will jell later. That sometimes has happened to me. I've known it myself, I've recognised it in myself. Sometimes they *have* jelled for the first night, and that's very exciting. But it's not often, not very often – I suppose twice out of fifteen, sixteen years on the stage. If there's a really big problem that I simply can't resolve, I do like to try and do it myself. I like to say 'This morning I'm going to do many many things, I'm going to make many mistakes.' Quietly I might say to a director 'I'm going to make many mistakes in this bit, but there's something I'm trying to get out of it.' And if there's one bit right or if a director says to me, 'No, that's not right – you need something', I might say to him 'Well, look, if in the whole of the next day or two I do two lines like you

mean, will you jot down what those two lines are and tell me?' It's like an enormous cross-word puzzle, a very complicated one. I do like the clues and I do like to work it out by myself. But if I really get stuck over ten across and twenty-five down, then I'll have to ask for a further clue or sometimes the answer. I don't like having to ask.

GLE: What if the answer that arrives to you by absolute conviction – your conviction I mean – turns out to be very different from the answer the director wants? What happens then?

JD: Then the director must win.

GLE: The director must win?

JD: I think so. Unless I could persuade him, by whatever reason, that I think this or this should be so. For instance just a little thing that happened recently working with Frank Hauser, whom I'm devoted to. I understand him very well – it's like tuning in to the same programme. There's one thing in the play we're doing at the moment where all three of us had to get up at one point, and Leo [McKern] has a line where he gets up and says the line. And just as he started the line we all used to get up. Frank said 'No, don't do that. Wait till he's said the line, *then* get up.' I said 'I know that's not right, I just know it's not right.' I said it to myself, because it's Leo's line and it's Frank's direction – I can't say it. Came the first night and, on that line – nothing. I said to Frank 'Would it be awful if we get up on the beginning of that line?' He said 'No, try it.' And Leo said he thought it was right too. And so we did it, up straight away. It was very interesting, because you always have to consider that there are several ways of getting a laugh, but it's not just a laugh, it's the quality of the thing that is important.

One thing I'm getting very clear about now which I've not recognised before. I make many many mistakes, but one thing I know is that I know the rhythm, very clearly, of a play. I can read it like music now.

GLE: Does this apply only to Shakespeare?

JD: It seems to. I can tell very much when the score's not right – and I've never recognised that in myself before. I just recognise it very much in Shakespeare. When you cut, for instance, in a play, I actually do feel a funny physical pain – there's a gap of a note missing. I don't want the whole of it in, but there might be just one note we've left out, like a piano that's gone a bit dead.

GLE: The RSC has, from time to time made some very interesting connections between plays and groups of plays. I'm thinking, for instance, of John Barton's *Twelfth Night* which seemed to be conceived much more in the spirit of the later plays than what we call the Romantic comedies. Going back to what you said earlier about your image as a tragedienne, what are your views about the so-called Romantic comedies? You've played Viola three times.

JD: I've played it more than that – but three times at Stratford. I played Viola before in Africa in John Neville's production. I played it then much more for comedy, much more. John Barton was the one who said it's such a bittersweet play, that if you do that it tips it over. It's not pure comedy, not even Maria – and I played Maria at the Vic. There's so much bittersweetness tinging all those characters, that you cannot play too much on the comic side and in that totally optimistic way (though Viola *is* an optimist and the catalyst of the play).

GLE: I'm concerned to ask you this because I think that although many people think of you as the grave classical actress, I am aware, every now and again, of a bubbly spirit inside you – as if there's a pixie trying to get out.

JD: I do hope so, Gareth!

GLE: Do you have to keep this pixie under firm control?

JD: Yes! It bursts out after the show. And I can get a laugh in almost any play! And I've never laughed so much as when we rehearsed *The Duchess of Malfi*. I joked till the last minute and then I suppressed myself enough to play. And then after the show it bursts out again. In rehearsals of the John Hopkins *Quartet* we laughed a great deal.

GLE: Is this a simple release or an attitude?

JD: It's both, because in order to do something that is extremely dramatic, like *Malfi* (you could say melodramatic), you have to open the valve and let that rush of pressure off. And then you've got a graver, more icy pressure underneath it. When the hot water's gone out, the cold water's there.

GLE: How would your pixie work with Lady Macbeth or Cleopatra?

JD: Oh it did! I've done that. It was excruciating. They thought we were the Morecambe and Wise of West Africa – John Neville and myself as the Macbeth family. I came on for the sleep-walking scene and someone said 'Oh my God she's washing her hands and there's no basin'! I don't know how I got through it. I just don't know how I got through it.

GLE: You've not played Lady Macbeth in England?

JD: No, and I would never be asked, Gareth. Nor Cleopatra. That's not my scene. I wouldn't know how to approach them, actually.

GLE: You've done Restoration Comedy . . .

JD: . . . The thing I adored most of all was *The Country Wife* and I long to do it again. I did it in Nottingham and it went like a bomb. I think it's probably one of the happiest parts I've ever played. And I've played the little girl Cynthia in *The Double Dealer*.

GLE: Millamant?

JD: I've not been asked to, but it's something I know I want to embark on.

GLE: Is there any actor or actress, past or present, who's been a special influence on you?

JD: There are many people actually. I've got in my mind so clearly certain performances that are really emblazoned on me – for many many different reasons. I remember before I went to the Vic for my audition – they wanted to see me about Ophelia – I saw Barbara Jefford in *The Two Gentlemen of Verona*. She was most marvellous in it, and that is very very clear to me. I remember seeing Marius Goring and Yvonne Mitchell in *The Shrew* and Michael Warr as Christopher Sly at Stratford. I think that might have been my first visit to Stratford and I was absolutely mesmerised, because I thought how amazing to get that amount of fun, to get so many people laughing out of that play that was written so many years ago. Later on I came to act in Stratford for the first time and I remember that I loved watching people and working with incredible technicians. Sir John [Gielgud] made an enormous impression on me as did Peggy [Ashcroft] when we did *The Cherry Orchard*.

There was that incredible way Sir John sat and did the crossword, and then he would get up. I used to think, 'when does he do the work, when does he get to do it?' In fact he gave me so much help in *The Cherry Orchard*, when I was most unhappy and couldn't do what Michel [St Denis] wanted at all. Sir John did it really. He encouraged me so much and I'm devoted to him.

I couldn't say to you that there's one person. I admire a great many actors and actresses for many many things, for many things I remember them doing. Oh, I remember John Clements and Kay Hammond when they did *The Little Glass Clock* and I recall they were like Dresden characters. And I think of Miles Malleson when we did *The Double Dealer* – something exquisite and eccentric – like something really perfect.

© GARETH LLOYD EVANS 1974

SHAKESPEARE STRAIGHT AND CROOKED: A REVIEW OF THE 1973 SEASON AT STRATFORD

PETER THOMSON

In *The Grass of Oblivion*, Valentin Katayev recalls how Meyerhold laid sudden plans for a new theatre:

'It's going to be an arena theatre. The audience all round. Nearly all round. Imagine it, comrades!' Meyerhold grew more and more excited, ruffling up his forest of hair, striding to and fro, now doubling up, now flinging his head back and swinging round. 'On the opening night we'll have *Othello*. The stage completely bare except for a huge carpet stretching right across it in only one colour. Bright crimson. What? Green? You see, Zina thinks it would be better green. *She's not quite right, but so much the better.* A huge dark-green carpet stretching right across the arena without a single wrinkle, dazzlingly lighted from above by all the floodlights; and in the centre of the carpet — no! Not in the centre, just a little off centre, somewhere near centre – a small . . .' He made a pause and, screwing up his face in delight, held out his hand, as though holding in his long, Paganini-like fingers something aethereally light, small, magical 'And in the middle of this brightly lit green . . .' he opened his fingers, 'something absolutely minute but startlingly visible from the farthest corner of the hall – a lace handkerchief with a small strawberry embroidered on one corner. Nothing else! That is *Othello*. That is the real, the essential Shakespeare. Brilliantly simple, isn't it?'[1]

Katayev writes in the evident conviction that Meyerhold was a genius. But what would his production of *Othello* have been like? I'm very much afraid it would have offended, even outraged, Shakespearian scholars. And yet Meyerhold is certainly among the very great figures of the twentieth-century theatre, with an imagination second to none. In the contem-porary British theatre only Peter Brook has a comparable vision and authority, and Brook has amply demonstrated his ability to offend scholars. The greater the director, the argument may run, the greater the danger that he will rival rather than serve Shakespeare's text. The experience of three years as the reviewer of the Stratford season for *Shakespeare Survey* has increased my awareness of the breach between universities and the theatre, a breach that has been made wider by the development of English studies. After attending a performance at Stratford, students and teachers of English will often talk as if Shakespeare were peculiarly their property. He is not. He belonged and should be restored to an excitable and unpretentious audience, from which most of us are, by inclination and training, debarred. We rarely contribute generously to the atmosphere in the audience of a Shakespeare play, since we are there for private, acquisitive reasons, self-centred rather than communal. Our tendency is either to reject or to hoard, to relish the experience more for the judgements it allows us to *make* than for anything we simply *receive*. We lack the ability to suspend judgement for a time that is a natural skill in the unsophisticated audience. I'm reminded of a point Northrop Frye makes about Shakespeare's comic plots:

it seems clear that no audience of Shakespeare, whether Elizabethan or modern, is allowed to think at all. They have the power to like or dislike the play, but no

[1] V. Katayev, *The Grass of Oblivion* (London, 1969), p. 170.

143

right to raise questions, as long as the action is going on, about the plausibility of the incidents or their correspondence with their habitual view of life.[1]

Nor should the theatre audience test what is done on stage against their habitual view of what *should* be done. Far too often, students, scholars, and scholarly critics ignore what is there in order to draw attention to what has been missed, or concentrate more on the distortion (which is, after all, not necessarily anything other than an alternative to a particular preconception) than on the experience. A performance should serve a text, certainly, but cannot answer to it at every point. Perhaps it should not. There is still much cogency in the sort of distinction George Hauger draws[2] between what lies on the page as a *script* and what becomes, in performance, a *play*. In these terms, a play is defined by a performance that it can never precede, and no play, not even one by Shakespeare, is a book. I do not wish to re-open an old debate, since I have nothing to add to it, but it does seem to me important that academics should be sympathetic to a theatrical question ('how can we make this script into a play?') they are unlikely ever to have to ask. Whatever the prevailing pieties, Shakespeare's work does not play itself, and much of what I hear castigated as directorial perversity is a faithful reflection of authorial complexity.

I'm not trying to defend against all comers the professional theatre in general and the Royal Shakespeare Company in particular. The power of the modern director has established patterns of behaviour, but not standards of performance. In the mind of a Meyerhold or a Brook, an image may translate itself almost instantaneously into its *mise en scène*, something to capture and contain his imaginative energy until it is released through rehearsal; but inspiration has become compulsory for all directors, and those who don't have it must be severely tempted to cultivate the appearance of having it. It has become the rule to adopt a leading idea about a play, and use every available theatrical method to force it across to the audience. Over-simplification is almost inevitable if the dramatist is Shakespeare, and this can have a dangerous charm in the theatre, as it did in John Barton's substitution of Bolingbroke in disguise for Richard II's friendly groom. Over-emphasis, on the other hand, is theatrically offensive too. I doubt whether this year's *Richard II* will have more friends among the purists than the *Romeo and Juliet*, yet it displayed a far greater theatrical intelligence than Terry Hands's vulgarly ingenious production, in which the over-emphases were sometimes hysterical. The 'director's theatre' post-dates Shakespeare by 400 years, and cannot lightly be assumed to be suitable for the production of his plays. Its English advocates have tended to look to Stanislavsky for authority. The vexed issue in this context is that of the 'super-objective': 'what we need is a super-objective which is in harmony with the intentions of the playwright and at the same time arouses a response in the soul of the actors. That means that we must search for it not only in the play but in the actors themselves'.[3] Stanislavsky stresses the collaboration of the whole company, but in a director's theatre (and whatever he *says*, Stanislavsky cannot escape all responsibility) it is the director who decides on the production's superobjective. Design will re-inforce that superobjective, and so will the director's more obviously 'original' ideas. There are times — as in this year's *Romeo and Juliet* and, sometimes, in *As You Like It* — when the resources seem to have been used to give a specious consistency to an unhappy idea, but Stanislavsky can furnish an alternative text:

[1] N. Frye, *A Natural Perspective* (New York, 1965), p. 13.

[2] G. Hauger, *Theatre – General and Particular* (London, 1966), pp. 24–5.

[3] C. Stanislavsky, *An Actor Prepares*, trans. E. R. Hapgood (Harmondsworth, 1967 ed.), pp. 274–5.

The usual impression is that a director uses all of his material means, such as the set, the lighting, sound effects and other accessories, for the primary purpose of impressing the public. On the contrary. We use these means more for their effect on the actors. We try in every way to facilitate the concentration of their attention on the stage.[1]

Where the director's theatre addresses its serious attention to the art of the actor, it is, I suggest, the highest development of western theatrical method *so far*.

It seems particularly worth reiterating that view here because directors have taken, and often enough deserved, a fair battering in the pages of *Shakespeare Survey* in recent years. We had in the same volume, for instance, Professor Muir ironically suggesting to a young director that 'the quickest way to acquire a reputation would be to play Shakespeare straight, without cuts and without gimmicks',[2] and Professor Brown, from the premise that 'most of us would agree that we cannot nail down his purpose or be sure that we understand', asking: 'Will anyone find a way of presenting Shakespeare freely? ... Could theatrical craftsmanship be allied to a production which seemed as unstrained, as "easy" and "natural", as Shakespeare's writing? And as ambiguous, reflective, invitingly difficult, and alive?'[3] Professor Brown's questions are fine, but his answers, not surprisingly, are disappointing and, with one exception, expressed as negatives. The positive suggestion is that audience and actors should be placed 'in the same unvarying light', primarily so that the audience 'can easily withdraw from the play and can look where they please'. It is optimistic to suppose that, as a result, 'the mere necessity of holding attention would enforce greater vitality and variety in the acting. A far quicker overall pace would be required and varied rhythms . . .' Perhaps. Or perhaps ham-acting, and a tendency to go hell-for-leather through the boring bits. Professor Brown is

looking for alternatives to the enforcing of the director's single-minded approach, but, despite his useful stress on audiences and his corrective concern for the actor, his quest is in its early stages. I have much sympathy for his wish to 'free' Shakespeare, but in the exigent theatrical situation every idea must be translated into a method of work. Where the scholar can afford to be tentative and exploratory, the theatre-professional must be concrete and complete. He cannot illuminate a *part* of the play. He has to present the *whole*. It is a more daunting task than that of most of us who lecture or write essays.

Professor Muir's call for 'straight' Shakespeare should be appraised in this context. It is easy enough to know approximately what he means – Gielgud, we might agree, is a 'straighter' actor than Olivier, and Glen Byam Shaw a 'straighter' director than Peter Brook – but very much harder to apply the adjective in detail. What is a 'straight' playing of *Macbeth*'s witches, or of Caliban, or of *Measure for Measure*? Why should we suppose that what cannot be agreed in the study should be defined in the theatre? It is the very attempt to straighten Shakespeare that has led to the imposition of directorial lines, with their accompanying over-simplifications and over-emphases. Playing Shakespeare straight is the notional idea of most professional directors. The difficulties come with the attempts to enact an intention. It is the fear of many Shakespearians, Professor Muir among them, that the modern director will become (or has become) more important in the theatre than the words. The call for straight playing is, above all, a plea that Shakespeare's text should

---

[1] *Ibid.*, p. 171.

[2] K. Muir, 'Shakespeare the Professional', in *Shakespeare Survey 24* (Cambridge, 1971), p. 46. Professor Muir's essay is reprinted in his *Shakespeare the Professional* (London, 1973).

[3] J. R. Brown, 'Free Shakespeare', in *Shakespeare Survey 24*, p. 134.

be allowed to declare itself. The director who knows when to stop *making* things happen, and *let* them happen instead is the only one suited to the staging of Shakespeare. But then, he is the only worthwhile director anyway. Even so, his achievement will not often be recognised by the scholar who knows what he wants, and would be a dictatorial, line-pushing director of the worst kind. 'Straight' Shakespeare is all too likely to mean 'Shakespeare as I'd make the actors do him'. There is no prospect of general agreement about any production. What I most regret is the naive intolerance of many academics in their discussion of Stratford productions, the assumption that the plays could *easily* have been better. It is not true of Professor Muir, but I have wondered whether the demand for 'straighter' Shakespearian productions masks a stronger demand for no productions at all. The exploitation of performances as evidence of the superiority of his own conceptions over the theatre's is the meanest use the academic makes of his role as audience.

The 1973 repertoire was informed by no master-plan. The mixed bag included *Romeo and Juliet*, *Richard II*, *As You Like It*, *Love's Labour's Lost*, and, opening too late for review here, *The Taming of the Shrew*. The 'straightest' was *Love's Labour's Lost* despite its eighteenth-century costumes and its undisguised pole-trees. The designers, Timothy O'Brien and Tazeena Firth, had covered the stage with a grass cloth and roofed it with a silk canopy sloping up from the rear to the proscenium. According to the programme the canopy was fifty feet by twenty-three feet, and its delicately veined tree-design had begun as a photographic negative enlarged 1,980 times, and transferred for printing to thirty-one silk screens, each of them used only four times 'to print an image which repeats itself as little as economically possible'. The souvenir programme's familiar

humorist must have chosen the word 'economically', but the idea was an interesting one, and the effect of enclosing the play in its rural setting successful. It gave to the production some of the pictorial effect that Pater anticipated in *Appreciations*. 'It is as if Shakespeare had intended to bind together, by some inventive conceit, the devices of an ancient tapestry, and give voices to its figures.'[1] David Jones opened the play with drums and solemn brass to accompany the coffin-bearing procession of Navarre and his court. In unison, Navarre and his three companions doffed their fine hats and tossed them into the empty coffin, to be followed there by cloaks and swords. Only then did the King begin:

> Let fame, that all hunt after in their lives,
> Live register'd upon our brazen tombs,
> And then grace us in the disgrace of death.

It was an over-labouring of the play's awareness of life's brevity, and not characteristic of the production's lighter touch. The company's evident confidence in the play's attractiveness owed much to the assurance of Ian Richardson's Berowne. It was good to hear this fine speaker of Shakespeare relishing the verbal challenge of *Love's Labour's Lost*. His separateness was immediately established in the repeated, but subtly differentiated, emphasis on 'Which I hope well is not enrolled there ... The which I hope is not enrolled there ... Which I hope well is not enrolled there.' In this first speech, Richardson had already found a way – a pause, a smirk, a turn of the head – of bringing the audience into the word-play without explicitly acknowledging their presence. It would earn him a delighted laugh on 'Let's see the penalty' (line 122), and our collaboration in his questioning of 'Necessity' (lines 147 and 152). All his major speeches were explored for their legitimate vocal

[1] W. Pater, *Appreciations* (London, 1907 edition), p. 163.

variety. The 'German clock' of III, i, 180 entered the rhythm of the previous line; every word of the punning prose that opens IV, iii was carried over to the audience; 'Have at you, then, affection's men-at-arms' began quietly and reached a controlled climax only at 'For wisdom's sake, a word that all men love ...' But the comic peak of the performance was reached with the tearing of his incriminating letter to Rosaline. He had come close to giving himself away in the lustful delivery of his reproach to the King:

> When shall you hear that I
> Will praise a hand, a foot, a face, an eye,
> A gait, a state, a brow, a breast, a waist,
> A leg, a limb? (IV, iii, 179–82)

The production was careful to indicate that every man in the play is uncritically fond of the female body. Berowne, despite both his sophistication and his mockery of sophistication, is no exception. Richardson had expended vast energy in concealment and in comic attack before Costard and Jaquenetta brought the letter. Now, in the attempt to preserve his secret, he not only tore the letter into tiny pieces but tried by whirling his arms like a possessed windmill to scatter the fragments.

The production's other major strength was in the performance of the villagers. Timothy Dalton's wild-haired, athletic Costard was a plausible rustic study, and the trio of Dull, Sir Nathaniel and Holofernes made sense and laughter out of almost all they did. I shall be lucky to see a better Holofernes than Derek Smith's; Goldsmith's village master in search of 'boding tremblers'. He carried a cane, and could only with difficulty restrain the urge to use it, firstly on Dull, later on Costard, and finally on Berowne during his interruption of one of the Worthies. His silencing of Armado with 'Shall I have audience?' (v, i, 114) had the astonished fury of an ignored headmaster, and he managed to speak as if dictating without

ever seeming slow. Most important of all, he had the determination and the skill to make his meaning clear. The 'sorel' pun was explained with the aid of chalk and a slate carried in the capacious pocket of his gown, but with or without props, he made me realise that the comic appeal of Holofernes in the modern theatre does not depend on ducking the issue and getting laughs out of conspicuous incomprehensibility. If Smith succeeded in explaining his comic lines to us, we laughed, and if he didn't, we laughed in appreciation of his faith in us. Jeffery Dench's Sir Nathaniel was nicely judged. With frizzy red hair, and wearing a beret, he stuck close to Holofernes, leaving Dull always slightly apart to vary the stage-picture. When Holofernes said 'peregrinate', Sir Nathaniel noted the word down. As Dull, Denis Holmes preserved a placid good humour and an endearingly vacant grin. It was a nice touch to have him respond to Holofernes's 'pauca verba' by rubbing his belly and licking his lips in anticipation of a good meal. The solidity of this group was an implicit criticism of the courtiers' posturing. There is no answer to the protest of Holofernes at Berowne's mockery of his performance as Judas – 'This is not generous, not gentle, not humble'. This production made no attempt to dignify Navarre's purposes, either in the taking or the breaking of the oath. He and his three favoured courtiers were witty but not likeable – and they were utterly exposed in the extravagant finery and elaborate staging of their Muscovite interlude. The Princess of France and her ladies were also presented as brittle, slight people against the substantial countrymen. It was not a good year for actresses, and not all the work that had gone into their scenes was rewarded in performance. There was imitation of gaiety more often than gaiety itself. Estelle Kohler as Rosaline was less successful than Ian Richardson in commanding our attention when she needed it. She and the others looked faintly embarrassed when they were required to do some complicated and energetic re-grouping during the reading of Armado's letter to Jaquenetta. Nevertheless, the re-discovery of the satirical sting in the presenta-tion of courtly shallowness was a substantial achievement. David Jones realised rightly that there was no need to make a feature of Marcade's entry. It was as unobtrusive as his exit, but it provided the necessary deepening of the lovers' experience. Afterwards – a typically thoughtful piece of direction – the first three lovers paired up in the centre leaving Rosaline and Berowne below them, separated by almost the whole width of the stage. This was the only production to allow the actors an uncluttered stage, and though more use might have been made of the upstage area, the rewards were obvious.

It is a pity, perhaps, to end on a quibble, but I was puzzled by Tony Church's Armado. He played the whole role towards the plaintive poverty of 'The naked truth of it is, I have no shirt.' He was a crumpled melancholy figure, without a hint of the braggart, and with no variation of his slow speaking pace. I hope the first scene with Moth improved later in the run, or that the alternative Moth (I do not know which of the two boys mentioned in the pro-gramme I saw) was better than the one I watched. As it was, I thought it shoddy and embarrassing. The boy understood nothing he said, and, since there was no relationship between them, Tony Church was unable to help. Are boy actors worth the risk?

If *Love's Labour's Lost* was the *straightest* production of the season, *As You Like It* bid fair to be the *crookedest*. It is characteristic of 'crooked' Shakespeare to pursue relevance at all costs, and to use the plays to say what *we* would like to. Let Charles Marowitz speak to it:

It was my belief that there was no great relevance in reviving 'Othello' today without accommodating the black revolutionary spirit irrationally lodged in an audience's expectations that made me want to tackle it; and by tackling it, I mean bypassing Shakespeare's original intentions and extracting only what I needed to achieve my own purposes.[1]

Marowitz does not claim to present Shake-speare's play. Stratford has not yet dared to monkey with the text as Marowitz does, but the prospect has, I expect, interested Buzz Goodbody now and then. I had heard rumours of wild inventiveness in this production of *As You Like It* before I saw it, and, having hated Miss Goodbody's work on *King John* in 1970, I was prepared for the worst. Both programme and poster talked of the woman's role, a modern *cause célèbre* – and we knew the pro-duction was to be in modern dress. The portents, then, were grim. The event was con-fused, popular, over-eclectic, and rather jolly. I discerned no underlying logic, 'what the hell', perhaps, rather than 'as you like it'; but there was theatrical flair, and an understanding of contemporary tastes in entertainment that could be, but was not always, vulgar.

To deal first with the updating. It was no help to Orlando to be asked to court Ganymede in modern dress. 'Soppy' was a word I heard whispered in the row behind me. In general, though, the main plot was allowed to speak for itself, only intermittently threatened by the spectacular modernism of some episodes. I doubt whether Professor Brown would agree, but this was, in many ways, an unusually 'free' production, not concerned to enforce an interpretation so much as to embellish a story. Charles the wrestler was one of the embellish-ments. Brian Glover, who played the role, wrestles professionally, and is familiar with the television style. The audience recognised him immediately in the finger-stretching gestures

[1] C. Marowitz, 'The Moor the Merrier', in *The Guardian*, 8 June 1972. Marowitz is writing in defence of his version of *Othello*, which he was careful to call an *Othello*.

which accompanied his dialogue, and the wicked relish with which he punched a fist into the palm of his other hand. The wrestling match, arranged by Glover, was a television spectacular which David Suchet handled with dexterity. It took place, improbably, in the plush casino that Duke Frederick's court had become. The Duke himself was an elderly playboy in a black eye-patch. At the opening of the scene, Rosalind and Celia were properly isolated downstage while the dinner-jacketed guests smoked and circulated upstage under a showy chandelier. Touchstone, a bookie rather than a gambler, was out of place too. His 'motley' would later be represented by a loud check suit. There were times in Arden when he looked like the comedian and Rosalind the principal boy in a Christmas pantomime. Duke Senior's forest court had a seedy, Chekhovian elegance that was a surprisingly apt setting for the histrionic misanthropy of Richard Pasco's brilliant Jaques. There were numerous smaller points. William had his name printed on his T-shirt. Phebe was an art student, who found the saw of might, 'Who ever lov'd that lov'd not at first sight' (III, v, 82), by looking it up in a Penguin Book of Verse. 'It was a lover and his lass' was sung to a pleasant rock tune, and turned into a considerable musical number by its accompaniment and choreography. I didn't enjoy it. Boy actors again. There was more rock and vigorous modern dancing to celebrate the weddings. After such conclusive celebrations, the unfortunate actor of Jaques de Boys must have felt even more like an unrequested encore.

Christopher Morley's design called for a variable quantity of thin vertical poles that could be easily raised or lowered. They were a neutral background, probably more 'indoor' than 'outdoor', and not, therefore, particularly suited to this play. When, after the interval, a large log, with the old-fashioned reality of a pantomime ground-row, was set centre stage, I

was surprised. It was a conflict of styles for which there seemed no explanation – other, perhaps, than the production's general eclecticism. The relationship of Rosalind and Celia was a close and strong one. Maureen Lipman's Celia could match Roslind passion for passion. It was a pity she was so tall, taller, in fact, than Eileen Atkins' Rosalind. Not only was it in conflict with the text, but it seemed to unsettle Eileen Atkins in the early scenes. Why, after all, should it have been she who put on the denim suit? Where was her 'pretty little coz'? It was a strangely modest performance, almost as if Celia had been strengthened at Rosalind's expense. Derek Smith's Touchstone was as eager as his Holofernes to explain his jokes. His dialogue with Corin (Jeffrey Dench's beautifully observed old countryman) was a fine example of the simultaneous acting of text and footnotes. Is Touchstone's modern equivalent a rather brash seaside comic, likely to make a song-and-dance act out of his Rosalind rhymes? The suggestion didn't offend me, and I enjoyed the magnificent patter of his 'quarrel on the seventh cause' set piece as much as any of the other people who applauded it. Finally there was Richard Pasco's Jaques, speaking for an older generation of theatregoers in his dislike of what was going on around him. It was an interpretation built round the 'libertine' and the 'scholar'. His white suit and hat had seen better days. He smoked without evident pleasure, wore glasses with cheap frames, and walked with his knees bent in a strange, small-stepping slouch. He had the air of a man faced with the alternative of alcoholism or indigestion. Not only did he know that his breath smelt vile, but also that no one would dare tell him. Graham Greene would have understood some of his motives, knowing that every smile can accompany an unpleasant memory. It was a complete enough performance to justify, even to demand, this kind of description. David Palmer pointed out to me how carefully each entrance and exit had been planned and executed. I was much impressed by the reticence with which a tensely loving relationship between Jaques and Duke Senior was indicated. Whilst liking to hear Jaques talk, the Duke was always nervous of his tongue. The party was never complete when he wasn't there, and never at ease when he was. Talking, it was implied, was Jaques's social art. A man confident enough to conclude a scene as Jaques concludes II, v, knows that his effects depend partly on what he says, and partly on the fact that it is he who says it: 'I'll go sleep if I can; if I cannot, I'll rail against all the first-born of Egypt.' I found myself honestly looking forward to 'All the world's a stage', and honestly enjoying it. 'Muling and puking' became funny through Pasco's disgust. Left alone at the dining-table, Jaques wheezed his way into a long belly-laugh – at the Duke, at life, at us – which became, in effect, the beginning of the interval. At the end of the play, having watched the modern frenzy of the wedding from off the raised stage, he spat out 'so, to your pleasures' disconcertingly. It was only with some difficulty that Duke Senior recovered sufficient poise to restart the dance:

> Proceed, proceed: we will begin these rites,
> As we do trust they'll end, in true delights.
>
> (v, iv, 191–2)

Against the strength of Pasco's Jaques, the Duke seemed dangerously sentimental.

I make no bones about my dislike of Terry Hands's production of *Romeo and Juliet*. It had the appearance of a rush job in which the director had tried to save time by telling the actors what to do instead of letting them discover their own style. Estelle Kohler was required to pitch her Juliet at least five years too young for her own ease, and Timothy Dalton's slender voice was often over-taxed in an attempt to rival the on-stage volume. The production was overloaded with directorial bright ideas, and the actors were kept constantly at stretch in the effort to control them. As a result the stage was possessed by a hysteria not far short of panic. It was, I assume, Hands's intention that the family quarrel should be viewed on the level of street-gang hysteria. Tybalt, certainly, was a skinhead bully and Mercutio perhaps a muscular advocate of gay liberation. What, though, are the advantages of likening these Veronese brawls to pop festival 'bother'? The 'relevance' of *Romeo and Juliet* is surely guaranteed by the plight of the lovers. I would much prefer a frankly 'crooked' adaptation to this kind of jerry-building on a Shakespearian foundation. The perils of a director's theatre were fully displayed here.

The dominant effect of Farrah's set was provided by the upstage black and gold grill, and by the two bridges that crossed the stage in front of it. The higher of these was set at about fourteen feet above the floor. The other, just upstage of it, was about seven feet high, and had steps behind it and also steps leading down onto the main playing area. The whole set bore in on the action, confining it, for the most part, to centre stage. The lower bridge was rarely used. The higher, Juliet's balcony and the scene of the lovers' parting, gave some of the audience a view of nothing higher than the actors' knees. A designer's job includes the consideration of sight-lines.

The performance began with a half-lit massed entry, the crowd both threatening and afraid. The prologue was spoken by the actor who would play Prince Escalus, and then the lights were raised, red bunting was spread diagonally across the stage (the first of several uses of the clothes-line principle), and the street-scene began. The production aimed to stress the linking of boredom and violence, but the first brawl, though vigorous, was not very dangerous. I missed the blow that left one body sprawled under the stage-left stairway, to be ignored for the rest of the scene. It was David Suchet's bullet-headed Tybalt, bursting out of brown leather, who introduced the first real chill. A blonde and vacuous Benvolio would have been no match for him. It was Bernard Lloyd's charismatic Mercutio who had Benvolio's puppyish loyalty. He made his first entrance carrying a life-size female doll, which would later be torn obscenely apart, item by item, to illustrate the conjuration 'by Rosaline's bright eyes' (II, i, 17f.). The playing of Mercutio as a flamboyant pervert and rival gang-leader to the sadistic bully Tybalt relegated the love of Romeo and Juliet to theatrical second place. The hysteria, which came to a climax in Romeo's scream as he stabbed· Tybalt in the groin with a short dagger, was toned down but not lost after Juliet had heard of her husband's banishment. For most of the time the gang scenes were stagy rather than theatrical, but Mercutio's death was an exception. A gradual dawning of awareness of the seriousness of his wound was expressed first on Mercutio's face, and then spread among his friends to reach its height in Benvolio's anguish. It was finely handled, and moving in defiance of its context.

I am not at all sure what Terry Hands intended us to think of Romeo and Juliet. Their corpses were finally huddled without beauty below the massive metal gates that defined the Capulets' monument, and this tended to confirm the reduced stature of their love. Here, as in the gang warfare itself, there was a suggestion that *West Side Story* was returning influence to its original. Estelle Kohler's unnecessarily kittenish Juliet gained authority in the balcony scene, but was sadly confined in delivering 'Gallop apace, you fiery-footed steeds' on a sheepskin rug right up against a background of two sheets, slung on the ubiquitous clothesline. (In II, v she had been required to beat a carpet hung on the clothes-line. Am I missing some point?) She was at her best in the parting from Romeo, and the subsequent defiance first of her mother ('He shall not make me there a joyful bride' was given a particularly subtle stress) and then of the Nurse ('Speakest thou from thy heart?'). It seems strange to say it, but Timothy Dalton was remarkably unobtrusive as Romeo, a gentle victim of the production's violence. I wondered whether his churchyard threat to tear Balthasar 'joint by joint' had given Terry Hands the hint for the destruction of Mercutio's doll, but I doubt whether the hint was necessary.

One other scene (IV, v) deserves description. Juliet was discovered, apparently dead, with her head towards the audience. Almost at once four keeners appeared on the lower of the two bridges. Capulet addressed the audience from downstage right on 'All things that we ordained festival, / Turn from their office to black funeral', but the solemn mood was challenged by the three grotesquely masked Musicians. While the keeners dressed Juliet in her wedding gown, they joked and peered at her. Even when the corpse was laid out their jarring comments continued, and they were a disturbing presence at the inset funeral song. It was now that the metal gates that would dominate act v were shut, and Juliet laid on a raked slab downstage centre. In this scene, at least, the actors were in tune with their director's ideas.

It would be easy to make John Barton's production of *Richard II* sound gimmicky and gratuitously theatrical, merely by listing some of its ingredients. The designers, Timothy O'Brien and Tazeena Firth, had flanked the central acting area with two escalators joined by a bridge which could ride noiselessly up and down them – a piece of refined visible mechanism that would have made Piscator jealous, and could carry Richard down to the base court like glistering Phaethon on the

Victoria Line. For their fight, Mowbray and Bolingbroke had been provided with elaborate hobby-horses similar to those used for *The Chances* during Chichester's opening season. The Percys, 'riding' bigger, ominous-black horses, had to walk on short stilts to carry them. Richard, returned from Ireland, sat *astride* a white horse, erected in the middle of the stage, like the centre-piece of a *tableau-vivant*. Gloucester's widow was played as a ghost, emerging from the downstage grave-trap with a skull in her hand, and speaking with the aid of echo-effects. v, ii began as a winter scene, with York and his Duchess wrapped against the cold, and a snowman ('a mockery king of snow') quirkily featured in a dominant central position. When York had completed his account of the entry into London of Bolingbroke and Richard, winter cloaks were doffed, the snowman melted, and spring colours greeted the lines:

> To Bolingbroke are we sworn subjects now,
> Whose state and honour I for aye allow.
>
> (v, ii, 39–40)

The Queen's ladies-in-waiting wore decorative masks in their first two scenes, and their movements were stylised throughout. I have no idea why they were required to slither around the stage during Richard's farewell to his wife. In the garden scene, their formality was matched by the gardeners, dressed, again for no clear reason, as monks. It was also as a monk, walking beside Northumberland's horse and chanting *Kyrie Eleison*, that Bolingbroke made his return to England in II, iii: and the cowl was again a disguise in the sensational substitution of Bolingbroke for Richard's groom in v, v. There is no doubt of the meretricious effectiveness of that theatrical moment when Bolingbroke lowered the hood to reassure Richard, 'What my tongue dares not, that my heart shall say'; but there is nothing else to say in defence of this invention

(despite the coincidental use of a groom's disguise by Robert de Vere, Richard's historical favourite). It related to the production's ruling decision – to play Richard and Bolingbroke as twin starring roles, along the lines indicated in Anne Barton's programme note: 'Richard's journey from king to man is balanced by Bolingbroke's progress from a single to a twin-natured being. Both movements involve a gain and a loss. Each, in its own way, is tragic.' Within the terms of what, despite the claims made there, was a wholly theatrical decision, John Barton's production was *not* gimmicky. On the contrary, it was the passionately sensed and consistently argued presentation of a vision.

It has been generally my impression of John Barton's work that ideas encountered in the study are, with some effort, translated into the theatre. This was not so with *Richard II*. The informing idea of this production was the alternation of Richard Pasco and Ian Richardson as Richard and Bolingbroke – in itself a fascinating contrast between an actor naturally warm and 'romantic' and one cooler and more 'classical'. It began with the two actors meeting downstage of the sun-king's draped golden cloak, consulting the prompt-book (which shall play the king tonight?), turning upstage to hold the crown together – and freezing for a moment until the Bolingbroke of the night dropped his hand, and the Richard smiled, laughed, and was ready to lead the play into action. The performance was often in touch with the make-believe of children's games. The horses were an aspect of this. At the end, the 'groom' gave the imprisoned Richard a toy 'roan Barbary', and the coffin carrying Richard's body was a child's. It was, perhaps, this awareness of the child's vision that gave new weight to the concern for kinship of cousin, uncle, aunt. Certainly the opening was as jaunty as a family charade until the sudden hardening of Richard's face at Bolingbroke's first mention of Gloucester's death (I, i, 100), and there was a nursery petulance in the expression of 'We were not born to sue, but to command.' The by-play between Bolingbroke and Aumerle in I, iii preserved the sense of uncertain innocence, as did the chuckle with which Richard preceded his announcement of the banishments. It was during Mowbray's final denial of his guilt that Bolingbroke began the conscious calculation that was to be reinforced when Gaunt's gesture of grace over his head turned into the mimed holding of a crown. Both Richard and Bolingbroke signalled their role-playing to the audience. The kind of part they were playing varied with the play's crises, but not the awareness of themselves as actors. Bored with his pretence as righteous accuser, Bolingbroke broke off before completing his charges against Bushy and Green (III, i), and the message to Richard in Flint Castle was turned into sportive deception when Northumberland, still on horseback, took it down in note form at Bolingbroke's dictation. When Northumberland assured Richard that Bolingbroke 'doth humbly kiss thy hand' (III, iii, 104), the usurping actor was, in fact, standing casually downstage right. After a splendidly mobile staging of the often painful gage-throwing scene, IV, i continued to enforce the *double* role-playing. There was a conscious reminiscence of the opening mime in Richard's insistence that he and Bolingbroke hold the crown together, and a comically histrionic use by Richard of the kerchief given to him by Northumberland. Most notably, the circular property mirror was given a prominence which it retained until Richard's death. When Richard had punched out the glass, Bolingbroke lifted the empty ring-frame and placed it over Richard's head deliberately enough for us to see it pass from halo to crown, and from crown to noose to the enormously stressed accompaniment of:

> The shadow of your sorrow hath destroy'd
> The shadow of your face. (IV, i, 292–3)

The stress on these lines, reinforced by repetition and echo-effects, was to be picked up in the final confrontation when Bolingbroke as Groom held the empty ring of the mirror between his face and Richard's, the mutual reflection of two shadows strutting and fretting their hour upon the stage. The death was a theatrical set-piece, with Richard hoisted by his chains some twelve feet above the stage and shot in the back by an arrow fired from upstage by Exton.

The use of so much that is conventionally associated with the stage's 'magic' – mechanical transformations, melting snowman, pantomime horses, stilt-walking, the tricky curtain-call – was consistent with the perception of the play's conscious theatricality. I am not so happy about the presentation of the narrative. By placing two detailed performances among so many generalised ones – varying from the domestic knockabout of Beatrix Lehmann's Duchess of York (the authority for this is Bolingbroke's comment on her entrance in v, iii, 'Our scene is alter'd from a serious thing'), through the sinister, black-clad Percys, to the emptily formal, emotionless Queen – Barton risked some obscuring of the action. The situation was not improved by the ill-advised doubling of Richard's sycophant Bagot and his murderer Exton (a grand piece of work in a small part by Anthony Pedley, who had a workmanlike season throughout). The production laid no stress on the misdemeanours of Richard's favourites, and thus gave no serious hint of his homosexuality. The latter was no loss, but audiences unfamiliar with the text might have benefited from a clearer notion of the background to the usurpation. The best director I ever worked with as a student used to shout 'Plot!' whenever he thought we were mishandling crucially informative lines.

This was certainly not a 'straight' production as Professor Muir would intend it. As the programme was at pains to point out, about 500 lines had been cut and twenty others imported from *2 Henry IV* to give extra body to the role of Bolingbroke. It was, however, an intelligent and outstandingly bold attempt to give the text a life not merely *in* but *of* the theatre.

© PETER THOMSON 1974

THE YEAR'S CONTRIBUTIONS TO SHAKESPEARIAN STUDY

1. CRITICAL STUDIES

reviewed by D. J. PALMER

Though the reach may exceed the grasp, an attempt to formulate the nature of Shakespearian tragedy is an ambitious enterprise. I. Morris[1] and R. Nevo[2] undertake it from very different points of view.

Morris sees Shakespearian tragedy in a religious perspective, although unlike most attempts to Christianise its meaning his argument does not depend on allegory or on explicit allusions to Christian doctrine within the plays. On the contrary, he insists upon the essentially secular nature of tragic experience, conceiving tragedy and Christian belief alike to be grounded upon the universal human condition in which worldly aspirations must inevitably end in failure and disaster, for 'in a Divine universe, every human aspiration short of the desire for God must come to naught'. 'The high duty of tragedy, in fact,' writes Morris, 'is to present the situation that faith must overcome.' It is the need for revelation, rather than the revelation itself, that he would have us recognise in the tragedies.

This argument, carefully stated and elaborately documented (though with relatively little direct reference to the plays themselves), seems open to question at several points. In stressing the basis of tragedy in human experience, for instance, Morris tends to obscure the distinction between life and art, and to overlook the fact that comedy has the same basis. Moreover, to describe tragedy as a 'confirmation', albeit implicit, of Christian truth contradicts the primacy and autonomy that are claimed for

experience, and suggests instead that the eye of faith can only look upon tragedy as a mirror of its own preconceptions. But if Christian belief so diminishes human values that it is compelled to reduce the complex individuality of Shakespeare's protagonists to the judgement that 'in their self-choosing, and their will to creaturely transcendence, they are all akin', then its relevance to Shakespearian tragedy must be doubted. To consider the tragic ordering and evaluation of experience in terms other than its own may be to see through a glass darkly.

Nevo approaches the tragedies through their dramatic structure, showing each of them to conform to the same basic five-part progression which she identifies as 'predicament, psychomachia, peripeteia, perspectives of irony and pathos, and catastrophe'. In this structure, which is conceived as a continuous dynamic sequence rather than a series of rhetorical divisions, the protagonist is 'the axis of development', moving through the corresponding phases of 'challenge, temptation or dilemma, disintegration, and despair, to the final recognition in which all that was hidden is revealed, and self and destiny fully and finally confronted'. The analysis of each tragedy is consistent without being rigidly schematic, with much lively and acute commentary,

[1] *Shakespeare's God: The Role of Religion in the Tragedies* (George Allen and Unwin, 1972).
[2] *Tragic Form in Shakespeare* (Princeton University Press, 1972).

particularly on the soliloquies, but there is an undue emphasis upon the tragic action as a vehicle for the protagonist's achievement of self-discovery. We are told, for instance, that in his death the hero 'in some way exhibits and affirms that in which he has had faith, that which defined his inmost being, or with which he has identified himself, despite his rejection of it or his previous failure to recognize it', a suggestion whose confidence disturbs the dramatic balance between enlightenment and inscrutability, and which therefore comes perilously close to an insidious form of consolation. No doubt, however, this is a finer response to tragedy than 'the moral distribution of praise or blame' from which it seeks to rescue the plays.

Such attempts to find a common denominator in the tragedies meet with the scepticism of K. Muir, for whom 'there is no such thing as Shakespearian Tragedy: there are only Shakespearian tragedies'. *Shakespeare's Tragic Sequence*[1] may therefore be a somewhat misleading title if it suggests a study of the features that relate the plays to each other as a group, since, although Muir deals with them in chronological order, pointing out the immaturities of the early tragedies and drawing occasional comparisons, his focus is upon the individual qualities of each play. Nevertheless, there does emerge from the book as a whole a strong insistence upon Shakespeare's artistic 'disinterestedness', that supreme quality of the dramatic imagination which critics of a more dogmatic turn of mind than Muir often fail to appreciate. There are a few contentious or incautious statements, such as the thrice-repeated conviction that 'it was Hamlet's bounden duty to avenge the murder', the assertion that Edgar cures his father of despair, and, also in discussing *King Lear*, the notion that principles of human decency are specifically Christian. But Muir's ability to deal directly and succinctly with large and complex

issues, his judicious sense of balance, and his flair for the precise, illuminating phrase, make this an eminently useful introduction to the tragedies.

Not surprisingly, the same qualities of critical wisdom characterise Muir's other book, *Shakespeare the Professional*,[2] which brings together a dozen essays originally published in various journals. The coherence of the collection is provided by its central chapters on image-patterns in the tragedies, but readers who are tiring of this kind of approach will find greater stimulus in the more miscellaneous essays on Shakespeare's professionalism, on his dramatic attitudes to poets, and on his achievement in the non-dramatic poems, which apart from the Sonnets have not won the esteem that Muir believes them to deserve. As far as *Venus and Adonis* is concerned, critical uncertainty about the nature of its achievement may have something to do with its moral ambivalence, a feature of the poem that Muir discusses, and that is further examined in J. D. Jahn's[3] provocative essay on Adonis, which sees him not as a figure of passive innocence but as a self-admiring and self-righteous coquette.

Sen Gupta[4] is another critic who prefers to deal with the major tragedies as separate plays, though he prefaces his 'fragmentary visions' with a sympathetic but not uncritical appraisal of A. C. Bradley's monumental work. The essays that follow treat the plays from different angles: style in *Antony and Cleopatra*, imagination in *Mabeth*, symbolism in *Othello*, nature in *King Lear*, and, most obliquely of all, '*Hamlet* in the light of Indian Poetics'. Yet, despite this variegated and unsystematic sequence of topics, there is a persistent con-

[1] Hutchinson University Library, 1972.
[2] Heinemann, 1973.
[3] 'The Lamb of Lust: The Role of Adonis in Shakespeare's *Venus and Adonis*', *Shakespeare Studies*, VI (1970), 11–34.
[4] *Aspects of Shakespearian Tragedy* (Oxford University Press, 1973).

cern with the relationships between reality and forms of imaginative truth that gives a tenuous unity to the book.

If the tragedies do not readily lend themselves to synthesis, neither does the multiplicity of interpretation that surrounds them. P. Gottschalk,[1] however, makes a worthwhile attempt to trace some sense of order and continuity in the proliferation of *Hamlet* criticism since Bradley. Needless to say, the scale of this endeavour is almost encyclopedic, but he skilfully steers a difficult course between historical relativism and reductive classification to offer a tidier perspective on the development and interaction of five distinctive lines of approach to the play. This essay in comparative criticism reveals the consequences of bringing different assumptions and interests to bear upon the play, but it does not consider how the play itself invites divided responses. That such ambivalences and imperfect recognitions are not only inherent in *Hamlet* but an important part of its meaning is argued by P. L. McNamara,[2] who examines the variety of mirroring devices used in the dramatic action to explore 'the communication, reception and reflection of situation, character and point of view'. 'The paradox at the heart of the play' according to McNamara, 'is that man can never accurately mirror what is since he can never fully know what is.' D. Pirie[3] finds in the play's use of theatrical metaphor a reflection of Hamlet's inability to become fully engaged in the reality of the world of Elsinore: 'his sense that action cannot faithfully reveal emotion is demonstrated by reference to the limitations of the art-form of drama'.

C. Havely,[4] on the other hand, takes a decidedly less equivocal view of the tragedy's most elaborate mirroring device, the play-within-the-play, in which she finds epitomised 'the qualities that the theatre possesses of being able to mimic, collate or clarify the complexity of life itself'. The significance of Hamlet's re-titling of the play as 'The Mouse-trap' is explored by J. Doebler[5] in relation to an iconographical tradition deriving from St Augustine's reference to the Cross as the mouse-trap set for the Devil. W. Schrickx[6] also uses the evidence of a traditional context, in this case the conventions of revenge tragedy, to interpret Hamlet's second soliloquy in terms of the revenge hero's formal dedication to his role. According to this reading, Hamlet's invocation to Heaven and Hell in the opening lines of the speech does not express doubts about the provenance of the Ghost, but rather represents a conventional submission of the hero to the powers that be, and a rejection of the 'momentary' thought of allegiance to Hell. Shakespeare does some strange things with literary tradition, however, as M. Grivelet[7] demonstrates in a characteristically subtle investigation of his treatment of the Troy legend and the figure of Pyrrhus in the Player's speech. Comparing this episode with Racine's use of classical myth, Grivelet concludes that for both dramatists 'Greece is the dwelling-place not so much of reason and good sense as of much darker powers of the mind'.

The reductiveness that has been characteristic of so much modern criticism of *Othello* is reflected in three essays, each making a

[1] *The Meanings of 'Hamlet'* (University of New Mexico Press, 1972).

[2] 'Hamlet's Mirrors', *Ariel*, IV (1973), 3–16.

[3] '*Hamlet* Without the Prince', *Critical Quarterly*, XIV (1972), 293–314.

[4] 'The Play Scene in *Hamlet*', *Essays in Criticism*, XXIII (1973), 217–35.

[5] 'The Play Within the Play: the *Muscipula Diaboli* in *Hamlet*', *Shakespeare Quarterly*, XXIII (1972), 161–9.

[6] 'The Background and Context of Hamlet's Second Soliloquy', *Modern Language Review*, LXVIII (1973), 241–55.

[7] 'Racine's "Dream of Passion"', *Shakespeare 1971: Proceedings of the World Shakespeare Congress, Vancouver, August 1971*, ed. C. Leech and J. M. R. Margeson (University of Toronto Press, 1973), pp. 144–55.

dogmatic claim to tell us what the tragedy is really about. To R. A. Yoder,[1] it is 'a dream of social alienation, a conflict between order and renewal', expressed not through character but through different kinds of ritual, as the old order of Venice, where 'the ceremonies and formal rhetoric of society disguise the actual condition of life', spreads its 'web of duplicity' over the 'festival of renewal' that begins on Cyprus. While Yoder treats the play as a myth of social decadence, in which 'it is beside the point to look for a flaw or character trait to explain what happens', R. M. Levitsky[2] firmly puts the blame for catastrophe upon 'the sins and weaknesses of the mind', particularly upon a misplaced confidence in the self-sufficiency of reason. This moralistic approach, however true to the canons of Christian doctrine that it invokes, has the doubtful merit of making Iago and Othello indistinguishable in the error of their ways. D. L. Jeffrey and P. Grant[3] also turn to moral theology for their joint interpretation of the play 'as basically concerned with good and bad fame', and their severity towards Othello's care for his worldly reputation leads them to adopt a singularly harsh view of the hero's anguish over his sense of dishonour: 'Many a soldier, we are prepared to believe, has been cuckolded and remained in the army nevertheless.' All three essays, despite their divergent emphases, share a tendency to impose inappropriately schematic ideologies on the play.

A timely protest against reductive criticism is registered by M. Rosenberg,[4] whose scepticism about narrowly thematic interpretations of *King Lear* lends itself in principle to the rest of Shakespeare's work: 'it reflects so many varieties of human possibility, from the transcendent to the animal – so many that it must defeat any attempt to enclose its meaning in limited formulae'. Rosenberg's extensive study of *King Lear* almost reaches the other extreme of total eclecticism in its use of the play's stage- and film-history to illustrate in scene-by-scene detail its complex and comprehensive possibilities for performance. The fashionable theatrical notion of sub-text can too easily be debased into mere pretext, but Rosenberg's attention to the importance of physical as well as verbal expressiveness is true to the nature of Shakespeare's acommodating art, demonstrating that there are more things of interest in the world of *King Lear* than may be dreamt of in your philosophical criticism. J. Levenson[5] corroborates this stress upon the importance of non-verbal effects in the play by her discussion of its use of silence 'to express, invoke, even define other kinds of reality', relating this dramatic device to the significances of silence in fairy-tale, folklore and biblical contexts. Rosenberg's confidence in the dramatic logic and coherence of the play's structure is shared by J. Ellis,[6] who defends the early scenes of the Gloster sub-plot against the charges of Bradley and others that they lack probability.

The structural coherence of *Macbeth* receives close attention in two articles that examine the play's use of repetition. J. Hartwig[7] perceives an ironic parallel between Macbeth's otherwise superfluous persuasion of Banquo's murderers and the spurious rationale by which the hero himself was earlier driven to murder Duncan: in both cases he finds that 'Macbeth moves

[1] 'The Two Worlds of *Othello*', *The South Atlantic Quarterly*, LXXII (1973), 213–25.

[2] 'All-in-All Sufficiency in *Othello*', *Shakespeare Studies*, VI, 209–21.

[3] '*Reputation in Othello*', ibid., pp. 197–208.

[4] *The Masks of King Lear* (University of California Press, 1972).

[5] 'What the Silence Said: Still Points in *King Lear*', *Shakespeare 1971*, ed. Leech and Margeson, pp. 215–29.

[6] 'The Gulling of Gloucester: Credibility in the Subplot of *King Lear*', *Studies in English Literature*, XII (1972), 275–89.

[7] 'Macbeth, the Murderers, and the Diminishing Parallel', *Yearbook of English Studies*, III (1973), 39–43.

from a powerful consideration of choice in soliloquy to a simplified and even reversed explanation in dialogue'. Another and more extended example of recapitulation is analysed by E. B. Lyle,[1] who finds that the sequence beginning with the Hecate scene and leading to Macbeth's second encounter with the Witches recollects the play's opening sequence, and therefore corresponds more closely than the act division of the Folio text to the principles of two-part structure recently proposed by E. Jones. It also suggests that in one form or another the Hecate scene is Shakespearian in conception. D. Amneus,[2] on the other hand, radically questions the play's structural integrity by arguing that Ross's reference to 'an earnest of a greater honour' must signify an original version of the play in which Duncan declared Macbeth Prince of Cumberland and heir to the throne: a solution that introduces greater perplexities than those it seeks to unravel. Focusing on 'the imaginative complexity of Macbeth's character', P. R. Moorthy[3] shifts the emphasis of interpretation from the moral conflict of good and evil to the anterior psychological struggle with fear: 'Macbeth needs fear for his conviction of the reality of life and death,' writes Moorthy, placing the core of the tragedy in the hero's inner compulsion 'to do what was to him the ultimate in his daring'. Yet Macbeth himself confesses to 'vaulting ambition', an image that C. Belsey[4] relates to the traditional representation of Pride as a figure falling from a horse.

Among studies of the Roman tragedies, the resurgent critical interest in *Titus Andronicus* is reflected in two essays. Reminding us of the dual tradition according to which the Goths were regarded both as barbarous and as naturally vigorous and noble in contrast to Roman decadence, R. Broude[5] sees the reconciliation of Goths and Romans at the end of the play as signifying the regeneration of the Empire. D. J. Palmer[6] considers the play as

'Shakespeare's thesis in tragedy', in which the use of literary allusion and the impulse to ritualised behaviour and formalised utterance serve as analogues to the playwright's own art.

A similar association of ritual with dramatic performance, occurring in the stage-imagery of the assassination scene in *Julius Caesar*, provides J. I. M. Stewart[7] with a point of departure for his British Academy lecture, which unfolds into an urbane reaffirmation of Shakespeare's highly personalised view of history, countering Jan Kott's notion of the historical process in Shakespeare as the ritual of the 'Great Staircase'. The treatment of historical awareness in *Julius Caesar* also interests R. Berman,[8] who finds in Brutus's desire to make history repeat itself by attempting to emulate his heroic ancestor 'the failure of modern man to equal legendary man'. R. M. Levitsky,[9] however, regards Brutus as a mixture of ancient and modern virtues, as Shakespeare combined in the character the Stoic ideals of firmness and fortitude with 'those qualities of pity, love, grief and vexation which distinguish him as Man'. She also attributes the complexity of Brutus's characterisation to a

[1] 'Act-Division in *Macbeth*', *Notes and Queries*, XX (1973), 140–1.

[2] 'Macbeth's "Greater Honor"', *Shakespeare Studies*, VI, 223–30.

[3] 'Fear in *Macbeth*', *Essays in Criticism*, XXIII, 154–66.

[4] 'Shakespeare's "Vaulting Ambition"', *English Language Notes*, X (1972), 198–201.

[5] 'Roman and Goth in *Titus Andronicus*', *Shakespeare Studies*, VI, 27–34.

[6] 'The Unspeakable in Pursuit of the Uneatable: Language and Action in *Titus Andronicus*', *Critical Quarterly*, XIV, 320–39.

[7] 'Shakespeare's Lofty Scene', Annual Shakespeare Lecture, *Proceedings of the British Academy*, LVII (1971), 181–95.

[8] 'A Note on the Motives of Marcus Brutus', *Shakespeare Quarterly*, XXIII, 197–200.

[9] 'The Elements were so Mix'd', *Publications of the Modern Language Association of America*, LXXXVIII (1973), 240–5.

certain ambivalence in Shakespeare's attitude towards Roman constancy.

Contrary tendencies in the characterisation of Cassius are seen by J. W. Velz[1] to amount to an ironic effect of 'radical inconsistency', as Cassius's ability to look quite through the deeds of men ultimately betrays him at Philippi. Through what Velz diagnoses as a temperamental inclination to see the worst in people and situations, 'the man whom Caesar justly called "a great observer" would be shown to fail egregiously in the last observation of his life'. Two other articles on the play note its indebtedness to Ovid's *Metamorphoses* in different respects. J. O. Wood[2] observes that the numerous references to the conspirators as hounds, and the recurrent puns on hart/heart, probably derive from Ovid's account of Actaeon, 'a mythic archetype that was often drawn into Shakespeare's mind as an emblem, whether of a heart acutely distressed or of a man suddenly turned upon by subjects or supposed friends'. In Golding's prefatory verses to the reader of his translation of Ovid, J. F. Forrest[3] locates the origin of the image of unfeeling mankind transformed into 'blocks and stones'.

Apart from J. L. Barroll's[4] rather laborious and unwieldy analysis of the character of Octavius, relatively little has been added to the criticism of *Antony and Cleopatra*. More attention has been paid to the last and least attractive of the tragedies, *Coriolanus*, including J. L. Halio's[5] sympathetic discussion of the hero's moral integrity and consequent dilemmas. Taking his title from A. C. Bradley's classic essay, Halio sees the play in terms of Coriolanus's final acceptance of a humanity he has previously tried to reject, pointing out that at the crisis of momentous choice Coriolanus is the only Shakespearian tragic protagonist to make the right decision. The language of the play is approached from different directions by C. M. Sickerman[6] and L. N. Danson.[7] Sickerman

illustrates Coriolanus's insensitivity to language, his 'fear and mistrust of words', while Danson draws attention to the use of metonymy as an important stylistic feature of the play, embodying the central thematic concern with the relationship of the part to the whole. To H. D. F. Kitto,[8] who as usual carries his learning lightly and with wit, this theme, expressed at the outset in Menenius's fable of the body and its rebellious members, exemplifies the true classical conception of tragedy, which Aristotle failed to grasp in his misplaced emphasis upon the hero as the sole focus of interest.

Two books explore aspects of the continuity and development in Shakespeare's art between the histories and the major tragedies. N. Council's[9] study of attitudes to honour in the plays from *1 Henry IV* to *King Lear* traces variations on a theme so complex and extensive that even its orthodox definition as 'the reward due to virtuous action' seems capable of infinite shades of interpretation in different contexts. In the pragmatism of Prince Hal, the self-sufficiency of Brutus, the subjectivism of Troilus and the scepticism of Hamlet, Council perceives the rejection of the conventional ideal of honour as a basis for action, and in the

[1] 'Cassius as a "Great Observer"', *Modern Language Review*, LXVIII, 256–9.
[2] 'Intimations of Actaeon in *Julius Caesar*', *Shakespeare Quarterly*, XXIV (1973), 85–9.
[3] '"Blocks" and "Stones" in *Julius Caesar*', *Notes and Queries*, XX, 134–5.
[4] 'The Character of Octavius', *Shakespeare Studies*, VI, 231–88.
[5] '*Coriolanus*: Shakespeare's "Drama of Reconciliation"', *ibid.*, pp. 289–303.
[6] '*Coriolanus*: The Failure of Words', *English Literary History*, XXXIX (1972), 189–207.
[7] 'Metonymy and *Coriolanus*', *Philological Quarterly*, LII (1973), 30–42.
[8] 'Why Blame Aristotle?', *Shakespeare 1971*, ed. Leech and Margeson, pp. 133–43.
[9] *When Honour's at the Stake: Ideas of Honour in Shakespeare's Plays* (George Allen and Unwin, 1973).

cases of Othello and Lear he observes a wider breach between notions of honour and virtue. It is far from clear, however, whether Council regards these deviations from the traditional meaning of honour as criticisms of its inadequacy, as perversions of an ideal, or as attempts to redefine its essence. If, for instance, Hotspur 'perfectly embodies all the characteristics of the honourable man', is this a comment on the limitations of such honour or an implied censure upon Hal's (and for that matter Hamlet's) more complex attitude to life? The main weakness of the book is its frequent uncertainty about the validity of the different kinds of honour portrayed.

M. Mack, Jr[1] also pursues the evolution of a theme from the history plays to the tragedies. In this case it is regicide and its dramatic implications in *Richard II*, *Hamlet* and *Macbeth*. The killing of a king, Mack argues, is a focal point in the tragic structure of each of these plays, because it exploits most directly the tensions inherent in the dual nature of kingship, sacramental and natural, theoretical and practical. He finds that the destruction of an established monarch produces psychological and moral disorientation as well as social and political disorder; it is the 'cause of both awareness and disintegration', as an increasingly introverted consciousness and drive to self-clarification corresponds in these tragedies to the ambiguity and inscrutability of the external world. In the dramatic progression that Mack traces, Richard is the forerunner of Hamlet as Bolingbroke anticipates Claudius, while the figure of Macbeth incorporates both the protagonist's capacities for introspection and the usurper's promotion of confusion. Though it is somewhat overwritten, Mack's book illuminates Shakespeare's ability to realise the potential of a single dramatic motif without repeating himself.

In a valuable and authoritative study, R. Ornstein[2] approaches the history plays, not as vehicles for Tudor ideology or embodiments of Elizabethan commonplaces, but as examples of dramatic art. He makes a detailed and penetrating analysis of the different dramatic structures into which Shakespeare shaped both his narrative material and his developing insight into political realities. Ornstein cogently reasserts the view that Shakespeare's conception of history has more to do with human behaviour than with abstract ideas or impersonal forces: 'He places as great a value on the sanctity of personal relations in the History Plays as in the tragedies, because he intuits that order depends, not on concepts of hierarchy and degree, but on the fabric of personal and social relationships which is woven by ties of marriage, kinship, and friendship, by communal interests, and ideals of loyalty and trust'. Consequently, instead of propounding a reductive thesis, the book brings fresh critical intelligence to bear on Shakespeare's increasingly complex and searching presentation of the inseparability of public and private life.

There have been surprisingly few articles on the histories this year. A somewhat pedestrian essay by V. M. Carr[3] on the animal imagery of *2 Henry VI* comes to the obvious conclusion that it 'supports the prey-predator-protector theme' of the play. H. B. Rothschild, Jr[4] proposes yet another conventional figure in Falstaff's complex literary and dramatic pedigree, namely the *picaro*, who like Shakespeare's fat knight thrives in conditions of social disorder and reduces all values to the satisfaction of the primal appetites. With a

[1] *Killing the King: Three Studies in Shakespeare's Tragic Structure* (Yale University Press, 1973).
[2] *A Kingdom for a Stage: The Achievement of Shakespeare's History Plays* (Harvard University Press, 1972).
[3] 'Animal Imagery in *2 Henry VI*', *English Studies*, LIII (1972), 408–12.
[4] 'Falstaff and the Picaresque Tradition', *Modern Language Review*, LXVIII, 14–21.

tentativeness that is entirely justified, J. D. A. Ogilvy[1] suggests that Hal's speech as king in the 'play extempore' of *1 Henry IV* is intended as a parody of Arcadian rhetoric to match Falstaff's preceding burlesque of Euphuism.

Quantitatively, at least, the comedies have had ample coverage this year, though no particular critical approach or conception of comic form emerges as currently predominant. R. Berry,[2] in fact, would discourage us from attempting to define the genre; to him, it appears, there is no such thing as Shakespearian Comedy, only Shakespearian comedies. Beyond stating their 'grand theme' to be illusion, Berry prefers to treat each of the first ten comedies separately, looking for 'the play's governing idea', or 'that element of repetition that guides us towards the play's principle of organisation, and thus its design'. This is not as schematic as it sounds, for between them the essays adopt a variety of angles on the plays. Berry's critical style is vigorous, informal and economic, and he writes especially well on *Much Ado* and *As You Like It*; but the main virtue of this attractive book is that it brings out both the charm and the seriousness of the comedies, a blend of qualities difficult to represent without becoming either whimsical or ponderous. J. R. Brown[3] covers the ten comedies in the scope of an essay, skilfully moving between the general and the particular in order to discuss Shakespeare's techniques of presentation and his management of the audience's responses. In terms of their wide focus and dispersal of dramatic interest, Brown places a welcome emphasis on the 'unassertive' quality of the comedies, which 'make few demands, but offer many opportunities' in interpretation.

Despite the diversity of Shakespeare's comic interests, several essays point to themes and motifs that recur from play to play. S. Wells,[4] for instance, observes that those comedies in which Shakespeare was not working from a narrative source, *Love's Labour's Lost*, *A Midsummer Night's Dream* and *The Tempest*, are distinguished both by their highly-patterned structures and by the dramatist's pre-occupation with his own art. 'The perspective of the playwright' in the two latter plays, and their manipulation of levels of dramatic illusion, are also the subject of an elegant essay by H. Hawkins,[5] who suggests that the progenitor of such devices may have been *The Spanish Tragedy*.

Three articles examine the serious aspects of the comedies. J. W. Sider's[6] sweeping survey of Shakespeare's progression from the relatively minor adversities of the first comedies, through the darker shadows of the problem plays (marred, according to Sider, by their 'abrupt final dispositions'), to the 'more meaningful optimism' of the last plays, is somewhat cursory in its judgements, and by focusing on narrative plot offers only a limited notion of 'seriousness'. A more substantial and penetrating study that also pursues a line of development through the plays is J. E. Siemon's[7] analysis of the different kinds of villainy embodied in Shylock, Angelo and Leontes, a sequence in which he examines how 'Shakespeare transforms the villain from a troublesome fellow who must be outwitted in

[1] 'Arcadianism in *1 Henry IV*', *English Language Notes*, x, 185–8.
[2] *Shakespeare's Comedies: Explorations in Form* (Princeton University Press, 1972).
[3] 'The Presentation of Comedy: The First Ten Plays', *Shakespearian Comedy* (Stratford-upon-Avon Studies 14), ed. M. Bradbury and D. Palmer (Edward Arnold, 1972), pp. 9–30.
[4] 'Shakespeare Without Sources', *ibid.*, pp. 58–74.
[5] 'Fabulous Counterfeits: Dramatic Construction and Dramatic Perspectives in *The Spanish Tragedy*, *A Midsummer Night's Dream*, and *The Tempest*', *Shakespeare Studies*, VI, 51–65.
[6] 'The Serious Elements of Shakespeare's Comedies', *Shakespeare Quarterly*, XXIV, 1–11.
[7] 'The Canker Within: Some Observations on the Role of the Villain in Three Shakespearian Comedies', *Shakespeare Quarterly*, XXIII, 425–43.

order for society to reassert its health into a sick member of society who must be cured if society is to regain its health'. A different kind of comic seriousness receives attention in R. A. Foakes's[1] essay on such 'voices of maturity' as those of Jaques, Theseus and Feste, whose attitudes are seen to counterbalance the impulse towards festive release. The specialised role of the fool adds another dimension to the increasing range and subtlety of Shakespeare's comic art, as G. Lloyd Evans[2] points out, suggesting that the association between the emergence of this figure in the comedies and the arrival of Robert Armin in Shakespeare's company reflects the intimate creative relationship between playwright, actor and role.

The critical orthodoxy that now recognises the qualities and defects of Shakespeare's early work as those of precocious sophistication rather than untrained simplicity continues to hold favour. Three of the first comedies are discussed by J. Arthos[3] in terms of their assimilation of the literary and philosophical interests of continental humanism, although the usefulness of this book is blighted by its impressionistic attitude to the plays and by an exasperating diffuseness of style. The ingenuity of dramatic technique in *The Comedy of Errors* is further investigated by G. Salgādo[4] in an article on the dislocation of the time-sense in the form, language and action of the comedy. 'Certain quite distinctive effects', he writes, 'are made possible by the fact that the actual unfolding of the drama must inevitably be in linear progression while the ordering of events implicitly questions that very progression'. I.-S. Ewbank[5] takes a fresh look at the problem of Shakespeare's attitude to convention in *The Two Gentlemen of Verona*, arguing that while it reveals 'a critical awareness that words may substitute for or falsify experience', the play's dependence on verbal techniques fails to realise in fully dramatic terms the truth to complex human relation-

ships that is achieved in the Sonnets. Two articles on *Love's Labour's Lost* illuminate different aspects of its background. T. Lennam[6] persuasively relates the form of the comedy to the 'Wit' moralities of the earlier sixteenth century, suggesting that it might be seen as an inversion of the educational precepts contained in those dramas, while J. D. Hunt[7] makes effective use of Castiglione, among others, to clarify the courtly values that are used and abused throughout the play.

The reassurances of *A Midsummer Night's Dream* are sweet after the disconcerting inconclusions of *Love's Labour's Lost*, and it is pleasant to record that neither J. P. Smith[8] nor R. A. Zimbardo[9] wish to diminish the sense of harmonious perfection celebrated by that comedy. In a slight but stylish piece, restating the play's concern with the transfiguring power of imagination, Smith focuses upon the audience's participation in the theatrical experi-

[1] 'The Owl and the Cuckoo: Voices of Maturity in Shakespeare's Comedies', *Shakespearian Comedy*, ed. Bradbury and Palmer, pp. 121–41.

[2] 'Shakespeare's Fools: The Shadow and the Substance of Drama', *ibid.*, pp. 142–59.

[3] *Shakespeare: The Early Writings* (Bowes and Bowes, 1972).

[4] '"Time's Deformed Hand": Sequence, Consequence, and Inconsequences in *The Comedy of Errors*', *Shakespeare Survey 25* (Cambridge University Press, 1972), pp. 81–91.

[5] '"Were man but constant, he were perfect": Constancy and Consistency in *The Two Gentlemen of Verona*', *Shakespearian Comedy*, ed. Bradbury and Palmer, pp. 31–57.

[6] '"The Ventricle of Memory": Wit and Wisdom in *Love's Labour's Lost*', *Shakespeare Quarterly*, XXIV, 54–60.

[7] 'Grace, Art and the Neglect of Time in *Love's Labour's Lost*', *Shakespearian Comedy*, ed. Bradbury and Palmer, pp. 75–96.

[8] 'Imaginary Forces and the Ways of Comedy', *Shakespeare in the New World* (Stratford Papers 1968–9), ed. B. A. W. Jackson (Irish University Press, 1972), pp. 1–20.

[9] 'Regeneration and Reconciliation in *A Midsummer Night's Dream*', *Shakespeare Studies*, VI, 35–50.

ence. More philosophically, Zimbardo works out the interaction of two Renaissance ideas, continuity through change and *discordia concors*, to show that 'concordance of seeming opposites by means of the reconciling faculty, imagination, is the dominant motif', uniting all levels of the dramatic action. Some well-trodden territory is revisited by J. Mandel's[1] essay which reminds us that *A Midsummer Night's Dream* is not the only occasion on which Shakespeare employs the analogy between dream and dramatic illusion to affirm the validity of imaginative creation.

There is, of course, little unanimity of opinion about *The Merchant of Venice*. R. C. Hassel, Jr[2] finds it pervaded by irony and by an awareness of human imperfectibility; unlike other Shakesperian comedy, he writes, 'there is no world which is sufficiently perfect to accommodate wisdom and festivity. Perceptiveness almost demands unhappiness'. To A. Wertheim,[3] at the other extreme, there is nothing problematical about the triumph of good over evil in the play: 'All the characters undergo education and conversion; but before they can do so they must lose their money or their commercial values. Certainly Shylock takes part in this central ritual; and if his financial loss is the most severe, the possibility of his salvation is also the greatest act of grace in the play'. No wonder that N. Rabkin[4] is moved to complain that criticism too often evades the problem posed by such divergent responses, radical differences of interpretation which he attributes to the critic's habit of intellectualising after the event. Doubtless Rabkin's exhortation 'to consider the play as a dynamic interaction between artist and audience' would alert critics to the ways in which it invites and provokes our reactions, but even then one suspects that a uniformity of understanding is neither probable nor desirable. Perhaps it is the function of the play to disturb us and to leave us something to think about,

and possibly it is better that we should be induced to relate our theatrical experience to life instead of confining our interests to the technical skills of dramaturgy. Yet another approach to *The Merchant of Venice* is proposed by D. J. Palmer,[5] who takes the view that the play's overt sententiousness is inimical to the comic spirit, which nevertheless manifests itself through the arbitrary and irrational motions of the affections, hatred and love, that are controlled by the artist rather than the moralist.

Social conformity is evidently a point at issue in the criticism of *Much Ado About Nothing*. M. Taylor[6] writes about 'the proper balance between sceptical individualism and social responsibility' in the play, and comes down on the side of 'the forces of social stability', though he manages to conceal all traces of humour in the play. On the other hand, both J. A. Allen[7] and D. Ormerod[8] take up the theme of 'fashion' to suggest that the action questions the claims of social convention on individual integrity, but only Allen, through his focus on Dogberry, seems to find anything amusing in the comedy.

Two articles on *The Merry Wives of Windsor* by J. A. Roberts stress its social and festive spirit. Defending the play against the

[1] 'Dream and Imagination in Shakespeare', *Shakespeare Quarterly*, XXIV, 61–8.
[2] 'Antonio and the Ironic Festivity of *The Merchant of Venice*', *Shakespeare Studies*, VI, 67–74.
[3] 'The Treatment of Shylock and Thematic Integrity in *The Merchant of Venice*', *Shakespeare Studies*, VI, 75–87.
[4] 'Meaning and Shakespeare', *Shakespeare 1971*, ed. Leech and Margeson, pp. 89–106.
[5] '*The Merchant of Venice*, or the Importance of Being Earnest', *Shakesperian Comedy*, ed. Bradbury and Palmer, pp. 97–120.
[6] '*Much Ado About Nothing*: the Individual in Society', *Essays in Criticism*, XXIII, 146–53.
[7] 'Dogberry', *Shakespeare Quarterly*, XXIV, 35–53.
[8] 'Faith and Fashion in *Much Ado About Nothing*', *Shakespeare Survey 25*, pp. 93–105.

disparagement that labels it a farce, she argues[1] that it fulfils the more positive aims of comedy: 'It reinforces our confidence in social forms, and asserts that there are orderly and beneficent forces at work in them'. In her other essay,[2] she suggests that its mood is appropriate to the festivities of Hallowe'en as 'a record of the transition from fall to winter – an effort to put the house in order, to become reconciled to the passing of fertility from the old to the young'. Both essays therefore bring the play more closely into line with the other comedies instead of taking the more usual view of it as an anomalous venture into citizen comedy.

Some singularly ponderous and platitudinous pieties are visited upon *As You Like It*. According to M. Taylor,[3] the play insists both on the inevitability of sin and suffering and on the possibility of redemption, 'enabling us to laugh at Adam's penalty without forgetting the need for salvation', though there seems little cause for laughter in the woeful pageant to which he reduces the comedy. An even greater solemnity invests R. E. Fortin's[4] approach to the play, in which, for instance, the oak trees of Arden are described as 'intimations of the sacred mystery of life and of the supernatural dimensions of human existence', and Orlando's 'action of redeeming Oliver by his own blood is clearly reminiscent of the Christian mystery of man's redemption'. At this sort of thing the 'mirth in heaven' is distinctly audible. T. Kelly,[5] however, stops a good way short of deifying Orlando in making a reasoned case for regarding this romantic hero as less 'peculiarly inept and slightly ridiculous' than his counterparts in the other comedies. The old question of whether Jaques represents Shakespeare's putting down of Jonson is re-examined by D. Bevington[6] in a consideration of Shakespeare's attitude to satire, and he concurs with the established view that the creation of Jaques reveals 'a complex appreciation of the theory of satire' rather than

'a particular hit at Jonson'. Studies of the play in relation to pastoral convention will be mentioned later.

A stylish and discerning essay by A. Barton[7] is addressed to Shakespeare's management of the comic resolution in *As You Like It* and *Twelfth Night*, distinguishing between 'the classical equilibrium' of the ending of *As You Like It* with its 'various and crowded dance', and the more disturbed conclusion of *Twelfth Night*, in which 'a world of revelry, of comic festivity, fights a kind of desperate rearguard action against the cold light of day'. The 'meditative' quality of *Twelfth Night* is described by J. S. Lawry,[8] who gives a somewhat laboured account of the 'sea-associated redemption of Illyria from affectation'. D. McPherson[9] plausibly suggests that the source of Malvolio's yellow stockings and cross-garters is the description of the emasculate Hercules in Seneca's *Hippolytus*.

Though we are accustomed to see a discontinuity between the romantic comedies and the problem plays, R. Warren[10] notes a number of 'interesting similarities of situation and

---

[1] '*The Merry Wives*: Suitably Shallow, But Neither Simple Nor Slender', *Shakespeare Studies*, VI, 109–23.

[2] '*The Merry Wives of Windsor* as a Hallowe'en Play', *Shakespeare Survey 25*, pp. 107–12.

[3] '*As You Like it*: the Penalty of Adam', *Critical Quarterly*, XV (1973), 76–80.

[4] '"Tongues in Trees": Symbolic Patterns in *As You Like It*', *Texas Studies in Literature and Language*, XIV (1972), 569–82.

[5] 'Shakespeare's Romantic Heroes: Orlando Reconsidered', *Shakespeare Quarterly*, XXIV, 12–24.

[6] 'Shakespeare vs Jonson on Satire', *Shakespeare 1971*, ed. Leech and Margeson, pp. 107–22.

[7] '*As You Like It* and *Twelfth Night*: Shakespeare's Sense of an Ending', *Shakespearian Comedy*, ed. Bradbury and Palmer, pp. 160–80.

[8] '*Twelfth Night* and "Salt Waves Fresh in Love"', *Shakespeare Studies*, VI, 89–108.

[9] 'Herculean Malvolio', *Notes and Queries*, XX, 135–6.

[10] '"Let Summer bear it out": a Note on *Twelfth Night* and *All's Well That Ends Well*', ibid., pp. 136–8.

phrase' between *Twelfth Night* and *All's Well That Ends Well*, 'almost as if the sombre mood of *All's Well* is developing from the sombre undertones underlying the gaiety of *Twelfth Night*'. A very different view of the mood of *All's Well*, however, is taken by R. L. Smallwood[1] in a comprehensive and well-argued exercise in defensive criticism, which claims it as 'a comedy, not a morality play'. 'A comparison of the play with its sources', writes Smallwood, 'reveals at every turn the dramatist's care to present the story and its principal characters in as mellow and engaging a light as possible'. Support for such an emphasis on the tolerance and good humour of the play is forthcoming in J. Rothman's[2] vigorous appreciation of Parolles as a figure who delights us in the theatre as a harmless foolish braggart, while moralistic critics stay at home and sternly deplore his wickedness. Yet to J. M. Silverman[3] the chief problem of *All's Well* is its structural shift 'from a deliberately naive and "miraculous" form of comedy to one more devious and filled with intrigue', suggesting that 'the complexities of the comic condition' are inextricably related to 'the confused and fallen world of contingency'. D. M. Bergeron[4] points to another kind of structural motif in the myth of Mars and Venus, which he regards as a shaping influence upon the play's concern with the opposing values of love and war, drawing upon the associations carried by the names of Diana and Helena.

The treatment of love and war in *Troilus and Cressida* continues to dismay modern criticism, or else to confirm its pessimistic convictions. E. Schwartz[5] notes the diverse elements of dramatic style, 'which need to be reconciled with each other', but it seems that all that can be salvaged from the vision of 'a meaningless chaos, to which one may respond in various ways, none of them really adequate' is the attempt of Troilus and Hector 'to act as though value were possible' in a world where,

according to Schwartz, it does not and cannot exist. A positive relish for the ugly nihilism of Thersites pervades R. A. Yoder's[6] essay, which asserts that both Greeks and Trojans seek to escape from unpleasant realities by clinging desperately to ceremony and formal rhetoric. Yoder charges both camps with betraying private integrity to 'a collective, public order which is absolute in its authority and which is geared to continuing the long, absurd war' (Shakespeare our contemporary?), and he pillories most modern interpretations for their tendency, as he sees it, to shirk the issues by seeking refuge in the multiplicity of the play's points of view instead of acknowledging that Thersites is Shakespeare's ultimate spokesman. By contrast, M. Sacharoff,[7] who has recently been challenging the approach to the play as a satire, argues that parts of it are written in the heroic style, and that despite notions to the contrary there is no substantial precedent in medieval tradition for the debasement of heroic legend.

Predictably, *Measure for Measure* provokes considerable critical activity, though little advance is made from the familiar and established positions. J. A. Lavin[8] provides a lucid and well-balanced introduction to the play for

1 'The Design of *All's Well That Ends Well*', *Shakespeare Survey* 25, pp. 45–61.
2 'A Vindication of Parolles', *Shakespeare Quarterly*, XXIII, 183–96.
3 'Two Types of Comedy in *All's Well That Ends Well*', *Shakespeare Quarterly*, XXIV, 25–34.
4 'The Mythical Structure of *All's Well That Ends Well*', *Texas Studies in Literature and Language*, XIV, 559–68.
5 'Tonal Equivocation and the Meaning of *Troilus and Cressida*', *Studies in Philology*, LXIX (1972), 304–19.
6 '"Sons and Daughters of the Game": An Essay on Shakespeare's *Troilus and Cressida*', *Shakespeare Survey* 25, pp. 11–25.
7 'The Traditions of the Troy-Story Heroes and the Problem of Satire in *Troilus and Cressida*', *Shakespeare Studies*, VI, 125–35.
8 '*Measure for Measure*', *Shakespeare in the New World*, ed. Jackson, pp. 97–113.

a non-specialist audience, outlining the background of sources, uses of literary and dramatic conventions, and critical reputation. Addressing the same audience, G. Durrant[1] takes a rather bland view of the play's predicaments in the assurance that the controlling presence of the Duke removes any anxieties we might otherwise feel. W. L. Godshalk[2] sees in the play a progression of its major characters through mutual involvement towards 'a stasis in which freedom and restraint are equally balanced'. In another article,[3] Godshalk also provides a gloss on the difficult ellipsis of Angelo's soliloquy referring to the devil's horn and crest. Turning attention to the theatrical structure of *Measure for Measure*, J. Powell[4] explores its ways of shifting focus as an 'imagistic' technique projecting the dramatic tension between forms of perception and experience.

The extreme reactions of many critics to the character of Isabella, as either saint or prude, are eschewed by A. Greco[5] in favour of a recognition of her vulnerability and lack of confidence in the first half of the play, followed by an emphasis upon the humanising process which she undergoes. But she has indeed become a tame creature by the end of the play if we can suppose that she consents to marry the Duke as a 'self-sacrifice', and there is something quite shocking in the proposition that 'since Isabella is more a woman of reason than of emotion, she will not insist on falling in love before marrying'.

The two camps of critical opinion about the Duke, or rather the critical and uncritical attitudes towards him, each find new recruits. According to D. M. Hamilton,[6] he 'is allowed to reveal his weaknesses and idiosyncrasies and even to become a target of the play's comedy', a view shared by H. S. Weil, Jr[7], in his disapprobation of Peter Brook's 1950 production of the play for cutting the text in order to present the Duke as an ideal ruler. S. C. Velz,[8]

on the other hand, seeks to persuade us that some rather tenuous links between the play and the parable of the seeds in Mark 4 provide further evidence for regarding the Duke as a Christ-figure. Another possible source for the play's treatment of religious issues is proposed by D. Kaula,[9] who finds a parallel between Angelo's religious hypocrisy, and abuse of his position, and a contemporary pamphlet relating to the Archpriest controversy, attacking the Jesuits for similar corrupt practices.

A prominent feature of the year's critical output has been the appearance of no less than five books on pastoral romance in the comedies and last plays: a veritable Babel of green fields. D. Young's[10] excellent study is the best of them, encompassing *As You Like It* and *King Lear* as well as *The Winter's Tale* and *The Tempest*. Recognising that the pastoral mode is not merely escapist, but a potentially complex and inclusive convention, he explores the versatility with which Shakespeare realised its possibilities in successive and different ways. The essential pastoral features of these four plays are shown to be a dialectic of opposing values and a romance structure of exile, sojourn in the natural world, and eventual

[1] '*Measure for Measure*: A Comedy', *ibid.*, pp. 21–39.

[2] '*Measure for Measure*: Freedom and Restraint', *Shakespeare Studies* VI, 137–50.

[3] '"The Devil's Horn": Appearance and Reality', *Shakespeare Quarterly*, XXIII, 202–5.

[4] 'Theatrical *Trompe l'oeil* in *Measure for Measure*', *Shakespearian Comedy*, ed. Bradbury and Palmer, pp. 181–209.

[5] 'A Due Sincerity', *Shakespeare Studies*, VI, 151–73.

[6] 'The Duke in *Measure for Measure*: "I Find an Apt Remission in Myself"', *Shakespeare Studies*, VI, 175–83.

[7] 'The Options of the Audience: Theory and Practice in Peter Brook's *Measure for Measure*', *Shakespeare Survey 25*, pp. 27–35.

[8] 'Man's Need and God's Plan in *Measure for Measure* and Mark iv', *ibid.*, pp. 37–44.

[9] '*Measure for Measure* and John Musk's Dialogue', *Shakespeare Studies*, VI, 185–95.

[10] *The Heart's Forest: A Study of Shakespeare's Pastoral Plays* (Yale University Press, 1972).

return, involving a process of readjustment, though Young finds that *King Lear* invokes the pastoral norms only to deny their consolation. He is particularly attentive to the intricate and flexible relationship of Art and Nature in the plays, which he sees as central to the patently fictive and artificial tradition of pastoral and its concern with the relativity of perspectives. His most suggestive and stimulating chapters are those on the two last plays, which are shown to embody their profundity of vision in terms of a self-referring interest in techniques of illusion and constructs of imagination. This appreciation of the formal and equivocal self-consciousness of the last plays as an important dimension of their meaning serves as a valuable reminder that the serious playfulness of fiction is very different from the certitudes of dogmatic theology.

H. Smith[1] approaches the last plays as the 'natural outgrowth of Shakespeare's experience in writing comedy and tragedy'. After two opening chapters illustrating and describing the more obvious characteristics of pastoral romance, the changing ways of Shakespeare's imagination are traced through his use of sources and through the anticipations of the last plays to be found in his earlier work. In this respect, Smith makes a good case for considering the influence of Sidney's *Arcadia* upon *King Lear*, 'not merely in the plot, but in image, in thought, and in total meaning', as a turning-point of crucial importance for the romance interests of the last plays. The book ranges over a multiplicity of issues, and quotation is lavishly used: indeed, its main weakness is its tendency to become an anthology of miscellaneous observations and examples, many of them dealt with only superficially. This lack of penetration is reflected in some of the critical judgements that are made: for instance in the limited view of pastoral that is implied by maintaining that *As You Like It* decreases the pastoral element of its source, and in the surprising remark that *The Winter's Tale* contains 'nothing like the emphasis on time, or the meaning of it, that we find in *As You Like It*'.

T. McFarland's[2] book has a highly personal emphasis that produces some provocative and eccentric points of view. His opening declaration that 'every work of art, indeed, is a consolation for the nothingness of our lives' prepares us for his insistence that happy fulfilment depends upon 'the security of being in a group'. Such a view hardly allows for the critical though tolerant scrutiny of human limitations that Shakespearian comedy presents, and McFarland's conception of comic fulfilment as a kind of total immunity from the hazards of living is reflected in some simplistic, sentimental and downright perverse interpretations of the plays. Marcade's disruption of the pastimes of *Love's Labour's Lost*, for instance, is held to reassure us that death exists only in the world outside, thus not disturbing but reinforcing 'the ease of the paradisal enclosure'. In the Forest of Arden, Orlando's romantic love, obscurely associated in McFarland's mind with the anti-social attitudes of the wicked brothers, is seen as the primary obstacle to the blissful outcome. Polixenes, on the other hand, is not allowed to upset the 'pastoral bliss' of Florizel and Perdita, while Caliban's threat to the 'tranquillity' and 'unchallengable potency' of Prospero's rule is 'hardly worth noticing', despite the distress that omnipotence itself evinces in the play. There is no mortal business, and very little that is recognisably Shakespearian, in the 'enchanted haven' of McFarland's imagination.

H. Felperin[3] describes romance as 'a success story in which difficulties of any number of kinds are overcome, and a tall story in which

[1] *Shakespeare's Romances: A Study of Some Ways of the Imagination* (The Huntington Library, 1972).
[2] *Shakespeare's Pastoral Comedy* (University of North Carolina Press, 1973).
[3] *Shakespearian Romance* (Princeton University Press, 1972).

they are overcome against impossible odds or by miraculous means'. This broad and basic definition enables him to relate Shakespeare's plays not merely to the conventions of a particular literary genre but also to medieval religious drama and even to the Christian story itself. Romance becomes, in fact, 'a mode of perceiving the world'. But because it offers such freedom to the imagination, he argues, the 'golden world' of romance is at odds with brazen reality; the best romances therefore contain a strong anti-romantic dimension: 'It is through this technique of shadowing or qualifying or problematizing the triumphs it presents that the best romance manages to pass itself off as an image of the real.' In the romance of Sidney and Spenser, for instance, Felperin finds that the Protestant ethic validates romance through the idea of trial and testing. With these considerations in mind, he approaches Shakespeare, and finds that romantic happiness in the comedies has few obstacles to overcome, and that it is constantly expected but always frustrated in the tragedies, particularly in *King Lear*, while the satisfying achievement of the last plays is that they 'earn their right to end happily by refusing to mitigate the severities they also present'. By making 'romance' stand for so many things at once, however, this argument sometimes confuses the distinction between the 'anti-romantic' elements of realism, adversity and moral earnestness. Miseries and misfortunes are as essential to romance convention as to the brazen world, while the miraculous endings of the last plays are as dependent upon their self-confessed artifice as upon their moral gravity. Nevertheless Felperin rightly stresses the capacity of the last plays to keep in touch with human realities even in their most fantastic moments.

D. Petersen's[1] confidence in 'the soundness of my approach' and its capacity 'to provide the kind of understanding of *The Tempest*

and the other romances that has been lacking' almost echoes the self-congratulation of Leontes, 'How blest am I in my true opinion'. According to Petersen, the affliction of the Sicilian king reflects 'the truth that the feelings and assumptions that we bring to bear in our act of perceiving "reality" determine our interpretation of what we see'. The naturalism of tragedy, it is argued, leaves us to infer the moral nature of the universe (assuming our thoughts tend in that direction), so that the significance of what happens depends on what we believe. The last plays, on the other hand, seem to Petersen 'more effective' in dealing with metaphysical problems because they 'figure forth a reality that is only inferentially revealed to the observer of phenomenal nature'. They are said to be exemplary actions, imitations of an ideal reality in the sense that Sidney conceived of poetic representation. However, it is difficult to see why the use of emblematic devices, which also abound in the tragedies, should make the last plays radically different in form as moral exempla, while the insistence on 'Shakespeare's subordination of representational imitation to ideological concerns' in his treatment of the improbabilities of romance is suspiciously like imprisoning Ariel in a cloven pine, figuratively speaking.

The fifth and concluding volume of G. Lloyd Evans's[2] succinct and lively series on Shakespeare's life and work brings him to the two final tragedies and to the romances, which, as he points out, Shakespeare himself might not have thought of as his last plays. Within a relatively brief scope, Lloyd Evans has to be concise and selective, but he is both reliably informative and engagingly fresh in his discussion of critical issues in the plays. This volume places the focus of commentary upon

[1] *Time, Tide, and Tempest: A Study of Shakespeare's Romances* (The Huntington Library, 1973).
[2] *Shakespeare V: 1606–1616*, Writers and Critics (Oliver and Boyd, 1973).

the stylistic and theatrical qualities of the plays, often referring to recent stage productions. It deserves to be widely read, by students and general readers alike.

Most of the year's articles on the last plays are devoted to *The Tempest*, but there are two that refer to the plays as a group. Warning us against overrating the influence of the court masque upon these plays, J. Jacquot[1] notes that in the period when Shakespeare was writing the romances the Jacobean masque was beginning to employ elaborate Italianate scenery with its perspectives and changes of setting, while 'what is evident in the plays themselves is the reliance on word-painting and the appeal to the mind's eye'. A marked increase in the use of internal rhyme is a feature of Shakespeare's style in the plays of the final period to which K. Muir[2] draws attention; it may well reinforce the evidence we already have for Shakespeare's hand in *The Two Noble Kinsmen* and *Henry VIII*, though Muir leaves us to speculate about its other possible significances.

Attitudes to art in *The Tempest* are debated from several points of view. S. R. Homan[3] argues that there is a duality of perspective which reflects 'the age's own ambivalence toward art as either airy nothing, a mockery of nature's truth, or something created out of nothing and thereby a testament to the artist's quasi-divine powers'. Prospero's 'assumption of god-like powers and responsibilities', according to R. Egan,[4] inevitably falls short of its aims, since 'his artistic ideal of a perfect world, given the nature of post-lapsarian humanity, can never be realised'. R. Henze,[5] in an allegorical interpretation of the play, also sees Prospero's devotion to his art as more of a liability than an asset, although the suggestion that Prospero 'discovers that man cannot live in a fantasy apart from the world, and the rejection of the masque becomes part of a larger rejection of passive life in general', if it is not anticipated by Prospero's conception of

his plot at the beginning of the play, hardly seems dependent on the notion that he represents the soul of man. An even more puritanical view of the play is taken by W. Rochett,[6] who draws from it the message that 'through disciplined intellectual and spiritual labor we must correct the "ill-husbandry" of the past', though he might have added that according to Shakespeare we shall have music and other forms of entertainment while we work. A. Pasternak Slater[7] finds an interesting but inconclusive parallel between *The Tempest* and Isaiah, 19, both reflecting a 'movement from sin, to punishment involving a trance-like state, to the final coming of understanding, justice and joy', while her description of the play as 'a dramatic sermon' is, sadly, all too true of the way it is treated in most of the criticism under review. All the more refreshing, therefore, to encounter A. D. Nuttall,[8] the critic as provocative agent, in his learned and witty perambulation around the perimeters of pastoral tradition, discovering an unlikely kinship between Caliban and Jaques as subversive figures who expose the 'mendacity' of the 'civility sequestered but unchanged' around them, and as libertines caught up in 'the main paradox of pastoral, which is that sexuality is natural, yet nature is pre-sexual'.

Among the miscellaneous items that come

1 'The Last Plays and the Masque', *Shakespeare 1971*, ed. Leech and Margeson, pp. 156–73.
2 'A Trick of Style and Some Implications', *Shakespeare Studies*, VI, 305–10.
3 '*The Tempest* and Shakespeare's Last Plays: The Aesthetic Dimensions', *Shakespeare Quarterly*, XXIV, 69–76.
4 'This Rough Magic: Perspectives of Art and Morality in *The Tempest*', *Shakespeare Quarterly*, XXIII, 171–82.
5 '*The Tempest:* Rejection of a Vanity', *Shakespeare Quarterly*, XXIII, 420–34.
6 'Labor and Virtue in *The Tempest*', *Shakespeare Quarterly*, XXIV, 77–84.
7 'Variations Within a Source: From Isaiah xix to *The Tempest*', *Shakespeare Survey 25*, pp. 125–35.
8 'Two Unassimilable Men', *Shakespearian Comedy*, ed. Bradbury and Palmer, pp. 210–40.

last but not least, merely because they defy the reviewer's chosen categories, are three books each in its own way both speculative and wide-ranging. M. Goldman's[1] exploration of the tensions and energies that relate audience, performers and play to each other makes an original contribution to the current growth of critical concern with the theatrical dynamics of the plays: a topic of greater interest and importance than the old-fashioned attitude to Shakespeare's 'stage-craft'. With some penetrating and imaginative insights into particular plays, Goldman's main approach is to consider the unfolding dramatic action as an experience in which characters and audience are moved to a more complex sense of self by the stress of encounter: 'the theater, like Prospero's island – and like festivity, mercy, love, or even the notion of freedom – is at once an escape from the self and a confrontation of it'.

A. Aronson's book[2] is also about conceptions of the self in Shakespeare, but from a very different standpoint, since Aronson is convinced that Jung's psychological theories 'furnish deeper insights into Shakespeare's work than any previously available'. In one sense this is not surprising, since Jung's system of concepts claims universal applicability. Its consequences as a tool of literary analysis, however, are fairly disastrous, as all the plays are reduced to a single subject: the individuation of self. Characters become archetypes, archetypes enact their myths, and myths turn out to be merely 'different symbols for the same psychic antagonism'. Moreover, if it works at all, this devastating technique would presumably come up with the same interpretation of any literary work, good, bad, or indifferent: it is heedless of precisely those qualities that makes Shakespeare worthwhile. It may be excellent theoretical psychology, but it certainly spells monotony for the reader or playgoer.

L. A. Fiedler[3] tilts at the bardolatrous establishment in his attempt to expose Shake-speare's male chauvinism and racial prejudice, in a book that is either highly exasperating or mildly amusing, depending on how it is taken. He makes three basic assumptions, none of which bears rigorous examination: that Shakespeare is entirely representative of the cultural attitudes of his time, that these attitudes included a general though usually concealed antagonism towards women, Jews, blacks and red Indians for being alien, and that the opinions expressed by dramatic characters can be identified with the views of their author. Using the same assumptions, he might have found that Shakespeare was suspicious, if not downright contemptuous, of poets and actors, those other 'strangers on the borders of his world'.

Aspects of Shakespeare's style are discussed in three papers originally delivered to the World Shakespeare Congress recently held in Vancouver. J. A. Barish[4] traces the use of prose in the plays, showing that while it undergoes less development than the verse, and although its comic function varies little between the earlier and later work, there is an increase in the occurrence of serious prose in passages of argument and close reasoning, as Shakespeare's art grows to maturity. The development of the dramatic verse is discussed by G. R. Hibbard,[5] who illustrates the problems of the early Shakespeare in relating poetic artifice to action and character, until in Berowne and Richard II he creates ways of indulging his delight in verbal exuberance while simultaneously recognising its limitations. The origins of Shakespeare's wordplay, R. Weimann[6] suggests, should be

[1] *Shakespeare and the Energies of Drama* (Princeton University Press, 1972).
[2] *Psyche and Symbol in Shakespeare* (Indiana University Press, 1972).
[3] *The Stranger in Shakespeare* (Croom Helm, 1972).
[4] 'Continuities and Discontinuities in Shakespearian Prose', *Shakespeare 1971*, ed. Leech and Margeson, pp. 59–75.
[5] 'The Forced Gait of a Shuffling Nag', *ibid.*, pp. 76–88.
[6] 'Shakespeare's Wordplay: Popular Origins and Theatrical Functions', *ibid.*, pp. 230–43.

sought in dramatic rather than rhetorical tradition, since verbal distortions and inversions function in the mystery cycles and in the Tudor moralities as a 'medium of interaction between the mimetic form of dialogue and the communal expression of festive release, between role and actor, drama and audience'.

In another paper from the World Shakespeare Congress, R. W. Ingram[1] considers the ways in which 'incidental' music can be used in the plays to emphasise significant dramatic moments or else to mark shifts of tone. A different aspect of music in the plays is the subject of P. T. Dircks'[2] essay, which focuses upon the dramatic functions of the 'catch' in

Twelfth Night and *The Tempest*, showing how in each case the clowns' song of revelry is integrated with the central concerns of the plot. Also related to the musical element in the play are the various forms of dance that A. Brissenden[3] identifies and discusses in relation to their dramatic contexts.

[1] 'Music as Structural Element in Shakespeare', *ibid.*, pp. 174–89.
[2] 'Shakespeare's Use of the Catch as Dramatic Metaphor', *Shakespeare Quarterly*, XXIV, 88–90.
[3] 'Shakespeare and Dance', *Shakespeare in the New World*, ed. Jackson, pp. 85–96.

© D. J. PALMER 1974

2. SHAKESPEARE'S LIFE, TIMES, AND STAGE

reviewed by NIGEL ALEXANDER

Two works of major importance must be treated first. With the publication of his seventh volume Geoffrey Bullough[1] brings his immense collection of Shakespeare's possible source material within sight of completion. Only the last volume, on the Romances, remains to be published. Like its predecessors, this is a volume which any serious student must have ready to hand. It is particularly convenient to have in one volume such materials as Saxo Grammaticus and Belleforest as well as the later *Fratricide Punished* for *Hamlet*; Cinthio, Bandello and Richard Knolles for *Othello*; the Annesly case, Holinshed, Higgins, Spenser, Sidney, Harsnett and *The True Chronicle History* for *King Lear*; Holinshed, Buchanan and Leslie for *Macbeth*. Professor Bullough provides much more than a collection of the standard sources. He has revived the suggestion that the play-within-the-play in *Hamlet* contains elements originally derived from some account of the murder of

Francesco Maria I, Duke of Urbino. Two passages are included, Luigi Gonzaga's protestation of his innocence and Pietro Aretino's apology to Gonzaga. In general this volume gives considerable weight to the possible effect of contemporary historical events. The marriage of James VI and Anne of Denmark is considered as a possible influence on the early play on the *Hamlet* story and current political issues may have been glanced at in the references to England and Poland. The show of kings in *Macbeth* may be derived from an anecdote about Catherine de Medici, and the character of Lady Macbeth may owe some touches to that presumed poisoner and instigator of the Massacre of St Bartholomew. Such accounts are valuable and this kind of 'historical' influence seems far more probable

[1] *Narrative and Dramatic Sources of Shakespeare.* Vol. VII – *Major Tragedies: Hamlet, Othello, King Lear, Macbeth* (Routledge and Kegan Paul and Columbia University Press, 1973).

than the elaborate historical allegories which have recently come again into fashion.

It is particularly satisfactory to have selections from Seneca's *Agamemnon* and *Troas* for *Hamlet* and the *Medea* and *Agamemnon* for *Macbeth*. The whole question of Shakespeare's debt to the classical tradition has recently been re-opened in stimulating fashion by Reuben A. Brower[1] in his very important book. It is a subject that has been infinitely obscured by the immense critical confusion which surrounds the idea of the 'classical'. It obviously has relevance to the Hecate scenes in *Macbeth*. Professor Bullough is not persuaded that these are an interpolation and thinks that Shakespeare may be seen deliberately trying out different styles of writing in the play.

Naturally not everything has been included and it is possible to disagree with some of the editor's judgements. If a chapter from Harsnett's *A Declaration of Egregious Popish Impostures* is to be included among the sources of *King Lear* (and of course it should be) should there not be a passage from Lavater's *Of Ghosts and Spirits Walking by Night* for *Hamlet*? A strong case for such inclusion is made out in a very interesting paper by Jean-Marie Maguin[2] pointing out that Robert Garnier's *Cornélie* incorporates this protestant attitude to ghosts at a time when France was rent by bitter religious feuds in which the question of Purgatory played an important part. If Kyd was the author of the early *Hamlet* play then his translation of Garnier's play as *Cornelia* acquires exceptional importance. Maguin's paper makes it clear that we do not yet know enough about this vexed and difficult question. Another surprising omission is Montaigne. There is only one reference to his work in the index and yet surely the strong probable influence of his *Essays* on *Hamlet* and *Lear* ought to be considered?

In his introductions to each play Professor Bullough is both comprehensive and judicious. Together with his excellent bibliographies, they provide a really first-rate survey of the historical and critical problems. Yet the very ease of the writing and the wealth of reference sometimes obscure difficulties. It is, for example, said to be probable that Thomas Kyd is the author of the earlier play on the *Hamlet* story which Professor Bullough then follows tradition by calling the *Ur-Hamlet*. This is still the orthodox view and Nashe's 'To the Gentlemen Students of Both Universities' is cited in evidence. Yet when this is taken with the two other references to the earlier *Hamlet* — the entry in Henslowe's *Diary* of the performance at Newington Butts and Lodge's reference to the ghost which cried miserably at the Theatre 'Hamlet, revenge' a very different interpretation becomes possible. The company at Newington Butts was an amalgamation of the Admiral's Men and those who were about to become the Chamberlain's Men. The list of plays performed unquestionably includes some Shakespearian titles and if Lodge saw *Hamlet* at the Theatre he was almost certainly watching a performance by Shakespeare's company. The possibility that the author of the earlier *Hamlet* was William Shakespeare cannot be ruled out.

The sudden appearance of the old play of *Leir* in 1605 is also more of a puzzle than commentators usually recognise. As R. W. Chambers, following Perrett, pointed out, the *Leir* play is extraordinary in having a happy ending. All other versions of the story up to that time end even more disastrously than

---

[1] *Hero and Saint: Shakespeare and the Graeco-Roman Heroic Tradition* (Oxford University Press, 1971).

[2] 'Of Ghosts and Spirits Walking by Night: a Joint Examination of the Ghost Scenes in Robert Garnier's *Cornélie*, Thomas Kyd's *Cornelia* and Shakespeare's *Hamlet* in the Light of Reformation Thinking as Presented in Lavater's Book', *Cahiers Elisabethains* (1972), 25–40.

Shakespeare's play. The desire for a 'happy ending' has led to countless revisions and adaptations since that time. It is possible that *Leir* is the beginning of this tradition. The automatic assumption that Shakespeare used the old play of *Leir* to produce *King Lear* seems to me not proven and in need of further careful scrutiny.

Professor Bullough has performed his task as editor in a way that adds greatly to our knowledge and understanding of the texts that he presents. The book is indispensable.

Not less so is Richard Southern's new book[1] on the problems involved in the presentation of the interesting but difficult body of drama usually known as the Tudor Interlude. It is divided into three main sections dealing with (1) 1466–1527, The Doors of Entrance; (2) 1527–53 The Travers; (3) 1553–77, The Rise of the Stage. Dr Southern is a complete master of his material and presents his evidence in a clear and forthright fashion. In a book of this kind, however, it is inevitable that some of the steps in the argument should depend upon probability and conjecture. Not everyone will find themselves in agreement with all of those made in this book. Disagreement over detail, however, should not obscure the fact that this book triumphantly demonstrates that the approach to these works through the technical details of staging and presentation is infinitely more illuminating and rewarding than any merely literary account of the texts. In this book *Nature*, *Fulgens and Lucrece*, *Godly Queen Hester* and *Gorboduc* all come alive as dramatic possibilities capable of holding the interest of an audience.

In his discussion of the nature of the traverse in *Godly Queen Hester* Dr Southern touches upon a point that is so fundamental for all Shakespearian production that it is worth quoting at length:

At this point it is worth recalling what I have said already about the scene of action in Interludes; any

serious study of them suggests that if one allows oneself to think of this scene of action as one thinks of the 'scene of action' of a modern play – that is to say as the place where the plot is *supposed* to take place instead of where the actual performance *is* taking place – then the whole nature of the presentation of an Interlude will be missed.

The action of an Interlude was emphatically not conceived as an imitation or re-presentation of some outside event supposed to be happening, or to have once happened, elsewhere, but as the entry into one's room of a group of players who came in and presented a story or a diverting argument *in one's own room*. It was indeed, from the presentation point of view, something more like having a home charade than going out to a theatre performance. The technicalities of setting were provided, or accepted, with the purpose of helping the players in presenting such a performance, not so as to turn part of one's room into the semblance of some other place. So long as the galvanizing and vivid custom of direct audience-address persisted, no other conception of the scene of action of a play could of course ever be entertained, for direct address to spectators *must* belie any fiction that the action is taking place somewhere where there are no spectators!

Thus when the King enters the traverse the audience assume that he has entered the traverse for the purposes of the action and the story – the traverse does not have to be anything else. This method and attitude, Dr Southern argues, was current right through the period of Shakespearian drama and our productions are not likely to be satisfactory until we have come to terms with that fact. Some confirmation of this view could have been found this year in Jonathan Miller's brilliant production of *The Malcontent* at the Nottingham Playhouse and the Bankside Globe. Here the actors were perpetually aware of performing to an audience and the unlocalised set was used as a series of aids in presenting the performance. The result was a 'Jacobean' production which was also a modern entertainment, a welcome

[1] *The Staging of Plays Before Shakespeare* (Faber, 1973).

change from such monstrosities as the Prospect *Pericles* extravaganza.

Dr Southern believes that we must approach the Shakespearian stage by studying what came before it – examining what the actors were accustomed to and then seeing how they had adapted these customs for their permanent theatres – rather than attempting a reconstruction by working backwards from later forms of the theatre. His view that the Elizabethan hall is the main factor conditioning the nature of the English stage receives support and confirmation in Richard Hosley's[1] important study of the presentation of plays in the Great Hall of Hampton Court Palace, with an acting area that must have been approximately 40 feet wide, in Trinity Hall of the church of St Botolph-without-Aldersgate, London, where the acting area must have only been 14 feet wide, and in the unidentified playhouse depicted in the frontispiece to Francis Kirkman's *The Wits* – an engraving published in 1662 but relating to a performance of drolls during the interregnum. This generation of theatre historians have made an enormous advance in our understanding of the nature of the Elizabethan theatre and Dr Southern's book is both in itself a major advance and now the best possible introduction to that fascinating subject.

The twenty-fifth anniversary of the Shakespeare Birthplace Trust occurred in 1972 and Levi Fox[2] has commemorated the occasion in a handsome volume containing many excellent colour photographs of the properties of the Trust and interesting facsimiles of title-pages and other documents. The text is admirably succinct and accurate and the whole publication forms an important record of the Trust's essential activities and an admirable souvenir of any visit to Stratford.

Two most ambitious projects have been launched by the University of Salzburg. Under the titles of *Elizabethan Studies* and *Jacobean Studies* and the editorship of Dr James Hogg it is proposed to publish 'doctoral theses and other learned studies in this field which, though they have failed in the present economic situation to find a commercial publisher, yet deserve to be made available to a wider public'. They are printed by photographic process from a specially prepared typescript and are, within the obvious limitations of such a process, attractively presented. The series itself is obviously 'commercial' to the extent that it must rely heavily on university librarians taking the whole series if it is to pay its way. Many will no doubt do so, but an examination of the first volumes on offer ought, perhaps, to give them pause. It is true that in view of what does get published no one can grudge these authors their at least equally worthy appearance in print. Although there are notable exceptions, the general standard of the volumes under review seems to me to give cause for concern. These strictures can only be supported here by a brief examination of the works in question but a more discriminating editorial policy ought to be urged on the editors of what is, potentially, an admirable venture.

Thomas Mark Grant[3] does not inspire confidence at the beginning of his study of Chapman's comedies by referring to the 'immense erudition' of Miller MacLure since, whatever the virtues of Professor MacLure's study of Chapman, it did not attempt, or claim, to deal with the immensely difficult and equally important question of Chapman's classical learning. Mr Grant has even fewer pretensions as he shows by his few remarks on *The Shadow of Night* or *Ovid's Banquet of Sence* – and yet whoever wants to understand the dramatist and the translator of Homer must first come to terms with the author of these

[1] 'Three Renaissance English Indoor Playhouses', *English Literary Renaissance*, III (1973), 166–82.
[2] *In Honour of Shakespeare* (Jarrold, 1972).
[3] *The Comedies of George Chapman: A Study in Development* (Universität Salzburg, 1972).

works. Mr Grant's analysis of the comic action of his chosen plays I found neither clear nor illuminating. His study of *The Widow's Tears* seemed particularly inadequate and his conclusion that 'The withering away of Chapman's moral energies and artistic talents is most clearly revealed in the deep estrangement which grows up increasingly after *The Widow's Tears* between tragic hero and dramatic action' is worthy of Edward Dowden. While a study of Chapman's comedies is badly needed Mr Grant cannot be said to have provided it.

Dekker is the object of Suzanne Blow's[1] study and her examination of his rhetoric is a competent and thorough academic study within its limits. Rhetoric is also the concern of Annette Drew-Bear[2] but her application of it is rather more illuminating. She argues that the main characters in *Sejanus*, *Volpone*, *The Alchemist* and *Bartholomew Fair* all assume 'faces' and that the key to their characters is to be found in the false *ethos* that they adopt and the rhetoric that they deploy in order to sustain it. It is satisfactory to see *Sejanus* receiving as careful and thorough investigation as the major comedies since it is still a greatly undervalued play. Two other studies of Jonson are provided by Mary C. Williams[3] and Derek de Silva.[4]

John F. McElroy[5] admirably sustains a new and interesting view of Thomas Middleton. He studies four generally neglected tragi-comedies, *More Dissemblers Besides Women*, *The Witch*, *The Old Law*, and *A Fair Quarrel*, and argues that in them 'the author's use (or rather abuse) of the Fletcherian mode and conventions is both deliberate and consistent'. In this context episodes like the 'charm' in *The Witch* (II, ii) 'can be appreciated only as a grotesque caricature of Fletcher's notorious bedroom scenes'. Despite his interesting defence of Middleton's art the author is still convinced that the works 'are obviously moribund'. It would be interesting if a theatrical director could be found to prove him wrong.

David Hard Zucker's[6] 1968 dissertation presented to Syracuse University ought to have undergone revision, or more thorough revision, before its publication now. His central thesis is clearly important – that the power of Marlowe's works lies in their combination of visual and verbal imagery into emblems of compelling emotional power. Yet he does not really make nearly enough of the visual effects of crowns and clothes in *Tamburlaine* and, while he rightly stresses the importance of the masque of the Seven Deadly Sins for *Faustus*, and the way in which Faustus himself acts as presenter for the dumb show of Alexander, Thais and Darius, he is still able to describe the scenes with the Duke of Vanholt as indicating the weakness and puerility of Faustus' designs. By far the best part of the book is the excellent chapter on *Edward II* and it is difficult to believe that this would not have found a commercial or learned publisher willing to print it as an article.

Even Alice Shalvi's[7] work suffers from its original format as a doctoral dissertation to the extent that once her original point about the concept of honour is made it is then laboured unnecessarily through every possible complication and combination in order to clinch the thesis. This is, however, criticism and commentary of a high order and the chapters on *Hamlet*, *Troilus and Cressida* and *Measure*

[1] *Rhetoric in the Plays of Thomas Dekker* (Universität Salzburg, 1972).

[2] *Rhetoric in Ben Jonson's Middle Plays: A Study of Ethos, Character Portrayal, and Persuasion* (Universität Salzburg, 1973).

[3] *Unity in Ben Jonson's Early Comedies* (Universität Salzburg, 1972).

[4] *Jonson: Wit and the Moral Sense in Volpone and the Major Comedies* (Universität Salzburg, 1972).

[5] *Parody and Burlesque in the Tragicomedies of Thomas Middleton* (Universität Salzburg, 1972).

[6] *Stage and Image in the Plays of Christopher Marlowe* (Universität Salzburg, 1972).

[7] *The Relationship of Renaissance Concepts of Honour To Shakespeare's Problem Plays* (Universität Salzburg, 1972).

for Measure are helpful and interesting readings of the plays. If all the volumes reached this standard it would be indeed an important publishing event.

Unfortunately they do not. There are at present three studies devoted to John Webster. Sanford Sternlicht[1] provides a competent enough account of Webster's imagery but our experience with mathematical counts of words and the study of style by computers is surely far enough advanced for it to be evident to anyone that the evidence is insufficient to reach the kind of certainty which would make his conclusions about authorship worth while. It is difficult to decide whether Richard Bodtke[2] or Robert P. Griffin[3] has written the duller book. Both seem to me muddled in thought and inexact in language and to add little or nothing to our understanding of a great dramatist. On the other hand William E. Mahaney[4] in his classified bibliography has provided a valuable research tool – valuable despite the fact that it is incomplete and its index unreliable. While, for example, Inga-Stina Ekeblad's excellent and well known article 'The Impure Art of John Webster' is included, her later and much more significant 'Webster's Realism or "A Cunning Piece Wrought Perspective"' is not. Mr Mahaney also says that he has marked any item which he has not personally examined. If that is so then his examination of some items must have been unbelievably cursory for a bibliographer.

Russell Fraser[5] has attempted a work of enormous synthesis designed to demonstrate that the present broke away from its medieval past in sixteenth-century England – two hundred years after a similar process had occurred on the continent. By the nature of the case this kind of thesis is unprovable and it need therefore surprise no one but Professor Fraser that he does not prove it. The author, however, is a man who has read long and deeply and has plenty of interesting things to say as he moves

from Mickey Spillane to *Measure for Measure* but since his categories are by definition infinitely elastic and can include or exclude anything he chooses there can be nothing approaching what is normally called an argument. Professor Fraser's erudition is obvious and the quality of his previously published books such that any reviewer who holds these opinions must search anxiously for the beam in his own eye. For this reader, at least, the synthesis was indefinitely postponed.

Equally synthetic, but with its own fascination, is Michael John Petry's[6] collection of everything that he can find which by any stretch of imagination, and he has a large imagination, can have anything to do with Herne the Hunter. The connection between Acteon, Woden, the wild hunt, Herne himself and various Green Men, is hardly susceptible of proof. It is, however, evident that the legend of the ghostly hunter of Windsor forest does fit into a pattern of wild huntsmen of folk-tale and legend. Mr Petry rightly treats his subject with the seriousness which it deserves and makes clear what a mild version of the legend was used by Shakespeare in *The Merry Wives of Windsor*. The wild huntsman and his spectral pack is not a benign figure and those who encounter him in a wood should stand stock still in the middle of the pathway or throw themselves to the ground making the sign of the cross and in no circumstances look up or speak. Mr Petry's dark tales remind one that Horatio, on the battlements of Elsinore,

[1] *John Webster's Imagery and the Webster Canon* (Universität Salzburg, 1972).
[2] *Tragedy and the Jacobean Temper: The Major Plays of John Webster* (Universität Salzburg, 1972).
[3] *John Webster: Politics and Tragedy* (Universität Salzburg, 1972).
[4] *John Webster: A Classified Bibliography* (Universität Salzburg, 1973).
[5] *The Dark Ages and the Age of Gold* (Princeton, 1973).
[6] *Herne the Hunter: A Berkshire Legend* (Reading, 1972).

was a man of extreme and even foolhardy courage.

Monsters of a less supernatural sort are the concern of James E. Savage.[1] This collection of essays by the late Professor Savage has been through the press by his friends and colleagues. The relationships of the choric, broker and humorous characters are examined in interesting and suggestive fashion.

A number of interesting contributions to knowledge have been made in the course of the year. John Feather[2] suggests that it is probable that Robert Armin played in *Two maids of More-clacke* in 1597/8 as a way of bringing himself to the attention of the London companies after his years in the provinces and that he joined the Chamberlain's Men for the playing season of 1598. E. D. Pendry[3] transcribes two recognizances taken out before a Middlesex justice which involve a Thomas Dekker of Whitechapel in 1608 and 1609. Suzanne Gossett[4] examines a unique English theatre on the continent, in the English College at Rome, between 1591 and 1660. The evidence comes from account books, architects' drawings, a brief MS. by a student and teacher at the college, the plays of Joseph Simons and a few reference books. William A. Ringler Jr and Stephen W. May[5] draw attention to a MS. poem in the Cambridge University Library (MS. Dd.5.75, folio 46) which is the epilogue of a play performed at court at Shrovetide 1598/9. Since only two plays are recorded as having been performed by the Admiral's and Chamberlain's Men they suggest that it is possibly an epilogue to a Shakespearian performance.

Arthur Freeman[6] publishes correct texts of the only two surviving letters from Essex to his sister Penelope Rich. Of possibly even greater interest is his recovery[7] of a full transcript of the document which triggered the action of the Privy Council in examining Thomas Kyd and Christopher Marlowe. It is a fifty-three line copy (*c.* 1600) of the poem which was removed from the wall of the Dutch Churchyard, Broadstreet ward. It has a note at the end *per. Tamburlaine* and it is Mr Freeman's thesis that this simple reference caused the Privy Council to try to interview Marlowe. Since he was out of town they examined his associate Thomas Kyd and in his papers found the damning atheistical pamphlet which caused Kyd's torture and perhaps Marlowe's murder. A. N. Kinkaid[8] examines R. C. Bald's decipherment of a Revels office scrap in the *Times Literary Supplement* (17 March 1927, p. 193), and now reads it as a note concerning a comedy, *Cupid's Festival*, deposited in the Revels Office for licensing purposes by an actor known as Dwarf Bob. Alvaro Ribeiro[9] investigates the life of Sir John Roe, the friend of Ben Jonson and claims to show conclusively that B. N. de Luna's theory of Jonson's complicity through Roe in the Gunpowder Plot is untenable.

Eliot Slater[10] compares the vocabulary of *Lucrece, Venus and Adonis* and *A Lover's Complaint* statistically and finds that the vocabulary of the first two is homogeneous but

[1] *Ben Jonson's Basic Comic Characters* (University and College Press of Mississippi, 1973).

[2] 'Robert Armin and the Chamberlain's Men', *Notes and Queries*, XIX (1972), 448–50.

[3] 'Thomas Dekker in the Magistrate's Court', *English Literary Renaissance*, III, 53–9.

[4] 'Drama in the English College, Rome, 1591–1660', *English Literary Renaissance*, III, 60–93.

[5] 'An Epilogue Possibly by Shakespeare', *Modern Philology*, LXX (1972), 138–9.

[6] 'Essex to Stella: Two letters from the Earl of Essex to Penelope Rich', *English Literary Renaissance*, III, f. p. 248.

[7] 'Marlowe, Kyd, and the Dutch Church Libel', *ibid.*, 44–52.

[8] 'A Revels Office Scrap Deciphered', *Notes and Queries*, XIX, 461–3.

[9] 'Sir John Roe: Ben Jonson's Friend', *Review of English Studies*, XXIV (1973), 153–64.

[10] 'A Statistical Note on A Lover's Complaint', *Notes and Queries*, XX (1973), 138–40.

that the third shows a real difference in vocabulary which may be due to different authorship or to the poems being composed at different times. Karl Wentersdorf[1] examines Armstrong's theory of image clusters and concludes that clusters are significant – though their exact significance is perhaps unclear. Imagery of a rather different kind is studied by Soji Iwaski[2] whose study of the emblem of truth as the daughter of time in *King Lear* and *The Winter's Tale* does not quite seem as illuminating as it ought to be.

In three notes on *Macbeth* M. J. C. Echeruo[3] concludes that the law of tanistry is not really applicable to the play, E. B. Lyle[4] argues that the Folio act divisions conceal the structure and George Walton Williams[5] uses the law of re-entry to demonstrate that Macbeth cannot be the Third Murderer. James F. Forrest[6] derives the use of 'blocks' and 'stones' in *Julius Caesar* from Arthur Golding. S. P. Zitner[7] traces 'Spartan dog' in *Othello* to *Metamorphoses* II. John Velz[8] finds a possible source for the wooing of Bianca under the guise of academic instruction. David McPherson[9] traces Malvolio's cross garters to Seneca's *Hippolytus*.

A. J. Gilbert[10] notes some similarities between Sonnet XXIV and Chapman's *Ovid's Banquet of Sence*. John C. Meagher[11] prints the text of Thomas Nelson's Lord Mayor's Show of 1590. Finally Martin Brunkhorst[12] gives a most interesting account of the fortunes of *Coriolanus* in translation and adaptation in Germany and *Shakespeare Jahrbuch* for 1973 contains some interesting articles on the film of *King Lear*[13].

© NIGEL ALEXANDER 1974

[1] 'Imagery as a Criterion of Authenticity: A Reconsideration of the Problem', *Shakespeare Quarterly*, XXIII (1972), 231–59.
[2] 'Veritas Filia Temporis and Shakespeare', *English Literary Renaissance*, III, 249–63.
[3] 'Tanistry, the "Due of Birth" and Macbeth's Sin', *Shakespeare Quarterly*, XXIII, 444–50.
[4] 'Act Division in *Macbeth*', *Notes and Queries*, XX, 140–1.
[5] 'The Third Murderer in *Macbeth*', *Shakespeare Quarterly*, XXIII, 261.
[6] '"Blocks" and "Stones"?' in *Julius Caesar*, *Notes and Queries*, XX, 134–5.
[7] 'Iago as Melampus', *Shakespeare Quarterly*, XXIII, 263–4.
[8] 'Gasgoigne, Lyly, and the Wooing of Bianca', *Notes and Queries*, XX, 130–3.
[9] 'Herculean Malvolio', *ibid.*, 135–6.
[10] 'Philosophical Conceits in Shakespeare and Chapman', *English Studies*, LIV (1973), 118–21.
[11] 'The London Lord Mayor's Show of 1590', *English Literary Renaissance*, III, 94–104.
[12] *Shakespeares Coriolanus in deutscher Bearbeitung* (de Gruyter, 1973).
[13] G. M. Kosinzew, 'Gedanken zum Film *König Lear*', 56–61; Robert Weimann, 'Lear und das Bild der armen nackten Elenden. Zum spezifischen Gehalt der filmischen Umsetzung von Shakespeares Tragödie', 62–73; Waltrad Fischer-Weimann, 'Der Film *König Lear*', 74–80; Wilfried Adling, 'Historizität und Aktualität in Kosinzews Film *König Lear*', 101–2.

3. TEXTUAL STUDIES

reviewed by RICHARD PROUDFOOT

The survey of this year's work in Shakespearian textual studies may well take as its point of departure the papers delivered by Charlton Hinman and Fredson Bowers to the World Shakespeare Congress at Vancouver in September 1971,[1] both of which take stock of

[1] Clifford Leech and J. M. R. Margeson (eds.), *Shakespeare 1971* (Toronto, 1972): C. Hinman,

the situation then current and concern themselves with the immediate prospect as well as with the vital needs of future editors of Shakespeare. Hinman recapitulates the major developments from 1964 to 1971, coming to rest on D. F. McKenzie's 'Printers of the Mind'[1] and assessing the damage sustained by the structure of bibliographical analysis of the early texts as the dust and smoke clear after that most severe assault on many of the assumptions underlying such analysis. He finds those parts of the structure most haunted by Shakespearians among the least shaken, namely, the identification of compositors on internal evidence and the establishment of their characteristics, the demonstration of setting by formes in the printing of the First Folio and the currency in the Elizabethan period of methods of proof-correction less rigorous than those described by Moxon in the 1680s. Points that he is willing to concede include the normality of concurrent printing in the Elizabethan period as well as later and the consequent invalidity of analyses, on internal evidence alone, of the interrelation of rates of composition and rates of presswork. Urging the need for more and better compositor studies, he simultaneously advocates the use by editors now of what we already know of given workmen as a guide towards a greater freedom to emend where good reason exists for doing so than has been usual in the past two decades: 'editors ought not any longer ... to proceed as if compositors, all alike, were almost always faithful to copy, and as if presuming to correct compositorial errors were the most heinous of the deadly sins' (p. 47). Three examples, from a page in Folio *King John* set by Jaggard's compositor B and from pages set by Simmes's compositor A in *Much Ado About Nothing* (1600) and *Richard II* (1597), all involve the same source of presumed error, the substitution of a word repeated from, or in, the immediate context for another closely resembling it which has

been adopted as an emendation by some editors on other good grounds. The knowledge that the two identified compositors were both given to this type of error supports the readings '*thy* charge' (*F* my) at *John* Through Line Number 269; 'than you *take* pains' (*Q* took) in Benedick's echo of Beatrice's words at *Much Ado*, 1072; and 'Whilst he from *one* side to the other turning' (*Q1* the one) at *Rich. II*, 2,385. The demonstration is clearly valid, but it raises broader questions about the use for editors of knowledge about the habits of identified compositors. Is the knowledge that these two workmen were liable to corrupt the text they were setting by verbal substitution of this kind evidence of the need for emendation or does it rather assist the rationalisation of emendations already recommended on other grounds? Is it the identity of the compositors or the general knowledge that this kind of error is one that type-setters can easily make that is necessary as the basis for an editorial decision? If it could be proved that the page in *Rich. II* was set, not by A after all but by his fellow-worker on the job, S, would the emendation lose any of its attraction? The identification of the work of a given compositor will always remain, in the absence of collateral external evidence, hypothetical, however strongly the internal evidence may recommend confidence in that hypothesis. What compositorial study has to offer editors is never going to be certainty about individual details in any text, and for many purposes the analysis of errors of setting in a given book, irrespective of their source in the habits of identifiable compositors, may be as useful as any but the most clearcut and demonstrably sound identifications. Whatever its value, compositor analysis is no panacea: no compositorial identification will

'Shakespearian Textual Studies: Seven More Years', pp. 37–49; F. Bowers, 'Seven or More Years?', pp. 50–8.

[1] *Studies in Bibliography*, XXII (1969), 1–75.

ever guarantee either the absence of error or the regular incidence of particular types of error or the uniform distribution of error in given pages of any printed text.

Professor Hinman's plea for more and better studies of compositors is nonetheless wholly justified as a signpost towards one of the few routes available in the direction of a fuller and more precise knowledge of the earliest texts and Professor Bowers, in his rejoinder, echoes and endorses that plea. Earlier in his paper, he stresses the superior practical importance for editors of knowledge of compositors as against hypotheses about the nature of the manuscripts used as printer's copy. He points out that in some instances knowledge of compositors can even contribute to establishing the character of copy: if the same two compositors set James Robert's Quartos of *The Merchant of Venice* (1600) and *Hamlet* (1604/5), then it is 'inconceivable ... that anyone could fancy both manuscripts were holograph as was generally assumed before the era of compositor analysis' (p. 58). If he is right, however, in claiming that 'we have built up this question of copy to inflated proportions for single-text plays', he can hardly evade his own share of responsibility for that inflation. But it may rather be that, like compositor analysis but to an even more extreme degree, the study of lost manuscripts through the medium of the printed editions in which alone they survive is worth-while only in direct proportion to the likelihood, in view of the nature of the evidence, that results can be achieved which shall have a sufficient substance and clarity of outline to establish confidence in them as the basis for editorial attitudes and decisions. The study of the Ralph Crane transcripts from which some Folio comedies were printed seems to argue against a pessimistic view of such inquiries, although there will be few cases which offer so satisfactory a quantity and range of evidence. These general discussions of compositorial studies have a particular importance at a moment when such studies are once more on the increase. Whatever our reservations about the likely sum total of knowledge to be derived from them, and whether we share the pessimism of Hinman or the optimism of Bowers about the long-term prospects for a 'definitive' text of Shakespeare, we must recognise compositor identification and analysis as among our slender means for continuing, in the words of P. H. Davidson, 'to strive to push back the moment when we have to make our conjectures – when the guessing must begin'.[1]

Meanwhile the work of analysis is itself progressing on several fronts, with new studies of the compositors of the First Folio, the 1619 Pavier/Jaggard Quartos and the Quartos printed by Valentine Simmes. A further monograph considers the printer's copy for five Folio comedies and the scribe who prepared it. Except in the case of T. H. Howard-Hill's study of Ralph Crane,[2] the new findings all tend to challenge familiar positions and often reintroduce doubt where some measure of assurance once seemed to have been attained. Considered together, they serve as a reminder of how far we yet are from the adoption of consistent and comprehensive methods in the detection and presentation of evidence for the identification of compositors and also of how essential it is that any such argument be not only accurate in its detail but as broadly-based as it can be made both in the range of compositorial characteristics isolated as significant and in the constant relation of these to whatever can be determined of the printing process as a whole.

[1] 'Marry, Sweet Wag', in D. Galloway (ed.), *Elizabethan Theatre II* (1970), p. 143.
[2] T. H. Howard-Hill, *Ralph Crane and Some Shakespeare First Folio Comedies* (Charlottesville, Bibliographical Society of the University of Virginia, 1972).

Andrew H. Cairncross[1] returns to the First Folio and continues his attempt not only to assign pages about which Hinman expressed doubt but to reassign wholesale others about which he was more confident. In the process, he is already prepared to revise his own earlier re-assignments, published in 1971.[2] His main new contention is that the compositor known as E and identified by Fredson Bowers[3] as John Leason, an apprentice who was bound to Jaggard in November 1622, and who, by Hinman's count, was employed only on the Tragedies, was neither Leason nor an apprentice but was employed throughout the Folio and set many pages usually assigned to B, whose most frequent spelling preferences E is known to have shared, as well as a few pages previously assigned to A and C. A subsidiary thesis is that pages in the early Comedies ($A-E G) assigned by Hinman to A or C should be given instead to an allegedly new fifth man whom Cairncross (like T. H. Howard-Hill) calls F. The overall effect of Cairncross's presentation of his evidence is sketchy and impressionistic, and indeed he endeavours to disarm criticism with the claim that he is dealing with differential forms which 'are not usually common enough to lend themselves to the impressive kind of tabulation used in compositorial studies' (p. 370). The obvious danger, that only a small part of what could be evidential may be presented, is not avoided, and much of what is consists of variant or individual spelling forms of too rare occurrence to be reliable evidence of anything. Readers are not helped by a wayward inconsistency in matters of layout, systems of reference (no use is made of Hinman's compact Through Line Numbers), and even typography.

That the work assigned by Hinman to B, or A, should turn out to be assignable, on a fuller understanding of the evidence, to another man need cause no surprise, so that Cairncross's position is not an impossible one. He points out

that inconsistencies have been accepted within B's pages, not only in the Folio but in the Pavier Quartos: thus his preferred forms *Glouster/Glou.* are mixed with the *Gloster/Glo.* forms held to identify E not only in F *King Lear*, where they differentiate between the two men, but in B's pages in some F Histories, such as *1* and *2 Henry VI* and *2 Henry IV* and in the Pavier *Contention* and *Lear* of 1619, which have been held to be entirely B's work. The record of instances (p. 373) shows, for example, 15 *Gloster* forms in B's pages of *1 Hen. VI*: what it fails to specify is that only one of these, at TLN 2393, is of the full name, the others being speech prefixes *Glo.*, that *Gloster* or *Glost.* are the dominant forms in the pages set by A and that the minority forms *Glocester* and *Gloucester* are preferred by B and A respectively. Granted that the forms quoted are inconsistent with B's recognised preferences in plays he set in F from printed copy, no allowance is here made for the possible influence of what might appear to have been the most frequent spellings of the name in the copy manuscript. The addition to the list of 'E' forms in B's pages of *1 Hen. VI* of a few spellings which run counter to B's preferences (p. 382) allows Cairncross to appropriate the pages for E (together, in a final summary list on p. 406, with l5, a page set by A, according to Hinman, and one which Cairncross nowhere discusses in detail). The second reassignment, of A's pages in the early comedies to F, depends largely on the coincidence of future tense forms such as *we'll* with *doe-goe-here* spelling preferences, which seems to rule out both A, who favours *wee'le*, and C, who is a *do-go-heere* man.

What is chiefly disturbing in this study is the

1 'Compositors E and F of the Shakespeare First Folio', *Papers of the Bibliographical Society of America*, 66 (1972), 369–406.

2 'Compositors C and D of the Shakespeare First Folio', *ibid.*, 65 (1971), 41–52.

3 *Bibliography and Textual Criticism* (Oxford, 1964), p. 181.

sense of *parti pris* for a particular answer to the questions asked, constantly apparent in the ease with which the very inconsistencies which are used as evidence against Hinman's identifications are turned into positive indications of the presence of E, who is granted a near monopoly of 'unstable usage'. We are left unsure how far we can trust any particular characteristic offered as distinctive of either E or F, simply because we are given no clear picture of the total evidence. This is the more unfortunate as it is quite clear that much of the material presented could be used to improve our knowledge of the Folio compositors if it were more coherently displayed, more fully and objectively examined and so appraised that the emergence of conclusions could be seen as a matter of demonstration rather than one of rhetoric and special pleading.

By way of contrast, the approach of T. H. Howard-Hill[1] to the more limited question of pages in the Comedies in F1 about which doubt remains after Hinman's work, is a model of caution and objectivity and although he too reaches the conclusion that the share of A in the comedies before *The Winter's Tale* should be reassigned, his new identifications differ widely in detail from those of Cairncross. Laying stress on the dangers of undue reliance on spellings as evidence in plays set from manuscript copy, he pays attention to habits of spacing after commas within short lines and at the ends of lines, the typographic handling of turnovers and preferences in handling elisions, allowing only a few selected variant spellings of common words among his evidence for the identification of compositors. His main concern is to achieve a finer discrimination between the work of compositors A, C and D than was attained by Hinman, who relied largely on *do-go-here* spelling patterns. His most consistent new pattern of preferences is in the spacing of commas. A and D prefer not to set a space after a mid-line comma, D's preference

being the stronger; B and C have the opposite habit, stronger in B; while of the four workmen, C alone sets a space before the comma at a line end with great regularity. The differentiation which is aided by this observation is between A and C, who share *doe-goe* spelling preferences. The other difficult discrimination, between A and D, is aided by D's usual practice of dealing with overrun lines by setting the words carried over as a new line indented from the left margin, an arrangement found only rarely in the pages of A and C. The application of all the criteria held to be strong enough to establish the presence of a given compositor rather than merely to confirm it, leads to the reassignment of most pages where Hinman was in doubt between A and another to the other, C or D, as well as to changes in a few of Hinman's identifications and confirmation of a few more (pp. 74–5). The great reduction of A's share in the Comedies leaves a small residue of 'A' pages in which Howard-Hill goes on to point out a pattern of preferential spellings inconsistent with Alice Walker's list of A spellings, to which his pages later in the Folio conform. It is only at this point that he feels compelled by the evidence to posit the presence of a fifth compositor (whom he first identified and christened F in 1969), in the Comedies section of the Folio. A table on p. 89 reveals the extent and kind of variation between the spellings in these 'A' pages in the early Folio comedies and those in *W. Tale*, with which the Folio work of the compositor hitherto called A is thought by Howard-Hill to begin. Appendices follow in which the characteristics used to distinguish the compositors are displayed in tables, together with their respective shares in the plays from *The Tempest* to *W. Tale* and a final list of additional differentiating forms of spelling. The strength of this analysis lies not only in the

[1] 'The Compositors of Shakespeare's Folio Comedies', *Studies in Bibliog.*, XXVI (1973), 61–106.

rigorous selection of evidence which is unlikely to reflect the character of the copy manuscripts underlying the majority of the plays considered, but in its acceptance of the conclusions to which that evidence points, even where those conclusions imply, as they do for much of *Measure for Measure*, a division of work in which many pages were divided between two compositors working from a single type-case. The whole is underpinned by its constant relation of the new evidence to what Hinman has demonstrated about the other aspects of the printing process. It is to be hoped that further studies will extend the analysis to the Histories and Tragedies.

There is inevitably an overlap between Howard-Hill's work on the Folio compositors and his study of Ralph Crane, the putative scribe of the copy from which they set five of the comedies. Again, the new analysis builds upon the work of earlier scholars, confirming it in its central conclusions, amplifying and clarifying its basis in critically assembled and tested detail and modifying it where a consideration of the whole evidence leads to conclusions not so clearly visible to investigators of single plays. Even this study accepts limits, though, by concentrating on Crane's extant manuscript transcripts of seven works by dramatic authors and on five Folio comedies, *Tempest*, *The Two Gentlemen of Verona*, *The Merry Wives of Windsor*, *M. for M.* and *W. Tale*. The possibility of Crane transcripts as copy for other Folio plays, such as *2 Henry IV*, is noted but not here explored, and reference is made to Webster's *Duchess of Malfi*, also printed from a Crane manuscript, only in passing and in corroboration of particular points in the argument.

The general import of the book is simple: the hypothesis that Crane transcripts underlie the Folio text of the five comedies is vindicated at every point on the dual evidence of the extant transcripts and of the habits of the Folio

compositors involved. Details of the accepted view of the matter are modified: thus, Crane is credited with no strictly 'editorial' function in preparing the transcripts and his own 'copy' for all five plays is cautiously identified as 'foul papers', although *W. Tale* is held to stand at one further remove from them, showing Crane's peculiarities more strongly than the other plays not only because it was the last of the five to be transcribed (late in 1622) but because its exemplar was a prompt-book reconstructed by Crane himself from 'foul papers' to replace the lost one. One of the most distinctive and perplexing features of two of the Folio plays, Crane's 'massed entries' at the beginning of scenes, is traced, not as often to the presumed influence of the Jonson Folio of 1616, but to the peculiarly difficult nature of the papers from which he was working for *Two Gent.* and *Merry Wives* (as well as for Webster's *Duchess*).

But the value of the book lies not only in the new confidence which it imparts to conclusions already familiar in outline, but in the quantity of precise and well-ordered detail which it makes available to future investigators of Crane. Chapter 3 gives a full account of Crane's scribal practices in the extant dramatic transcripts, which documents Howard-Hill's contention that Crane's own habits varied more than has been generally recognised at different times and in preparing transcripts for various purposes: it ends with a list of Crane's preferred forms of spelling and contraction which, although selective, will provide the necessary basis for any attempt to detect Crane copy behind further dramatic texts. The equally detailed account of the five Folio comedies which constitutes Chapter 5 will be an indispensable reference for all future editors, although here one might question the choice of the New Arden Shakespeare as the sole criterion for the incidence of corruption in these plays. A rare lapse of logic apparently occurs in relation to a misreading at *W. Tale*, TLN 368: 'Crane's spelling "holly" might explain the printing of "Holy-Horse" for "hobby-horse"' (p. 132). This could only be so if we suppose the error to originate with Crane: to credit compositor A with first misreading "hobby" as "holly" and then altering it to "Holy" because of his familiarity with Crane's habit of doubling medial *l* in *holy* seems too elaborate a series of coincidences – but perhaps no such explanation is implied.

The broader editorial implications of the study are not very encouraging. Crane emerges as 'a sophisticating scribe, with strong opinions about what kind of orthography was desirable' and one whose concern for legibility and for turning in an intelligible manuscript was stronger than his obligation to preserve the details of his copy, especially in such features as the precise wording of stage directions; still worse, 'There is little hope, although his influence on orthography is clear enough, that all points at which he altered the substantives of his copy texts have been detected by modern scholars and much of his influence will continue to elude detection' (p. 138). On the credit side, the fidelity of the Folio compositors to the 'orthographical characteristics of their copy' turns out to be unexpectedly great, features characteristic of Crane which do not occur in their pages elsewhere in the Folio being found in the work of all of them in the 'Crane comedies' (p. 133).

Returning to more strictly compositorial investigations, two new inquiries into the setting of the Pavier Quartos share, and amplify, the scepticism of A. S. Cairncross about the attribution of the whole of the ten plays to Jaggard's compositor B.[1] P. M. W. Blayney[2] sets out merely to reopen the two questions, whether B was employed in the setting of the 1619 collections and, if so, whether he was their only compositor. The first question raises the problem of how a compositor's habits may be expected to change over a period of years. Here a critical examination of evidence adduced by W. S. Kable in favour of B's presence reveals both substantial inaccuracy and extensive omissions and leads to the conclusions that 'If one makes the untested assumption that only one man worked on the [Pavier] collection, then it must be recognized that he had some preferences which are the reverse of those found in the examined part of B's Folio settings' and that even 'If we are dealing with the same man, it hardly seems safe to base any arguments on his long-term consistency' (p. 193). The question of division of the work receives a more tentative answer. On the rather scanty evidence of Greg's table of watermarks in the Pavier Quartos,[3] the order of printing established in 1910 by W. Neidig[4] is revised to place *A Midsummer Night's Dream* as the seventh play, between *Merry Wives* and *Lear*, instead of at the end. This permits Blayney to postulate the use of a two-skeleton pattern of imposition throughout seven plays which would have been at least compatible with a division of composition between two compositors. However, his subsequent scrutiny of *Mer. Ven.* and *MND* in search of two compositorial patterns related to the two skeletons produces no more than suggestive hints for *Mer. Ven* and is wholly negative for *MND*. The results of another investigator of the same question, J. F. Andrews, are summarised in *Shakespeare Newsletter*.[5] On the basis of a wide range of

[1] See W. S. Kable, 'Compositor B, The Pavier Quartos, and Copy Spellings', *Studies in Bibliography*, XXI (1968), 131–61; and *The Pavier Quartos and the First Folio* (Dubuque, Iowa, 1970).

[2] '"Compositor B" and the Pavier Quartos: Problems of Identification and their Implications', *Library*, 5th series, XXVII (1972), 179–206.

[3] *Library*, 2nd series, IX (1908), before p. 381.

[4] *Modern Philology*, VIII (1910–11), 145–63.

[5] XXII (Feb. 1972), p. 6: abstract of 'The Pavier Quartos of 1619 – Evidence for Two Compositors', doctoral dissertation, Vanderbilt University, 1971.

evidence, he has divided the ten plays between two compositors, assigning to B the whole of *Oldcastle* and a share in the two parts of *The Contention*, *Mer. Ven.*, *Lear* and *Henry V*; the remaining sections of these five plays and the whole of *Pericles*, *A Yorkshire Tragedy*, *Merry Wives* and *MND* are assigned to another compositor called (confusingly enough in the light of recent Folio studies) F. We may hope that a fuller account of this investigation is to be published and that when it is Andrews will be prepared to rename F, perhaps associating him with the 1619 Quartos by the use of the letter P.

Analysis of Quarto texts continues in two new articles by Alan E. Craven on the composition of play Quartos in the shop of Valentine Simmes.[1] The work of three compositors, A, B and S, is considered in eight Quartos printed between 1597 and 1603. Craven's point of departure is the analysis of A and B in *2 Hen. IV*, *Much Ado*, *The Shoemaker's Holiday* and *1 Contention* (all 1600) by W. Craig Ferguson,[2] with whose identifications he disagrees only in assigning *Contention*, like *2 Hen. IV* and *Much Ado*, to A alone. Adding some preferential forms to Ferguson's list of A's characteristics, Craven proceeds to allocate to him the whole of *Ham.* (1603) (in spite of much variation in it from A's habits in 1600); fifty-seven and a half pages of *Rich. II* (1597) (though which pages they are is never specified); and the whole of Simmes's share ($A-G) in *Richard III* (1597). He is further credited with the whole of *Rich. II*, Q2 (1598). Even if these identifications could be relied upon, it would be hard to have much confidence in estimates of A's reliability and characteristic types of error based on so narrow a range of evidence about them as is offered. This is a pity, because he is characterised as having the habit of taking 'more material into his head than he could deal with accurately' and of being peculiarly prone, on the evidence

of Q2 *Rich. II*, to verbal substitution. If this were substantiated, it would have far-reaching implications for editors of *2 Hen. IV*, *Much Ado*, *Rich. II* and even *Rich. III*, where some memorial elements usually accounted for as reflecting copy might instead be attributable to compositor A. Unfortunately, too many questionable and untested assumptions underlie these conclusions, which should restrain the eagerness of editors to see corruption boil and bubble in the plays examined. Chief among these are the assumptions that compositor A has been identified beyond reasonable doubt and that his rate of error was constant whether his copy was printed or manuscript. When Craven proceeds to consider Simmes's compositors B and S, he may be right in confirming the presence of B as A's partner in *The Shoemakers' Holiday* and in suggesting that he also shared *Rich. II*, Q3 (1598) with the third man, S, who, in turn, had been A's partner for *Rich. II*, Q1, in which he set fifteen and a half unspecified pages. The doubts begin when, on the basis of this small quantity of setting, for which the copy included both printed and manuscript material, Craven proceeds to generalise about the characteristics and reliability of these men too. His general conclusion 'that the textual integrity of any Simmes quarto depends, perhaps to a degree not heretofore suspected, on the identity of the compositor or compositors who set it' (p. 171) may be just, but is not, in the present state of our knowledge, very useful. The way is open for further work on Simmes: three play

[1] 'Simmes' Compositor A and Five Shakespeare Quartos', *Studies in Bibliography*, xxv 37–60; 'Two Valentine Simmes Compositors', *Papers of the Bibliographical Society of America*, 67 (1973), 161–71.

[2] 'The Compositors of *Henry IV, Part 2, Much Ado About Nothing, The Shoemakers' Holiday*, and *The First Part of the Contention*', *Studies in Bibliography*, xiii (1960), 19–29: reprinted as Chapter iii of *Valentine Simmes* (Charlottesville, Bibliographical Society of the University of Virginia, 1968).

Quartos from the years of his Shakespeare editions have yet to be analysed, Chapman's *Humorous Day's Mirth* (1599), *A Warning for Fair Women* (1599) and *1 Sir John Oldcastle* (1600). The last of these may even call in question a major axiom of Simmes compositor studies, namely that A is clearly identified by the habit of setting unabbreviated speech prefixes without a following period. In *Oldcastle*, where the possibility of 'foul papers' copy in the hands of more than one author certainly complicates the issue, such speech prefixes are found on all but seven of the seventy-six text pages, but with a variation of frequency in relation to stopped abbreviated prefixes which fluctuates widely and not in any apparent response either to a need to justify lines or to fluctuation from scene to scene such as could have existed in the copy. In this play, the unstopped speech prefix test for A will have to be applied with care and it seems even possible that the habit held to be distinctive of one compositor will turn out to have been shared by another, or at least that the relative frequency of abbreviated and unabbreviated prefixes in short lines may turn out to be significant too. The suitability of Simmes as a subject for immediate further work is increased by the availability of W. C. Ferguson's brief but comprehensive monograph on his career, his stocks of type, ornaments and paper, and his publications.

As the use of computers for literary research increases both in range and frequency, in spite of the daunting technical and economic problems posed by them, the collection of essays edited by R. A. Wisbey[1] deserves the attention of all potential editors and textual investigators. Only one of the essays deals directly with a Shakespearian topic: Ruth L. Widmann[2] describes her use of a computer in collating multiple editions of *MND*. Her account of the technical problems of preparing texts on punched cards for computer reading will serve as a timely caution to any scholar who imagines computers to be labour-saving devices. The punching of some 2,300 cards occupied student card-punchers (who were also surprisingly entrusted with the job of proof-reading their own work) for some 160 hours, enabling Professor Widmann to obtain a print-out of the full collation of sixty editions, graphically presented so that details, even of punctuation and capitalisation, are easily visible (although in the sample printed, of TLN 2178–83, the much more significant omission from F4 of a whole word, *it* in line 2179, is not). Two major grounds for unease are at once apparent, granted the value of so close a collation of so many derivative editions of a printed text in the first place: the first is that the input method is inadequately safeguarded against frequent minor error, the second that the display of the print-out is misleading in its emphasis, if not simply inefficient. Misgivings can only increase as we find coincidences in punctuation or capitalisation in some eighteenth-century editions presented as evidence of direct derivation, as if Capell needed the authority of Rowe's third edition to capitalise *Hand* at 2182 or of Theobald's first to introduce a comma after *sing* at 2183. The chief point that should be made is that wishful metaphorical thinking about computers has its dangers. To imagine one 'in the role of a high-grade clerical assistant' is as risky as to attribute human characteristics to any other electronic tool, however swift, efficient and tireless it may seem. The risk lies in the distraction of attention from the crucial role of the human servants of the machine, the researching scholar and her team of card-punchers, on whose accuracy and intelligence the significance of any results ob-

---

[1] *The Computer in Literary and Linguistic Research* (Cambridge, 1971).
[2] 'The computer in historical collation: use of the IBM 360/75 in collating multiple editions of *A Midsummer Night's Dream*', ibid., pp. 57–63.

tained must wholly depend, and to impute to the whole operation a sense of guaranteed accuracy and efficiency which only properly attaches to the mechanical enabling phases of the work performed by the tool.

The uses and limitations of computers in literary editing are the subject of a paper by Harold Love[1] in which the main question posed is whether the computer is indeed only a new and more efficient tool for performing conventional and familiar tasks or whether it holds out the possibility of entirely new methods of handling some aspects of the editorial task. The conclusion is balanced: as tool, the computer promises to increase the accuracy and flexibility of work on authorial, scribal and compositorial practices; on the collation of multiple copies (especially of machine-printed books, until more sophisticated scanners are developed) and of multiple editions; on the classification of variants and the construction of stemmata; and on all forms of linguistic analysis. Ultimately, once standards of production attain a generally acceptable level, the computer-setting of edited texts and their apparatus should constitute a truly new method of editing and one which promises a higher degree of accuracy of detail than can be attained by even the most costly of proof-correction (a process which will simply become obsolete). Cost remains one disabling objection, and, until computer scanning of texts can be relied on for all varieties of type-material, human error will still be a vitiating factor affecting input. One of the principal criticisms which has justly been levelled at T. H. Howard-Hill's Oxford Shakespeare Concordances, now completed with the publication of *Hamlet* from the Q2 text,[2] has been that the process of pre-editing by which the texts were prepared involved the introduction of error in perceptible quantity. Two main potential sources of error have been identified as the use of microfilm, which Neil Taylor[3] has shown as

motivating two editorial 'corrections' of non-existent misprints in Q *2 Hen. IV* (a procedure which, however, leaves the text of the concordance unaffected), and the correction, as misprints, of readings which some editors have found grounds for retaining as authentic or have emended in plausible ways other than those adopted by Professor Howard-Hill.[4] But, though just, these criticisms can hardly be thought to detract seriously from the value of a work of reference whose likeliest users will be working closely enough with the original texts to identify the rare slip or error where it occurs and whose editor has from the outset expected that, where the quantity of material concorded was so great, some such small residue would be left for his readers to detect and to report.

Editions of plays received for review include a reprint in paperback of Clifford Leech's New Arden *Two Gent.*[5] and new volumes in three other series. *The Comedy of Errors*, edited by Stanley Wells in the New Penguin Shakespeare,[6] maintains the high standards of the series. One new reading depends on interpretation rather than emendation: at II, i, 79, Dromio's line begins with 'An', rather than the usual 'And', which increases the humour of his helpless resignation when ordered back to Antipholus by Adriana with the threat 'or I will break thy pate across' – 'An he will bless that cross with other beating / Between you I shall have a holy head'. Such regard for nuance is in keeping with the tone of respect for Shakespeare's art which informs the introduction. Dr Wells contributes to the current

[1] 'The computer and literary editing: achievements and prospects', *ibid.*, pp. 47–56.

[2] Oxford, 1973.

[3] *Notes and Queries*, 218 (1973), 134.

[4] Review of Concordances to *Cymbeline* and *Hamlet* in *The Times Literary Supplement* (29 Sept. 1973), p. 1090.

[5] London, 1972.

[6] Harmondsworth, 1972.

revaluation of a play once easily dismissed as a derivative farce. He is ready to claim it as, in the strictest sense, Shakespeare's 'masterpiece', the first work 'in which mastery of a craft is displayed', and to describe it as 'both the most brilliant comedy that had so far been written in English, and . . . a completely assured work for which no excuses need be made'. The question of its date of composition is left open, partly because the editor wishes to see it as a later work than *Two Gent.*, which he finds lacking in 'theatrical craftsmanship' (though without considering the possible status of the text of it printed in F), but because he also recognises that stylistic evidence points to the priority of *Com. Errors*. If the play gives us our best evidence for Shakespeare the country schoolmaster, we must also remember Shakespeare the father of twins, given to pondering the potentially frightening concept of the 'absolute external identity of one person with another', whose more disturbing resonances, though closer to the heart of *Twelfth Night*, are not overlooked in this very early work. An unfortunate slip makes the author of *Ralph Roister Doister* into Thomas, not Nicholas, Udall, and the suggestion of a late dating, even 1594, might have invited at least passing reference to the existence of an English analogue in the manuscript play of Amphitryon called *The Birth of Hercules* (c. 1595), to which a German theatre historian, Dieter Schamp of Dusseldorf, has recently and implausibly attempted to attach the name of Shakespeare.

As You Like It, edited by Christine Trautvetter,[1] follows *M. for M.* in the 'Old-Spelling and Old-Meaning' Shakespeare series launched by Ernest Leisi. It is hard to do justice to the real and solid merits of this edition, because both in detail and in policy it constantly undermines the reader's confidence. First there is the text itself, printed in near facsimile from the Yale Folio facsimile with the claim that for *AYLI* 'this text is in no way inferior to that of the Norton fascimile prepared by Charlton Hinman'. The issue remains academic, though, as Dr Trautvetter's own text is marred by frequent minor errors and, while she reveals no interest in the possible effect of compositorial habit on the orthographical matters which are among her concerns, retains such linguistically insignificant features as the use of vv for w resulting from type shortage. The notes, which are largely compilations from earlier editions and from such works of reference as Abbott's *Shakespearian Grammar*, Kökeritz's *Shakespeare's Pronunciation* and Eric Partridge's *Shakespeare's Bawdy* (though not Tilley's *Dictionary of Proverbs*), mix matter with impertinency with a fine impartiality, admirably defending and clarifying F '*turne his merrie Note*', at II, v, 3, or providing an informative discussion of 'Attalanta's *better part*', at III, ii, 142, but spending pages on the possible and impossible sexual undertones of Touchstone's mustard and pancakes or his 'right Butter-womens ranke' (III, ii, 94) and even descending to the egregious error of defending F's misreading *his* in '*Helens cheeke, but not his heart*' (III, ii, 140) on the non-existent grounds of an alleged analogy of usage in *Hen. V* (III, vii, 64), 'my mistress wears his own hair', where the 'mistress' in question is the Dauphin's horse. The two most damaging shortcomings of this edition, in terms of its aim of clarifying the meaning of the words, are its editor's insufficiently sure sensitivity to normal English idiom and her total lack of theatrical awareness, which leads to an assumed definition of 'context' in terms mainly of lexical possibility and allows her, for instance, to grope for her bawdy trout in the speeches of Celia as willingly as in those of Touchstone.

The edition of *Lear* prepared for the Bobbs-Merrill Shakespeare Series by E. A. Horsman,[2]

[1] Heidelberg, 1972.
[2] Indianapolis: New York, 1973.

is an example of what a modernised students' reading edition should be. Textually it is conservative, relying more on F than, for example, G. K. Hunter did in his recent New Penguin edition, and its introduction, notes (which are especially helpful with 'old meanings' of familiar words, though unfashionably reticent where sexual innuendo may be imagined or invented) and appendices provide a full, factual and thoroughly digested account of the play in all its major aspects. With characteristic thoroughness, the editor makes his own contribution, in an appendix on the transmission of the text, to one of the outstanding problems, that of the nature of the Quarto copy used to set Folio *Lear*. His suggestion that the evidence for use of composite copy, including leaves from both Q1 and Q2, corresponds with Hinman's division of the F text between compositors B and E in such a way as to associate B with Q1 copy and E with Q2 copy deserves more extended exposition than has been possible within the present volume.

The new *Shakespeare Variorum Handbook*, jointly compiled by Richard Hosley, Richard Knowles and Ruth McGugan,[1] brings welcome promise of revival for a leading American edition. It announces modifications of policy which include a move from type-facsimile to diplomatic reprinting of the copy-text and a more selective account of variants and emendations than hitherto in the textual apparatus, but the commentary and critical appendices will 'continue to be as inclusive as the bulk of modern scholarship will allow'. International interest in Shakespearian textual studies is further reflected by the inclusion of a full and meticulous account of the history of the text and of scholarly investigation of it by Hans Walter Gabler in the new German *Shakespeare-Handbuch*[2] and by the publication of *Shakespeare's First Folio*,[3] in which R. S. Varma provides an enthusiastic introduction to his subject which will convey its outlines to an

Indian audience but which is flawed by a few minor errors of fact and by many misprints.

J. P. Feather[4] comments on the apparent use of two distinct measures, a long and a short, often corresponding with prose and verse respectively, in the setting of some play texts, including Q1 *Lear*, and points out the need for investigators of compositorial spelling habits to take account of the variation and its effect on justification. An explanation for this phenomenon is offered by D. F. McKenzie,[5] who draws attention to Moxon's instructions for 'indenting the stick' by placing large quads at one end of it to reduce the measure for setting a sequence of short lines, a procedure which he holds responsible for errors in Q1 *Lear* on K1 and K4[5]. On the latter page, the words 'and ap-/(pointed guard,)', omitted by the compositor and added as a stop-press correction, fall outside the shortened measure used to set the page. In a further note,[6] McKenzie describes eight proof-sheets from an English translation of Lambert Daneau printed in 1594 by John Legate (STC 6227), and rescued from the binding of another book in the Cambridge University Library. These quarto sheets afford both new details of late sixteenth-century methods of proof-correction and clear evidence of quarto type-setting by formes, the innermost forme of the gathering having been set first. R. J. Roberts[7] describes 'an uncut though tattered sheet on which the title-page [dated

[1] New York, 1971.
[2] Ina Schabert (ed.) (Stuttgart, 1972); III. *Teil: Das Werk*. A. Der Text, 194–242.
[3] Kitab Mahal, Allahabad, 1970.
[4] 'Some Notes on the Setting of Quarto Plays', *Library*, 5th series, XXVII, 237–44.
[5] '"Indenting the Stick" in the First Quarto of *King Lear* (1608)', *Papers of the Bibliographical Society of America*, 67, pp. 125–30.
[6] 'Eight Quarto Proof Sheets of 1594 Set by Formes: *A fruitfull commentarie*', *Library*, 5th series, XXVIII (1973), 1–13.
[7] 'Rowe's Shakespeare: an Experiment of 1708', *ibid.*, 56–61.

1708] and first eight pages of *The Tempest* have been imposed in octavo' which has recently been acquired by the British Museum. The sheet is apparently a trial for Rowe's 1709 edition of Shakespeare, printed by Jacob Tonson, who had bought the copyright in the plays in May 1707 from the heirs of John Herringman. The format of the trial sheet was adopted for the 1709 collection, but its text suggests that if Rowe prepared it his editorial principles had moved away, by 1709, from reliance on F2 (of which he owned a copy) towards a greater dependence on F4 and a more thorough modernisation of spelling and punctuation than even that of F4. Were another editor of the 1708 fragment to be sought, he might be John Hughes, whose edition of Spenser Tonson published in 1715.

John C. Meagher[1] considers *Much Ado*, III, iii, 160–1, and proposes an ingenious new solution to Q's clearly erroneous attribution of the speech to Conrade. He sees the Q speech prefix '*Conr.*', used here and at line 156, 'Masters, masters', as the compositor's misinterpretation of a copy form '*Con,*' and argues that both lines should be spoken by Dogberry, for whom the prefix '*Const.*' is used in v, i. His arrival would be in response to the instruction given to Hugh Oatcake, the third Watchman, who has no other function in the scene, to 'Call vppe the right maister Constable' (line 151). This rearrangement gives the malapropism 'let vs obey you to go with vs' to the character best suited to speak it, but leaves a new problem in the lack of an entry direction for Dogberry before line 155. T. W. Craik ('"Berowne Steppes Forth"')[2] would emend the Q/F stage direction at *Love's Labour's Lost*, v, ii, 655, to read '*Clowne steppes forth*', suggesting that it anticipates the interruption of Armado at line 661 by Costard, who is described as *Clowne* elsewhere in the scene, and that the compositor might have been guided by the end of the word in his copy to misread its beginning.

J. C. Maxwell[3] attacks the Latin quotation at *2 Hen. VI*, IV, i, 117, '*Pine gelidus timor occupat artus*, it is thee I feare' by taking the English words as paraphrase of the Latin, which recommends the emendation of *Pine* to *Prae te*.

W. F. Bolton ('Menenius's "scale't": a New Defense')[4] defends F at *Coriolanus*, I, i, 95, by reference to *OED* 'scale' $v.^2$ 2.b., '? To split off scales or flakes from (coin) for the purpose of fraud', a sense which the phrase 'fobbe off' in the reply of the Second Citizen seems to support. Joseph S. G. Bolton[5] argues against the common editorial practice of omitting three and a half lines of the 1594 Q1 text of *Titus Andronicus*, I, i, 'because of their reference to a later event in the play as having already taken place'. The emendation of line 35 from 'at this day' to 'at this door' (assuming a copy-spelling *daie* misread as *dore*) removes the difficulty of apparent reference to the killing of Alarbus before the event, while providing precedent for it from the earlier triumphs of Titus. H. F. Brooks[6] supports the preference of R. Levin[7] for Q1 'stand to' over Q2 'speake' in the Nurse's speech at *Romeo and Juliet*, II, iv, 144, accounting for 'speake' as a copyist's erroneous repetition of a word from the previous speech. James O. Wood,[8] arguing that the imagery of dogs frequently applied to the conspirators in *Julius Caesar* implies a reference to the myth of Actaeon 'that was often drawn into Shakespeare's mind as an emblem, whether of a heart acutely distressed or of a man

---

[1] 'Conrade Conned: or, the Career of Hugh Oatcake', *Shakespeare Quarterly*, XXIV (1973), 90–2.
[2] *Notes and Queries*, 218, p. 133.
[3] 'Three Notes on *2 Henry VI*', *ibid.*, 133–4.
[4] *English Language Notes*, X (1972), 110–11.
[5] 'A Plea for $3\frac{1}{2}$ Rejected Shakespearian Lines', *Shakespeare Quarterly*, XXIII (1972), 261–3.
[6] *Review of English Studies*, XXIII (1972), 459.
[7] *Ibid.*, p. 56.
[8] 'Intimations of Actaeon in *Julius Caesar*', *Shakespeare Quarterly*, XXIV, 85–8.

suddenly turned upon by subjects or supposed friends', incidentally reinforces F's reading at v, i, 53–4, 'Neuer till *Caesars* three and thirtie wounds / Be well aueng'd' against Theobald's correction, 'three and twenty'. Though the ancient historians give the number of Caesar's wounds as twenty-three, Actaeon in Ovid's *Metamorphoses* has a pack of thirty-three named hounds. Henning Krabbe[1] reconsiders Dover Wilson's emendation, 'time-server' (F 'time') at *Macbeth*, II, iii, 6. He notes that Shakespeare does not use the word elsewhere and offers as an alternative 'time-pleaser', which occurs in *TN* and also in *Cor.*, in a passage 'closely connected with the supply of corn in a time of dearth' and thus similar in subject to the Porter's lines about the farmer 'that hang'd himself on th'expectation of plenty'. Leslie Brisman ('A Better Way: *King Lear* IV, iii, 20')[2] defends Hudson's punctuation, 'Were like. A better way: those happy smilets', taking 'A better way' to express the Gentleman's repeated endeavour to improve on his description of the mingled smiles and tears of Cordelia, 'who stands for the inability to translate emotion into words'. K. P. Wentersdorf[3] cuts through paleographic controversy with a fresh defence of the manuscript form 'momtanish' at line 263 of the Hand D scene in *Sir Thomas More*, which he understands as a 'readily conceivable Elizabethan' spelling of 'mahometanish', an epithet which would certainly fit the context of More's rebuke to the mob for its inhumanity towards foreigners.

© RICHARD PROUDFOOT 1974

[1] 'The "Time-Server" in the Porter's Speech in *Macbeth*', *Notes and Queries*, 218, 141–2.
[2] *Shakespeare Quarterly*, XXIII (1972), 205–6.
[3] 'A Crux in the Putative Shakespearian Addition to *Sir Thomas More*', *English Language Notes*, X, 8–10.

INDEX

Adams, Joseph Q., 93, 111n., 112, 113, 118, 121n., 129
Adiing, Wilfried, 179n.
Admiral's Men, 130, 133, 134n., 136, 173, 178
Alexander, Nigel, 46n., 49, 54, 55, 56n., 172–9
Alexander, Peter, 62n., 119n., 129n., 132n., 135
Alexander the Great, 72, 75, 78, 79
Allen, J. A., 164
Alleyn, Edward, 134
Ames, William, 90
Amneus, D., 159
Andrews, J. F., 185
Andrews, Mark Edwin, 95, 98, 104
Anne of Denmark, 172
Aristotle, 78, 160
Armin, Robert, 163, 178
Armstrong, W. A., 23n., 31n., 179
Arnold, Aerol, 26n.
Aronson, A., 171
Arthos, J., 163
Ashcroft, Dame Peggy, 142
Ashe, Thomas, 97
Atkins, Eileen, 149
Austin, Warren B., 130n.

Bacon, Sir Francis, 95
Bald, R. C., 178
Baldwin, T. W., 59n., 105, 106n., 127n., 129, 132n., 134n.
Bandello, Matteo, 172
Barish, J. A., 171
Barker, Felix, 34n.
Barnet, Sylvan, 16n.
Barroll, J. Leeds, 31n., 160
Barton, Anne, 44, 152, 165
Barton, John, 141, 144, 151, 152, 153
Battenhouse, Roy, 71–9
Baxter, Richard, 87n.
Belleforest, F. de, 172
Belsey, C., 159
Bergeron, D. M., 166
Berman, Ronald, 24n., 159
Berry, R., 162
Bevington, David, 72, 165
Birch, T. & Oldys, W., 56
Bland, D. S., 118n.
Blayney, P. M. W., 185
Blow, Suzanne, 176

Bodtke, Richard, 177
Bolton, Joseph S. G., 191
Bolton, W. F., 191
Bond, R. Warwick, 111n., 112, 113, 119
Bonheim, Jean, 24n.
Bonnard, Georges A., 112, 113, 119
Booth, Edwin, 34n.
Botticelli, 139
Bowen, Catherine Drinker, 100n.
Bowers, T., 45n.
Bradbrook, Muriel, 11n., 89–90, 91n., 113–14, 115, 116–17, 118, 119, 122, 127, 130n.
Bradbury, M., & Palmer, D. J., 162n., 163n., 164n., 165n., 167n., 170n.
Bradley, A. C., 72, 156, 157, 160
Brae, A. E., 107, 108
Brandes, George, 106n.
Brisman, Leslie, 192
Brissenden, A., 172
Bromley, John, 72n.
Brook, Peter, 143, 145, 167
Brooke, C. F. Tucker, 98n., 99n., 112n., 119
Brooke, Christopher, 120
Brooke, Nicholas, 1n., 31n., 34, 35, 40n.
Brooks, H. F., 191
Broude, R., 159
Brower, Reuben A., 173
Brown, J. R., 145, 148, 162
Brunkhorst, Martin, 179
Buchanan, George, 172
Bull, George, 46n.
Bullough, Geoffrey, 16n., 19n., 28n., 112, 172, 173, 174
Bulman, James C., Jr. 111–27
Bunyan, John, 91
Burckhardt, Sigurd, 83, 91

Cairncross, Andrew S., 132n., 135, 181–2, 183, 185
Calderwood, James L., 27n.
Campbell, Oscar James, 120n.
Capell, Edward, 187
Carew (Cary), Sir George, 99, 101, 103, 104
Carlyle, Thomas, 21
Carr, V. M., 161
Castiglione, Baldesar, 56, 163
Cecil, Sir Robert, 94
Cecil, William (Lord Burghley), 94

Chaderton, Laurence, 83n.
Chaloner, Thomas, 59, 60, 61, 62, 63, 65, 66n., 67, 68, 69
Chamberlain's Men, 134n., 136, 173, 178
Chambers, E. K., 1n., 95n., 98n., 106n., 127n., 129n., 132, 134n., 135
Chambers, R. W., 173
Chapman, George, 175, 176, 179, 186
Charlton, H. B., 25n.
Chaucer, Geoffrey, 109n.
Chettle, Henry, 130n.
Christ, 66
Church, Tony, 148
Cinthio, Giraldi, 172
Clemen, W. H., 11n., 24n., 25n., 26n., 29n., 32n.
Clements, John, 142
Coghill, Nevill, 82n.
Coke, Edward, 95n.
Combes, John, 99
Combes, Thomas, 99
Combes, William, 99
Council, N., 160–1
Craig, Hardin, 96n., 106n.
Craik, T. W., 191
Crane, Ralph, 181, 184, 185
Craven, Alan E., 186
'C.T.S.', 116n.
Cubeta, P. M., 39n.

Daiches, David, 54n.
Dalton, Timothy, 147, 150, 151
Danby, John F., 22n., 31n.
Daneau, Lambert, 190
Daniel, Samuel, 131
Danson, L. N., 160
Danter, John, 135–6
Davidson, P. H., 181
Dawson, Giles, E. 93, 134n.
Dekker, Thomas, 176, 178
De la Primaudaye, Pierre, 45n.
De Luna, B. N., 178
De Medici, Catherine, 172
Dench, Jeffery, 147, 149
Dench, Judi, 137–42
Derby's Men, 133n., 135, 136
De Selincourt, E., 96n.
De Silva, Derek, 176
Digges, Thomas, 45n.
Dircks, P. T., 172
Doebler, J., 157

Donne, John, 93, 94, 109, 120
Dowden, Edward, 176
Drew-Bear, Annette, 176
Dudley, Robert, 118n.
Dugdale, William, 115n.
Dunkel, Wilbur, 93n., 94n.
Durrant, G., 167
Dutton, John, 134
Dutton, Lawrence, 134
'Dwarf Bob', 178
Dyce, Alexander, 111n., 112, 115n., 116n., 117n.

Eccles, Mark, 99, 102n., 129n.
Echeruo, M. J. C., 179
Egan, Richard, 71, 72, 170
Egerton, Sir Thomas (Lord Ellesmere), 94, 95, 99, 100
Ekeblad, Inga-Stina, 177
Eliot, T. S., 11
Elizabeth I, 93, 100, 134
Ellis, J., 158
Elton, Oliver, 106n.
Emery, J. K., 104n.
Erasmus, 59–69
Essex, Earl of, 129n
Everitt, E. B., 129n
Ewbank, I.-S., 163

Farmer, Richard, 106
Farnham, Willard, 111n.
Farrah, 150
Feather, John P., 178, 190
Felperin, H., 168–9
Fenner, Dudley, 84
Ferguson, W. Craig, 186, 187
Fiedler, L. A., 171
Finkelpearl, Philip J., 114n, 119, 120n.
Firth, Tazeena, 146, 151
Fisch, Harold, 81–92
Fischer-Weimann, Waltrad, 179n.
Fleay, Frederick, 106n., 107
Fleissner, Robert F., 105–10
Fletcher, John, 176
Florio, John, 45n., 50n., 52n., 54n.
Foakes, R. A., 134n., 163
Folger Library, 104
Forrest, James F., 160, 179
Fortescue, Sir John, 72
Fortin, R. E., 165
Fowler, Alastair, 109n.
Fox, Levi, 175
Fraser, Russell, 177
Freeman, Arthur, 178
French, A. L., 31n.
Frye, N., 144n.
Furness, H. H., 43n., 107, 108n.
Furnivall, F. J., 132

Gabler, Hans Walter, 190
Galloway, D., 181n.

Gardner, William, 94
Garnier, Robert, 173
Gervinius, 106n.
Gielgud, Sir John, 142, 145
Gilbert, A. J., 179
Glover, Brian, 148–9
Goddard, H. C., 72
Godshalk, W. L., 92n., 167
Golding, Arthur, 160, 179
Goldman, M., 171
Goldsmith, Robert H., 59n., 113n.
Goodbody, Buzz, 148
Goring, Marius, 142
Gossett, Suzanne, 178
Gottschalk, P., 157
Gouge, William, 90
Grammaticus, Saxo, 172
Grant, P., 158
Grant, Thomas Mark, 175–6
Granville Barker, Harley, 48
Gray, Henry David, 106, 107, 108
Greco, A., 167
Green, A. Wigfall, 114n., 115, 116n., 118n.
Green, Thomas, 99
Greene, Graham, 149
Greene, Robert, 16, 130, 132, 134
Greg, Sir Walter, 133, 185
Greville, Fulke, 117n.
Griffin, Robert P., 177
Grivelet, M., 157

Halio, J. L., 160
Hall, Edward, 28n., 72
Halliday, F. E., 106n.
Halliwell-Phillipps, J. O., 97n., 106n.
Hamilton, A. C., 11n., 17n., 18
Hamilton, D. M., 167
Hammond, Kay, 142
Hands, Terry, 144, 150, 151
Hanmer, Theobald, 49n.
Hapgood, E. R., 144n.
Harington, Sir John, 136n.
Harrison, G. B., 16n., 21n.
Harsnett, Samuel, 172, 173
Hart, H. C., 112, 119, 120, 121, 122
Hartwig, J., 158
Harvey, Gabriel, 117n., 130
Hassell, R. C., Jr., 164
Hauger, George, 144
Hauser, Frank, 140
Havely, C., 157
Hawkins, H., 162
Hazlitt, W. C., 111n.
Heilman, Robert B., 27n., 28n.
Henslowe, Philip, 134, 135, 136, 173
Henze, R., 170
Herford, C. H., 106n., 112n., 118, 120, 123, 124, 125, 126
Herringman, John, 191
Heywood, Thomas, 129

Hibbard, G. R., 171
Hieatt, A. Kent, 109n.
Higgins, J, 172
Hill, R. F., 33
Hinman, Charlton, 179, 181, 182, 183, 184, 189, 190
Hobson, Harold, 34n.
Hoby, Sir Thomas, 56n.
Hogg, James, 175
Holinshed, Raphael, 35, 36, 131, 172
Holmes, Denis, 147
Homan, S. R., 170
Homer, 119
Honigmann, E. A. J., 112n., 113, 116n. 132n.
Hopkins, John, 141
Horace, 62, 119, 122
Horsman, E. A., 189
Hoskyns, John, 120
Hosley, R., 77n., 135, 175, 190
Hotson, Leslie, 94, 119n.
Howard, Leslie, 138
Howard-Hill, T. H., 181, 182, 183, 184, 188
Huberd, Edward, 99, 101, 102
Hudson, H. N., 192
Hughes, John, 191
Humphreys, A. R., 37n., 131n.
Hunt, Christopher, 106n.
Hunt, J. D., 163
Hunt, John, 101, 102, 103
Hunt, W., 129n.
Hunter, G. K., 1–9, 106n., 190

Ingram, R. W., 172
Iwaski, Soji, 179

Jackson, B. A. W., 163n., 166n., 172
Jacquot, J., 170
Jaggard, William, 180, 181, 182, 185
Jahn, J. D., 156
James I, 95, 133
James VI, 172
Jeffrey, D. L., 158
Jefford, Barbara, 142
Jepson, Laura, 11n.
Johnson, James T., 90n.
Jones, David, 146, 148
Jones, E., 159
Jones, W. J., 94n., 101, 103
Jonson, Ben, 83, 112, 119, 120, 121, 122, 123, 124, 126, 127, 135, 176, 178
Joseph, Sister Miriam, 84n.
Julius Caesar, 72
Jung, 171
Juvenal, 119

Kable, W. S., 185
Kantorowitz, Ernst, 44
Katayev, Valentin, 143
Kaula, D., 167

INDEX

Kelly, T., 165
Kennet, W., 61, 62, 63, 64, 65, 66, 67, 68
Kenny, T., 106n.
Kinkaid, A. N., 178
Kirkman, Francis, 175
Kitto, H. D. F., 160
Kittredge, G. L., 130n.
Knight, Charles, 106n.
Knight, Wilson, 71, 82n.
Knight, W. Nicholas, 93–104
Knights, L. C., 54n.
Knowles, Richard, 172, 190
Kohler, Estelle, 147, 150, 151
Kökeritz, H., 189
Kosinzew, G. M., 179n.
Kott, Jan, 159
Krabbe, Henning, 192
Kyd, Thomas, 173, 178

Lambarde, William, 93–104
Lambert, Edmund, 97, 98, 102, 103, 104
Lambert, John, 98–104
Lane, Richard, 99
Lanham, John, 134
Laski, Harold, 83n.
Lavater, L., 173
Lavin, J. A., 166
Law, R. A., 133n.
Lawry, J. S., 165
Leason, John, 182
Leavis, F. R., 82n.
Leech, C., 157n., 158n., 164n., 165n., 170n., 179n., 188
Legate, John, 190
Legh, Gerard, 114n., 118n.
Lehmann, Beatrix, 153
Leicester, Earl of, 129
Leisi, Ernest, 189
Lennam, T., 163
Leslie, John, 172
Levenson, J., 158
Lever, J. W., 92n.
Levin, Harry, 61n., 63n., 65n., 67n.
Levin, R., 191
Levitsky, R. M., 158, 159
Lipman, Maureen, 149
Lloyd, Bernard, 151
Lloyd Evans, Gareth, 137–42, 163, 169–70
Lodge, Thomas, 130, 173
Love, Harold, 188
Lovejoy, Arthur, 44
Lowe, R., 106n.
Lucian, 111, 116n., 117, 119, 121n., 127
Lyle, E. B., 159, 179

McAvoy, William Charles, 59n.
McCombie, Frank, 59–69
McElroy, John F., 176
McFarland, T., 168

McGugan, Ruth, 190
Machiavelli, Nicolò, 45, 46, 53, 72, 74–5
Mack, M., Jr., 161
McKenzie, D. F., 180, 190
McKern, Leo, 140
McLauchlan, Juliet, 43–57
MacLure, Miller, 175
McNamara, P. L., 157
McPherson, D., 165, 179
Maguin, Jean-Marie, 173
Mahaney, William E., 177
Malleson, Miles, 142
Malone, Edmund, 107, 111n., 129
Mandel, J., 164
Margeson, J. M. R., 157n., 158n., 164n., 165n., 170n., 179n.
Marlowe, Christopher, 18, 31, 71–9, 130, 132, 135, 176, 178
Marowitz, Charles, 148
Marriott, W. K., 46n.
Marston, John, 99
Martin, Richard, 120
Masefield, John, 106n.
Maxwell, J. C., 106n., 111n., 112n., 136n., 191
May, Stephen W., 178
Meagher, John C., 179, 191
Meres, Francis, 105, 107, 108, 132
Meyerhold, V. E., 143, 144
Middleton, Thomas, 176
Miller, Arthur, 81
Miller, Jonathan, 174
Miller, Perry, 83n.
Mitchell, Yvonne, 142
Montaigne, 44–5, 50, 52n., 56, 173
Montemayor, J. de, 131
Moore Smith, G. C., 112, 118
Moorthy, P. R., 159
Morley, Christopher, 149
Morris, I., 155
Moxon, J., 180, 190
Muir, Kenneth, 18n., 24n., 34, 59n., 133, 145, 146, 154, 156, 170
Musk, John, 167n.

Nashe, Thomas, 130, 135
Neidig, W., 185
Nelson, Norman E., 84
Nelson, Thomas, 179
Neville, John, 34n., 141
Nevo, R., 155–6
Nosworthy, J. M., 111, 116, 118n., 122n., 127n., 133n.
Nunn, Trevor, 137, 138–9
Nuttall, A. D., 170

Ogilvy, J. D. A., 162
Oldys, W. & Birch, T., 56
Oliver, H. J., 111n., 112n., 113
Olivier, Lord, 145
Ormerod, D., 164

Ornstein, R., 161
O'Brien, Timothy, 146, 151
Overbury, Nicholas, 100
Overbury, Sir Thomas, 100
Ovid, 2, 16–17, 19. 160, 192

Palmer, D. J., 149, 155–92, 159, 163n., 164 and n., 165n., 167n., 170n.
Palmer, John, 31n., 32n.
Partridge, Eric, 18, 189
Pasco, Richard, 149, 150, 152
Pater, Walter, 146
Pavier, T., 181, 182, 185
Pedley, Anthony, 153
Peele, George, 130, 132, 135
Pembroke, Earl of, 134
Pembroke's Men, 129–36
Pendry, E. D., 178
Perkins, William, 83n., 84, 85–8, 90, 91
Perrett, W., 173
Petersen, D., 169
Petry, Michael John, 177
Pinciss, G. M., 129–36
Pirie, D., 157
Pitcher, Seymour, 131n.
Plautus, 2, 18, 119
Plutarch, 111, 112n.
Pollard, A. W., 129
Poole, R., 129n.
Potter, Lois, 33–41
Powell, J., 167
Powle, Stephen, 100
Powle, Thomas, 100, 101, 102, 103
Praetorius, C., 132n.
Price, Hereward T., 11n.
Price, Joseph G., 106n.
Proudfoot, Richard, 179–92

Queen's Men, 129–36
Quiller-Couch, Sir A., 106n.

Rabkin, N., 164
Racine, 157
Raleigh, Sir Walter, 56, 112n.
Ramus, Peter, 83, 84
Raphael, 55
Rea, John D. 59n.
Reese, M. M., 32n., 41
Ribeiro, Alvaro, 178
Ribner, Irving, 71
Ricci, Luigi, 46n.
Rich, Penelope, 178
Richardson, Ian, 146–7, 152
Rickert, R. T., 134n.
Ricks, Christopher, 44
Riggs, David, 78–9
Ringler, William A., Jr., 178
Roberts, J. A., 164
Roberts, James, 136n., 181
Roberts, R. J., 190
Rochett, W., 170

Roe, Sir John, 178
Romei, Annibale, 45n.
Rosenberg, M., 158
Rossiter, A. P., 24n., 31n.
Rothman, J., 166
Rothschild, H. B., Jr., 161
Rowe, Nicholas, 187, 191
Rowley, Samuel, 129
Rudyerd, Sir Benjamin, 114n.

Sacharoff, M., 166
St Augustine, 157
St Denis, Michel, 142
St Germain, Christopher, 95, 96, 97
St Paul, 83, 86
Salgãdo, G., 163
Sanders, Gerald, 106n.
Sargent, Ralph M., 16n.
Savage, James E., 178
Schäfer, Jürgen, 59n.
Schamp, Dieter, 189
Schrickx, W., 157
Schwartz, E., 166
Sebonde, Raymond, 45n.
Sen Gupta, S. C., 72n., 156
Seneca, 16, 17, 19, 165, 173, 179
Shakespeare, Hamnet, 94, 98
Shakespeare, John, 94, 98–104
Shakespeare, Mary, 98–104
Shakespeare, William
    editions
        Arden, 34n., 38n., 92n., 133
        Cambridge, 132n.
        Folios, 49n., 105n., 106n., 108, 132, 135; editorial research on, 187–92; textual studies of, 179–92 *passim*; facsimiles of, 189
        Malone Society, 130n.
        Neilson-Hill, 105n.
        New Arden, 34n., 38n., 92n., 106n., 111n., 133
        New Cambridge, 62n., 71n., 106n.
        New Penguin, 188, 190
        Quartos, 45n., 113, 135; textual studies of, 179–92
        Rowe, 191
        Signet, 34n.
        Variorum, 28n., 29n., 43n., 69, 106, 107, 108n.
    plays
        All's Well that Ends Well, 106, 107, 108, 165n., 166
        Antony and Cleopatra, 3, 65, 156, 160
        As You Like It, 59, 69, 108, 130, 131, 144, 146, 148, 162, 165, 167, 168, 189
        Comedy of Errors, The, 2, 18, 93, 95, 163, 188, 189
        Coriolanus, 69, 160, 179, 192
        Cymbeline, 133n.

Hamlet, 1n., 43–57, 59–69, 85, 90, 130, 132, 133, 136, 157, 161, 172, 173, 176, 181, 186
Henry IV, 64, 94
1 Henry IV, 24, 27n., 75, 160, 161
2 Henry IV, 76, 131, 154, 182, 184, 186, 188
Henry V, 71–9, 109, 186, 189
Henry VI, 22, 79, 136
1 Henry VI, 1n., 182
2 Henry VI, 132n., 135, 154, 161, 182, 191
3 Henry VI, 22, 23n., 132n., 135
Henry VIII, 110, 170
Julius Caesar, 1, 159, 179, 191
King John, 106n., 148, 180
King Lear, 2, 3, 18n., 43, 59, 98, 109, 112n., 113, 127, 132, 133, 156, 158, 160, 168, 169, 172, 173, 174, 179, 182, 185, 186, 190, 192
Love's Labour Lost, 105, 106n., 107, 108, 131, 146, 148, 162, 163, 168, 191
Macbeth, 43, 47, 48n., 55, 145, 156, 158, 161, 172, 173, 179, 192
Measure for Measure, 81, 82–3, 84–92, 108, 109n., 145, 166, 167, 176, 177, 184, 189
Merchant of Venice, The, 81, 82, 90, 91, 93–104, 107, 108, 131, 164, 181, 185, 186
Merry Wives of Windsor, The, 108, 164, 165n., 177, 184, 185, 186
Midsummer Night's Dream, A, 7n., 59, 95, 107, 108, 162, 163, 164, 185, 186, 187
Much Ado About Nothing, 105–10, 162, 164, 180, 186, 191
Othello, 43, 143, 148n., 157, 172, 179
Pericles, 89, 175, 186
Richard II, 1n., 21, 33–41, 144, 146, 151, 152, 161, 180, 186
Richard III, 1n., 18, 21–32, 132, 133, 135n., 186
Romeo and Juliet, 1–9, 131, 135n., 137, 144, 146, 150, 191
Taming of the Shrew, The, 2, 106, 107, 108, 109, 132, 135, 136, 142, 146
Tempest, The, 60, 88, 89, 108, 162, 167, 170, 172, 183, 184, 191
Timon of Athens, 111–27
Titus Andronicus, 1–9, 11–19, 135, 136, 159, 191
Troilus and Cressida, 22, 59n., 69, 119, 127, 166, 176
Twelfth Night, 82, 91, 107n., 108, 110, 131, 141, 165, 166, 172, 189, 192

Two Gentlemen of Verona, The, 108, 109, 131, 142, 163, 184, 188, 189
Winter's Tale, The, 57, 86, 89, 103, 108, 137, 139, 167, 168, 179, 180, 184
poems
    Lover's Complaint, A, 178
    Rape of Lucrece, The, 2, 178
    Sonnet xxiv, 179
    Venus and Adonis, 2, 130n., 156, 178
Shalvi, Alice, 176
Shaw, George Bernard, 34n.
Shaw, Glen Byam, 145
Sickermann, C. M., 160
Sider, J. W., 162
Sidney, Sir Philip, 117n., 168, 169, 172
Siegel, Paul N., 81n., 91n.
Siemon, J. E., 162
Silverman, J. M., 166
Simmes, Valentine, 180, 181, 186, 187
Simons, Joseph, 178
Simpson, Percy and Evelyn, 112n., 118, 120, 123, 124, 125, 126
Singleton, Charles S., 56n.
Slater, A. Pasternak, 170
Slater, Eliot, 178
Small, R. A., 122n.
Smallwood, R. L., 166
Smith, Derek, 147, 149
Smith, H., 168
Smith, J. C., 96n.
Smith, J. P., 163
Smyth, Richard, 102
Somerset, Earl of, 100
Sommers, Alan, 11n.
Southampton, Earl of, 129n.
Southern, Richard, 174–5
Spencer, Theodore, 51n., 56n.
Spenser, Edmund, 96, 99–100, 109, 117n., 169, 172, 191
Spillane, Mickey, 177
Spivack, Bernard, 23n.
Sprague, A. C., 34n.
Stanislavsky, C., 144
Stauffer, Donald A., 22n.
Steevens, George, 69, 111n., 112, 119
Sternlicht, Sanford, 177
Stewart, J. I. M., 45n., 159
Stirling, Brents, 39n.
Stone, Harlan F., 104
Storey, Graham, 31n.
Stovell, J., 98
Stow, John, 131
Strange's Men, 129, 134, 136
Stride, John, 138
Stride, John, 138
Suchet, David, 149, 151
Suddard, Mary, 18
Suetonius, 119
Sussex's Men, 134, 135, 136

Tarlton, Richard, 133, 136
Taylor, M., 164, 165
Taylor, Neil, 188
Taylor, Rupert, 132n.
Theobald, Lewis, 187, 192
Thomson, Peter, 143–54
Tilley, M. P., 189
Tillyard, E. M. W., 11n., 12n.
Titian, 55
Toliver, Harold E., 27n.
Tolman, Albert H., 106–7, 108
Tonson, Jacob, 191
Toole, William B., 21–32
Trautvetter, Christian, 189
Traversi, Derek, 72
Tree, Beerbohm, 34n.
Tricomi, Albert H., 11–19

Udall, Nicholas, 189
Underhill, Thomas, 99
Ungerer, Gustav, 136n.
Urbino, Duke of (Francesco Maria I),
    172
Ure, Peter, 33n., 34n., 38n.

Varma, R. S., 190
Velz, John W., 59n., 160, 179
Velz, S. C., 167
Vergil, Polydore, 28n.
Verplanck, Gulian, 106n.
Vickers, Brian, 83
Vincent, E. R. P., 46n.

Waith, Eugene, 11n., 16, 111n.
Walker, Alice, 183
Warner, David, 34n.
Warr, Michael, 142
Warren, R., 165
Webster, John, 177, 184
Weil, H. S., 167
Weimann, R., 171–2, 179n.
Wells, Stanley, 39, 162, 188
Welsford, Enid, 59n.
Wendell, B., 106n.
Wentersdorf, Karl P., 129n., 179, 192
Wertheim, A., 164
West, William, 95, 96, 97
Whitgift, Archbishop, 135
Widmann, Ruth L., 187

Wigfall, A., 114n.
Williams, George Walton, 179
Williams, Mary C., 176
Williams, Michael, 139
Williamson, Audrey, 34n.
Wilson, J., 61
Wilson, Edwin, 34n.
Wilson, F. P., 83n.
Wilson, John Dover, 11n., 51n., 62,
    71n., 106n., 132n., 135, 192
Wilson, Robert, 130n.
Wingfield, A., 112
Winny, James, 45n.
Wisbey, R. A., 187
Wood, J. O., 160, 191
Woodward, Fraunces, 99

Yates, Frances, 45n.
Yoder, R. A., 158, 166
Young, D., 167, 168

Zimbardo, R. A., 163–4
Zitner, S. P., 179
Zucker, David Hard, 176

92805

DATE DUE

822.332 N645	v.27	92805
AUTHOR		
TITLE Shakespeare Survey...v.27.		

DATE DUE	BORROWER'S NAME

822.332   v.27
N645
Shakespeare Survey...v.27.

OHIO DOMINICAN COLLEGE
LIBRARY
COLUMBUS, OHIO 43219

DEMCO